THE
VICTORS

ALSO BY STEPHEN E. AMBROSE

Eisenhower and Berlin, 1945
The Supreme Commander
Rise to Globalism
Crazy Horse and Custer
Pegasus Bridge
Nixon: The Education of a Politician
Nixon: The Triumph of a Politician, 1962–72
Nixon: Ruin and Recovery, 1973–1990
Band of Brothers
Upton and the Army
D-Day
Halleck
Eisenhower
Undaunted Courage
Citizen Soldiers
Americans at War
Duty, Honor, Country
Ike's Spies
Comrades
Nothing Like It In The World
Wild Blue
To America

THE VICTORS

THE MEN OF WORLD WAR II

STEPHEN E. AMBROSE

SIMON &
SCHUSTER

London · New York · Sydney · Toronto · Dublin

A VIACOM COMPANY

This edition published by Simon & Schuster UK Ltd, 2004
A Viacom Company

3 5 7 9 10 8 6 4 2

Simon & Schuster UK Ltd
Africa House
64–78 Kingsway
London WC2B 6AH

www.simonsays.co.uk

Simon & Schuster Australia
Sydney

A CIP catalogue record for this book is available
from the British Library

ISBN 0-7432-6366-9

Printed and bound in Great Britain by
Mackays of Chatham plc

FOR ELIZABETH STEIN

Contents

Introduction

My EXPERIENCES with the military have been as an observer. The only time I wore a uniform was in naval ROTC as a freshman at the University of Wisconsin, and in army ROTC as a sophomore. I was in second grade when the United States entered World War II, in sixth grade when the war ended. When I graduated from high school in 1953, I expected to go into the army, but within a month the Korean War ended and I went to college instead. Upon graduation in 1957, I went straight to graduate school. By the time America was again at war, in 1964, I was twenty-eight years old and the father of five children. So I never served.

But I have admired and respected the men who did fight since my childhood. When I was in grade school World War II dominated my life. My father was a navy doctor in the Pacific. My mother worked in a pea cannery beside German POWs (Afrika Korps troops captured in Tunisia in May 1943). Along with my brothers—Harry, two years older, and Bill, two years younger—I went to the movies three times a week (ten cents six nights a week, twenty-five cents on Saturday night), not to see the films, which were generally real clinkers, but to see the newsreels, which were almost exclusively about the fighting in North Africa, Europe, and the Pacific. We played at war constantly: "Japs" vs. marines, GIs vs. "Krauts."

In high school I got hooked on Napoleon. I read various biographies and studied his campaigns. As a seventeen-year-old freshman in naval ROTC, I took a course on naval history, starting with the Greeks and ending with World War II (in one semester!). My instructor had been a submarine skipper in the Pacific and we all worshiped him. More important, he was a gifted teacher who loved the navy and history. Although I was a premed student with plans to take up my father's practice in Whitewater, Wisconsin, I found the history course to be far more interesting than chemistry or physics. But in the second semester of naval ROTC, the required course was gunnery. Although I was an avid hunter and thoroughly familiar with shotguns and rifles, the workings of the five-inch cannon baffled me, so in my sophomore year I switched to army ROTC.

Also that year, I took a course entitled "Representative Americans" taught by Professor William B. Hesseltine. In his first lecture he announced that in this course we would not be writing term papers that summarized the conclusions of three or four books; instead, we would be doing original research on nineteenth-century Wisconsin politicians, professional and business leaders, for the purpose of putting together a dictionary of Wisconsin biography that would be deposited in the state historical society. We would, Hesseltine told us, be contributing to the world's knowledge.

The words caught me up. I had never imagined I could do such a thing as contribute to the world's knowledge. Forty-five years later, the phrase continues to resonate with me. It changed my life. At the conclusion of the lecture—on General Washington —I went up to him and asked how I could do what he did for a living. He laughed and said to stick around, he would show me. I went straight to the registrar's office and changed my major from premed to history. I have been at it ever since.

As for this book, Alice Mayhew made me do it. Two years ago I sent in to her the manuscript of a book she eventually titled *Citizen Soldiers* (she picks all my titles, including the one for this book). That was the eleventh manuscript I had sent her—three volumes on Eisenhower, three volumes on Nixon, one on a British airborne company in World War II, one on an American airborne company in that war, one on D-Day, and one on Meriwether Lewis.

All but the Nixon volumes and the Lewis book were on war, and there was plenty of war in the second and third Nixon volumes—and Lewis led a military expedition.

So when I put the manuscript of what became *Citizen Soldiers* in the mail, I promised my wife, Moira, "I ain't going to study war no more." I had seen enough destruction, enough blood, enough high explosives. To remove temptation, I gave my library of World War II books to the Eisenhower Center at the University of New Orleans. Like the Civil War veterans after Appomattox, like the GIs after the German and Japanese surrenders, I wanted to build. Alice accepted my decision and told me to write a book on the building of the first transcontinental railroad. I loved the idea and put in a year of research.

Then Alice called and said I should do a book on Ike and the GIs, drawing on my previous writings to put together a coherent narrative. She said it would be the easiest book I'd ever write. That didn't turn out to be so, as there was lots of hard work involved. But it has been the most fun. The challenge of writing a history of the Supreme Commander and the junior officers, NCOs, and enlisted men carrying out his orders—generally ignoring the ranks in between—has given me a new appreciation of both.

The older I get, the more of his successors as generals and presidents I see, the more I appreciate General and President Eisenhower's leadership. And the more I realize that the key to his success as a leader of men was his insistence on teamwork and his devotion to democracy.

General Eisenhower liked to speak of the fury of an aroused democracy. It was in Normandy on June 6, 1944, and in the campaign that followed, that the Western democracies made their fury manifest. The success of this great and noble undertaking was a triumph of democracy over totalitarianism. President Eisenhower said he wanted democracy to survive for all ages to come. So do I. It is my fondest hope that this book, which in its essence is a love song to democracy, will make a small contribution to that great goal.

1

Preparation

AT THE BEGINNING of World War II, in September 1939, the Western democracies were woefully unprepared for the challenge the totalitarians hurled at them. The British army was small and sad, the French army was large but inefficient and demoralized from top to bottom, while the American army numbered only 160,000 officers and men, which meant it ranked sixteenth in the world, right behind Romania. The totalitarian armies of Imperial Japan, the Soviet Union, and Nazi Germany, meanwhile, were larger and better prepared than their foes. As a consequence, between the early fall of 1939 and the late fall of 1941, the Japanese in China, Indochina, at Pearl Harbor, and in the Philippines and Malaya; the Red Army in Poland and the Baltic countries; the Germans in Poland, Norway, Belgium, Holland, and France, won great victories. The only bright spots for the democracies were the British victory in the Battle of Britain in the summer and fall of 1940 (but that was a defensive victory only) and Adolf Hitler's decision to attack his ally Joseph Stalin in the spring of 1941.

Because of the last two events, the apparently certain totalitarian victory of May 1940 was now in question. Perhaps the democracies would survive, perhaps even prevail and emerge as the victors. That depended on many things, but most of all on the abilities of the British and Americans to put together armies that could challenge the Japanese and German armies in open combat. That required producing leaders and men. How that was done is the central theme of this book.

We begin with Dwight David Eisenhower, the man who became the Supreme Commander of the British and American armies that formed the Allied Expeditionary Force. His personality dominated the AEF. He was the man who made the critical decisions. In the vast bureaucracy that came to characterize the high command of the AEF, he was the single person who could make judgments and issue orders. He had many high-powered subordinates, most famously Gen. Bernard Law Montgomery and Gen. George S. Patton, but from the time of his appointment as Supreme Commander to the end of the war, he was the one who ran the show. For that reason, he gets top billing here.

Eisenhower was a West Point graduate (1915) and professional soldier. When the war broke out, he was a lieutenant colonel serving on the staff of Gen. Douglas MacArthur in the Philippines. By mid-1941 he had become a brigadier general and chief of staff at the Third Army, stationed at Fort Sam Houston, Texas. He was there that December 7; on December 12 he got a call from the War Department ordering him to proceed immediately to Washington for a new assignment. What he did over the next few weeks, and what happened to him, illustrate how ill-prepared the American army was for war, and how fortunate it was to have Eisenhower in its ranks.

On Sunday morning, December 14, Eisenhower arrived at Union Station in Washington. He went immediately to the War Department offices in the Munitions Building on Constitution Avenue (the Pentagon was then under construction) for his initial conference with the Chief of Staff, Gen. George C. Marshall. After a brief, formal greeting Marshall quickly outlined the situation in the Pacific—the ships lost at Pearl Harbor, the planes lost at Clark Field outside Manila, the size and strength of Japanese attacks elsewhere, troop strength in the Philippines, reinforcement possibilities, intelligence estimates, the capabilities of America's Dutch and British allies in Asia, and other details. Then Marshall leaned forward across his desk, fixed his eyes on Eisenhower's, and demanded, "What should be our general line of action?"

Eisenhower was startled. He had just arrived, knew little more than what he had read in the newspapers and what Marshall had just told him, was not up to date on the war plans for the Pacific, and had no staff to help him prepare an answer. After a second or two of hesitation Eisenhower requested, "Give me a few hours."

"All right," Marshall replied. He had dozens of problems to deal with that afternoon, hundreds in the days to follow. He needed help and he needed to know immediately which of his officers could give it to him. He had heard great things about Eisenhower from men whose judgment he trusted, but he needed to see for himself how Eisenhower operated under the pressures of war. His question was the first test.

Eisenhower went to a desk that had been assigned to him in the War Plans Division (WPD) of the General Staff. Sticking a sheet of yellow tissue paper into his typewriter, he tapped out with one finger, "Steps to Be Taken," then sat back and started thinking. He knew that the Philippines could not be saved, that the better part of military wisdom would be to retreat to Australia, there to build a base for the counteroffensive. But the honor of the army was at stake, and the prestige of the United States in the Far East, and these political factors outweighed the purely military considerations. An effort had to be made. Eisenhower's first recommendation was to build a base in Australia from which attempts could be made to reinforce the Philippines. "Speed is essential," he noted. He urged that shipment of planes, pilots, ammunition, and other equipment be started from the West Coast and Hawaii to Australia immediately.

It was already dusk when Eisenhower returned to Marshall's office. As he handed over his written recommendation, he said he realized that it would be impossible to get reinforcements to the Philippines in time to save the islands from the Japanese. Still, he added, the United States had to do everything it could to bolster MacArthur's forces because "the people of China, of the Philippines, of the Dutch East Indies will be watching us. They may excuse failure but they will not excuse abandonment." He urged the advantages of Australia as a base of operations—English-speaking, a strong ally, modern port facilities, beyond the range of the Japanese offensive—and advised Marshall to begin a program of expanding the facilities there and to secure the line of communications from the West Coast to Hawaii and then on to New Zealand and Australia. "In this," Eisenhower said, ". . . we dare not fail. We must take great risks and spend any amount of money required."

Marshall studied Eisenhower for a minute, then said softly, "I agree with you. Do your best to save them." He thereupon placed Eisenhower in charge of the Philippines and Far Eastern Section of the War Plans Division. Then Marshall leaned forward—Eisenhower recalled years later that he had "an eye that seemed to me awfully cold"—and declared, "Eisenhower, the Department is filled with able men who analyze their problems well but feel compelled always to bring them to me for final solution. I must have assistants who will solve their own problems and tell me later what they have done."

Over the next two months Eisenhower labored to save the Philippines. His efforts were worse than fruitless, as MacArthur came to lump Eisenhower together with Marshall and President Franklin D. Roosevelt as the men responsible for the debacle on the islands. But throughout the period, and in the months that followed, Eisenhower impressed Marshall deeply, so deeply that Marshall came to agree with MacArthur's earlier judgment that Eisenhower was the best officer in the army.

Marshall was not an easy man to impress. He was a cold, aloof person—"remote and austere," Eisenhower called him—a man who forced everyone to keep his distance. President Roosevelt had tried at their first meeting to slap him on the back and call him George, but Marshall drew back and let the President know that the name was General Marshall, and General Marshall it remained. He had few intimate friends. When he relaxed he did it alone, watching movies or puttering in his garden. He kept a tight grip on his emotions and seldom displayed any sign of a sense of humor. His sense of duty was highly developed. He made small allowance for failings in others, but to those who could do the work, Marshall was intensely loyal. He also felt deep affection toward them, though he seldom showed it.

Hardly anyone, for example, could resist Eisenhower's infectious grin, and he was known throughout the army by his catchy nickname, but Marshall did resist. In all their years together, Marshall almost always called him Eisenhower (except after November 4, 1952, when he called him Mr. President).

Marshall slipped only once, at the victory parade in New York City in 1945, and called him Ike. "To make up for it," Eisenhower recalled with a smile, "he used the word 'Eisenhower' five times in the next sentence."

For his part, Eisenhower always called Marshall "General." After ten years with MacArthur, he found Marshall to be the ideal boss, both as a man to work for and as a teacher. In October 1942 he told an assistant, "I wouldn't trade one Marshall for fifty MacArthurs." He thought a second, then blurted out, "My God! That would be a lousy deal. What would I do with fifty MacArthurs?" As he later wrote more formally, Eisenhower conceived "unlimited admiration and respect" for Marshall, and came to have feelings of "affection" for him. Marshall came to have the dominant role not only in Eisenhower's career, but also in his thinking and in his leadership techniques. He was the model that Eisenhower tried to emulate; he set the standards Eisenhower tried to meet.

The two men, although ten years apart in age, had much in common. Marshall had the build and grace of an athlete, was about Eisenhower's height (six feet), and was equally well proportioned. He had been a football player in college. Like Eisenhower, he loved exploring the Civil War battlefields and habitually illustrated his points or strengthened his arguments by drawing on examples from past battles and campaigns. The way he exercised leadership coincided nicely with Eisenhower's temperament. He never yelled or shouted, almost never lost his temper. He built an atmosphere of friendly cooperation and teamwork around him, without losing the distinction between the commander and his staff—there was never any doubt as to who was the boss.

Marshall headed a stupendous organization. To do so effectively he needed assistants he could trust. In picking them, he took professional competence for granted and concentrated on personality traits. Certain types were, in his view, unsuited for high command. Foremost among these were those who were self-seeking in the matter of promotion. Next came those who always tried to "pass the buck." Officers who tried to do everything themselves and consequently got bogged down in detail were equally unsatisfactory. Men who shouted or pounded on the desk were as unacceptable to Marshall as men who had too great a love of the limelight. Nor could he abide the pessimist. He surrounded himself with men who were offensive-minded and who concentrated on the possibilities rather than the difficulties.

In every respect, Eisenhower was exactly the sort of officer Marshall was looking for.

Worn-out, angry at his country for not having prepared for the war, angry at MacArthur and the navy for the way they were fighting it, angry at being stuck in Washington, one day Eisenhower almost lost his temper completely with Marshall. It happened on March 20 in Marshall's office. Marshall and Eisenhower had settled a detail about an officer's promotion. Marshall then leaned forward to say that in the last war staff officers had gotten the promotions, not the field officers who did the fighting, and that he intended to reverse the process in this war. "Take your case," he added. "I know that you were recommended by one general for division command and by another for corps command. That's all very well. I'm glad that they have that opinion of you, but you are going to stay right here and fill your position, and that's that!" Preparing to turn to other business, Marshall muttered, "While this may seem a sacrifice to you, that's the way it must be."

Eisenhower, red-faced and resentful, shot back, "General, I'm interested in what you say, but I want you to know that I don't give a damn about your promotion plans as far as I'm concerned. I came into this office from the field and I am trying to do my duty. I expect to do so as long as you want me here. If that locks me to a desk for the rest of the war, so be it!"

He pushed back his chair and strode toward the door, nearly ten paces away. By the time he got there he decided to take the edge off the outburst, turned, and grinned. He thought he could see a tiny smile at the corners of Marshall's mouth.

Whether Marshall smiled or not, Eisenhower's anger returned full force after he left the office. He went to his desk and filled his diary with his feelings. The thought of spending the war in Washington, missing combat again, was maddening. It seemed so unfair. Marshall's cold, impersonal attitude just added to the anger. He cursed Marshall for toying with him; he cursed the war and his own bad luck.

The next morning Eisenhower read what he had written,

shook his head, and tore the page out of his diary, destroying it. Then he wrote a new entry. "Anger cannot win, it cannot even think clearly. In this respect," he continued, "Marshall puzzles me a bit." Marshall got angrier at stupidity than anyone Eisenhower had ever seen, "yet the outburst is so fleeting, he returns so quickly to complete 'normalcy,' that I'm certain he does it for effect." Eisenhower envied Marshall that trait and confessed, "I blaze for an hour! So, for many years I've made it a religion never to indulge myself, but yesterday I failed."

A week later Marshall recommended Eisenhower for promotion to major general (temporary). In his recommendation to the President, Marshall explained that Eisenhower was not really a staff officer but was his operations officer, a sort of subordinate commander. Surprised and delighted, Eisenhower first reacted, "This should assure that when I finally get back to the troops, I'll get a division." Decades later, in his memoirs, he wrote that he "often wondered" if his outburst and the way in which he had been able to control his emotions and end the session with one of his big lopsided grins had led Marshall to take a greater interest in him.

Perhaps, but unlikely. Marshall had already been pushing Eisenhower ahead, increasing his responsibilities at a rapid pace. In January he had taken Eisenhower along as his chief assistant to the first wartime conference with the British, and had given Eisenhower the task of preparing the basic American position on organization and strategy for global war. In mid-February he made Eisenhower his principal plans and operations officer. This steady progress surely indicated that Marshall, with or without the display of what MacArthur called "Ike's damn Dutch temper," thought Eisenhower's potential unlimited.

By the beginning of April, Eisenhower had 107 officers working directly under him. As his responsibilities included both plans and operations, he was concerned with all army activities around the world, which gave Eisenhower a breadth of vision he could not have obtained in any other post.

Working in daily contact with the units in the field, as well as preparing plans on grand strategy, gave Eisenhower a realistic sense of the scope of modern war. In late February he had been complaining in his diary about both MacArthur and Adm. Ernest J. King,

Chief of Naval Operations. He called King "an arbitrary, stubborn type, with not too much brains and a tendency toward bullying his juniors." The outburst led him to write a sentence that described the essence of Eisenhower's leadership style, both as a general and as president. "In a war such as this, when high command invariably involves a president, a prime minister, six chiefs of staff, and a horde of lesser 'planners,' there has got to be a lot of patience—no one person can be a Napoleon or Caesar."

Of all the generals, Eisenhower himself came closest to a Napoleonic role, but he would never make such a comparison. Having been a staff officer for so long himself, he was acutely aware of the importance of his staff to him; he was just as acutely aware of the indispensability of the subordinates in the field commands who carried out his orders. He had no false modesty, was conscious of the crucial nature of the role he played, but he never thought of himself as a Napoleon. Always, his emphasis was on the team. He was not self-effacing but realistic, aware that there were definite limits on his powers, and keeping his self-image in perspective.

While the Americans badly needed Marshall, Eisenhower, and other generals to ram their feet into the stirrups and take command, they needed even more desperately to build and equip an army. This was done through conscription and the tremendous output of American industry, which had been flat on its back in 1939 but was by the beginning of 1942 turning out the tools and weapons of war in an ever-increasing, record-setting pace. But weapons without soldiers are useless. The creation of the U.S. Army in 1942–43 was one of the great achievements of the American Republic in the twentieth century. How it was accomplished is a long story, one part of which is told in this account of the beginnings of a company of elite volunteers who were part of the 101st Airborne Division.

The men of Easy Company, 506th Parachute Infantry Regiment, 101st Airborne Division, U.S. Army, came from different backgrounds, different parts of the country. They were farmers and coal miners, mountain men and sons of the Deep South. Some were desperately poor, others from the middle class. One came from Harvard, one from Yale, a couple from UCLA. Only one was from the Old Army, only a few came from the National Guard or reserves. They were citizen soldiers.

Each of the 140 men and seven officers who formed the original company followed a different route to its birthplace, Camp Toccoa, Georgia, but they had some things in common. They were young, born since the Great War. They were white because the U.S. Army in World War II was segregated. With three exceptions they were unmarried. Most had been hunters and athletes in high school.

They were special in their values. They put a premium on physical well-being, hierarchical authority, and being part of an elite unit. They were idealists, eager to merge themselves into a group fighting for a cause, actively seeking an outfit with which they could identify, join, be a part of, relate to as a family.

They volunteered for the paratroopers, they said, for the thrill, the honor, and the $50 (for enlisted men) or $100 (for officers) monthly bonus paratroopers received. But they really volunteered to jump out of airplanes for two profound, personal reasons. First, in Pvt. Robert Rader's words, "The desire to be better than the other guy took hold." Each man in his own way had gone through what Lt. Richard Winters experienced: a realization that doing his best was a better way of getting through the army than hanging around with the sad excuses for soldiers they met in the recruiting depots or basic training. They wanted to make their army time positive, a learning and maturing and challenging experience.

Second, they knew they were going into combat, and they did not want to go in with poorly trained, poorly conditioned, poorly motivated draftees on either side of them. As to choosing between being a paratrooper spearheading the offensive and an ordinary infantryman who could not trust the guy next to him, they decided the greater risk was with the infantry. When the shooting started they wanted to look up to the guy beside them, not down.

They had been kicked around by the Depression and had the scars to show for it. They had grown up, many of them, without enough to eat, with holes in the soles of their shoes, with ragged sweaters and no car and often not a radio. Their educations had been cut short, either by the Depression or by the war.

"Yet, with this background, I had and still have a great love for my country," Lt. Harry Welsh declared forty-eight years later. Whatever their legitimate complaints about how life had treated them, they had not soured on it or on their country.

They came out of the Depression with many other positive features. They were self-reliant, accustomed to hard work and to taking orders. Through sports or hunting or both, they had gained a sense of self-worth and self-confidence.

They knew they were going into great danger. They knew they would be doing more than their part. They resented having to sacrifice years of their youth to a war they never made. They wanted to throw baseballs, not grenades, shoot a .22 rifle, not an M-1. But having been caught up in the war, they decided to be as positive as possible in their army careers.

Not that they knew much about airborne, except that it was new and all-volunteer. They had been told that the physical training was tougher than anything they had ever seen, or that any other unit in the army would undergo, but these young lions were eager for that. They expected that when they were finished with their training, they would be bigger, stronger, tougher than when they started, and they would have gone through the training with the guys who would be fighting beside them.

"The Depression was over," Pvt. Carwood Lipton recalled of that summer of 1942, "and I was beginning a new life that would change me profoundly." It would all of them.

First Lt. Herbert Sobel of Chicago was the initial member of E Company, and its commanding officer. His executive officer (XO) was 2nd Lt. Clarence Hester from northern California. Sobel was Jewish, urban, with a commission from the National Guard. Hester had started as a private, then earned his commission from officer candidate school (OCS). Most of the platoon and assistant platoon leaders were newly commissioned graduates of OCS, including 2nd Lts. Dick Winters from Pennsylvania, Walter Moore from California's racetracks, and Louis Nixon from New York City and Yale. S. L. Matheson was an ROTC graduate from UCLA. At twenty-eight years of age Sobel was the old man in the group; the others were twenty-four or younger.

The company, along with Dog, Fox, and Battalion HQ Companies, made up the 2nd Battalion of the 506th PIR. The battalion commander was Maj. Robert Strayer, a thirty-year-old reserve officer. The regimental commander was Col. Robert Sink, a 1927

West Point graduate. The 506th was an experimental outfit, the first parachute infantry regiment in which the men would take their basic training and their jump training together as a unit. It would be a year before it was attached to the 101st Airborne Division, the Screaming Eagles. The officers were as new to this paratrooping business as the men; they were teachers who sometimes were not much more than one day ahead of the class.

The original NCOs were Old Army. "We looked up to them," Pvt. Walter Gordon of Mississippi remembered, "as almost like gods because they had their wings, they were qualified jumpers. But, hell, if they knew how to do an about-face, they were ahead of us, we were raw recruits. Later, looking back, we regarded them with scorn. They couldn't measure up to our own people who moved up to corporals and sergeants."

The first privates in Easy were Frank Perconte, Herman Hansen, Wayne Sisk, and Carwood Lipton. Within a few days of its formation, Easy had a full complement of 132 men and eight officers. It was divided into three platoons and a headquarters section. There were three twelve-man rifle squads plus a six-man mortar team squad to a platoon. A light infantry outfit, Easy had one machine gun to each of the rifle squads, and a 60mm mortar in each mortar team.

Few of the original members of Easy made it through Toccoa. "Officers would come and go," Winters remarked. "You would take one look at them and know they wouldn't make it. Some of those guys were just a bowl of butter. They were so awkward they didn't know how to fall." This was typical of the men trying for the 506th PIR; it took 500 officer volunteers to produce the 148 who made it through Toccoa, and 5,300 enlisted volunteers to get 1,800 graduates.

As the statistics show, Toccoa was a challenge. Colonel Sink's task was to put the men through basic training, harden them, teach them the rudiments of infantry tactics, prepare them for jump school, and build a regiment that he would lead into combat. "We were sorting men," Lieutenant Hester recalled, "sorting the fat to the thin and sorting out the no guts."

The only rest came when they got lectures on weapons, map

and compass reading, infantry tactics, codes, signaling, field telephones, radio equipment, switchboard and wire stringing, and demolitions. For unarmed combat and bayonet drills, it was back to using those trembling muscles.

When they were issued their rifles, they were told to treat the weapon as they would treat a wife, gently. It was theirs to have and to hold, to sleep with in the field, to know intimately. They got to where they could take it apart and put it back together blindfolded.

To prepare the men for jump school, Toccoa had a mock-up tower some thirty-five feet high. A man was strapped into a parachute harness that was connected to fifteen-foot risers, which in turn were attached to a pulley that rode a cable. Jumping from the tower in the harness, sliding down the cable to the landing, gave the feeling of a real parachute jump and landing.

All these activities were accompanied by shouting in unison, chanting, singing together, or bitching. The language was foul. These nineteen- and twenty-year-old enlisted men, free from the restraints of home and culture, thrown together into an all-male society, coming from all over America, used words as one form of bonding. The one most commonly used, by far, was the *f*-word. It substituted for adjectives, nouns, and verbs. It was used, for example, to describe the cooks: "those f——ers," or "f——ing cooks"; what they did: "f——ed it up again"; and what they produced. Pvt. David Kenyon Webster, a Harvard English major, confessed that he found it difficult to adjust to the "vile, monotonous, and unimaginative language." The language made these boys turning into men feel tough and, more important, insiders, members of a group. Even Webster got used to it, although never to like it.

The men were learning to do more than swear, more than how to fire a rifle, more than that the limits of their physical endurance were much greater than they had ever imagined. They were learning instant, unquestioning obedience.

Although the British army had been in somewhat better shape than the American army in 1939, and although by the time Easy Company began to take shape Britain had been at war for two and a half years, it was not much better off. The Royal Navy and the Royal Air Force (RAF) had been engaged in an all-out struggle, but except for Eighth Army in the North African desert and some engagements in Greece and Crete, the British army had seen no action against the German army. Even in North Africa, the struggle had not yet taken on the all-out ferocity it would later assume, as Col. Hans von Luck of the German army was discovering. Luck had been in the van in the drive to the Channel coast in May 1940, and again in the invasion of the Soviet Union in June 1941. In the fall of 1941 he had led his reconnaissance unit across the Leningrad-Moscow canal, and thus become the only German officer to get east of Moscow. But he had been compelled to withdraw, and then was called to North Africa by his old mentor, Gen. Erwin Rommel of Afrika Korps. He found that the fighting there against the British was very much different from what he had experienced fighting the Red Army in Russia.

In North Africa, Colonel Luck was fighting in the only war he ever enjoyed. He commanded the armed reconnaissance battalion on Rommel's extreme right (southern) flank. He thus enjoyed a certain independence, as did his British opposite number. The two commanding officers agreed to fight a civilized war. Every day at 5 P.M. the war shut down, the British to brew up their tea, the Germans their coffee. At about quarter past five, Luck learned that the British commander would communicate over the radio. "Well," Luck might say, "we captured so-and-so today, and he's fine, and he sends his love to his mother, tell her not to worry." Once Luck learned that the British had received a month's supply of cigarettes. He offered to trade a captured officer—who happened to be the heir to the Players cigarette fortune—for one million cigarettes. The British countered with an offer of 600,000. Done, said Luck. But the Players heir was outraged. He said the ransom was insufficient. He insisted he was worth the million and refused to be exchanged.

One evening an excited corporal reported that he had just stolen a British truck jammed with tinned meat and other delicacies. Luck looked at his watch—it was past 6 P.M.—and told the corporal he would have to take it back, as he had captured it after 5 P.M. The corporal protested that this was war, and anyway, the troops were already gathering in the goods from the truck. Luck called Rommel, his mentor in the military academy. He said he was suspicious of

British moves farther south and thought he ought to go out on a two-day reconnaissance. Could another battalion take his place for that time? Rommel agreed. The new battalion arrived in the morning. That night, at 5:30 P.M., just as Luck had anticipated, the British stole *two* supply trucks.

Back in England, among the elite units, there were no high jinks, but the essential problem of too many drills, too many parades, and no action remained. Throughout its ranks the British army still suffered from the humiliation of Dunkirk in May 1940. In no way was it ready for the challenge of going back to France. But it contained leaders who were determined to get it ready.

Throughout the British army at home, boredom reigned. The so-called phony war was from September 1939 to May 1940, but for thousands of young men who had enlisted during that period, the time from spring 1941 to the beginning of 1944 was almost as bad. There was no threat of invasion. The only British army doing any fighting at all was in the Mediterranean; almost everywhere else duties and training were routine—and routinely dull. Discipline had fallen off, in part because of the boredom, in part because the War Office had concluded that martinet discipline in a democracy was inappropriate, and because it was thought it dampened the fighting spirit of the men in the ranks.

Many soldiers, obviously, rather enjoyed this situation and would have been more than content to stick out the war lounging around the barracks, doing the odd parade or field march, otherwise finding ways of making it look as if they were busy. But there were thousands who were not content, young men who had joined up because they really did want to be soldiers, really did want to fight for King and Country, really did seek some action and excitement. In the spring of 1942 their opportunity came when a call went out for volunteers for the airborne forces.

Britain had made a decision to create an airborne army. The 1st Airborne Division was being formed up. Maj. Gen. F.A.M. "Boy" Browning would command it. Already a legendary figure in the army, noted especially for his tough discipline, Browning looked like a movie star and dressed with flair. In 1932 he had married the novelist Daphne du Maurier, who in 1942 suggested a red beret for airborne troops, with Bellerophon astride winged Pegasus as the airborne shoulder patch and symbol.

Pvt. Wally Parr was one of the thousands who responded to the call to wear the red beret. He had joined the army in February 1939, at the age of sixteen (he was one of more than a dozen in D Company, Oxfordshire and Buckinghamshire Light Infantry—Ox and Bucks—who lied about their age to enlist). He had been posted to an infantry regiment and had spent three years "never doing a damn thing that really mattered. Putting up barbed wire, taking it down the next day, moving it. . . . Never fired a rifle, never did a thing." So he volunteered for airborne, passed the physical, and was accepted into the Ox and Bucks, just then forming up as an air landing unit, and was assigned to D Company. After three days in his new outfit he asked for an interview with the commander, Maj. John Howard.

"Ah, yes, Parr," Howard said as Parr walked into his office. "What can I do for you?"

"I want to get out," Parr stated.

Howard stared at him. "But you just got in."

"Yeah, I know," Parr responded, "and I spent the last three days weeding around the barracks block. That's not what I came for. I want to transfer from here to the paras [paratroopers]. I want the real thing, what I volunteered for, not these stupid gliders, of which we don't have any anyway."

"You take it easy," Howard replied. "Wait." And he dismissed Parr without another word.

Leaving the office, Parr thought, I'd better be careful with this fellow.

In truth, Parr as yet had no idea just how tough his new company commander was. Howard had come out of a background that was as working class as any of the Cockneys in his company. He started as an enlisted man, earned a commission, and by 1941 was a captain with his own company, which he trained for the next year. At the beginning of 1942 he learned that a decision had been taken to go airborne with the Ox and Bucks, and that his battalion would be gliderborne troops. No one was forced to go airborne; every officer and trooper was given a choice. About 40 percent declined the opportunity to wear the red beret. Another 10 percent were weeded out in the physical exam. It was meant to be an elite regiment.

The sergeant major came to the Ox and Bucks specially posted from the outside. Wally Parr made the man's overpowering personality vivid in a short anecdote. "That first day," said Parr, "he called the whole bleeding regiment together on parade. And he looked at us, and we looked at him, and we both knew who was boss."

Howard himself had to give up his company and his captaincy to go airborne, but he did not hesitate. He reverted to lieutenant and platoon leader in order to become an airborne officer. In three weeks his colonel promoted him and gave him command of D Company. Shortly after that, in May 1942, he was promoted to major.

By July, Howard was pretty much on his own, allowed by his colonel to set his own training pace and schedule. Initially, he put the emphasis on teaching the men the skills of the light infantryman. He taught them to be marksmen with their rifles, with the light machine gun, with the carbine and the pistol, with the Piat (projector infantry antitank) and other antitank weapons. He instructed them in the many types of grenades, their characteristics and special uses.

Most of all, Howard put the emphasis on learning to think quickly. They were elite, he told the men; they were gliderborne troops, and wherever and whenever it was they attacked the enemy, they could be sure the premium would be on quick thinking and quick response.

Howard's emphasis on technical training went a bit beyond what the other company commanders were doing, but only just a bit. All of Howard's associates were commanding top-quality volunteers, and were volunteers themselves, outstanding officers. What was different about D Company was its commander's mania for physical fitness. It went beyond anything anyone in the British army had ever seen before. The regiment prided itself on being fit (one officer from B Company described himself as a physical-fitness fanatic), but all were amazed by, and a bit critical of, the way Howard pushed his fitness program.

D Company's day began with a five-mile cross-country run, done at a seven- or eight-minute-to-the-mile pace. After that the men dressed, policed the area, ate breakfast, and then spent the day on training exercises, usually strenuous. In the late afternoon Howard insisted that everyone engage in some sport or another. His own favorites were the individual endeavors, cross-country running, swimming, and boxing, but he encouraged soccer, rugby, and any sport that would keep his lads active until bedtime.

Those were regular days. Twice a month Howard would take the whole company out for two or three days, doing field exercises, sleeping rough. He put them through grueling marches, until they became an outstanding marching unit. Wally Parr swore—and a number of his comrades backed him up—that they could do twenty-two miles, in full pack, including the Brens (light machine guns) and the mortars, in five and one-half hours. When they got back from such a march, Parr related, "you would have a foot inspection, get a bite to eat, and then in the afternoon face a choice: either play soccer or go for a cross-country run."

All the officers, including Howard, did everything the men did. All of them had been athletes themselves, and loved sports and competition. The sports and the mutually endured misery on the forced marches were bringing officers and men closer together. Lt. David Wood was exceedingly popular with his platoon, as was Lt. H. J. "Tod" Sweeney, in his own quiet way, with his. But Lt. Den Brotheridge stood out. He played the men's game, soccer, and as a former corporal himself he had no sense of being ill at ease among the men. He would go into their barracks at night, sit on the bed of his batman (aide), Cpl. Billy Gray, and talk soccer with the lads. He got to bringing his boots along and shining them as he talked. Wally Parr never got over the sight of a British lieutenant polishing his boots himself while his batman lay back on his bed, gassing on about Manchester United and West Ham and other soccer teams.

Howard's biggest problem was boredom. He racked his brains to find different ways of doing the same things, to put some spontaneity into the training. His young heroes had many virtues, but patience was not one of them. The resulting morale problem extended far beyond D Company, obviously, and in late summer 1942, General Browning sent the whole regiment to Devonshire for two months of cliff climbing. He then decided to march the regiment

back to Bulford, some 130 miles. Naturally, it would be a competition between the companies.

The first two days were the hottest of the summer, and the
men were marching in serge, wringing wet. After the second day
they pleaded for permission to change to lighter gear. It was
granted, and over the next two days a cold, hard rain beat down on
their inadequately covered bodies.

Howard marched up and down the column, urging his men
on. He had a walking stick, an old army one with an inch of brass on
the bottom. His company clerk and wireless operator, Cpl. Edward
Tappenden, offered the major the use of his bike. "Not likely,"
Howard growled. "I'm leading my company." His hands grew more
blisters than Tappenden's feet, from his grip on the stick, and he
wore away all the brass on the end of it. But he kept marching.

On the morning of the fourth day, when Howard roused the
men and ordered them to fall in, Wally Parr and his friend Pvt. Jack
Bailey waddled out on their knees. When Howard asked them what
they thought they were doing Wally replied that he and Jack had
worn away the bottom half of their legs. But they got up and
marched. "Mad bastard," the men whispered among themselves
after Howard had moved off. "Mad, ambitious bastard. He'll get us
all killed." But they marched.

They got back to base on the evening of the fifth day. They
marched in at 140 steps to the minute, singing loudly, "Onward,
Christian Soldiers." They came in first in the regiment, by half a
day. Only two of Howard's men out of 120 had dropped out of the
march. (His stick, however, was so worn he had to throw it away.)

Howard had radioed ahead, and had hot showers and meals
waiting for the men. As the officers began to undress for their
showers, Howard told them to button up. They had to go do a foot
inspection of the men, then watch to make sure they all showered
properly, check on the quality and quantity of their food, and inspect the barracks to see that the beds were ready. By the time the
officers got to shower, the hot water was gone; by the time they got
to eat, only cold leftovers remained. But not one of them had let
Howard down.

"From then on," Howard recalled, "we didn't follow the normal pattern of training." His colonel gave him even more flexibility,
and the transport to make it meaningful. Howard started taking his

company to Southampton, or London, or Portsmouth, to conduct street-fighting exercises in the bombed-out areas. There were plenty to choose from, and it did not matter how much damage D Company did, so all the exercises were with live ammunition.

Howard was putting together an outstanding light-infantry company.

Howard also set out, on his own, to make D Company into a first-class night-fighting unit. It was not that he had any inkling that he might be landing at night, but rather he reckoned that once in combat, his troops would be spending a good deal of their time fighting at night. He was also thinking of a favorite expression in the German army that he had heard: "The night is the friend of no man." In the British army the saying was that "the German does not like to fight at night."

The trouble was, neither did the British. Howard decided to deal with the problem of fighting in unaccustomed darkness by turning night into day. He would rouse the company at 2000 hours, take the men for their run, get them fed, and then begin twelve hours of field exercises, drill, the regular paperwork—everything that a company in training does in the course of a day. After a meal at 1000 hours, he would get them going on the athletic fields. At 1300 hours he sent them to the barracks to sleep. At 2000 hours they were up again, running. This would go on for a week at a time at first; by early 1944, as Parr recalled, "We went several weeks, continuous weeks of night into day and every now and then he would have a change-around week." And Parr described the payoff: "Oh, we were used to it, we got quite used to operating in nighttime, doing everything in the dark."

D Company was developing a feeling of independence and separateness. All the sports fanaticism had produced, as Howard had hoped it would, an extreme competitiveness. The men wanted D Company to be first in everything, and they had indeed won the regimental prizes in boxing, swimming, cross-country, soccer, and other sports. When Brig. James Kindersley asked to observe a race among the best runners in the brigade, D Company had entered twenty runners, and took fifteen of the first twenty places. According to Howard, Kindersley "was just cock-a-hoop about it."

That was exactly the response Howard and his company had

been working so hard for so long to get. The ultimate competitiveness would come against the Germans, of course, but next best was competing against the other companies. D Company wanted to be first among all the gliderborne companies, not just for the thrill of victory, but because victory in this contest meant a unique opportunity to be a part of history. No one could guess what it might be, but even the lowest private could figure out that the War Office was not going to spend all that money building an elite force and then not use it in the invasion of France—whenever that came. It was equally obvious that airborne troops would be at the van, almost certainly behind enemy lines—this a heroic adventure of unimaginable dimensions. And, finally, it was obvious that the best company would have the leading role at the van. That was the thought that sustained Howard and his company through the long dreary months, now stretching into two years, of training.

That thought sustained them because, whether consciously or subconsciously, to a man they were aware that D-Day would be the greatest day of their lives. Nothing that had happened before could possibly compare to, while nothing that happened afterward could possibly match, D-Day. D Company continued to work at a pace that bordered on fanaticism in order to earn the right to be the first to go.

2

Getting Started

THE AMERICANS were eager to get going on defeating the Germans. Eisenhower's first task as Marshall's principal advisor had been to save the Philippines, which by January 1942 was already obviously impossible. Meanwhile, Eisenhower was beginning to think on a worldwide scale. On January 22 he scribbled in his diary, "We've got to go to Europe and fight, and we've got to quit wasting resources all over the world, and still worse, wasting time." He had concluded that the correct strategy was "Germany first," on the grounds that the Germans were the main threat, that it was imperative to help keep the Red Army in the war by putting pressure on Germany from the west, and that once Germany was defeated the Americans could go over to the offensive against the Japanese. He recommended to Marshall a program: spend 1942 and the first months of 1943 building an American force in Britain, then invading France. Marshall agreed and told Eisenhower to prepare a draft directive for the American commander in Britain.

Eisenhower came up with a name—the European Theater of Operations (ETO)—and produced the draft. He urged "that absolute unity of command should be exercised by the Theater Commander," who should organize, train, and command the American ground, naval, and air forces assigned to the theater. As he handed the draft to Marshall, he asked the Chief of Staff to study it carefully because it could be an important document in the further waging of the war. Marshall replied, "I certainly do want to read it. You may be the man who executes it. If that's the case, when can you leave?" Three days later Marshall appointed Eisenhower to the command of ETO.

That June 24, Eisenhower arrived in England. There were no bands to greet him, no speeches at the airport, no ceremonies. It was almost the last time in his life he would have such a quiet arrival anywhere. That day he was still unknown to the general public, in America as well as in Britain. But the day following his arrival in London he held a press conference. An announcement was passed out identifying him as the commander of the American forces in Britain.

From that moment forth his life was dramatically and unalterably changed. He suddenly became a world figure—in the jargon of World War II, a Very Important Person, or VIP. It hardly mattered that his role was more that of an administrator than a commander, or that the number of men under him was relatively small (55,390 officers and men). Precisely because there were so few American forces in Britain, in fact, and because they were not involved in combat, Eisenhower received more coverage. His appointment was a front-page story. Every reporter in London, whether British or American, who could do so attended Eisenhower's first-ever press conference.

Eisenhower proved to be outstanding at public relations. There was, first and foremost, the man himself. He *looked* like a soldier. He stood erect, with his square, broad shoulders held back, his head high. His face and hands were always active, his face reddening with anger when he spoke of the Nazis, lighting up as he spoke of the immense forces gathering around the world to crush them. To cameramen, he was pure gold—for them a good photo of Eisenhower, whether tight-lipped or grim or laughing heartily, was usually worth at least two columns on the front page. His relaxed, casual manner was appealing, as was the nickname "Ike," which seemed to fit so perfectly. His good humor and good looks attracted people. Most reporters found it impossible to be in Eisenhower's presence and not like him.

His mannerisms complemented his good looks. Recording before a newsreel camera for the movie-theater audience back in the States, he spoke with great earnestness directly into the camera, his eyes riveted on the invisible audience. It was a perfect expression of a devotion to duty that he felt deeply, and it electrified viewers. So too did his manner of speaking bluntly about the difficulties ahead, the problems that had to be met and overcome, all followed by that big grin and a verbal expression of Eisenhower's bouncy enthusiasm.

He habitually used expressions that immediately identified him as just plain folks. He would speak of someone who "knows the score," someone else as a "big operator," or he would say, "I told him to go peddle his papers somewhere else." He called his superiors the "Big Shots." He made innumerable references to "my old hometown, Abilene," and described himself as a "simple country boy," sighing and responding sadly to a question, "That's just too complicated for a dumb bunny like me."

Eisenhower, in short, was an extremely likable person who came to the public's attention at exactly the right moment in the war. Nothing was happening in the European Theater to write about, but London was overrun with reporters looking for copy.

Throughout the war Eisenhower manipulated the press for his own purposes and for the good of the Allied cause. He was more aware of the importance of the press, and better at using it, than any other public figure of his day. This recognition was a result of his instincts and his common sense. In addition, he enjoyed meeting with the press, liked reporters as individuals, knew some of them himself from his long years in Washington, called them by their first names, posed for their photographs, flattered them not only by the attention he paid to them but by telling them that they had a crucial role to play in the war. Eisenhower believed that a democracy could not wage war without popular, widespread support for and understanding of the war effort, which only the press could create. At his first press conference he told the reporters that he considered them "quasi members of my staff," part of the "team," a thought that delighted the reporters no end, and he promised to be open and honest with them always. Only the most cynical of reporters could fail to respond to such blandishments.

Eisenhower's sense of public relations extended far beyond himself. He used the press to sell the idea of Allied unity. He believed that Anglo-American friendship was a sine qua non of final victory, and did all he could to make that friendship genuine and lasting. In the summer of 1942 his major effort was to smooth relations between the British public and the American soldiers, airmen, and sailors who were coming to the British Isles in ever-increasing numbers—eventually, more than two million came to the United Kingdom.

Eisenhower, the man at the top, was the most important individual in molding the British attitude toward the U.S. Army. He was aware of it, accepted the responsibility, and met it magnificently. London took him to its heart. He was so big, so generous, so optimistic, so intelligent, so outspoken, so energetic—so American.

Besides being good copy personally, he represented the American military machine that was coming to win the war, so inevitably he was a center of attention. His relations with the London press were as good as with the American. The British appreciated reports that he took them as they were, neither trying to ape their mannerisms nor make fun of their ways. They laughed at an item that related Eisenhower's practice of levying on the spot a fine of twopence on any American who used a British expression such as "cheerio."

Another favorite London story concerned Eisenhower's heavy smoking—he consumed four packs of Camels a day. The American ambassador, deeply embarrassed, had told Eisenhower after a dinner party that it was the custom in England not to smoke at the dinner table before the toast to the King had been drunk. Eisenhower's response was that he would attend no more formal dinners.

When Adm. Lord Louis Mountbatten nevertheless invited him to a dinner, Eisenhower said no. When Mountbatten pressed the point and assured Eisenhower he would not have to curtail his smoking, Eisenhower reluctantly agreed to go. After the sherry the party sat down to soup. As soon as it was consumed Mountbatten jumped to his feet and snapped, "Gentlemen, the King!" After the toast he turned to Eisenhower and said, "Now, General, smoke all you want."

With such stories making the rounds, and with his picture in the papers frequently, Eisenhower became a great favorite in London. Taxi drivers would wave; people on the street would wish him good luck.

Beyond the rapport he established with the British public, he got on well with British leaders, best of all with Prime Minister Winston Churchill himself. He soon became a regular weekend visitor at Churchill's country home, Chequers. Eisenhower's informality appealed to Churchill, and the Prime Minister responded to him in kind. On the evening of July 5, for example, Eisenhower recorded in his diary, "We spent the early part of the evening on the lawn in front of the house, and . . . took a walk . . . into the neighboring woods, discussing matters of general interest in connection with the war." After dinner they saw a movie, then talked until 2:30 A.M. Eisenhower slept that night in a bed Cromwell had slept in.

The "matters of general interest" the two men discussed included Ultra, the British system of breaking the German code and thus being able to read German radio messages. Next to the research on building an atomic bomb, it was the most closely guarded secret of the war. Only a handful of the British high command even knew of its existence; among the Americans, only Marshall, Roosevelt, and now Eisenhower knew about it.

Although the British and Americans were starting the process of creating the closest alliance in history, they had sharp disagreements. In the summer of 1942 they were engaged in a fierce argument over where they should launch their first offensive. Marshall and Eisenhower were insistent on waiting until 1943 and then invading France; the British, led by Churchill and Field Marshal Alan Brooke, wanted to invade French North Africa in the fall of 1942. For a number of reasons, but chiefly because the American armed forces were still more a potential than an actual force and thus the British would provide the bulk of the troops for the first offensive, the British won the argument. Reluctantly, the Americans agreed to a fall 1942 invasion of North Africa. In a nice twist of fate, the Combined Chiefs of Staff, or CCS (consisting of the British and American high commands), appointed Eisenhower to command the operation he had so strenuously opposed. The code name was Torch.

It was Eisenhower's first command (he had not gotten to Europe in World War I and had never been in combat). Necessarily, it was a learning experience for him.

Eisenhower planned to go to Gibraltar on November 2, to take command of the Rock, the best communications center in the area, and direct the invasion from there. Bad weather prevented the flight on November 2 and again on the third; on the fourth Eisenhower ordered his reluctant pilot, Maj. Paul Tibbets (by reputation the best flier in the Army Air Force; he later flew the *Enola Gay* on the first atomic-bomb mission), to ignore the weather and take off. Six B-17 Flying Fortresses, carrying Eisenhower and most of his staff, got through safely, but only after engine trouble, weather problems, and an attack by a German fighter airplane had been overcome.

After a bumpy landing Eisenhower went to his headquarters, which were in the subterranean passages. Offices were caves where the cold, damp air stagnated and stank. Despite the inconveniences Eisenhower got a great kick out of being in actual command of the Rock of Gibraltar, one of the symbols of the British Empire. "I simply must have a grandchild," he scribbled in his diary, "or I'll never have the fun of telling this when I'm fishing, gray-bearded, on the banks of a quiet bayou in the deep South."

He had little time to gloat or enjoy. British and American troops under his command were about to invade a neutral territory, without a declaration of war, without provocation, and with only a hope, not a promise, that the French colonial army would greet them as liberators rather than aggressors. He hoped he could find a high-ranking French officer who would cooperate, but was frustrated. Disgusted, he exploded, "All of these Frogs have a single thought—'ME.' "

General Patton was leading an invading force that had loaded, combat-ready, in Norfolk, Virginia, thousands of miles away from its destination at Casablanca, where to add to the worries the surf was one of the highest in the world. The British contingent had to sail past Gibraltar, where the Spanish might turn on them. What the French would do, no one knew.

In short, Eisenhower, in his first experience in combat or in command, faced problems that were serious in the extreme, and as much political as military. His staff was at least as tense as he was, and looked to him for leadership. It was a subject he had studied for decades. It was not an art in his view, but a skill to be learned. "The one quality that can be developed by studious reflection and practice is the leadership of men," he wrote his son John at West Point. Here was his chance to show that he had developed it.

In the event, he not only exercised it, but learned new lessons. It was "during those anxious hours" in Gibraltar, he later wrote in a draft introduction to his memoirs that he finally decided to discard, "that I first realized how inexorably and inescapably strain and tension wear away at the leader's endurance, his judgment and his confidence. The pressure becomes more acute because of the duty of a staff constantly to present to the commander the worst side of an eventuality." In this situation, Eisenhower realized, the commander had to "preserve optimism in himself and in his command. Without confidence, enthusiasm and optimism in the command, victory is scarcely obtainable."

Eisenhower also realized that "optimism and pessimism are infectious and they spread more rapidly from the head downward than in any other direction." He saw two additional advantages to a cheerful and hopeful attitude by the commander: First, the "habit tends to minimize potentialities within the individual himself to become demoralized." Second, it "has a most extraordinary effect upon all with whom he comes in contact. With this clear realization, I firmly determined that my mannerisms and speech in public would always reflect the cheerful certainty of victory—that any pessimism and discouragement I might ever feel would be reserved for my pillow. I adopted a policy of circulating through the whole force to the full limit imposed by physical considerations. I did my best to meet everyone from general to private with a smile, a pat on the back and a definite interest in his problems."

He did his best, from that moment to the end of his life, to conceal with a big grin the ache in his bones and the exhaustion in his mind.

There was a great deal more that went into Eisenhower's success as a leader of men, of course. As he put it on another occasion, the art of leadership is making the right decisions, then getting men to *want* to carry them out. But the words he wrote about his learning experience on the Rock, words that he was too modest to put into the published version of his memoirs, are a classic expression of one of the most critical aspects of leadership, perfectly said by a man who knew more about the subject than almost anyone else.

On November 8, American troops went ashore in Morocco and Algeria, while British troops landed near Oran. The initial opposition, consisting of French colonial troops, was light, but as the Allies moved east into Tunisia, they ran up against German troops rushed in from Italy. Resistance stiffened. Further, the winter rains turned the roads into quagmires. The first great Allied offensive of World War II came to a dispiriting halt.

Eisenhower, who had serious political problems to deal with in his relations with the French, paid too little attention to what was happening at the front. He delegated his command to Gen. Lloyd Fredendall, an officer who had come highly recommended by Marshall. But in the event, Fredendall proved incapable of meeting the test of combat. Despite his serious and well-placed misgivings, Eisenhower allowed Fredendall to stay in command, merely giving him an occasional pep talk.

Rommel, meanwhile, having been driven out of Egypt and across Libya by General Montgomery's Eighth Army, in the offensive that had begun in November at El Alamein, arrived in Tunisia. He decided to counterattack the Americans. His object was to divide the American and British forces in Tunisia, and even more to inflict a stinging defeat on the Americans in their first encounter with the German army. Rommel's aim was to give the Americans an inferiority complex. On February 14 he began the attack. By the sixteenth he was at the Kasserine Pass and had inflicted major losses on the green American troops. Fredendall all but collapsed. It appeared that Rommel was about to drive the Allies out of Tunisia.

Despite the embarrassing and costly losses, Eisenhower was not disheartened. He realized that all his lectures on the need to eliminate complacency and instill battlefield discipline among the American troops had had little effect, but he also realized that the shock of encountering the Wehrmacht on the offensive was accomplishing his objectives for him.

"Our soldiers are learning rapidly," he told Marshall at the height of the battle, "and while I still believe that many of the lessons we are forced to learn at the cost of lives could be learned at home, I assure you that the troops that come out of this campaign are going to be battle wise and tactically efficient." The best news of all was that American soldiers, who had previously shown a marked disinclination to advance under enemy fire, were recovering rapidly from the initial shock of Rommel's attack. The troops did not like being kicked around and were beginning to dig in and fight.

Nevertheless, on February 21, Rommel got through Kasserine Pass. Eisenhower regarded this development as less a threat, more an opportunity, because by then his efforts had produced a preponderance of American firepower at the point of attack, especially in artillery. Rommel had a long, single supply line that ran through a narrow pass, which made him vulnerable.

"We have enough to stop him," Eisenhower assured Marshall, but he expected to do more than that. He urged Fredendall to launch an immediate counterattack on Rommel's flanks, seize the pass, cut off the Afrika Korps, and destroy it. But Fredendall disagreed with Eisenhower's conclusion that Rommel had gone as far as he could; he expected him to make one more attack and insisted on staying on the defensive to meet it. Rommel, accepting the inevitable, began his retreat that night. It was successful, and a fleeting opportunity was lost.

In a tactical sense Rommel had won the victory. At small cost to himself, he had inflicted more than five thousand American casualties, destroyed hundreds of tanks and other equipment. But he had made no strategic gain, and in fact had done Eisenhower a favor. In his pronouncements before Kasserine, Eisenhower had consistently harped on what a tough business war is and on the overwhelming need to impress that fact on the troops.

But the man most responsible for American shortcomings was Eisenhower himself, precisely because he was not tough enough. Despite his serious and well-founded doubts he had allowed Fredendall to retain command. Eisenhower had allowed a confused command situation to continue. He had accepted intelligence reports based on insufficient sources. And at the crucial moment, when Rommel was at his most vulnerable, he had failed to galvanize his commanders, which allowed Rommel to get away.

Kasserine was Eisenhower's first real battle; taking it all in all, his performance was miserable. Only American firepower, and German shortages, had saved him from a humiliating defeat.

But Eisenhower and the American troops profited from the experience. The men, he reported to Marshall, "are now mad and ready to fight." So was he. "All our people," he added, "from the very highest to the very lowest have learned that this is not a child's game and are ready and eager to get down to . . . business." He promised Marshall that thereafter no unit under his command "will ever stop training," including units in the front line. And he fired Fredendall, replacing him with Patton.

When Patton arrived Eisenhower gave him advice that might better have been self-directed. "You must not retain for one instant," Eisenhower warned Patton, "any man in a responsible position where you have become doubtful of his ability to do the job. . . . This matter frequently calls for more courage than any other thing you will have to do, but I expect you to be perfectly cold-blooded about it."

To his old friend Gen. Leonard Gerow, then training an infantry division in Scotland, Eisenhower expanded on the theme. "Officers that fail," he said, "must be ruthlessly weeded out. Considerations of friendship, family, kindliness, and nice personality have nothing whatsoever to do with the problem. . . . You must be tough." He said it was necessary to get rid of the "lazy, the slothful, the indifferent or the complacent." Whether Eisenhower could steel himself sufficiently in this regard remained to be seen.

Patton tightened discipline to a martinet standard while his whirlwind tours in his open command car, horns blaring and outriders roaring ahead and behind him, impressed his presence on everyone in the corps. His flamboyant language and barely concealed contempt for the British created pride in everything American. When British officers made slighting remarks about American fighting qualities, Patton thundered, "We'll show 'em," and then demanded to know where in hell the Brits had been during the crisis of Kasserine. But British Gen. Harold Alexander told Patton to avoid pitched battles and stay out of trouble.

Not being allowed to attack, forced to stand to one side while

Montgomery delivered the final blow to the Afrika Korps, was galling to Patton. He asked Eisenhower to send him back to Morocco, where he could continue his planning for the invasion of Sicily. Eisenhower did so, replacing Patton with the recently arrived Gen. Omar Bradley, his old West Point classmate. Then Eisenhower told Alexander that it was essential that the Americans have their own sector in the final phase of the Tunisian campaign. Alexander replied that the Americans had failed at Kasserine and thus their place was at the rear.

Eisenhower held his temper, but his words were firm. He told Alexander that the United States had given much of its best equipment to the British. If the American people came to feel that their troops would not play a substantial role in the European Theater, they would be more inclined to insist on an Asia-first strategy. But most of all, Eisenhower insisted, Alexander had to realize that in the ultimate conquest of the Nazis, the Americans would necessarily provide the bulk of the fighting men and carry most of the load. It was therefore imperative that American soldiers gain confidence in their ability to fight the Germans, and they could not do so while in the rear. Alexander tried to debate the point, but Eisenhower insisted, and eventually Alexander agreed to place II Corps on the line, on the north coast.

Having persuaded the reluctant Alexander, Eisenhower turned his attention to Bradley. He told Bradley that he realized the sector assigned to II Corps was poorly suited to offensive action, but insisted that Bradley had to overcome the difficulties and prove that the U.S. Army "can perform in a way that will at least do full credit to the material we have." He instructed Bradley to plan every operation "carefully and meticulously, concentrate maximum fire power in support of each attack, keep up a constant pressure and convince everyone that we are doing our full part. . . ." He concluded by warning Bradley to be tough. Eisenhower said he had just heard of a battalion of infantry that had suffered a loss of ten men killed and then asked permission to withdraw and reorganize. That sort of thing had to cease. "We have reached the point where troops *must* secure objectives assigned," Eisenhower said, "and we must direct leaders to get out and *lead and to secure the necessary results.*"

Eisenhower spent the last week of April touring the front lines, and was pleased by what he saw. Bradley was "doing a great job," he concluded, and he was delighted to hear a British veteran say that the U.S. 1st Infantry Division was "one of the finest tactical organizations that he had ever seen."

By the first week in May, the German bridgehead was reduced to the area immediately around the cities of Bizerte and Tunis. On May 7, British troops moved into Tunis itself; that same day Bradley sent Eisenhower a two-word message—"Mission accomplished." His II Corps had captured Bizerte. Only mopping-up operations remained to clear the Axis completely out of Tunisia.

Eisenhower spent the last week of the campaign at the front, and it made a deep impression on him. In February he had told his wife, Mamie, that whenever he was tempted to feel sorry for himself he would think of "the boys that are living in the cold and rain and muck, high up in the cold hills of Tunisia," and be cured.

In May he heard about a story in the American press on his mother; the story stressed Ida's pacifism and the irony of her son being a general. Ike wrote his brother Arthur that their mother's "happiness in her religion means more to me than any damn wise-crack that a newspaperman can get publicized," then said of the pacifists generally, "I doubt whether any of these people, with their academic or dogmatic hatred of war, detest it as much as I do."

He said that the pacifists "probably have not seen bodies rotting on the ground and smelled the stench of decaying human flesh. They have not visited a field hospital crowded with the desperately wounded." Ike said that what separated him from the pacifists was that he hated the Nazis more than he did war. There was something else. "My hated of war will never equal my conviction that it is the duty of every one of us . . . to carry out the orders of our government when a war emergency arises." Or, as he put it to his son John, "The only unforgivable sin in war is not doing your duty."

On May 13 the last Axis forces in Tunisia surrendered. Eisenhower's forces captured 275,000 enemy troops, more than half of them German, a total bag of prisoners even larger than the Russians had gotten at Stalingrad three and a half months earlier. Congratulations poured in on Eisenhower from all sides. He told Marshall he wished he had a disposition that would allow him to relax and enjoy a feeling of self-satisfaction, but he did not. "I always anticipate and discount, in my own mind, accomplishment, and am, therefore, mentally racing ahead into the next campaign. The consequence is that all the shouting about the Tunisian campaign leaves me utterly cold."

Eisenhower knew that the North African campaign had taken too long—six months—and cost too much: his forces had lost 10,820 men killed, 39,575 wounded, and 21,415 missing or captured, a total of 71,810 casualties. But it was over, and his men had won. His own great contribution had been not so much directing the Anglo-American victory, but insisting that they won as Allies. Thanks in large part to Eisenhower, the Alliance had survived its first test and was stronger than ever.

Rommel realized that it was all up for his Afrika Korps. His bold bid at Kasserine Pass had failed and now it was only a question of time.

In March 1943, Rommel called Col. Hans von Luck to come see him at his headquarters near Benghazi. Luck drove up and together they dealt with some of the supply problems. Then Rommel asked Luck to go for a walk. Rommel regarded Luck as almost a second son, and he wanted to talk. "Listen," Rommel said, "one day you will remember what I am telling you. The war is lost."

Luck protested hotly. "We are very deep in Russia," he exclaimed. "We are in Scandinavia, in France, in the Balkans, in North Africa. How can the war be lost?"

"I will tell you," Rommel answered. "We lost Stalingrad, we will lose Africa, with the body of our best-trained armored people. We can't fight without them. The only thing we can do is to ask for an armistice. We have to give up all this business about the Jews, we have to change our minds about the religions, and so on, and we must get an armistice now at this stage while we still have something to offer."

Rommel asked Luck to fly to Hitler's headquarters and plead with the Fuhrer to execute a Dunkirk in reverse. It was all up in North Africa for the Axis, Rommel said, and he wanted to save his Afrika Korps. Luck went, but did not get past Field Marshal Alfred Jodl, who told Luck that the Fuhrer was in political discussions with the Romanians and nobody wanted to butt in with military decisions. "And anyway," Jodl concluded, "there's no idea at all to withdraw from North Africa." Luck never returned to Tunisia. Rommel flew out. The Afrika Korps was destroyed or captured.

Luck went on to teach at the military academy for half a year. In the late fall of 1943 he got orders to join the 21st Panzer Division in Brittany as one of the two regimental commanders. He had been specially requested by the division commander, Brig. Gen. Edgar Feuchtinger, who was close to Hitler and thus got the officers he wanted. Feuchtinger was reviving 21st Panzer from the dead, but his contact with Hitler made it a feasible task. His officers were exclusively veterans, most from Africa or the Eastern Front. The troops—almost sixteen thousand of them, as this was a full-strength division—were volunteers, young, eager, fit. The equipment was excellent, the tanks especially so. In addition, the new 21st Panzer had an abundance of SPVs (self-propelled vehicles), put together by a Major Becker, a reserve officer who was a genius with transport. He could transform any type of chassis into an SPV. On the SPVs he would mount all sorts of guns, but his favorite was the multibarreled rocket launcher, the so-called Stalin organ, with forty-eight barrels.

Luck set to with his regiment. Among many other exercises, he began to give the men extended night-training drills. At the end of 1943, Rommel—as commander of Army Group B—took control of the German Seventh Army in Normandy and Brittany. His arrival and his personality injected badly needed enthusiasm and professional skill into the building of the Atlantic Wall to protect Hitler's Fortress Europe.

Following the victory in North Africa, the Allies continued offensive operations in the Mediterranean. This came about by default. Eisenhower and Marshall continued to believe that only an invasion of France could be decisive, that nibbling at the periphery of the German empire would never bring the Nazis to surrender, but by mid-1943 it was too late to mount Operation Roundup (the proposed 1943 invasion of France) because the immense buildup of British and American forces in North Africa had come at the expense of a buildup in Britain. So, with North Africa as a base, the Allies went after Sicily (July) and the Italian mainland, landing at

Salerno (September). Eisenhower commanded in each case. It took his forces almost three months to overrun Sicily, while in Italy the Germans were able to impose a stalemate south of Rome.

It had been a year marked by great gains on the map. The forces under Eisenhower's command had conquered Morocco, Algeria, Tunisia, Sicily, and southern Italy. The strategic gains, however, had been small at best. Germany had not lost any territory that was critical to its defense. It had not been forced to reduce its divisions in France or Russia. Taken as a whole, Eisenhower's campaigns from November 1942 to December 1943 must be judged a strategic failure.

By no means was it altogether his fault. In the summer of 1942 he had warned his political bosses about what was going to happen if they turned down Roundup for Torch. But some of the blame was his. The excessive caution with which he opened the campaign, his refusal to run risks to get to Tunis before the Germans, his refusal to take a chance and rush troops into Sardinia, his refusal to relieve Fredendall, his refusal to take a grip on the battle in Sicily, his refusal to seize the opportunity to take Rome with the 82nd Airborne, all contributed to the unhappy situation he left behind in Italy. The Allied armies were well south of Rome as winter set in, with little hope of any rapid advance. The Allies had expended great resources for small gains.

But there was one clear gain from 1943 for the Allies—it gave the high command in general, and Eisenhower particularly, badly needed experience. The troops, too, learned what a tough business war is. Further, Eisenhower learned which of his subordinates could stand up to the strain of battle and which could not. Had it not been for Torch, had Roundup been launched in 1943 instead of Overlord in 1944, the Allies would have gone ashore with an insecure Eisenhower in command of inexperienced troops led by Lloyd Fredendall. The idea of Fredendall in charge at Omaha Beach during the crisis is by itself enough to justify the Mediterranean campaign.

In his first combat experience Eisenhower had been unsure of himself, hesitant, often depressed, irritable, likely to make snap judgments on insufficient information, defensive in both his mood and his tactics. But he had learned how critical it was for him to be always cheery and optimistic in the presence of his subordinates, how costly caution can often be in combat, and whom he could rely upon in critical moments.

In the Mediterranean campaign Eisenhower and his team had improved dramatically. As they now prepared for the climax of the war, the invasion of France, they were vastly superior to the team that had invaded North Africa in November 1942. In that respect, the payoff for Torch was worth the price.

3

Planning and Training for Overlord

FROM THE TIME America entered the war against Germany, Stalin had been demanding that the Western Allies open a second front by invading France, in order to relieve the German pressure on Russia. Roosevelt had promised to do so in 1943, but Roundup got scuttled in favor of operations in North Africa, Sicily, and Italy. By the late fall of 1943, Stalin's demands had grown irresistible—and anyway invading France was exactly what Eisenhower and Marshall wanted to do. So when Stalin met with Roosevelt and Churchill at Teheran, Iran, in December, Roosevelt assured him that Overlord was definitely on for the spring of 1944. Stalin wanted to know who was in command. Roosevelt replied that the appointment had not yet been made. Stalin said in that case he did not believe the Americans and British were serious about the operation. Roosevelt promised to make the selection in three or four days.

But the President shrank from making the decision. He wanted to give the command to Marshall, who had built the army that would carry out Overlord, but he also wanted Marshall to continue to serve as Chief of Staff, with worldwide responsibility. In early December, after leaving Teheran for Cairo, Egypt, he asked Marshall to express his personal preference, and thus, he hoped, make the decision for him. Marshall replied that while he would gladly serve wherever the President told him to, he would not be the judge in his own case. Roosevelt thereupon asked Marshall to write a message to Stalin for him. As Roosevelt dictated, Marshall wrote, "From the President to Marshal Stalin. The immediate appointment of General Eisenhower to command of Overlord operations has been decided upon." Roosevelt then signed it.

It was the most coveted command in the history of warfare. It gave Eisenhower his great, unique opportunity. Without it, he would have been only one among a number of famous Allied generals rather than the Great Captain of World War II and, as a consequence, President of the United States.

He got the appointment, it seemed, by default. In explaining his reasoning afterward, Roosevelt said that he just could not sleep at night with Marshall out of the country. Eisenhower was the logical choice because Marshall was too important to be spared, even for Overlord. Since the commander had to be an American, a process of elimination brought it down to Eisenhower.

There were, nevertheless, manifold positive reasons for Eisenhower's selection. Overlord, like Torch, was going to be a joint operation, and Eisenhower had proved that he could create and run an integrated staff and successfully command combined British-American operations. No other general had done so. Adm. Andrew Cunningham, now a member of the CCS (he had assumed the duties of First Sea Lord in mid-October), had said it well when he left the Mediterranean. He told Eisenhower it had been a great experience for him to see the forces of two nations, made up of men with different upbringings, conflicting ideas on staff work, and basic, "apparently irreconcilable ideas," brought together and knitted into a team. "I do not believe," Cunningham said, "that any other man than yourself could have done it."

The key word was "team." Eisenhower's emphasis on teamwork, his never-flagging insistence on working together, was the single most important reason for his selection, much more important than his generalship, which in truth had been cautious and hesitant. Eisenhower's dedication to teamwork was, of course, a theme that had characterized his whole life, stretching back to Abilene High School baseball and football games.

Gathering the disparate forces for Overlord, welding them into a genuine team, making the plans for the actual engagement, and directing the action once the conflict began were challenges rather like coaching a football team, albeit on an immensely larger scale. The job required an ability to spot and exploit each player's strength, and to force each player—many of them "stars," egotistical and self-centered—to merge his talents with the others in order to fight together in a common cause. Marshall, for all his awesome abilities, did not have the patience required to work smoothly and efficiently with prima donnas, especially British prima donnas. Nor did Marshall have Eisenhower's experience in commanding amphibious operations. General Brooke, a man who was consistently and scathingly critical of Eisenhower's professional competence, recognized this truth. "The selection of Eisenhower instead of Marshall," he wrote, "was a good one."

Another, related factor in Roosevelt's choice was Eisenhower's popularity. Everyone liked him, responded positively to his outgoing personality, even when they disagreed with his decisions. His hearty laugh, infectious grin, relaxed manner, and consistent optimism were irresistible.

Equally important, he was physically strong enough to withstand the rigors and pressures of a long and arduous campaign. Fifty-three years old, he was tough enough to get along on four or five hours' sleep a night, to shake off a cold or the flu, to rouse himself from near-total exhaustion and present a cheerful face to his subordinates. It was not that he did not pay a price for all his activity, but that he did not let it show. In September 1943 a friend told him that he was pleased to see from some snapshots taken in Sicily that Eisenhower looked so healthy. In reply, Eisenhower said, "I must admit that sometimes I feel a thousand years old when I struggle to my bed at night." Nevertheless, the overriding impression he gave was one of vitality. Dwight Eisenhower was an intensely alive human being who enjoyed his job immensely.

That quality showed in his speech, his mannerisms, his physical movements, most of all in his eyes. They were astonishingly expressive. As he listened to his deputies discuss future operations, his eyes moved quickly and inquisitively from face to face. His concentration was intense, almost a physical embrace. The eyes always showed his mood—they were icy blue when he was angry, warmly blue when he was pleased, sharp and demanding when he was concerned, glazed when he was bored.

Most of all, they bespoke his supreme self-confidence, a cer-

tainty of belief in himself and his abilities. It was neither a blind nor
an egotistical confidence. As has been seen, he was a sharp and
insightful critic of his own decisions. Like the successful football
coach studying the movies of the preceding week's game, his self-
criticism was searching and positive, designed to eliminate errors
and improve performance.

He had made, and would have to make, countless decisions,
decisions that involved the lives of tens of thousands of men, not to
speak of the fate of great nations. He did so with the certainty
that he had taken everything into account, gathered all relevant
information, and considered all possible consequences. Then he
acted. This is the essence of command.

His self-confidence inspired confidence in him. When associates, be they superiors or subordinates, described Eisenhower, there
was one word that almost all of them used. It was trust. People
trusted Eisenhower for the most obvious reason—he was trustwor-
thy. Disagree as they might (and often did) with his decisions, they
never doubted his motives. Montgomery did not think much of
Eisenhower as a soldier, but he did appreciate his other qualities.
While he thought Eisenhower intelligent, "his real strength lies in
his human qualities. . . . He has the power of drawing the hearts of
men towards him as a magnet attracts the bit of metal. He merely
has to smile at you, and you trust him at once."

With his staff and with his troops, with his superiors and with
his subordinates, as with foreign governments, Eisenhower did
what he said he was going to do. His reward was the trust they
placed in him. Because of that trust, and because of the qualities he
possessed that brought it about, he was a brilliant choice as Supreme Commander, Allied Expeditionary Force, quite possibly the
best appointment Roosevelt ever made.

The buildup in Britain for Overlord was on a vast scale. Troops
of all kinds were coming to Scotland, Wales, Northern Ireland, and
England from the United States and Canada, along with refugees
from occupied Europe who were forming their own regiments,
divisions, and naval and air units, including Poles, Frenchmen,
Norwegians, Belgians, and Dutchmen. Thousands, tens of thousands, hundreds of thousands, ultimately more than three million

of them. Most of all, American infantry, armored, and airborne divisions. The 29th Infantry Division arrived first. It was a National Guard division from Virginia, Delaware, and Maryland, nicknamed the "Blue and Gray."

The 29th Division sailed for England in September 1942 aboard the *Queen Mary,* converted from luxury liner to troop transport. The *Queen Mary* sailed alone, depending on her speed to avoid submarines. At five hundred miles out from the Continent, and thus within range of the Luftwaffe, an escort of British warships appeared. A cruiser, HMS *Curaçao,* cut across the bow of the 83,000-ton *Queen Mary.* The *Queen* knifed into the 4,290-ton cruiser and cut her in half, killing 332 members of her crew. It was not an auspicious beginning to the great Allied invasion.

The division took over Tidworth Barracks, near Salisbury. These were the best barracks in England but woefully short of what GIs had become accustomed to in the training camps in the States. For men who had trained in the American South, the English weather was miserable. Pvt. John R. Slaughter of D Company, 116th Regiment, recalled, "Morale was not good during those first few months in the British Isles. Homesickness, dreary weather, long weeks of training without pause caused many of us to grumble."

In September 1943, Easy Company, 501st PIR, 101st Airborne, shipped over to England, where it took up barracks in the village of Aldbourne. The training that ensued was intense. The airborne officers, like their counterparts in the infantry and armored divisions, had been imbued with the spirit Eisenhower had insisted on ever since the American army had discovered, at Kasserine Pass, that it wasn't anywhere near as tough as it thought it was. The company did practice jumps, night exercises, on its own and with infantry, artillery, and tanks. Men learned how to jump at night, how to anticipate the ground coming up, how to stay in a foxhole while a tank ran over it, how to distinguish various German weapons by their sound, and most of all that most basic lesson for combat infantry, how to love the ground, how to read it, how to dig in it, how to survive. They went at the training so hard that every man in the company was convinced "combat can't be worse than this."

But it wasn't all misery. Weekend passes and the excellent British rail service gave the men a break from the tension. England in the late fall and early winter was a wonderland for the boys from the States. Most of the British boys their age were off in Italy or in training camps far from their homes, so there were lonely, bored, unattached young women everywhere. The American soldiers were well paid, much better than the British, and the paratroopers had that extra $50 per month. Beer was cheap and plentiful, once out of Aldbourne all restraints were removed, they were getting ready to kill or be killed, and they were for the most part twenty or twenty-one years old.

Pvt. David Kenyon Webster described the result in an October 23 diary entry: "Although I do not enjoy the army, most of the men in this outfit find it a vacation. Boys who had been working steadily at home enter the army and are relieved of all responsibilities. It is unanimously agreed that they never pitched such glorious drunks back home."

The excitement of the time, the kaleidoscope of impressions that were continually thrust upon them, the desperate need to escape the rigors of training, the thought of upcoming combat and Captain Sobel's chickenshit, combined to make this an unforgettable time and impel most of the men to make the most of it. "London to me was a magic carpet," Pvt. Gordon Carson wrote. "Walk down any of its streets and every uniform of the Free World was to be seen. Their youth and vigor vibrated in every park and pub. To Piccadilly, Hyde Park, Leicester Square, Trafalgar Square, Victoria they came. The uniform of the Canadians, South Africans, Australians, New Zealanders, the Free French, Polish, Belgians, Dutch, and of course the English and Americans were everywhere.

"Those days were not lost on me because even at twenty years of age, I knew I was seeing and being a part of something that was never to be again. Wartime London was its own world."

There was an excess of drinking, whoring, fighting. Older British observers complained, "The trouble with you Yanks is that you are overpaid, oversexed, and over here." (To which the Yanks would reply, "The trouble with you Limeys is that you are underpaid, undersexed, and under Eisenhower.")

□

The U.S. 2nd and 5th Ranger Battalions were composed of volunteers. Others referred to them as "suicide squads," but Lt. James Eikner of the 2nd Rangers disagreed: "We were simply spirited young people who took the view that if you are going to be a combat soldier, you may as well be one of the very best; also we were anxious to get on with the war so as to bring things to a close and get home to our loved ones as soon as possible."

Naturally, such fine troops had a special mission, to capture the German battery at Pointe-du-Hoc. As this would require scaling a 200-meter-high cliff, the rangers got into superb physical condition. In March they went to the Highlands of Scotland, where Brigadier Lord Lovat's No. 4 Commando put them through grueling speed marches (averaging twenty-five miles a day, culminating in a thirty-seven-mile march) across what was reputedly the toughest obstacle course in the world. They climbed mountains, scaled cliffs, practiced unarmed combat. They learned stealth, how to conduct quick-hitting strikes. In ten days of such training, one private's weight dropped from 205 to 170 pounds.

Next they practiced amphibious landing operations on the Scottish coast, hitting beaches specially prepared with barbed wire, beach obstacles, and every type of anti-assault landing device that Rommel had waiting for them. In April the rangers went to the Assault Training Center. In early May it was off to Swanage for special training in cliff scaling with ropes, using grappling hooks trailing ropes propelled to the top of the cliff by rockets, and with extension ladders donated by the London Fire Department and carried in DUKWs (amphibious vehicles).

Lt. Walter Sidlowski, an engineer, marveled at the rangers. "My guys had always felt we were in good shape physically," he remembered, "but watching the rangers using most of their time double-timing, with and without arms and equipment, push-ups and various other physical exercise whenever they were not doing something else, was cause for wonder."

"I can assure you," Lieutenant Eikner of the 2nd Ranger Battalion commented, "that when we went into battle after all this training there was no shaking of the knees or weeping or praying; we knew what we were getting into; we knew every one of us had volunteered for extra hazardous duty; we went into battle confident;

of course we were tense when under fire, but we were intent on getting the job done. We were actually looking forward to accomplishing our mission."

There were many other special units, including underwater demolition teams, midget-submarine crews to guide the incoming landing craft, tiny one-man airplanes with folded wings that could be brought in on rhino ferries (42-by-176-foot flat-bottomed pontoon barges with a capacity of forty vehicles, towed across the Channel by LSTs—landing ship, tanks—powered for the run into the beach by large outboard motors), put into operation on the beach, and used for naval gunfire spotting. The 743rd Tank Battalion, like the other DD tankers,* spent months learning how to maneuver their tanks in the Channel. The 320th Barrage Balloon Battalion (Colored) practiced setting up their balloons on the beach. The Cherokee code talkers (forty in all, twenty for Utah, twenty for Omaha) worked on their radios—they could speak in their own language, confident the Germans would never be able to translate.

Overlord was planned as a direct frontal assault against a prepared enemy position. The German line, or Atlantic Wall, was continuous, so there was no possibility of outflanking it. The Germans had a manpower advantage and the benefit of land lines of communication, so Eisenhower's forces could not hope to overwhelm them. Eisenhower's advantages were control of the air and of the sea, which meant that Allied bombers and ships could pound the enemy emplacements and trenches on a scale even larger than the World War I artillery barrages. In addition, he was on the offensive, which meant that he knew where and when the battle would be fought. Even better, he had no defensive lines to maintain, so he could concentrate all his resources on a relatively narrow front in Normandy, while the Germans had to spread their resources along the coast.

The Allied bombers would play a key role. There was no dispute about this point; all agreed that on the eve of D-Day every bomber that could fly would participate in the attack on the Nor-

* Swimming tanks, called DD for Direct Drive

mandy coastal defenses. There was, however, intense debate over the role of the bombers in the two months preceding the invasion. Eisenhower persisted in his demand that the bombers come under SHAEF (Supreme Headquarters, Allied Expeditionary Force) control, and that they then be used to implement the so-called Transportation Plan, designed to destroy the French railway system and thus hamper German mobility.

On March 6, Patton came to visit Eisenhower at his headquarters. His was shown into Eisenhower's office while Eisenhower was on the telephone with British Air Marshal Arthur Tedder, his deputy supreme commander.

"Now, listen, Arthur," Eisenhower was saying, "I am tired of dealing with a lot of prima donnas. By God, you tell that bunch that if they can't get together and stop quarreling like children, I will tell the Prime Minister to get someone else to run this damn war. I'll quit." Patton took careful note of the tone of command in his voice; Eisenhower was obviously taking charge, and Patton could not help being impressed.

Marshall supported Eisenhower in the dispute; Churchill supported Air Vice Marshal Arthur Harris and Gen. Tooey Spaatz, who wanted to bomb industrial targets inside Germany, not bridges and railroads in France. Eisenhower then told Churchill that if his bosses refused to make anything less than a full commitment to Overlord by holding back the bombers, he would "simply have to go home."

This extreme threat brought Churchill around. Tedder then prepared a list of more than seventy railroad targets in France and Belgium. The bombers went to work on the French railway system. By D-Day the Allies had dropped seventy-six thousand tons of bombs on rail centers, bridges, and open lines. The Seine River bridges west of Paris were virtually destroyed. Based on an index of 100 for January and February 1944, railway traffic dropped from 69 in mid-May to 38 by D-Day.

Eisenhower had dozens of major and hundreds of minor disagreements with Churchill and the CCS during the war, but the only occasion on which he threatened to resign was over the issue of command of the strategic air forces. He was certain at the time that he was right, and he never saw any reason to question that belief. In 1968, in one of his last interviews, he told this author that he felt the greatest single contribution he personally made to the success of Overlord was his insistence on the Transportation Plan.

There were many aspects to Overlord in which Eisenhower's role was more supervisory than direct, including such items as the artificial harbors, the specially designed tanks, assault techniques, the deception plan, the logistical problems involved in getting the men and equipment to the southern English ports, transporting them across the Channel, and supplying them in Normandy.

Overlord was the greatest amphibious assault in history, with the largest air and sea armadas ever assembled. It required, and got, painstakingly detailed planning, with thousands of men involved. SHAEF alone had a total strength of 16,312, of whom 2,829 were officers (1,600 Americans, 1,229 British). There were in addition the staffs of the U.S. and British armies, corps, and divisions, all devoting their entire energy to Overlord.

These vast bureaucracies did very well what they were created to do, but their limitations were obvious. They could suggest, plan, advise, investigate, but they could not act. Nor could any single member of the bureaucracies see the problem whole. Every individual involved had a specific given role to play and could concentrate on one set of problems; each staff officer was an expert struggling with his specialty. The officers could study and analyze a problem and make recommendations, but they could not decide and order.

Someone had to give the bureaucracies direction; someone had to be able to take all the information they gathered, make sense out of it, and impose order on it; someone had to make certain that each part meshed into the whole; someone had to decide; someone had to take the responsibility and act.

It all came down to Eisenhower. He was the funnel through which everything passed. Only his worries were infinite, only he carried the awesome burden of command. This position put enormous pressure on him, pressure that increased geometrically with each day that passed.

"Ike looks worn and tired," Eisenhower aide Capt. Harry Butcher, USN, noted on May 12. "The strain is telling on him. He looks older now than at any time since I have been with him." It would get worse as D-Day got closer and innumerable problems came up each day, many unsolved and some unsolvable. Still, Butcher felt that all would turn out all right, that Eisenhower could take it. "Fortunately he has the happy faculty of bouncing back after a night of good sleep."

Unfortunately, such nights were rare. Eisenhower's tension and tiredness began to show in his face, especially when he was inspecting training exercises, watching the boys he would be sending against Hitler's Atlantic Wall. The anxieties also showed in his letters to Mamie. Almost without exception, every letter he wrote her in the pre-Overlord period had a fantasy about his retirement plans when the war was over. The emphasis was on loafing in a warm climate.

Writing to Mamie was practically the only time he was free to think about issues that went beyond Overlord. He took the opportunity to express some of his deepest feelings. He loathed war and hated having to send boys to their death. "How I wish this cruel business of war could be completed quickly," he told Mamie. He was the man who had to total up all the casualties, bad enough in the air war, with worse to come when Overlord began. Counting the human costs was "a terribly sad business." It made him heartsick to think about "how many youngsters are gone forever," and although he had developed "a veneer of callousness," he could "never escape a recognition of the fact that back home the news brings anguish and suffering to families all over the country. Mothers, fathers, brothers, sisters, wives and friends must have a difficult time preserving any comforting philosophy and retaining any belief in the eternal rightness of things. War demands real toughness of fiber—not only in the soldiers that must endure, but in the homes that must sacrifice their best."

"I think that all these trials and tribulations must come upon the world because of some great wickedness," he said in another letter, "yet one would feel that man's mere intelligence to say nothing of his spiritual perceptions would find some way of eliminating war. But man has been trying to do so for many hundreds of years, and his failure just adds more reason for pessimism when a man gets really low!"

The contrast between Eisenhower and those generals who gloried in war could not have been greater. Small wonder that millions of Americans in the 1940s felt that if their loved one had to join the fight, Eisenhower was the general they wanted for his commander. Patton, MacArthur, Bradley, Marshall, and the others all had their special qualities, but only Eisenhower had such a keen sense of family, of the way in which each casualty meant a grieving family back home.

Eisenhower's concern was of such depth and so genuine that it never left him. In 1964, when he was filming with Walter Cronkite a television special entitled "D-Day Plus 20," Cronkite asked him what he thought about when he returned to Normandy. In reply, he spoke not of the tanks, the guns, the planes, the ships, the personalities of his commanders and their opponents, or the victory. Instead, he spoke of the families of the men buried in the American cemetery in Normandy. He said he could never come to this spot without thinking of how blessed he and Mamie were to have grandchildren, and how much it saddened him to think of all the couples in America who had never had that blessing because their only son was buried in France.

One reason, more rational than emotional, that Eisenhower was concerned about his troops was his realization that while he, SHAEF, the generals, and the admirals could plan, prepare the ground, provide covering support, ensure adequate supplies, deceive the Germans, and in countless other ways try to ensure victory, in the end success rested with the footslogger carrying a rifle over the beaches of Normandy. If he was willing to drive forward in the face of German fire, Overlord would succeed. If he cowered behind the beached landing craft, it would fail. The operation all came down to that.

For that reason, Eisenhower spent much of his pre–D-Day time visiting troops in the field. He wanted to let as many men as possible see him. He made certain that every soldier who was to go ashore on D-Day had the opportunity to at least look at the man who was sending him into battle; he managed to talk to hundreds personally. In the four months from February 1 to June 1 he visited twenty-six divisions, twenty-four airfields, five ships of war, and countless depots, shops, hospitals, and other installations. He would have the men break ranks, gather around him while he made a short speech, then go around shaking hands.

He always managed to talk to the enlisted men as individuals. Other generals did so too, of course, but none had Eisenhower's touch. Bradley, Patton, Montgomery, and the rest would ask a man about his military specialty, his training, his unit, his weapons.

Eisenhower's first question invariably was, "Where are you from?" He wanted to know about their families, what they did in civilian life back in the States, what their postwar plans were. He enjoyed discussing cattle ranching in Texas with them, or dairy farming in Wisconsin, or logging in Montana. To Eisenhower's associates, the men were soldiers; to Eisenhower, they were citizens temporarily caught up in a war none of them wanted, but which they realized was necessary. His face would light up whenever he met a boy from Kansas; he kept hoping to find one from Abilene, but never did. The British and Canadians responded as enthusiastically to Eisenhower's friendliness, informality, curiosity about them as individuals, and sincerity as did the Americans.

To the graduating class at Sandhurt, the British officer school, in the spring of 1944, Eisenhower delivered an impromptu address that ranks as one of his best. He spoke of the great issues involved, and made each individual aware that his own chances for a happy, decent life were directly tied up in the success of Overlord. He reminded them of the great traditions of Sandhurst. He told the newly commissioned officers that they must be like fathers to their men, even when the men were twice their age, that they must keep the enlisted men out of trouble, and stand up for them when they committed a transgression. Their companies, he said, returning to his favorite theme, must be like a big family, and they must be the head of the family, ensuring that the unit was cohesive, tough, well trained, well equipped, ready to go. The response of the Sandhurst graduates, according to Thor Smith, a public-relations officer at SHAEF, was "electric. They just loved him."

In early May all over the British Isles men went through final exercises for D-Day. From May 9 to 12 the 101st held its dress rehearsal, code-named Exercise Eagle. The entire division participated. Easy Company used the same airfield it would use on D-Day,

Uppottery. Personnel and equipment were loaded onto the same aircraft the company would use on the real thing; the takeoff, drop, and assembly followed the plan as close to the letter as possible, including spending the same amount of time in flight.

Climbing aboard the C-47s was difficult because of all the gear each man carried. Individuals were overloaded, following the age-old tendency of soldiers going into combat to attempt to be ready for every conceivable emergency. The vest and long drawers issued each man were impregnated, to ward off a possible chemical attack; it made them cumbersome, they stank, they itched, they kept in body heat and caused torrents of sweat. The combat jacket and trousers were also treated. The men carried a pocketknife in the lapel of their blouses, to be used to cut themselves out of their harness if they landed in a tree. In their baggy trousers pockets they had a spoon, razor, socks, cleaning patches, flashlight, maps, three-day supply of K-rations, an emergency ration package (four chocolate bars, a pack of Charms, powdered coffee, sugar, and matches), ammunition, a compass, two fragmentation grenades, an antitank mine, a smoke grenade, a Gammon bomb (a two-pound plastic explosive powerful enough to damage a tank), and cigarettes, two cartons per man. The soldier topped his uniform with a webbing belt and braces, a .45 pistol (standard for noncoms and officers; privates had to get their own, and most did), water canteen, shovel, first-aid kit, and bayonet. Over this went his parachute harness, his main parachute in its backpack, and reserve parachute hooked on in front. A gas mask was strapped to his left leg and a jump knife/bayonet to his right. Across his chest the soldier slung his musette bag (knapsack) with his spare underwear and ammunition, and in some cases TNT sticks, along with his broken-down rifle or machine gun or mortar diagonally up and down across his front under his reserve chute pack, leaving both hands free to handle the risers. Over everything he wore his Mae West life jacket. Finally, he put on his helmet.

Some men added a third knife. Others found a place for extra ammunition. Private Gordon, carrying his machine gun, figured he weighed twice his normal weight. Nearly every man had to be helped into the C-47. Once aboard, the men were so wedged in they could not move.

General Maxwell Taylor had moved heaven and earth to get enough C-47s for Exercise Eagle. The planes were in constant demand for logistical support throughout ETO, and Troop Carrier Command came last on the list. It was cheated on equipment. The fuel tanks did not have armor protection from flak.

Easy got its briefing for Eagle on May 10–11. The objective was a gun battery covering the beach. At dusk on May 11, Easy took off. The planes made "legs" over England, flying for about two and a half hours. Shortly after midnight the company jumped. For Easy, the exercise went smoothly; for other companies, there were troubles. Second Battalion headquarters company was with a group that ran into a German air raid over London. Flak was coming up; the formation broke up; the pilots could not locate the DZ (Drop Zone). Eight of the nine planes carrying Company H of the 502nd dropped their men on the village of Ramsbury, nine miles from the DZ. Twenty-eight planes returned to their airfields with the paratroopers still aboard. Others jumped willy-nilly, leading to many accidents. Nearly five hundred men suffered broken bones, sprains, or other injuries.

The only consolation the airborne commanders could find in this mess was that by tradition a bad dress rehearsal leads to a great opening night.

On the last day of May the company marched down to trucks lined up on the Hungerford Road. Half the people of Aldbourne, and nearly all the unmarried girls, were there to wave good-bye. There were many tears. The baggage left behind gave some hope that the boys would be back.

Training had come to an end. There had been twenty-two months of it, more or less continuous. The men were as hardened physically as it was possible for human beings to be. Not even professional boxers or football players were in better shape. They were disciplined, prepared to carry out orders instantly and unquestioningly. They were experts in the use of their own weapons, knowledgeable in the use of other weapons, familiar with and capable of operating German weapons. They could operate radios, knew a variety of hand signals, could recognize various smoke signals. They were skilled in tactics, whether the problem was attacking a battery or a blockhouse or a trench system or a hill defended by machine guns. They knew the duties and responsibilities of a squad or platoon leader and each was prepared to assume those duties if necessary. They knew how to blow bridges, how to render artillery pieces inoperative. They could set up a defensive position in an instant. They could live in the field, sleep in a foxhole, march all day and through the night. They knew and trusted each other. Within Easy Company they had made the best friends they had ever had, or would ever have. They were prepared to die for each other; more important, they were prepared to kill for each other.

They were ready. But, of course, going into combat for the first time is an ultimate experience for which one can never be fully ready. It is anticipated for years in advance; it is a test that produces anxiety, eagerness, tension, fear of failure, anticipation. There is a mystery about the thing, heightened by the fact that those who have done it cannot put into words what it is like, how it feels, except that getting shot at and shooting to kill produce extraordinary emotional reactions. No matter how hard you train, nor however realistic the training, no one can ever be fully prepared for the intensity of the real thing.

And so the men of Easy Company left Aldbourne full of self-confidence and full of trepidation.

They were part of a vast movement of men to the embarkation ports in the south of England. Overlord was staggering in its scope. In one night and day, 175,000 fighting men and their equipment, including 50,000 vehicles of all types, ranging from motorcycles to tanks and armored bulldozers, were to be transported across sixty to a hundred miles of open water and landed on a hostile shore against intense opposition. They would be either carried by or supported by 5,333 ships and craft of all types and almost 11,000 airplanes. They came from southwestern England, southern England, the east coast of England. It was as if the cities of Green Bay, Racine, and Kenosha, Wisconsin, were picked up and moved— every man, woman and child, every automobile and truck—to the east side of Lake Michigan in one night.

The effort behind this unique movement—which British prime minister Winston S. Churchill rightly called "the most diffi-cult and complicated operation ever to take place"—stretched back two years in time and involved the efforts of literally millions of people. The production figures from the United States, in landing craft, ships of war, airplanes of all types, weapons, medicine, and so much more, were fantastic. The figures in the United Kingdom and Canada were roughly similar.

But for all that American industrial brawn and organizational ability could do, for all that the British and Canadians and other allies could contribute, for all the plans and preparations, for all the brilliance of the deception scheme, for all the inspired leadership, in the end success or failure in Operation Overlord came down to a relatively small number of junior officers, noncoms, and privates or seamen in the American, British, and Canadian armies, navies, air forces, and coast guards. If the paratroopers and gliderborne troops cowered behind hedgerows or hid out in barns rather than actively sought out the enemy, if the coxswains did not drive their landing craft ashore but instead, out of fear of enemy fire, dropped the ramps in too-deep water, if the men at the beaches dug in behind the seawall, if the noncoms and junior officers failed to lead their men up and over the seawall to move inland in the face of enemy fire—why, then, the most thoroughly planned offensive in military history, an offensive supported by incredible amounts of naval firepower, bombs, and rockets, would fail.

It all came down to a bunch of eighteen- to twenty-eight-year-olds. They were magnificently trained and equipped and supported, but only a few of them had ever been in combat. Only a few had ever killed or seen a buddy killed. Most had never heard a shot fired in anger. They were citizen soldiers, not professionals.

It was an open question, toward the end of spring 1944, as to whether a democracy could produce young soldiers capable of fighting effectively against the best that Nazi Germany could produce. Hitler was certain the answer was no. Nothing that he had learned of the British army's performance in France in 1940, or again in North Africa and the Mediterranean in 1942–44, or what he had learned of the American army in North Africa and the Mediterranean in 1942–44, caused him to doubt that, on anything approaching equality in numbers, the Wehrmacht would prevail. Totalitarian fanaticism and discipline would always conquer democratic liberalism and softness. Of that Hitler was sure.

If Hitler had seen the junior officers and men preparing for the assault he might have had second thoughts. They were young men born into the false prosperity of the 1920s and brought up in the bitter realities of the Depression of the 1930s. The literature they had read as youngsters was antiwar, cynical, portraying patriots as suckers, slackers as heroes. None of them wanted to be part of another war. They wanted to be throwing baseballs, not hand grenades, shooting .22s at rabbits, not M-1s at other young men. But when the test came, when freedom had to be fought for or abandoned, they had to fight. They were soldiers of democracy. On them depended the fate of the world.

4

"OK, Let's Go"

D-DAY FOR OVERLORD was scheduled for June 5. At the end of May troops and equipment of all kinds began to move to the southern British ports and airfields. Tens of thousands of them. Once into their secure areas, they got their first briefings on where they were going to land. The armada of transports that would be carrying them across the English Channel gathered in the harbors; little LCVPs, Higgins boats,* carried the men from the quays to the transports. The armada of warships that would protect the transports began to gather off the coast—battleships, cruisers, destroyers, minesweepers, and more.

The AEF was set to go, living on the edge of fearful anticipation. "The mighty host," in Eisenhower's words, "was tense as a coiled spring," ready for "the moment when its energy should be released and it would vault the English Channel."

SHAEF had prepared for everything except the weather. It now became an obsession. It was the one thing for which no one could plan, and the one thing that no one could control. In the end, the most completely planned military operation in history was dependent on the caprice of winds and waves. Tides and moon

---

* Named for its inventor and producer, Andrew Higgins of New Orleans. The Navy designated it landing craft vehicle, personnel.

conditions were predictable, but storms were not. From the beginning, everyone had counted on at least acceptable weather for D-Day. There had been no contingency planning. Eisenhower's inclination, as he noted in his diary, was to go, whatever the weather, but if he held to a rigid timetable and conditions became really bad, the invasion might fail. Wind-tossed landing craft could founder before reaching the shore, or the waves might throw the troops up on the beaches, seasick and unable to fight effectively. The Allies would not be able to use their air superiority to cover the beaches. If Overlord failed, it would take months to plan and mount another operation, too late for 1944.

The evening of June 3, Eisenhower met in the mess room at Southwick House* with his commanders and RAF Group Capt. J. M. Stagg, his chief weatherman. Stagg had bad news. A high-pressure system was moving out and a low was coming in. The weather on June 5 would be overcast and stormy, with a cloud base of five hundred feet to zero and Force 5 winds. Worse, the situation was deteriorating so rapidly that forecasting more than twenty-four hours in advance was highly undependable. It was too early to make a final decision, but word had to go out to the American navy carrying Bradley's troops to Omaha and Utah Beaches, since they had the farthest to travel. Eisenhower decided to let them start the voyage, subject to a possible last-minute cancellation. He would make the final decision at the regular weather conference the next morning.

At 4:30 A.M. on Sunday, June 4, Eisenhower met with his subordinates at Southwick House. Stagg said sea conditions would be slightly better than anticipated, but the overcast would not permit the use of the air forces. Montgomery said he wanted to go ahead anyway. Tedder and Air Vice Marshal Trafford Leigh-Mallory wanted postponement. Adm. Bertram Ramsay said the navy could do its part but remained neutral when asked whether or not the whole operation should go.

Eisenhower remarked that Overlord was being launched with ground forces that were not overwhelmingly powerful. The operation was feasible only because of Allied air superiority. If he could

* SHAEF headquarters for the invasion, outside Portsmouth

not have that advantage, the landings were too risky. He asked if anyone present disagreed, and when no one did he declared for a twenty-four-hour postponement. The word went out to the American fleet by prearranged signal. Displaying superb seamanship, the fleet drove through the incoming storm, regained its ports, refueled, and prepared to sail again the next day.

That evening Eisenhower ate at Southwick House. After dinner he moved into the mess room. Montgomery, Tedder, SHAEF Chief of Staff Walter B. Smith, Ramsay, Leigh-Mallory, and various high-ranking staff officers were already there. The wind and the rain rattled the window frames in the French doors in staccato sounds. The mess room was large, with a heavy table at one end and easy chairs at the other. Two sides of the room were lined with bookcases, most of which were empty and forlorn. A third side consisted of the French doors; the fourth wall was covered with a huge map of southern England and Normandy, filled with pins, arrows, and other symbols of Allied and German units. The officers lounged in easy chairs. Coffee was served and there was desultory conversation. Stagg came in about nine-thirty with the latest weather report. Eisenhower called his associates to order and they all sat up to listen intently.

Stagg reported a break. Gen. Kenneth Strong, the SHAEF G-2 (intelligence officer), recalled that at Stagg's prediction, "a cheer went up. You never heard middle-aged men cheer like that!" The rain that was then pouring down, Stagg continued, would stop in two or three hours, to be followed by thirty-six hours of more or less clear weather. Winds would moderate. The bombers and fighters ought to be able to operate on Monday night, June 5–6, although they would be hampered by clouds.

Leigh-Mallory remarked that it seemed to be only a moderately good night for air power. Tedder, his pipe clenched between his teeth and forcibly blowing out smoke, agreed that the operations of heavy bombers were going to be "chancy." Eisenhower countered by pointing out that the Allies could call on their large force of fighter-bombers.

The temptation to postpone again and meet the following morning for another conference was strong and growing, but Ramsay put a stop to that idea by pointing out that Adm. Alan G. Kirk, commanding the American task force, "must be told in the next half hour if Overlord is to take place on Tuesday [June 6]. If he is told it is on, and his forces sail and are then recalled, they will not be ready again for Wednesday morning. Therefore, a further postponement would be forty-eight hours." A two-day delay would put everything back to June 8, and by that time the tidal conditions would not be right, so in fact postponement now meant postponement until June 19.

Whatever Eisenhower decided would be risky. He began pacing the room, head down, chin on his chest, hands clasped behind his back.

Suddenly he shot his chin out at Smith. "It's a helluva gamble but it's the best possible gamble," Smith said. Eisenhower nodded, tucked his chin away, paced some more, then shot it out at Montgomery, huddled in his greatcoat, his face almost hidden.

"Do you see any reason for not going Tuesday?" Montgomery straightened up, looked Eisenhower in the eye, and replied, "I would say—Go!"

Eisenhower nodded, tucked away his chin, paced, looked abruptly at Tedder. Tedder again indicated he thought it chancy. Finally Eisenhower halted, looked around at his commanders, and said, "The question is just how long can you hang this operation on the end of a limb and let it hang there?"

If there was going to be an invasion before June 19, Eisenhower had to decide now. Smith was struck by the "loneliness and isolation of a commander at a time when such a momentous decision was to be taken by him, with full knowledge that failure or success rests on his individual decision." Looking out at the wind-driven rain, it hardly seemed possible that the operation could go ahead. Eisenhower calmly weighed the alternatives, and at 9:45 P.M. said, "I am quite positive that the order must be given."

Ramsay rushed out and gave the order to the fleets. More than five thousand ships began moving toward France. Eisenhower drove back to his trailer and slept fitfully. He awoke at 3:30 A.M. A wind of almost hurricane proportions was shaking his trailer. The rain seemed to be traveling in horizontal streaks. He dressed and gloomily drove through a mile of mud to Southwick House for the last meeting. It was still not too late to call off the operation.

In the now-familiar mess room, steaming hot coffee helped shake the gray mood and unsteady feeling. Stagg said that the break he had been looking for was on its way and that the weather would be clearing within a matter of hours. The long-range prediction was not good, to be sure, but even as he talked the rain began to stop and the sky started to clear.

A short discussion followed, Eisenhower again pacing, shooting out his chin, asking opinions. Montgomery still wanted to go, as did Smith. Ramsay was concerned about proper spotting for naval gunfire but thought the risk worth taking. Tedder was ready. Leigh-Mallory still thought air conditions were below the acceptable minimum.

Everyone stated his opinion. Stagg withdrew to let the generals and admirals make the decision. No new weather reports would be available for hours. The ships were sailing into the Channel. If they were to be called back, it had to be done now. The Supreme Commander was the only man who could do it. Eisenhower thought for a moment, then said quietly but clearly, "OK, let's go." And again, cheers rang through Southwick House.

Then the commanders rushed from their chairs and dashed outside to get to their command posts. Within thirty seconds the mess room was empty except for Eisenhower. The outflow of the others and his sudden isolation were symbolic. A minute earlier he had been the most powerful man in the world. Upon his word the fate of thousands of men depended, and the future of great nations. The moment he uttered the word, however, he was powerless. For the next two or three days there was almost nothing he could do that would in any way change anything. The invasion could not be stopped, not by him, not by anyone. A captain leading his company onto Omaha or a platoon sergeant at Utah would for the immediate future play a greater role than Eisenhower. He could now only sit and wait.

That morning he visited South Parade Pier in Portsmouth to see some British soldiers climb aboard their landing craft, then returned to his trailer. He played a game of checkers on a cracker box with Butcher, who was winning, two kings to one, when Eisenhower jumped one of his kings and got a draw. At lunch they exchanged political yarns. After eating, Eisenhower went into a tent with representatives of the press and announced that the invasion was on. Smith called with more news about Free French leader Charles de Gaulle. After hanging up, Eisenhower looked out the tent flap, saw a quick flash of sunshine, and grinned.

When the reporters left, Eisenhower sat at his portable table and scrawled a press release on a pad of paper, to be used if necessary. "Our landings . . . have failed . . . and I have withdrawn the troops," he began. "My decision to attack at this time and place was based upon the best information available. The troops, the air and the Navy did all that bravery and devotion to duty could do. If any blame or fault attaches to the attempt it is mine alone."

At the quays, in Portsmouth, Southampton, Poole, and the smaller harbors, the men from the U.S. 1st, 29th, and 4th Divisions, the rangers, and assorted other units, along with the Canadian and British divisions, began to load up.

As the troops filed onto their transports and landing craft, they were handed an order of the day from General Eisenhower. It began, "Soldiers, Sailors and Airmen of the Allied Expeditionary Force:

"You are about to embark upon the Great Crusade, toward which we have striven these many months. The eyes of the world are upon you. The hope and prayers of liberty-loving people everywhere march with you. . . .

"You task will not be an easy one. Your enemy is well trained, well equipped and battle-hardened. He will fight savagely.

"But this is the year 1944! . . . The tide has turned! The free men of the world are marching together to Victory!

"I have full confidence in your courage, devotion to duty and skill in battle. We will accept nothing less than full victory!

"Good luck! And let us all beseech the blessing of Almighty God upon this great and noble undertaking."

Sgt. John Slaughter of the 29th Infantry Division had his buddies sign his copy. He wrapped it in plastic, put it in his wallet, and carried it through Normandy all the way to the Elbe River in eastern Germany. "I still have that document framed hanging over my writing desk," Slaughter said. "It is my most treasured souvenir of the war."

Thousands of those who received Eisenhower's order of the day saved it. I cannot count the number of times I've gone into the den of a veteran of D-Day to do an interview and seen it framed and hanging in a prominent place. I have one on my office wall.

Pvt. Felix Branham of the 116th Infantry got everyone on his ship to sign a 500-franc note he had won in a poker game. "One guy asked, 'Why?' and I said, 'Fellows, some of us are never getting out of this alive. We may never see each other again. We may be crippled, or whatever. So sign this.' I have that hanging on my wall in a frame. I wouldn't take *anything* for it."

On the afternoon of June 5 the Allied airborne troopers began dressing for battle. Each rifleman carried his M-1 (either broken down in a padded case called a Griswold container or already assembled), 160 rounds of ammunition, two fragmentation hand grenades, a white phosphorus and an orange-colored smoke grenade, and a Gammon grenade. Most carried a pistol—the paratroopers' greatest fear was getting shot out of the sky, next was being caught on the ground at the moment of landing, before they could put their rifles into operation—plus a knife and a bayonet. An unwelcome surprise was an order to carry a Mark IV antitank mine, weighing about ten pounds. The only place to fit it was in the musette bag, which led to considerable bitching and rearrangement of loads.

Machine gunners carried their weapons broken down, and extra belts of ammunition. Mortars, bazookas, and radios were rolled into A-5 equipment bundles with cargo chutes attached. Every man carried three days' worth of field rations and, of course, two or three cartons of cigarettes. One sergeant carried along a baseball. He wrote on it "To hell with you, Hitler," and said he intended to drop it when his plane got over France (he did). There were gas masks, an ideal place to carry an extra carton of cigarettes (Capt. Sam Gibbons of the 501st PIR stuck two cans of Schlitz beer in his). The men had first-aid kits with bandages, sulfa tablets, and two morphine Syrettes, "one for pain and two for eternity." They were also handed a child's toy cricket with the instructions that it could be used in lieu of the normal challenge and password. One click-click was to be answered with two click-clicks.

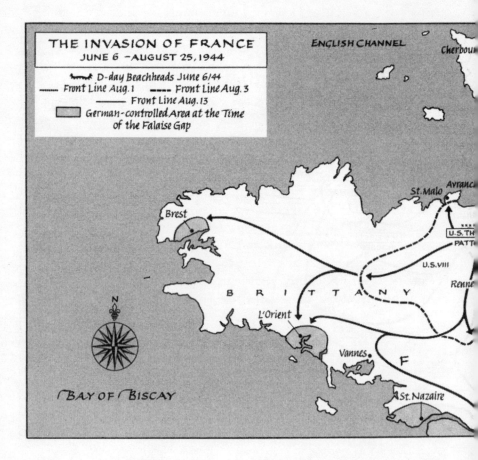

THE INVASION OF FRANCE
JUNE 6 – AUGUST 25, 1944

〰〰 D-day Beachheads June 6/44
——— Front Line Aug. 1   ‑‑‑‑ Front Line Aug. 3
——— Front Line Aug. 13
▨ German-controlled Area at the Time
    of the Falaise Gap

ENGLISH CHANNEL

Cherbour

D

Avranc

St. Malo

U.S. TH
PATT

U.S. VIII

Renne

Brest

B R I T T A N Y

L'Orient

Vannes.

F

N

BAY OF BISCAY

St. Nazaire

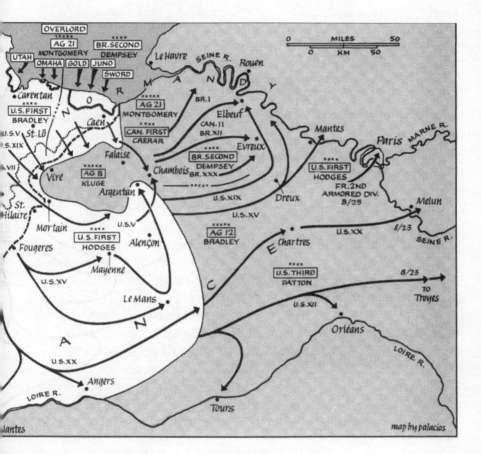

map by palacios

Pathfinders would go first to mark the drop zone with a gadget called the Eureka/Rebecca Radar Beacon System, which could send a signal up to the lead C-47 in each flight. Cpl. Frank Brumbaugh, a pathfinder with the 508th PIR, had not only the sixty-five-pound Eureka to carry, but two containers with carrier pigeons as well. After he set up his Eureka, he was supposed to make a note to that effect and put it in the capsule on the first pigeon's leg, then turn it loose. He was told to release the second pigeon at 0630 with information on how things were going. But when he got to the marshaling area, he discovered he had no way to feed or water the pigeons, so he let them go. Stripped, Brumbaugh weighed 137 pounds. With all his equipment, including his main and reserve chutes, he weighed 315 pounds.

Around 2000 hours, "Axis Sally," the "bitch of Berlin," came on the radio. "Good evening, 82nd Airborne Division," she said. "Tomorrow morning the blood from your guts will grease the bogey wheels on our tanks." It bothered some of the men; others reassured them—she had been saying something similar for the previous ten days.

Still, it made men think. Pvt. John Delury of the 508th PIR talked to his friend Pvt. Frank Tremblay about their chances of coming through alive. "He thought he'd get a slight wound and survive. I thought I was going to be killed. That was the last time I saw him."

Pvt. Tom Porcella, also of the 508th, was torturing himself with thoughts of killing other human beings (this was common; the chaplains worked overtime assuring soldiers that to kill for their country was not a sin). "Kill or be killed," Porcella said to himself. "Here I am, brought up as a good Christian, obey this and do that. The Ten Commandments say, 'Thou shalt not kill.' There is something wrong with the Ten Commandments, or there is something wrong with the rules of the world today. They teach us the Ten Commandments and then they send us out to war. It just doesn't make sense."

When every man was ready, the regiments gathered around their commanders for a last word. Most COs stuck to basics—to assemble quickly was the main point—but one or two added a pep talk. The most famous was delivered by Col. Howard "Jumpy"

Johnson, in command of the 501st PIR. Every man in the regiment remembered it vividly and could quote word for word his conclusion. As Lt. Carl Cartledge described Johnson's talk, "He gave a great battle speech, saying victory and liberation and death to the enemy and some of us would die and peace cost a price and so on. Then he said, 'I want to shake the hand of each one of you tonight, so line up.' And with that, he reached down, pulled his knife from his boot and raised it high above his head, promising us in a battle cry: 'Before the dawn of another day, I'll sink this knife into the heart of the foulest bastard in Nazi land!' A resounding yell burst forth from all 2,000 of us as we raised our knives in response."

After the regimental meetings the companies grouped around their COs and platoon leaders for a final word. The officers gave out the challenge, password, and response: "Flash," "Thunder," and "Welcome." "Welcome" was chosen because the Germans would pronounce it "Velcom." When Capt. Charles Shettle of the 506th PIR gave out the signals, Dr. Samuel Feiler, the regimental dental officer who had volunteered to accompany the assault echelon, approached him. Feiler was a German Jew who had escaped Berlin in 1938. "Captain Shettle," Feiler asked, "*Vat* do I do?"

"Doc," Shettle replied, "when you land, don't open your mouth. Take along some extra crickets and if challenged, snap twice." Later, as Shettle was inspecting each planeload prior to takeoff, he found Feiler with crickets strapped to both arms, both legs, and an extra supply in his pockets.

At 6 P.M. Eisenhower and a group of aides drove to Newbury, where the 101st Airborne was loading up for the flight to Normandy. The 101st was one of the units Leigh-Mallory feared would suffer 70 percent casualties. Eisenhower wandered around among the men, whose blackened faces gave them a grotesque look, stepping over packs, guns, and other equipment.

A group recognized him and gathered around. He chatted with them easily. He told them not to worry, that they had the best equipment and leaders. A sergeant said, "Hell, we ain't worried, General. It's the Krauts that ought to be worrying now." When he met a trooper from Dodge City, Eisenhower gave him a thumbs up and said, "Go get 'em, Kansas!" And a private piped up, "Look out,

Hitler, here we come." A Texan promised Eisenhower a job after the war on his cattle ranch. Eisenhower stayed until all the big C-47s were off the runway.

As the last plane roared into the sky Eisenhower turned to Kay Summersby, who was his driver that night, with a visible sagging in his shoulders. She saw tears in his eyes. He began to walk slowly toward his car. "Well," he said quietly, "it's on."

For Major Howard and the Ox and Bucks, June 5 had been a long day. In the morning the officers and men checked and re-checked their weapons. At noon they were told that it was on, that they should rest, eat, and then dress for battle. The meal was fatless, to cut down on airsickness. Not much of it was eaten. Pvt. Wally Parr explained why: "I think everybody had gone off of grub for the first time possibly in years." Then they sat around, according to Parr, "trying to look so keen, but not too keen like."

Toward evening the men got into their trucks to drive to their gliders. They were a fearsome sight. They each had a rifle or a Sten gun or a Bren gun, six to nine grenades, four Bren-gun magazines. Some had mortars; one in each platoon had a wireless set strapped to his chest. They had all used black cork or burned coke to blacken their faces. (Pvt. Darky Baines, as he was called, one of the two black men in the company, looked at Parr when Parr handed him some cork and said, "I don't think I'll bother.") Lt. David Wood remarked that they all, officers and men, were so fully loaded that "if you fell over it was impossible to get up without help." (Each infantryman weighed 250 pounds, instead of the allotted 210.) Parr called out that the sight of them alone would be enough to scare the Germans out of their wits.

As the trucks drove toward the gliders, Billy Gray could re-member "the girls along the road, crying their eyes out." On the trucks the men were given their code words. The recognition signal was "V," to be answered by "for Victory." The code word for the successful capture of the canal bridge was "Ham," for the river bridge "Jam." "Jack" meant the canal bridge had been captured but destroyed; "Lard" meant the same for the river bridge. Ham and Jam. D Company liked the sound of it, and as the men got out of their trucks they began shaking hands and saying, "Ham and Jam, Ham and Jam."

Howard called them together. "It was an amazing sight," he remembered. "The smaller chaps were visibly sagging at the knees under the amount of kit they had to carry." He tried to give an inspiring talk, but as he confessed, "I am a sentimental man at heart, for which reason I don't think I am a good soldier. I found offering my thanks to these chaps a devil of a job. My voice just wasn't my own."

Howard gave up the attempt at inspiration and told the men to load up. The officers shepherded them aboard, although not before every man, except Billy Gray, took a last-minute leak. Wally Parr chalked "Lady Irene" on the side of S. Sgt. Jim Wallwork's glider. As the officers fussed over the men outside, those inside their gliders began settling in.

A private bolted out of his glider and ran off into the night. Later, at his court-martial, he explained that he had had an unshakable premonition of his own death in a glider crash.

The officers got in last. Before climbing aboard, Lt. Den Brotheridge went back to Lt. R. "Sandy" Smith's glider, shook Smith's hand, and said, "See you on the bridge."

Howard went around to each glider, shook hands with the platoon leader, then called out some words of cheer. He had just spoken to the commander of the Halifax squadron, he said, who had told him, "John, don't worry about flak; we are going through a flak gap over Cabourg, one that we have been using to fly supplies in to the Resistance and to bring information and agents out."

Finally Howard, wearing a pistol and carrying a Sten gun, climbed into his own glider, closed the door, and nodded to Wallwork. Wallwork told the Halifax pilot that everything was go. At 2256 hours, June 5, they took off, the other gliders following at one-minute intervals.

The flight over the Channel of the American paratroopers in the 82nd and 101st Airborne Divisions was uneventful, but when the C-47s crossed the coast the skies erupted. German anti-aircraft gunners had gone to work and were firing with every gun they had.

In the body of the planes the troopers were terrified, not at what was ahead of them but because of the hopeless feeling of getting shot at and tumbled around and being unable to do anything about it. As the planes twisted and turned, climbed or dove, many sticks (one planeload of paratroopers) were thrown to the floor in a hopeless mess of arms, legs, and equipment. Meanwhile, bullets were ripping through the wings and fuselage. To Pvt. John Fitzgerald of the 502nd PIR, "they made a sound like corn popping as they passed through." Lt. Carl Cartledge likened the sound to "rocks in a tin can."

Out the open doors, the men could see tracers sweeping by in graceful, slow-motion arcs. They were orange, red, blue, yellow. They were frightening, mesmerizing, beautiful. Most troopers who tried to describe the tracers used some variation of "the greatest Fourth of July fireworks display I ever saw." They added that when they remembered that only one in six of the bullets coming up at them was a tracer, they couldn't see how they could possibly survive the jump.

For Pvt. William True of the 506th, it was "unbelievable" that there were people down there "shooting at *me!* Trying to kill Bill True!" Lt. Parker Alford, an artillery officer assigned to the 501st, was watching the tracers. "I looked around the airplane and saw some kid across the aisle who grinned. I tried to grin back but my face was frozen." Private Porcella's heart was pounding. "I was so scared that my knees were shaking and just to relieve the tension, I had to say something, so I shouted, 'What time is it?' " Someone called back, "0130."

The pilots turned on the red light and the jumpmaster shouted the order "Stand up and hook up." The men hooked the lines attached to the backpack covers of their main chutes to the anchor line running down the middle of the top of the fuselage.

"Sound off for equipment check." From the rear of the plane would come the call "sixteen OK!" then "fifteen OK!" and so on. The men in the rear began pressing forward. They knew the Germans were waiting for them, but never in their lives had they been so eager to jump out of an airplane.

"Let's go! Let's go!" they shouted, but the jumpmasters held them back, waiting for the green light.

"My plane was bouncing like something gone wild," Pvt. Dwayne Burns of the 508th remembered. "I could hear the machine-gun rounds walking across the wings. It was hard to stand up and troopers were falling down and getting up; some were throwing up. Of all the training we had, there was not anything that had prepared us for this."

In training, the troopers could anticipate the green light; before the pilot turned it on he would throttle back and raise the tail of the plane. Not this night. Most pilots throttled forward and began to dive. Pvt. Arthur "Dutch" Schultz and every man in his stick fell to the floor. They regained their feet and resumed shouting "Let's go!"

Sgt. Dan Furlong's plane got hit by three 88mm shells. The first struck the left wing, taking about three feet off the tip. The second hit alongside the door and knocked out the light panel. The third came up through the floor. It blew a hole about two feet across, hit the ceiling, and exploded, creating a hole four feet around, killing three men and wounding four others. Furlong recalled, "Basically the Krauts just about cut that plane in half.

"I was in the back, assistant jumpmaster. I was screaming 'Let's go!' " The troopers, including three of the four wounded men, dove headfirst out of the plane. The pilot was able to get control of the plane and head back for the nearest base in England for an emergency landing (those Dakotas—C-47s—could take a terrific punishment and still keep flying). The fourth wounded man had been knocked unconscious; when he came to over the Channel he was delirious. He tried to jump out. The crew chief had to sit on him until they landed.

On planes still flying more or less on the level, when the green light went on the troopers set a record for exiting. Still, many of them remembered all their lives their thoughts as they got to the door and leaped out. Eager as they were to go, the sky full of tracers gave them pause. Four men in the 505th, two in the 508th, and one each in the 506th and 507th "refused." They preferred, in historian John Keegan's words, "to face the savage disciplinary consequences and total social ignominy of remaining with the aeroplane to stepping into the darkness of the Normandy night."

Every other able-bodied man jumped. Private Fitzgerald had taken a cold shower every morning for two years to prepare himself for this moment. Pvt. Arthur DeFilippo of the 505th could see the tracers coming straight at him "and all I did was pray to God that he would get me down safely and then I would take care of myself."

Pvt. John Taylor of the 508th was appalled when he got to the door; his plane was so low that his thought was "We don't need a parachute for this; all we need is a step ladder." Pvt. Sherman Oyler, a Kansas boy, remembered his hometown as he got to the door. His thought was, "I wish the gang at Wellington High could see me now—at Wellington High."

When Pvt. Len Griffing of the 501st got to the door, "I looked out into what looked like a solid wall of tracer bullets. I remember this as clearly as if it happened this morning. It's engraved in the cells of my brain. I said to myself, 'Len, you're in as much trouble now as you're ever going to be. If you get out of this, nobody can ever do anything to you that you ever have to worry about.' "

At that instant an 88mm shell hit the left wing and the plane went into a sharp roll. Griffing was thrown to the floor, then managed to pull himself up and leap into the night.

Over the Channel, at 0000 hours, two groups of three Halifax bombers flew at seven thousand feet toward Caen. With all the other air activity going on, neither German searchlights nor antiaircraft gunners noticed that each Halifax was tugging a Horsa glider.

Inside the lead glider, Pvt. Wally Parr of D Company, Ox and Bucks, a part of the Air Landing Brigade of the 6th Airborne Division of the British army, was leading the twenty-eight men in singing. With his powerful voice and strong Cockney accent, Parr was booming out "Abby, Abby, My Boy." Cpl. Billy Gray, sitting down the row from Parr, was barely singing because all that he could think about was the pee he had to take. At the back end of the glider, Cpl. Jack Bailey sang, but he also worried about the parachute he was responsible for securing.

The pilot, twenty-four-year-old S. Sgt. Wallwork, of the Glider Pilot Regiment, anticipated casting off any second now because he could see the surf breaking over the Norman coast. Beside him his copilot, S. Sgt. John Ainsworth, was concentrating intensely on his stopwatch. Sitting behind Ainsworth, the commander of D Company, Maj. John Howard, a thirty-one-year-old former regimental sergeant major and an ex-cop, laughed with everyone else when the song ended and Parr called out, "Has the major laid his kitt yet?" Howard suffered from airsickness and had vomited on every training flight. On this flight, however, he had not been sick. Like his men, he had not been in combat before, but the prospect seemed to calm him more than it shook him.

As Parr started up "It's a Long, Long Way to Tipperary," Howard touched the tiny red shoe in his battle-jacket pocket, one of his two-year-old son Terry's infant shoes that he had brought along for good luck. He thought of Joy, his wife, and Terry and their baby daughter, Penny. They were back in Oxford, living near a factory, and he hoped there were no bombing raids that night. Beside Howard sat Lieutenant Brotheridge, whose wife was pregnant and due to deliver any day (five other men in the company had pregnant wives back in England). Howard had talked Brotheridge into joining the Ox and Bucks, and had selected his platoon for the #1 glider because he thought Brotheridge and his platoon the best in his company.

One minute behind Wallwork's glider was #2, carrying Lieutenant Wood's platoon. Another minute behind that Horsa was #3 glider, with Lieutenant Smith's platoon. The three gliders in this group were going to cross the coast near Cabourg, well east of the mouth of the Orne River.

Parallel to that group, to the west and a few minutes behind, Capt. Brian Priday sat with Lt. Tony Hooper's platoon, followed by the gliders carrying the platoons of Lts. Tod Sweeney and Dennis Fox. This second group was headed toward the mouth of the Orne River. In Fox's platoon, Sgt. M.C. "Wagger" Thornton was singing "Cow Cow Boogie" and—like almost everyone else on all the gliders—chain-smoking Players cigarettes.

In #2 glider, with the first group, the pilot, S. Sgt. Oliver Boland, who had just turned twenty-three years old a fortnight past, found crossing the Channel an "enormously emotional" experience, setting off as he was "as the spearhead of the most colossal army ever assembled. I found it difficult to believe because I felt so insignificant."

At 0007, Wallwork cast off his lead glider as he crossed the coast. At that instant, the invasion had begun.

5

The Opening Hours
of D-Day

WALLWORK MANAGED to land right next to the bridge, with the trailing two gliders landing right behind him. This was exactly where Major Howard had wanted to be. Air Vice Marshal Trafford Leigh-Mallory later called this "the finest feat of flying in World War II."

It was 0014, June 6, 1944. Howard's men jumped out of their gliders and began attacking the trenches around the bridge, where the German defenders had come alert and started firing. One squad, led by Lt. Den Brotheridge, started across the bridge to attack the Germans on the far side.

Brotheridge, when almost across the bridge, pulled a grenade out of his pouch and threw it at the machine gun to his right. As he did so, he was knocked over by the impact of a bullet in his neck. Just behind him, also running, came Billy Gray, his Bren gun at his hip. Gray also fired at the sentry with the Verey pistol, then began firing toward the machine guns. Brotheridge's grenade went off, wiping out one of the gun pits. Gray's Bren, and shots from others crossing the bridge, knocked out the other machine gun.

Gray was standing at the end of the bridge, at the northwest corner. Brotheridge was lying in the middle of the bridge, at the west end. Other men in the section were running onto the bridge. Wally Parr was with them, Pvt. Charlie Gardner beside him. In the middle of the bridge, Parr suddenly stopped. He was trying to yell "Able, Able," as the men around him had started doing as soon as the shooting broke out. But to his horror, "my tongue was stuck to the roof of my mouth and I couldn't spit sixpence. My mouth had dried up of all saliva and my tongue was stuck."

His attempts to yell only made the sticking worse. Parr's frustration was a terrible thing to behold—Parr without his voice was an impossible thing to imagine. His face was a fiery red, even through the burned cork, from the choking and from his anger. With a great effort of will Parr broke his tongue loose and shouted in his great Cockney voice, "COME OUT AND FIGHT, YOU SQUARE-HEADED BASTARDS," with a very long drawn-out *A* and the last syllable pronounced "turds." Pleased with himself, Parr started yelling "Ham and Jam, Ham and Jam," as he ran the rest of the way over, then turned left to go after the bunkers that were his task.

By 0021, the three platoons at the canal bridge had subdued most resistance from the machine-gun pits and the slit trenches— the enemy had either been killed or run off. Men previously detailed for the job began moving into the bunkers. Sandy Smith remembered that "the poor buggers in the bunkers didn't have much of a chance and we were not taking any prisoners or messing around, we just threw phosphorous grenades down and high-explosive grenades into the dugouts there and anything that moved we shot."

Wally Parr and Charlie Gardner led the way into the bunkers on the left. When they were underground, Parr pulled open the door to the first bunker and threw in a grenade. Immediately after the explosion, Gardner stepped into the open door and sprayed the room with his Sten gun. Parr and Gardner repeated the process twice; then, having cleaned out that bunker, and with their eardrums apparently shattered forever by the concussion and the sound, they went back up to the ground.

Their next task was to meet with Brotheridge, whose command post was scheduled to be the cafe, and take up firing positions. As they rounded the corner of the cafe, Gardner threw a phosphorous grenade toward the sound of sporadic German small-arms fire.

Parr shouted at him, "Don't throw another one of those bloody things, we'll never see what's happening."

Parr asked another member of D Company, "Where's Danny?" (To his face, the men all called him Mr. Brotheridge. The officers called him Den. But the men thought of him and referred to him as Danny.)

"Where's Danny?" Parr repeated. The soldier did not know, had not seen Lieutenant Brotheridge. Well, Parr thought, he's here, Danny must be here somewhere. Parr started to run around the cafe. "I ran past a bloke lying on the ground in the road opposite the side of the cafe." Parr glanced at him as he ran on. Hang on, he said to himself, and went back and knelt down.

"I looked at him, and it was Danny Brotheridge. His eyes were open and his lips moving. I put my hand under his head to lift him up. He just looked. His eyes sort of rolled back. He just choked and he laid back. My hand was covered with blood.

"I just looked at him and thought, My God. Right in the middle of that thing I just knelt there and I looked at him and I thought, What a waste! All the years of training we put in to do this job—it lasted only seconds and he lay there and I thought, My God, what a waste."

Jack Bailey came running up. "What the hell's going on?" he asked Parr.

"It's Danny," Parr replied. "He's had it."

"Christ Almighty," Bailey muttered.

Sandy Smith, who had thought that everyone was going to be incredibly brave, was learning about war. He was astonished to see one of his best men, a chap he had come to depend on heavily during exercises and who he thought would prove to be a real leader on the other side, cowering in a slit trench, praying. Another of his lads reported a sprained ankle from the crash and limped off to seek protection. He had not been limping earlier. Lieutenant Smith lost a lot of illusions in a hurry.

On the other (east) side of the bridge, David Wood's platoon was clearing out the slit trenches and the bunkers. The task went quickly enough, most of the enemy having run away. Wood's lads were shouting "Baker, Baker, Baker" as they moved along, shooting at any sign of movement in the trenches. Soon they were pronounced clear of enemy. Wood discovered an intact MG 34 with a complete belt of ammunition on it that had not been fired. He detailed two of his men to take over the gun. The remainder of his men filled in the trenches, and Wood went back to report to Howard that he had accomplished his mission.

As he moved back, he was telling his platoon, "Good work, lads," and "Well done," when there was a burst from a Schmeisser. Three bullets hit virtually simultaneously in his left leg, and Wood went down, frightened, unable to move, bleeding profusely.

All three platoon leaders gone, and in less than ten minutes! But the well-trained sergeants were thoroughly familiar with the various tasks and could take over; in Wood's platoon, a corporal took charge. In addition, Smith was still on his feet, although hardly mobile and in great pain. Howard had no effective officers at the canal bridge, and did not know what was happening at the river bridge. Gloom might have given way to despair had he known that his second-in-in-command, Captain Priday, and one-sixth of his fighting strength had landed twenty kilometers away, on the River Dives.

Howard kept asking Corporal Tappenden, "Have you heard anything from the river, from numbers four, five, and six?" "No," Tappenden kept replying, "no, no."

Over the next two minutes there was a dramatic change in the nature of the reports coming in, and consequently in Howard's mood. First, Lt. Jock Neilson of the sappers (combat engineers) came up to him: "There were no explosives under the bridge, John." Neilson explained that the bridge had been prepared for demolition, but the explosives themselves had not been put into their chambers. The sappers removed all the firing mechanisms, then went into the line as infantry. The next day they found the explosives in a nearby shed.

Knowing that the bridge would not be blown was a great relief to Howard. Just as good, the firing was dying down, and from what Howard could see through all the smoke and in the on-again, off-again moonlight, his people had control of both ends of the canal bridge. Just as he realized that he had pulled off Ham, Tappenden tugged at his battle smock. A message was coming in from Sweeney's platoon: "We captured the bridge without firing a shot."

Ham *and* Jam! D Company had done it. Howard felt a tremendous exultation and a surge of pride in his company. "Send it out," he told Tappenden. "Ham and Jam, Ham and Jam, keep it up until you get acknowledgment." Tappenden began incessantly calling out, "Ham and Jam, Ham and Jam."

In Ste.-Mere-Eglise, a fire in a barn was raging out of control. It was around 0200. The men of the U.S. 506th who had landed in and near the town had scattered. At 0145, the second platoon of F Company, 505th, had the bad luck to jump right over the town, where the German garrison was fully alerted.

Pvt. Ken Russell was in that platoon. "Coming down," he recalled, "I looked to my right and I saw this guy, and instantaneously he was blown away. There was just an empty parachute coming down." Evidently a shell had hit his Gammon grenades.

Horrified, Russell looked to his left. He saw another member of his stick, Pvt. Charles Blankenship, being drawn into the fire (the fire was sucking in oxygen and drawing the parachutists toward it). "I heard him scream once, then again, before he hit the fire, and he didn't scream anymore."

The Germans filled the sky with tracers. Russell was trying "to hide behind my reserve chute because we were all sitting ducks." He got hit in the hand. He saw Lt. Harold Cadish and Pvts. H. T. Bryant and Ladislaw Tlapa land on telephone poles around the church square. The Germans shot them before they could cut themselves loose. "It was like they were crucified there."

Pvt. Penrose Shearer landed in a tree opposite the church and was killed while hanging there. Pvt. John Blanchard, also hung up in a tree, managed to get his trench knife out and cut his risers. In the process he cut one of his fingers off "and didn't even know it until later."

Russell jerked on his risers to avoid the fire and came down on the slate roof of the church. "I hit and a couple of my suspension lines went around the church steeple and I slid off the roof." He was hanging off the edge. "And Steele, [Pvt.] John Steele, whom you've heard a lot about [in the book and movie *The Longest Day*], he came down and his chute covered the steeple." Steele was hit in the foot.

Sgt. John Ray landed in the church square, just past Russell and Steele. A German soldier came around the corner. "I'll never forget him," Russell related. "He was red-haired, and as he came around he shot Sergeant Ray in the stomach." Then he turned toward Russell and Steele and brought his machine pistol up to shoot them. "And Sergeant Ray, while he was dying in agony, he got his .45 out and he shot the German soldier in the back of the head and killed him."

Through all this the church bell was constantly ringing. Russell could not remember hearing the bell. Steele, who was hanging right outside the belfry, was deaf for some weeks thereafter because of it. (He was hauled in by a German observer in the belfry, made prisoner, but escaped a few days later.)

Russell, "scared to death," managed to reach his trench knife and cut himself loose. He fell to the ground and "dashed across the street and the machine-gun fire was knocking up pieces of earth all around me, and I ran over into a grove of trees on the edge of town and I was the loneliest man in the world. Strange country, and just a boy, I should have been graduating from high school rather than in a strange country."

There was a flak wagon in the grove, shooting at passing Dakotas. "I got my Gammon grenade out and I threw it on the gun and the gun stopped." He moved away from town. A German soldier on a bicycle came down the road. Russell shot him. Then he found an American, from the 101st (probably a trooper from the 506th who had landed in Ste.-Mere-Eglise a half hour earlier).

Russell asked, "Do you know where you are?"

"No," the trooper replied. They set out to find someone who did know.

Howard's success at the Orne Canal bridge came about because his three gliders landed together and thus a platoon-size force of more than thirty men was able to go into combat as a unit within seconds of landing. For the paratroopers it was altogether different. The parachutists of the British 6th Division and the American 82nd and 101st were badly scattered, due to the evasive action their C-47 pilots took when they encountered flak. There was almost no unit cohesion. Still, the men had been well trained and well briefed; they knew what to do and set out to accomplish their objectives as best they could. All over Normandy individuals, a pair of men, or small groups acted aggressively and effectively.

Easy Company of the 506th PIR was especially effective. Its CO had been killed when his plane crashed; Lt. Richard Winters took command. He had landed on the edge of Ste.-Mere-Eglise and managed to gather a dozen of the men. The company's objective was Ste.-Marie-du-Mont, some ten kilometers away. Winters set out for the village. When he arrived he was given orders to attack a German battery.

Winters went to work instinctively and immediately. He told the men of E Company to drop all the equipment they were carrying except weapons, ammunition, and grenades. He explained that the attack would be a quick frontal assault supported by a base of fire from different positions as close to the guns as possible. He set up the two machine guns to give covering fire as he moved the men forward to their jump-off positions.

The field in which the cannon were located was irregular in shape, with seven acute angles in the hedgerow surrounding it. This gave Winters an opportunity to hit the Germans from different directions.

Winters placed his machine guns (manned by Pvts. John Plesha and Walter Hendrix on one gun, Cleveland Petty and Joe Liebgott on the other) along the hedge leading up to the objective, with instructions to lay down covering fire. As Winters crawled forward to the jump-off position, he spotted a German helmet— the man was moving down the trench, crouched over, with only his head above ground. Winters took aim with his M-1 and squeezed off two shots, killing the Jerry.

Winters told Lt. Lynn Compton to take Sgts. Bill Guarnere and Don Malarkey, get over to the left, crawl through the open field, get as close to the first gun in the battery as possible, and throw grenades into the trench. He sent Sgts. Carwood Lipton and Mike Ranney out along the hedge to the right, alongside a copse, with orders to put a flanking fire into the enemy position.

Winters would lead the charge straight down the hedge. With

him were Pvts. Gerald Lorraine (of regimental HQ; he was Col. Robert Sink's jeep driver) and Popeye Wynn, and Cpl. Joe Toye.

Here the training paid off. "We fought as a team without standout stars," Lipton said. "We were like a machine. We didn't have anyone who leaped up and charged a machine gun. We knocked it out or made it withdraw by maneuver and teamwork or mortar fire. We were smart; there weren't many flashy heroics. We had learned that heroics was the way to get killed without getting the job done, and getting the job done was more important."

When Lipton and Ranney moved out along the hedge, they discovered they could not see the German positions because of low brush and ground cover. Lipton decided to climb a tree, but there were none of sufficient size to allow him to fire from behind a trunk. The one he picked had many small branches; he had to sit precariously on the front side, facing the Germans, exposed if they looked his way, balancing on several branches. About seventy-five meters away he could see about fifteen of the enemy, some in the trenches, others prone in the open, firing toward E Company, too intent on the activity to their front to notice Lipton.

Lipton was armed with a carbine he had picked up during the night. He fired at a German in the field. The enemy soldier seemed to duck. Lipton fired again. His target did not move. Not certain that the carbine had been zeroed in, Lipton aimed into the dirt just under the man's head and squeezed off another round. The dirt flew up right where he aimed; Lipton now knew that the carbine's sights were right and his first shot had killed the man. He began aiming and firing as fast as he cold from his shaky position.

Lieutenant Compton was armed with a Thompson subma-chine gun that he had picked up during the night (he got it from a lieutenant from D Company who had broken his leg in the jump). Using all his athletic skill, he successfully crawled through the open field to the hedge, Guarnere and Malarkey alongside him. The Germans were receiving fire from the machine gun to their left, from Lipton and Ranney to their rear, and from Winters's group in their front. They did not notice Compton's approach.

When he reached the hedge, Compton leaped over and through it. He had achieved complete surprise and had the German gun crew and infantry dead in his sights. But when he pulled the trigger on the borrowed tommy gun, nothing happened. It was jammed.

At that instant Winters called, "Follow me," and the assault team went tearing down the hedge toward Compton. Simultaneously, Guarnere leaped into the trench beside Compton. The German crew at the first gun, under attack from three directions, fled. The infantry retreated with them, tearing down the trench, away from Compton, Guarnere, and Malarkey. The Easy Company men began throwing grenades at the retreating enemy.

Compton had been an All-American catcher on the UCLA baseball team. The distance to the fleeing enemy was about the same as from home plate to second base. Compton threw his grenade on a straight line—no arch—and it hit a German in the head as it exploded. He, Malarkey, and Guarnere then began lobbing grenades down the trench.

Winters and his group were with them by now, firing their rifles, throwing grenades, shouting, their blood pumping, adrenaline giving them Superman strength.

Wynn was hit in the butt and fell down in the trench, hollering over and over, "I'm sorry, Lieutenant, I goofed off, I goofed off, I'm sorry." A German potato-masher grenade sailed into the trench; everyone dived to the ground.

"Joe, look out!" Winters called to Toye. The grenade had landed between his legs as he lay facedown. Toye flipped over. The potato masher hit his rifle and tore up the stock as it exploded, but he was uninjured. "If it wasn't for Winters," Toye said in 1990, "I'd be singing high soprano today."

Winters tossed some grenades down the trench, then went tearing after the retreating gun crew. Private Lorraine and Sergeant Guarnere were with him. Three of the enemy infantry started running cross-country, away toward Brecourt Manor.

"Get 'em!" Winters yelled. Lorraine hit one with his tommy gun; Winters aimed his M-1, squeezed, and shot his man through the back of his head. Guarnere missed the third Jerry, but Winters put a bullet in his back. Guarnere followed that up by pumping the wounded man full of lead from his tommy gun. The German kept yelling, "Help! Help!" Winters told Malarkey to put one through his head.

A fourth German jumped out of the trench, about a hundred

yards up the hedge. Winters saw him, lay down, took careful aim, and killed him. Fifteen or twenty seconds had passed since he had led the charge. Easy had taken the first gun.

Winters's immediate thought was that there were plenty of Germans farther up the trench, and they would be counterattacking soon. He flopped down, crawled forward in the trench, came to a connecting trench, looked down, "and sure enough there were two of them setting up a machine gun, getting set to fire. I got in the first shot and hit the gunner in the hip; the second caught the other boy in the shoulder."

Winters put Toye and Compton to firing toward the next gun, sent three other men to look over the captured cannon, and three to cover to the front. By this time Lipton had scrambled out of his tree and was working his way to Winters. Along the way he stopped to sprinkle some sulfa powder on Wynn's butt and slap on a bandage. Wynn continued to apologize for goofing off. Warrant Officer (WO) Andrew Hil, from regimental HQ, came up behind Lipton.

"Where's regimental HQ?" he shouted.

"Back that way," Lipton said, pointing to the rear. Hill raised his head to look. A bullet hit him in the forehead and came out behind his ear, killing him instantly.

After that, all movement was confined to the trench system, and in a crouch, as German machine-gun fire was nearly continuous, cutting right across the top of the trench. But Malarkey saw one of the Germans killed by Winters, about thirty yards out in the field, with a black case attached to his belt. Malarkey thought it must be a Luger. He wanted it badly, so he ran out into the field, only to discover that it was a leather case for the 105mm sight. Winters was yelling at him, "Idiot, this place is crawling with Krauts, get back here!" Evidently the Germans thought Malarkey was a medic; in any case the machine gunners did not turn on him until he started running back to the trench. With bullets kicking up all around him, he dived under the 105.

Winters was at the gun, wanting to disable it but without a demolition kit. Lipton came up and said he had one in his musette bag, which was back where the attack began. Winters told him to go get it.

Time for the second gun, Winters thought to himself. He left three men behind to hold the first gun, then led the other five on a charge down the trench, throwing grenades ahead of them, firing their rifles. They passed the two Jerries at the machine gun who had been wounded by Winters and made them prisoners. The gun crew at the second gun fell back; Easy took it with only one casualty.

With the second gun in his possession, and running low on ammunition, Winters sent back word for the four machine gunners to come forward. Meanwhile six German soldiers decided they had had enough; they came marching down the connecting trench to the second gun, hands over their heads, calling out "No make dead! No make dead!"

Pvt. John D. Hall of A Company joined the group. Winters ordered a charge on the third gun. Hall led the way and got killed, but the gun was taken. Winters had three of his men secure it. With eleven men, he now controlled three 105s.

At the second gun site Winters found a case with documents and maps showing the positions of all the guns and machine-gun positions throughout the Cotentin Peninsula. He sent the documents and maps back to the battalion, along with the prisoners and a request for more ammunition and some reinforcements, because "we were stretched out too much for our own good." Using grenades, he set about destroying the gun crew's radio, telephone, and range finders.

Capt. Clarence Hester came up, bringing three blocks of TNT and some phosphorous incendiary grenades. Winters had a block dropped down the barrel of each of the three guns, followed by a German potato masher. This combination blew out the breeches of the guns like half-peeled bananas. Lipton was disappointed when he returned with his demolition kit to discover that it was not needed.

Reinforcements arrived, five men led by Lt. Ronald Speirs of D Company. One of them, Pvt. "Rusty" Houch of F Company, rose up to throw a grenade into the gun positions and was hit several times across the back and shoulders by a burst from a machine gun. He died instantly.

Speirs led an attack on the final gun, which he took and destroyed, losing two men killed.

Winters then ordered a withdrawal because the company was

The commanders, Gen. Dwight D. Eisenhower and Field Marshal Erwin Rommel. They were tough, professional, determined men who carried immense responsibilities, as can be seen in the set of their jaws.

A prayer service on a landing craft, June 5, 1944. Statistically, every one of these men was going to get wounded or killed before victory was attained.
Below: Eisenhower at Le Havre, France, February 22, 1944, greeting reinforcements coming from England. He always established eye contact with his boys.

U.S. ARMY SIGNAL CORPS

Ike with the 101st Airborne, dusk, June 5, 1944, just before the paratroopers loaded up for their flight over the Channel. Lt. Wallace Strobel wears a card around his neck carrying the number of his plane, 23. Pvt. Sherman Oyler *(center)*, his head above Ike's thumb, wore the same uniform fifty years later at a celebration of the anniversary of D-Day in Abilene, Kansas. Strobel was also there, but not his uniform, which no longer fit. *Below:* Ike and Monty observe armored maneuvers before D-Day. Their concentration is complete.

UPI/BETTMANN

HANS WESENHAGEN

Pvt. David Webster, a Harvard English lit. major in 1942, a member of Easy Company in 1943, here seen in Holland in September 1944. *Right:* Lt. Richard Winters in training in the States, 1943. He was a platoon commander in Easy Company, 506th Parachute Infantry Regiment, 101st Airborne Division, just out of college.

FORREST GUTH

Below: Captain Winters, by now Easy Company's commander, in Holland, October 1944. He rose to become the CO of the 2nd Battalion, 506th PIR.
Right: He is under the same gate in 1991, looking as if he could pick up right where he left off forty-seven years earlier.

HOLLIS ANN HANDS

AL.KROACHKA/ARMY SIGNAL CORPS

The German defenses began at the low tide line (here German troops run for cover as the Allied plane flies low over the beach); Rommel had a half-million of these obstacles in place, along with 'Belgian gates', which were topped with mines and were underwater at high tide (these were piled up by American bulldozers on Utah Beach, June 8).

Ashore, fortified positions with steel-reinforced concrete walls as much as thirteen feet thick held 105mm cannon.

The Higgins assembly line in New Orleans, where Andrew Higgins, the designer and producer of the landing craft, vehicle personnel (LCVP, popularly known as the Higgins boat), built more than 20,000 of them.
Below: American troops got to England in every kind of ship imaginable. The lucky ones rode on the Queen Mary, shown here in mid-1944 during a lifeboat drill.

IMPERIAL WAR MUSEUM

Landing craft at Southampton, June 1 1944, part of the enormous build up in southern England for the invasion. These are landing craft, tanks (LCTs) and landing craft, headquarters (LCHs).

Below: American landing ship, tanks (LSTs), oceangoing vessels, at Brixham loading up on May 27. Altogether there were more than five thousand landing craft and ships of all types that participated in the invasion.

Maj. John Howard, CO of D Company, a part of the gliderborne Ox and Bucks Regiment, 6th Airborne Division. His company inaugurated the battle at 0016 hours, June 6, when the gliders touched down at Pegasus Bridge over the Orne River Canal.
Below: Lt. Den Brotheridge, one of Howard's platoon commanders and the first Allied officer killed on D-Day.

GIs line up for cigarettes just before loading up on the landing craft. One soldier said, 'No thanks, I don't smoke.' 'You might as well take them,' the quartermaster replied, 'because by the time you get where you're going, you will.' He was right. *Below:* Unidentified troops in a Higgins boat approaching Omaha Beach, about mid-morning, June 6. When the ramp went down, these men became visitors to hell.

The first waves of GIs at Omaha were hit by a tremendous barrage of machine-gun fire, rifle bullets, 88mm and 75mm cannon, exploding mines, mortars, and hand grenades. A Company of the 116th Regiment, 29th Division, was the first ashore. It took more than 90 percent casualties. Here a shell-shocked 29th Division soldier collapses by the chalk cliff below Colleville.

Below: Men from the 16th Regiment, 29th Division, under the cliff below Colleville. At this point, about 0800, the assault plan at Omaha was dead, and the troops – who had lost their weapons in getting ashore – were leaderless and dispirited.

TWO PHOTOS: U.S. ARMY SIGNAL CORPS

OPPOSITE:

Top: Wounded men from the 1st Division at Omaha Beach. Medics, universally acknowledged to be the bravest of the brave, had patched them up as best they could, but no amount of medical aid could take away what they had seen and experienced that morning.

Bottom: Survivors from a destroyed Higgins boat are helped onshore. This may have been the only battle in history in which the wounded were brought forward, toward the front line, for first aid from the medics.

U.S. COAST GUARD

Top: Men from the 4th Infantry Division moving ashore at Utah Beach, late afternoon, June 6. The opposition at Utah was relatively slight; for the 4th Division, the visit to hell began on June 7 and didn't end until May 1945.

Bottom: Light opposition doesn't mean no casualties; here medics give first aid to wounded 4th Division troops at Les Dunes de Madeleine, Utah Beach.

U.S. ARMY SIGNAL CORPS

TWO PHOTOS: WIDE WORLD

Robert Capa of *Life* magazine went in with the second wave at Easy Red sector, Omaha Beach, with E Company, 16th Regiment, 29th Division. He took 106 photos, got off the beach and back to Portsmouth late on June 6, then took the train to London and turned in the film for development. The darkroom assistant was so eager to see the photos that he turned on too much heat while drying the negatives. The emulsions melted and ran down. Only eight photos survive and they have a grainy quality to them. Capa was furious; he took pride in shooting clean and sharp. They became the best known of all D-Day photographs. Here are two of them.

The cliff at Pointe-du-Hoc. The rangers climbed it in the face of fierce resistance. Returning to the scene ten years later, the ranger CO, Col. James Earl Rudder, looked up, scratched his head, and asked a reporter, 'Will you tell me how we did this?'

COURTESY OF MRS. JAMES EARL RUDDER

U.S. COAST GUARD

A landing craft, tank (LCT) brings out wounded assault troops from Omaha Beach, June 7. They were taken to LSTs serving as hospital ships, then to England. The medical team, from the medics to the hospital ships to the hospitals back in England, did a magnificent job.

drawing heavy machine-gun fire from the hedges near Brecourt Manor, and with the guns destroyed there was no point to holding the position. The machine gunners pulled back first, followed by the riflemen. Winters was last. As he was leaving he took a final look down the trench. "Here was this one wounded Jerry we were leaving behind trying to put a MG on us again, so I drilled him clean through the head." It was 1130. About three hours had passed since Winters had received the order to take care of those guns.

With twelve men, what amounted to a squad (later reinforced by Speirs and the others), E Company had destroyed a German battery that was looking straight down causeway No. 2 and onto Utah Beach. That battery had a telephone line running to a forward observer who was in a pillbox located at the head of causeway No. 2. He had been calling shots down on the 4th Infantry as it unloaded. The significance of what Easy Company had accomplished cannot be judged with any degree of precision, but it surely saved a lot of lives, and made it much easier—perhaps even made it possible in the first instance—for tanks to come inland from the beach. It would be a gross exaggeration to say that Easy Company saved the day at Utah Beach, but reasonable to say that it made an important contribution to the success of the invasion.

Winters's casualties were four dead, two wounded. He and his men had killed fifteen Germans, wounded many more, and taken twelve prisoners; in short, they had wiped out the fifty-man platoon of elite German paratroops defending the guns, and scattered the gun crews. In an analysis written in 1985, Lipton said, "The attack was a unique example of a small, well-led assault force overcoming and routing a much larger defending force in prepared positions. It was the high morale of the E Company men, the quickness and audacity of the frontal attack, and the fire into their positions from several different directions that demoralized the German forces and convinced them that they were being hit by a much larger force."

There were other factors, including the excellent training the company had received and their combat inexperience. The men had taken chances they would not take in the future. Lipton said he never would have climbed that tree and so exposed himself had he been a veteran. "But we were so full of fire that day."

"You don't realize, your first time," Guarnere said. "I'd never, never do again what I did that morning." Compton would not have burst through that hedge had he been experienced. "I was sure I would not be killed," Lipton said. "I felt that if a bullet was headed for me it would be deflected or I would move."

(Paul Fussell, in *Wartime*, writes that the soldier going into combat the first time thinks to himself, "It *can't* happen to me. I am too clever / agile / well-trained / good-looking / beloved / tightly laced, etc." That feeling soon gives way to "It *can* happen to me, and I'd better be more careful. I can avoid the danger by watching more prudently the way I take cover / dig in / expose my position by firing my weapon / keep extra alert at all times, etc.")

In his analysis Winters gave credit to the army for having prepared him so well for this moment ("my apogee," he called it). He had done everything right, from scouting the position to laying down a base of covering fire, to putting his best men (Compton, Guarnere, and Malarkey in one group, Lipton and Ranney in the other) on the most challenging missions, to leading the charge personally at exactly the right moment.

Winters felt that if Captain Sobel had still been in command, he would have led all thirteen men on a frontal assault and lost his life, along with the lives of most of the men. Who can say he was wrong about that? But then, who can say that the men of Easy would have had the discipline, the endurance (they had been marching since 0130, after a night of little or no real sleep; they were battered and bruised from the opening shock and the hard landing), or the weapons skills to carry off this fine feat of arms, had it not been for Sobel?

Sink put Winters in for the Congressional Medal of Honor. Only one man per division was to be given that ultimate medal for the Normandy campaign; in the 101st it went to Lt. Col. Robert Cole for leading a bayonet charge; Winters received the Distinguished Service Cross. Compton, Guarnere, Lorraine, and Toye got the Silver Star; Lipton, Malarkey, Ranney, Liebgott, Hendrix, Plesha, Petty, and Wynn got Bronze Stars.

With the first light the Allied bombers approached the Norman coast, wave after wave of the four-engine B-17 Flying Fortresses and B-24 Liberators and the two-engine B-26 Marauders filling the sky. Their task was to drop their 500-pound bombs right at the water's edge, to stun or kill the German defenders in their pillboxes, fortifications, and trenches.

As the low-flying Marauders approached Utah Beach, the sky brightened and the crews saw a sight unique in world history. None of them ever forgot it; all of them found it difficult to describe. Below them, hundreds of landing craft were running into shore, leaving white wakes. Behind the landing craft were the LSTs and other transports, and the destroyers, cruisers, and battleships. "As I looked down at this magnificent operation," Lt. Allen Stephens, a copilot in a B-26 of the 397th Bomb Group, said, "I had the surging feeling that I was sitting in on the greatest show ever staged."

Lt. William Moriarity, a B-26 pilot, said, "As we approached the coast, we could see ships shelling the beach. One destroyer, half sunk, was still firing from the floating end. The beach was a bedlam of exploding bombs and shells."

Lt. A. H. Corry remembered that "the water was just full of boats, like bunches of ants crawling around down there. I imagined all those young men huddled in the landing craft, doubtless scared to death. I could see what they were heading into and I prayed for all those brave young men. I thought, man, I'm up here looking down at this stuff and they're out there waiting to get on that beach."

For the B-17 crews, flying mainly at 20,000 feet, up above the clouds, there was no such sight. They could see nothing but other B-17s. Those that could tucked in behind a pathfinder plane carrying radar. With radar, the lead bombardier would be able to mark a general target area. When the lead plane dropped its bombs, so would the ones following. That was not a textbook method of providing close-in ground support; such bombing was clearly inappropriate to its purpose. Eisenhower had said when he postponed the invasion that he was counting heavily on the air bombardment to get ashore; he added that the Allies would not have undertaken the operation without that asset.

Eventually Eisenhower learned the lesson that the B-17 was not a suitable weapon for tactical ground support. The testimony from the B-17 pilots and crews describing their experiences on D-Day suggests that the asset was wasted on D-Day, and that the proper use would have been to do what the B-17 was built to do, pound away at big targets inside Germany (oil refineries, train depots, factory complexes, airfields) and leave the beach bombardment to the Marauders and A-20s (Havocs).

But not even the commanders most dedicated to the idea that strategic airpower would win the war, the ones who had opposed the Transportation Plan so strongly, ever considered for an instant not participating in D-Day. They wanted to be there, and Eisenhower wanted them there.

At 20,000 feet, with heavy clouds below and the sky just beginning to lighten, where "there" was could be a mystery. Many pilots never got themselves located. The orders were, If you can't see the target, or get behind a radar plane, bring the bombs home. In the 466th Bomb Group, sixty-eight B-17s took off, carrying 400,000 pounds of bombs. Only thirty-two were able to drop their bombs. Those that did dropped them blind through the clouds over the British beaches.

Lt. Carl Carden had a brother down below. "I did not know where he was, but I wanted to be accurate. We were a little bit late because of the weather, which affected the bombing accuracy of almost every group up there with us." They delayed on the split-second timing so as to avoid hitting men coming ashore; as a consequence, all the bombs from the B-17s fell harmlessly two or even three miles inland.

"It was a day of frustration," said Lt. Werner Meyer. "We certainly didn't do as we had planned." The good part for the B-17s was that the flak was light and there was no Luftwaffe. "It was a milk run," Meyer concluded.

At Utah Beach, it was no milk run for the Marauders. They went in low enough for the Germans "to throw rocks at us." Sgt. Roger Lovelace recalled seeing "the first wave just a couple of hundred yards offshore, zigzagging toward the beach. We were running right down the shoreline looking for a target. We were drawing a lot of fire, not the usual 88mm but smaller rapid-fire stuff. I have this frozen image of a machine gunner set up by a barn, firing at us. For a short second I could look right down the barrel of that gun. A waist gunner or a tail gunner could return fire, but up in the top turret I felt helpless. I couldn't bring my guns below horizontal, therefore I couldn't fire on anything."

Lt. J. K. Havener saw a plane in his box take a flak hit, do a complete snap roll, recover, and carry on. "Unbelievable!" he remarked. "Now we're on our bomb run and another of our ships takes a direct hit, blows up, and goes down. Damn that briefer and his milk run. What's with all this flak!"

Sgt. Ray Sanders was in Havener's plane. "We were accustomed to heavy flak," he said, "but this was the most withering, heavy, and accurate we ever experienced."

On his bomb run, bombardier Lieutenant Corry was well below 1,000 feet, too low to use his bombsight. He could see men jumping out of the landing craft, guys who fell and were floating in the surf, tracers coming from the bunkers, spraying that beach. He used his manual trip switch, with his foot providing the aiming point. He made no attempt to be accurate; he figured, "I was making good foxholes for some of those guys coming ashore."

In Havener's B-26, Sergeant Sanders "heard our ship sound like it was being blown or ripped to bits. The sound was much louder than anything I had ever heard and seemed to come from every surface of our ship. Before the terrible noise and jolting had quit, I grabbed the intercom and yelled, 'We've been hit!' And our copilot, Lieutenant Havener, came back on the intercom and said, 'No, we haven't been hit. That was our bombs going off.' We were flying that low."

Lt. John Robinson recalled, "The explosions really bumped my wings at that altitude. It was like driving a car down the ties of a railroad track." Many others had similar experiences, a good indication of how much of the explosive power of those bombs went up in the air.

In contrast to the near-total success of the B-26s at Utah, the great bombing raids by B-17s and B-24s of June 6 against Omaha and the British beaches turned out to be a bust. The Allies managed to drop more bombs on Normandy in two hours than they had on Hamburg, the most heavily bombed city of 1943, but because of the weather and the airmen's not wanting to hit their own troops most of the blockbusters came down in Norman meadows (or were carried back to England), not on the Atlantic Wall. Yet the B-17 pilots and crews did their best and in some cases made important contributions, certainly far more than the Luftwaffe bomber force.

At the top of the elite world of the Allied air forces stood the fighter pilots. Young, cocky, skilled, veteran warriors—in a mass war fought by millions, the fighter pilots were the only glamorous individuals left. Up there all alone in a one-on-one with a Luftwaffe fighter, one man's skill and training and machine against another's, they were the knights in shining armor of World War II.

They lived on the edge, completely in the present, but young though they were, they were intelligent enough to realize that what they were experiencing—wartime London, the Blitz, the risks— was unique and historic. It would demean them to call them star athletes because they were much more than that, but they had some of the traits of the athlete. The most important was the lust to compete. They wanted to fly on D-Day, to engage in dogfights, to help make history.

The P-47 pilots were especially eager. In 1943 they had been on escort duty for strategic bombing raids, which gave them plenty of opportunity to get into dogfights. By the spring of 1944, however, the P-47 had given up that role to the longer-ranged P-51 (the weapon that won the war, many experts say; the P-51 made possible the deep penetrations of the B-17s and thus drove the Luftwaffe out of France).

The P-47 Thunderbolt was a single-engine fighter with classic lines. It was a joy to fly and a gem in combat. But for the past weeks the P-47s had been limited to strafing runs inside France. The pilots were getting bored.

Lt. Jack Barensfeld flew a P-47. At 1830 June 5, he and every other fighter pilot in the base got a general briefing. First came an announcement that this was "The Big One." That brought cheers and "electric excitement I'll never forget," Lt. James Taylor said. "We went absolutely crazy. All the emotions that had been pent-up for so long, we really let it all hang out. We knew we were good pilots, we were really ready for it."

The pilots, talking and laughing, filed out to go to their squadron areas, where they would learn their specific missions.

Barensfeld had a three-quarter-mile walk. He turned to Lt. Bobby Berggren and said, "Well, Bob, this is what we've been waiting for—we haven't seen any enemy aircraft for two weeks and we are going out tomorrow to be on the front row and really get a chance to make a name for ourselves."

Berggren bet him $50 that they would not see any enemy aircraft.

Lieutenant Taylor learned that his squadron would be on patrol duty, 120 miles south of the invasion site, spotting for submarines and the Luftwaffe. They would fly back and forth on a grid pattern.

"We were really devastated," Taylor remembered. "I looked at Smitty and Auyer and they were both looking at the ground, all of us felt nothing but despair. It was a horrible feeling, and lots of the fellows were groaning and moaning and whatnot." Taylor was so downcast he could not eat breakfast. Instead of a knight in shining armor, he was going to be a scout.

The first P-47s began taking off at about 0430. They had not previously taken off at night, but it went well. Once aloft, they became part of the air armada heading for France. Above them were B-17s. Below them were Marauders (B-26s) and Dakotas (C-47s). The Dakotas were tugging gliders. Around them were other fighters.

Lt. (later Maj. Gen.) Edward Giller was leader for a flight of three P-47s. "I remember a rather harrowing experience in the climb out because of some low clouds. There was a group of B-26s flying through the clouds as we climbed through, and each formation passed through the other one. That produced one minute of sheer stark terror."

It was bittersweet for the P-47 pilots to pass over the Channel. Lt. Charles Mohrle recalled: "Ships and boats of every nature and size churned the rough Channel surface, seemingly in a mass so solid one could have walked from shore to shore. I specifically remember thinking that Hitler must have been mad to think that Germany could defeat a nation capable of filling the sea and sky with so much ordnance."

Lieutenant Giller's assignment was to patrol over the beaches, to make certain no German aircraft tried to strafe the landing craft. "We were so high," he remembered, "that we were disconnected, essentially, from the activity on the ground. You could see ships smoking, you could see activities, but of a dim, remote nature, and no sense of personal involvement." Radar operators in England radioed a report of German fighters; Giller and every other fighter pilot in the area rushed to the sector, only to discover it was a false alarm.

Lieutenant Mohrle also flew a P-47 on patrol that day. "Flying back and forth over the same stretch of water for four hours, watching for an enemy that never appeared, was tedious and boring."

In the afternoon, Barensfeld flew support for a group of Dakotas tugging gliders to Normandy. The P-47s, flying at 250 miles per hour, had to make long, lazy S-turns to keep the C-47s in visual contact; otherwise they would overrun the glider formation. "Battle formation, 200–300 yards apart, then a turn, crossover, then we'd line up again. We were so busy we had no sense of time. Of course, we were looking for enemy aircraft, there weren't any. Mouth dry. Edge of seat. Silence. Very exciting time."

6

Utah Beach

CODE NAMES for the landing beaches, running from right to left as seen from the Channel, or west to east, were Utah, Omaha, Gold, Juno, and Sword. The 82nd and 101st Airborne Divisions landed inland from Utah; the British 6th Airborne inland from Sword. The U.S. 4th Infantry Division was scheduled to land at Utah; the U.S. 1st and 29th Infantry Divisions at Omaha; the British 50th Infantry Division at Gold; the Canadian 3rd Division at Juno; the British 3rd at Sword. The landings began an hour or so after dawn, following the air bombardment and an hour-long naval bombardment. As noted, the air strike did little good, except at Utah; the naval bombardment was too short in duration and too long in its targeting to do significant harm to the Germans in their fortifications at the water's edge. The swimming tanks were supposed to provide fire support at the beach itself, but nearly all of them swamped on their way in. So, as so often in war, it all came down to the poor bloody infantry. If the Allies were going to establish a beachhead in Normandy, it was up to the rifle-carrying privates and their NCOs and junior officers to do it.

The plan was for DD tanks to land first, at 0630, immediately after the naval warships lifted their fire and the LCT(R)s (landing craft, tank [rocket]) launched their thousand rockets. There were thirty-two of the swimming tanks at Utah, carried in eight LCTs (landing craft, tank). In their wake would come the 2nd Battalion, 8th Infantry Regiment, 4th Division, in twenty Higgins boats, each carrying a thirty-man assault team. Ten of the craft would touch down on Tare Green Beach opposite the strong point at Les-Dunes-de-Varreville, the others to the south at Uncle Red Beach.

The second wave of thirty-two Higgins boats carrying the 1st Battalion, 8th Infantry, plus combat engineers and naval demolition teams, was scheduled to land five minutes later. The third wave was timed for H plus fifteen minutes; it included eight LCTs with some bulldozer tanks as well as regular Shermans. Two minutes later the fourth wave, mainly consisting of detachments of the 237th and 299th Engineer Combat Battalions (ECBs), would hit the beach.

None of this worked out. Some craft landed late, others early, all of them a kilometer or so south of the intended target. But thanks to some quick thinking and decision-making by the high command on the beach, and thanks to the initiative and drive of the GIs, what could have been mass confusion or even utter chaos turned into a successful, low-cost landing.

Tides, wind, waves, and too much smoke were partly responsible for upsetting the schedule and landing in the wrong place, but the main cause was the loss to mines of three of the four control craft. When the LCCs (landing craft, control) went down it threw everything into confusion. The LCT skippers were circling, looking for direction. One of them hit a mine and blew sky-high. In a matter of seconds the LCT and its four tanks sank.

At this point Lts. Howard Vander Beek and Sims Gauthier on LCC 60 took charge. They conferred and decided to make up for the time lost by leading the LCTs to within three kilometers of the beach before launching the tanks (which were supposed to launch at five kilometers), giving them a shorter and quicker run to the shore. Using his bullhorn, Vander Beek circled around the LCTs as he shouted out orders to follow him. He went straight for the beach —the wrong one, about half a kilometer south of where the tanks were supposed to land. When the LCTs dropped their ramps and the tanks swam off, they looked to Vander Beek like "odd-shaped sea monsters with their huge, doughnut-like skirts for flotation wallowing through the heavy waves and struggling to keep in formation."

The Higgins boats carrying the first wave of assault teams were supposed to linger behind the swimming tanks, but the tanks were so slow that the coxswains drove their craft right past them. Thus it was that E Company of the 2nd Battalion was the first Allied company to hit the beach in the invasion. The tidal current, running from north to south, had carried their craft father left so they came in a kilometer south of where they should have been.

Gen. Theodore Roosevelt, Jr., T.R.'s son, was in the first boat to hit the shore. Maj. Gen. Ray Barton had initially refused Roosevelt's request to go in with the 8th Infantry, but Roosevelt had argued that having a general land in the first wave would boost morale for the troops. "They'll figure that if a general is going in, it can't be that rough." Roosevelt had also made a personal appeal, saying, "I would love to do this." Barton had reluctantly agreed.

Luck was with E Company. The German fixed fortifications at the intended landing site at exit 3 were far more formidable than those where the landing actually happened, at exit 2 opposite La Madeleine, thanks to the Marauder pounding the battery there had taken. The German troops in the area were from the 919th Regiment of the 709th Division. They had been badly battered by the combined air and sea bombardment and were not firing their weapons. There was only some small-arms fire from riflemen in trenches in the sand dune just behind the four-foot concrete seawall.

In those trenches were the Germans driven from their fixed positions by the bombardment. Their leader was Lt. Arthur Jahnke. He looked out to sea and was amazed. "Here was a truly lunatic sight," he recalled. "I wondered if I were hallucinating as a result of the bombardment." What he saw was a DD tank. "Amphibious tanks! This must be the Allies' secret weapon." He decided to bring his own secret weapon into action, only to discover that his Goliaths* would not function—the bombardment had destroyed the radio controls.

"It looks as though God and the world have forsaken us,"

* Miniature tanks loaded with explosives

Jahnke said to the runner by his side. "What's happened to our airmen?"

At that instant, Sgt. Malvin Pike of E Company was coming in on a Higgins boat. He had a scare: "My position was in the right rear of the boat and I could hear the bullets splitting the air over our heads and I looked back and all I could see was two hands on the wheel and a hand on each .50-caliber machine gun, which the Navy guys were firing. I said to my platoon leader, Lieutenant Rebarcheck, 'These guys aren't even looking where they are going or shooting.' About that time the coxswain stood up and looked at the beach and then ducked back down. The machine gunners were doing the same and we just prayed they would get us on the beach."

The boat hit a sandbar two hundred meters from the shore. (The water was shallower off exit 2 than at exit 3, which was why the Navy had insisted on going in at exit 3.) The coxswain said it was time for the infantry to go, that he was getting out of there.

Lieutenant Rebarcheck responded, "You are not going to drown these men. Give her another try." The coxswain backed off the bar, went 30 meters to the left, tried to go in, and hit the bar again. Rebarcheck said, "OK, let's go," but then the ramp got stuck.

"The hell with this," Rebarcheck called out. He jumped over the side; his men followed.

"I jumped out in waist-deep water," Sergeant Pike recalled. "We had 200 feet to go to shore and you couldn't run, you could just kind of push forward. We finally made it to the edge of the water, then we had 200 yards of open beach to cross, through the obstacles. But fortunately most of the Germans were not able to fight, they were all shook up from the bombing and the shelling and the rockets and most of them just wanted to surrender."

Capt. Howard Lees, commander of E Company, led his men over the seawall to the top of the dunes. "What we saw," Sergeant Pike remembered, "was nothing like what we saw on the sand table back in England. We said, 'Hey, this doesn't look like what they showed us.'" Roosevelt joined them, walking calmly up to their position, using his cane (he had had a heart attack), wearing a wool knit hat (he hated helmets), ignoring the fire. About this time (0640) the Germans to the north in the fortifications at Les-Dunes-de-

Varreville began shooting at 2nd Battalion with 88mm cannon and machine guns, but not accurately. Roosevelt and Lees conferred, studied their maps, and realized they were at the wrong place.

Roosevelt returned to the beach. By now the first Sherman tanks had landed and were returning the German fire. Commodore James Arnold, the navy control officer for Utah, was just landing with the third wave. "German 88s were pounding the beachhead," he recalled. "Two U.S. tanks were drawn up at the high-water line pumping back. I tried to run to get into the lee of these tanks. I realize now why the infantry likes to have tanks along in a skirmish. They offer a world of security to a man in open terrain who may have a terribly empty sensation in his guts." Arnold found a shell hole and made it his temporary headquarters.

"An army officer wearing the single star of a brigadier jumped into my 'headquarters' to duck the blast of an 88.

" 'Sonsabuzzards,' he muttered, as we untangled sufficiently to look at each other. 'I'm Teddy Roosevelt. You're Arnold of the Navy. I remember you at the briefing at Plymouth.' "

Roosevelt was joined by the two battalion commanders of the 8th Infantry, Lt. Cols. Conrad Simmons and Carlton MacNeely. As they studied the map, Col. James Van Fleet, CO of the regiment, came wading ashore. He had landed with the fourth wave, carrying the 237th and 299th ECBs.

"Van," Roosevelt exclaimed, "we're not where we were supposed to be." He pointed to a building on the beach. It was supposed to be to the left. "Now it's to our right. I figure we are more than a mile further south." Van Fleet reflected that ironically they were at the exact spot he had wanted the navy to land his regiment, but the navy had insisted it was impossible because the water was too shallow.

"We faced an immediate and important decision," Van Fleet wrote. "Should we try to shift our entire landing force more than a mile down the beach, and follow our original plan? Or should we proceed across the causeways immediately opposite where we had landed?" Already men were crossing the seawall and dunes in front of the officers, while navy demolition men and engineers were blowing up obstacles behind them.

Roosevelt became a legend for reportedly saying at this point,

"We'll start the war from right here." According to Van Fleet that was not the way it happened. In an unpublished memoir, Van Fleet wrote: "I made the decision. 'Go straight inland,' I ordered. 'We've caught the enemy at a weak point, so let's take advantage of it.' "

The important point was not who made the decision but that it was made without opposition or time-consuming argument. It was the right decision and showed the flexibility of the high command. Simmons and MacNeely immediately set about clearing the German beach opposition, preparing to seize the eastern ends of exits 1 and 2, then cross the causeways to drive west. First, however, they needed to get their men through the seawall and over the dunes.

Lt. Elliot Richardson was CO of a medic detachment that landed with the fourth wave. "I waded ashore with my guys. There were occasional shell bursts on the beach but it didn't amount to much as most of the German guns had been put out of action. I walked up to the top of the dune and looked around. There was this barbed wire area and a wounded officer who had stepped on an antipersonnel mine calling for help."

Richardson held a brief debate with himself. It was obviously dangerous to go into the area. Nevertheless, "I decided that I should go. I walked in toward him, putting each foot down carefully, and picked him up and carried him back." Richardson's men got the wounded officer on a stretcher and carried him down to an aid station on the beach.

"That was my baptism," Richardson said. "It was the sort of behavior I expected of myself."

Capt. George Mabry, S-3 (operations officer) of 2nd Battalion, 8th Infantry, crossed the dunes and found himself with several members of G Company caught in a minefield. Three men stepped on S-mines. Colonel Van Fleet described what happened: "Mabry had a choice: to withdraw to the beach or go after the enemy. Each alternative meant crossing the minefield. Mabry chose to charge. Firing as he ran, Mabry charged twenty-five yards to an enemy foxhole. Those Germans who resisted, he killed; the others surrendered. Next he gathered a handful of G Company men, sent for two tanks, and assaulted a large pillbox guarding the causeway at exit 1."

Sergeant Pike of E Company joined Mabry's group. As Mabry led the men across the causeway, headed toward Pouppeville, he caught up with Lieutenant Tighe of the 70th Tank Battalion. Tighe had lost three tanks to land mines but was moving cautiously ahead with his remaining two Shermans. Mabry put infantry in front and pushed on, urging speed because they were so exposed on the causeway and were taking mortar fire, simultaneously urging caution because of the mines. They came to a bridge over a culvert and figured it must be prepared for demolition; further, the scouts reported that they had seen some Germans duck into the culvert.

Mabry sent troops out into the flooded fields to pinch in on both sides of the culvert. The Germans surrendered without putting up a fight. Mabry had them disconnect the charges, then sent the prisoners back to the beach and pushed on.

After the guards put the prisoners into a landing craft, to be taken back to the USS *Bayfield* for interrogation, they reported to Van Fleet. It was 0940. Van Fleet radioed General Barton on *Bayfield,* "I am ashore with Colonel Simmons and General Roosevelt, advancing steadily." As new waves of landing craft came in, Van Fleet and Roosevelt sent them through the holes in the seawall with orders to move inland. Already the biggest problem they faced was congestion on the beach. There were too many troops and vehicles, not enough openings. Sporadic incoming artillery fire and the ubiquitous mines made the traffic jam horrendous. Still, at 1045, Van Fleet was able to radio Barton, "Everything is going OK." The beach area was comparatively secure, the reserve battalions were coming ashore.

Mabry pushed forward on the causeway. He kept cautioning his scouts. "You know," he said to Sergeant Pike, "the paratroopers are supposed to have taken this town Pouppeville, but they may not have. Let's not shoot any of our paratroopers." Pike said OK.

The scouts got to the western edge of the flooded area. "We could see the bushes and a few trees where the causeway ended," Pike recalled, "and then I saw a helmet and then it disappeared, and I told Captain Mabry that I saw a helmet up there behind those bushes and he said, 'Could you tell if it was American or German?' and I said, 'I didn't see enough, I don't know, sir.' "

The men on the far end of the causeway shot off an orange flare. "And these two guys stood up and the first thing we saw was the American flag on their shoulder and it was two paratroopers. They said, '4th Division?' and we said, 'Yes.' "

Lt. Eugene Brierre of the 101st was one of the two paratroopers. He greeted Pike and asked, "Who is in charge here?" Mabry came up and replied, "I am."

Brierre said, "Well, General Taylor is right back here in Pouppeville and wants to meet you."

It was 1110. The linkup between the 101st and 4th Divisions had been achieved. Exit 1 was in American hands.

Mabry talked to Taylor, who said he was moving out to accomplish further objectives, then proceeded through Pouppeville in the direction of Ste.-Marie-du-Mont. There were forty or so dead German soldiers in Pouppeville, testimony to the fight the 101st had been engaged in. Near Ste.-Marie-du-Mont, Lt. Louis Nixon of Easy Company, 506th, 101st asked Mabry for a bit of help from the two tanks; Mabry detached them and they went to work. Then it was on to Ste.-Marie-du-Mont, where the Mabry force helped the paratroopers secure the town.

The 4th Division and attached units were pouring ashore. Their main problem was with the sea, not the Germans. The waves were pitching the landing craft around, coming over the gunwales to hit the troops smack in the face, making many of the men so miserable they could not wait to get off. "The boats were going around like little bugs jockeying for position," Pvt. Ralph Della-Volpe recalled. "I had had an extra, extra big breakfast thinking it would help, but I lost it."

So did many others. Seaman Marvin Perrett, an eighteen-year-old coast guardsman from New Orleans, was coxswain on a New Orleans–built Higgins boat. The thirty members of the 12th Regiment of the 4th Division he was carrying ashore had turned their heads toward him to avoid the spray. He could see concern and fear on their faces. Just in front of him stood a chaplain. Perrett was concentrating on keeping his place in the advancing line. The chaplain upchucked his breakfast, the wind caught it, and Perrett's face was covered with undigested eggs, coffee, and bits of bacon.

One of Perrett's crew dipped a bucket in the Channel and threw the water over his face. "How's that, skipper?" he asked.

"That was great," Perrett replied. "Do it again." The crew member did, and the infantrymen broke into laughter. "It just took the tension right away," Perrett said.

Sgt. John Beck of the 87th Mortar Battalion had taken sea-sickness pills. They did not work; he threw up anyway. But they had an unintended effect—he fell asleep while going in.

"The explosion of shells awakened me as we approached the coast," he remembered "My best friend, Sgt. Bob Myers from New Castle, Pa., took a number of those pills and it drove him out of his mind. He didn't become coherent until the next day. He made the invasion of Normandy and doesn't remember one thing about it!"

Behind the sand dunes at Utah were flooded fields, difficult to cross. Behind the fields the ground rose and small hills dominated the landscape, most of them with a village on it. The American paratroopers had landed all over the area and in many cases had taken the villages, as Easy Company, 506th, 101st had done at Ste.-Marie-du-Mont. Other groups of troopers, ranging from three or four men to a platoon-size force, had moved to the beaches, to open the causeways leading through the fields for the incoming 4th Division.

Capt. L. "Legs" Johnson led a patrol of paratroopers down the causeway to the beach. He saw German soldiers in one of the batteries waving a white flag. "They were underground, part of the coastal defense group, and they were relatively older men, really not very good soldiers. We accepted their terms of surrender, allowing them to come up only in small groups. We enclosed them with barbed wire fencing, their own barbed wire, and they were pretty well shocked when they learned that there were a lot more of them than there were of us—there were at least fifty of those guys."

Johnson took his helmet off, set it down, lay on the ground with his helmet as a headrest, "really taking it sort of easy, waiting for the 4th Infantry Division to come up." At about 1100 the infantry were there, "and it was really sort of amusing, because we were on the beach with our faces all blackened, and these guys would come up in their boats and crash down in front of us and man, when they came off those boats, they were ready for action. We quickly hollered to them and pointed to our American flags."

Inland by about a kilometer from St.-Martin-de-Varreville there was a group of buildings holding a German coastal-artillery barracks, known to the Americans from its map signification as WXYZ. Lt. Col. Patrick Cassidy, commanding the 1st Battalion of the 502nd, short of men and with a variety of missions to perform, sent Sgt. Harrison Summers of West Virginia with fifteen men to capture the barracks. That was not much of a force to take on a full-strength German company, but it was all Cassidy could spare.

Summers set out immediately, not even taking the time to learn the names of the men he was leading, who were showing considerable reluctance to follow this unknown sergeant. Summers grabbed one man, Sgt. Leland Baker, and told him, "Go up to the top of this rise and watch in that direction and don't let anything come over that hill and get on my flank. Stay there until you're told to come back." Baker did as ordered.

Summers then went to work, charging the first farmhouse, hoping his hodgepodge squad would follow. It did not, but he kicked in the door and sprayed the interior with his tommy gun. Four Germans fell dead, others ran out a back door to the next house. Summers, still alone, charged that house; again the Germans fled. His example inspired Pvt. William Burt to come out of the roadside ditch where the group was hiding, set up his light machine gun, and begin laying down a suppressing fire against the third barracks building.

Once more Summers dashed forward. The Germans were ready this time; they shot at him from loopholes but, what with Burt's machine-gun fire and Summers's zigzag running, failed to hit him. Summers kicked in the door and sprayed the interior, killing six Germans and driving the remainder out of the building.

Summers dropped to the ground, exhausted and in emotional shock. He rested for half an hour. His squad came up and replenished his ammunition supply. As he rose to go on, an unknown captain from the 101st, misdropped by miles, appeared at his side. "I'll go with you," said the captain. At that instant he was shot through the heart and Summers was again alone. He charged another building, killing six more Germans. The rest threw up their hands. Summers's squad was close behind; he turned the prisoners over to his men.

One of them, Pvt. John Camien from New York City, called out to Summers: "Why are you doing it?"

"I can't tell you," Summers replied.

"What about the others?"

"They don't seem to want to fight," said Summers, "and I can't make them. So I've got to finish it."

"OK," said Camien. "I'm with you."

Together, Summers and Camien moved from building to building, taking turns charging and giving covering fire. Burt meanwhile moved up with his machine gun. Between the three of them, they killed more Germans.

There were two buildings to go. Summers charged the first and kicked the door open, to see the most improbable sight. Fifteen German artillerymen were seated at mess tables eating breakfast. Summers never paused; he shot them down at the tables.

The last building was the largest. Beside it were a shed and a haystack. Burt used tracer bullets to set them ablaze. The shed was used by the Germans for ammunition storage; it quickly exploded, driving thirty Germans out into the open, where Summers, Camien, and Burt shot some of them down as the others fled.

Another member of Summers's makeshift squad came up. He had a bazooka, which he used to set the roof of the last building on fire. The Germans on the ground floor were firing a steady fusillade from loopholes in the walls, but as the flames began to build they dashed out. Many died in the open. Thirty-one others emerged with raised hands to offer their surrender.

Summers collapsed, exhausted by his nearly five hours of combat. He lit a cigarette. One of the men asked him, "How do you feel?"

"Not very good," Summers answered. "It was all kind of crazy. I'm sure I'll never do anything like that again."

Summers got a battlefield commission and a Distinguished Service Cross. He was put in for the Medal of Honor, but the paperwork got lost. In the late 1980s, after Summers's death from cancer, Sergeant Baker and others made an effort to get the medal awarded posthumously, without success. Summers is a legend with American paratroopers nonetheless, the Sergeant York of World War II. His story has too much John Wayne/Hollywood in it to be believed, except that more than ten men saw and reported his exploits.

D-Day was a smashing success for the 4th Division and its attached units. Nearly all objectives were attained even though the plan had to be abandoned before the first assault waves hit the beach. Casualties were astonishingly light, thanks in large part to the paratroopers coming in on the German defenders from the rear. In fifteen hours the Americans put ashore at Utah more than 20,000 troops and 1,700 motorized vehicles. By nightfall, the division was ready to move out at first light on June 7 for its next mission, taking Montebourg and then moving on Cherbourg.

7

Omaha Beach

IF THE GERMANS were going to stop the invasion anywhere, it
would be at Omaha Beach. It was an obvious landing site, the
only sand beach between the mouth of the Douve to the west
and Arromanches to the east, a distance of almost forty kilometers. On both ends of Omaha the cliffs were more or less perpendicular.

The sand at Omaha Beach is golden in color, firm and fine,
perfect for sunbathing and picnicking and digging, but in extent
the beach is constricted. It is slightly crescent-shaped, about ten
kilometers long overall. At low tide, there is a stretch of firm sand
of three hundred to four hundred meters in distance. At high tide,
the distance from the waterline to the one- to three-meter bank of
shingle (small round stones) is but a few meters.

In 1944 the shingle, now mostly gone, was impassable to vehicles. On the western third of the beach, beyond the shingle, there
was a part-wood, part-masonry seawall from one to four meters in
height (now gone). Inland of the seawall there was a paved, promenade beach road, then a V-shaped antitank ditch as much as two
meters deep, then a flat swampy area, then a steep bluff that as-
cended thirty meters or more. A man could climb the bluff, but a
vehicle could not. The grass-covered slopes appeared to be feature-
less when viewed from any distance, but in fact they contained

many small folds or irregularities that proved to be a critical physical feature of the battlefield.

There were five small "draws," or ravines, that sloped gently up to the tableland above the beach. A paved road led off the beach at exit D-1 to Vierville; at Les Moulins (exit D-3) a dirt road led up to St.-Laurent; the third draw, exit E-1, had only a path leading up to the tableland; the fourth draw, E-3, had a dirt road leading to Colleville; the last draw had a dirt path at exit F-1.

No tactician could have devised a better defensive situation. A narrow, enclosed battlefield, with no possibility of outflanking it; many natural obstacles for the attacker to overcome; an ideal place to build fixed fortifications and a trench system on the slope of the bluff and on the high ground looking down on a wide, open killing field for any infantry trying to cross no-man's-land.

The Allied planners hated the idea of assaulting Omaha Beach, but it had to be done. This was as obvious to Rommel as to Eisenhower. Both commanders recognized that if the Allies invaded in Normandy, they would have to include Omaha Beach in the landing sites; otherwise the gap between Utah and the British beaches would be too great.

The waters offshore were heavily mined, so too the beaches, the promenade (which also had concertina wire along its length), and the bluff. Rommel had placed more beach obstacles here than at Utah. He had twelve strong points holding 88s, 75s, and mortars. He had dozens of Tobruks and machine-gun pillboxes, supported by an extensive trench system.

Everything the Germans had learned in World War I about how to stop a frontal assault by infantry Rommel put to work at Omaha. He laid out the firing positions at angles to the beach to cover the tidal flat and beach shelf with crossing fire, plunging fire, and grazing fire, from all types of weapons. He prepared artillery positions along the cliffs at either end of the beach, capable of delivering enfilade fire from 88s all across Omaha. The trench system included underground quarters and magazines connected by tunnels. The strong points were concentrated near the entrances to the draws, which were further protected by large cement roadblocks. The larger artillery pieces were protected to the seaward by concrete wing walls. There was not one inch of the beach that had not been presighted for both grazing and plunging fire.

□

Capt. Robert Walker of HQ Company, 116th Regiment, 29th Division later described the defenses in front of Vierville: "The cliff-like ridge was covered with well-concealed foxholes and many semipermanent bunkers. The bunkers were practically unnoticeable from the front. Their firing openings were toward the flank so that they could bring flanking crossfire to the beach as well as all the way up the slope of the bluff. The bunkers had diagrams of fields of fire, and these were framed under glass and mounted on the walls beside the firing platforms." To reporter A. J. Liebling, who climbed the bluff a few days later, it looked like "a regular Maginot Line."

The men attacking this formidable position had been on their Higgins boats since midnight. They were seasick, exhausted, their legs trembling from standing so long in the bouncing boats. Still, the misery caused by the spray hitting them in the face with each wave and by their seasickness was such that they were eager to hit the beach, feeling that nothing could be worse than riding on those damned landing craft. Adding to the problems for the Americans, no unit landed where it was supposed to. Companies were a kilometer or more off target.

When the ramps went down, the Germans opened fire. "We hit the sandbar," one coast guardsman recalled, "dropped the ramp, and then all hell poured loose on us. The soldiers in the boat received a hail of machine-gun bullets. The army lieutenant was immediately killed, shot through the head." In the lead boat, LCA (landing craft, assault) 1015, Capt. Taylor Fellers and every one of his men were killed before the ramp went down. LCA 1015 just vaporized. No one ever learned whether it was the result of hitting a mine or getting hit by an 88 shell.

All across the beach the German machine guns were hurling fire of monstrous proportions on the hapless Americans—one German gunner fired 12,000 rounds that morning.

Pvt. John Barnes, A Company, 116th, was in an LCA. As it approached the shoreline abreast with eleven other craft, someone shouted, "Take a look! This is something that you will tell your grandchildren!"

If we live, Barnes thought.

The LCA began to sink. "Suddenly, a swirl of water wrapped

around my ankles," Barnes remembered. "The water quickly reached our waist. I squeezed the CO2 tube in my life belt. The buckle broke and it popped away. I was going down under. I climbed on the back of the man in front of me and pulled myself up in a panic."

Some men had wrapped Mae Wests around their weapons and inflated them. Barnes saw a rifle floating by, then a flamethrower with two Mae Wests around it. "I hugged it tight but still seemed to be going down. I couldn't keep my head above the surface. I tried to pull the release straps on my jacket but I couldn't move. Lieutenant Gearing grabbed my jacket and used his bayonet to cut the straps and release me from the weight. I was all right now, I could swim."

The assault team was about a kilometer offshore. Sergeant Laird wanted to swim in, but Lieutenant Gearing said, "No, we'll wait and get picked up by some passing boat." But none would stop; the coxswains' orders were to go on in and leave the rescue work to others.

After a bit, "we heard a friendly shout of some Limey voice in one of the LCAs. He stopped, his boat was empty. He helped us to climb on board. We recognized the coxswain. He was from the *Empire Javelin*. He wouldn't return to the beach. We asked how the others made out. He said he had dropped them off OK. We went back to the *Empire Javelin*, which we had left at 0400 that morning. How long had it been? It seemed like just minutes. When I thought to ask, it was 1300."

Barnes and his assault team were extraordinarily lucky. About 60 percent of the men of A Company came from one town, Bedford, Virginia; for Bedford, the first fifteen minutes at Omaha was an unmitigated disaster. G and F Companies were supposed to come in to the immediate left of A Company, but they drifted a kilometer farther east before landing, so all the Germans around the heavily defended Vierville draw concentrated their fire on A Company. When the ramps on the Higgins boats dropped, the Germans just poured the machine-gun, artillery, and mortar fire on them. It was a slaughter. Of the 200-plus men of the company, only a couple of dozen survived, and virtually all of them were wounded.

Sgt. Thomas Valance survived, barely. "As we came down the

ramp, we were in water about knee-high and started to do what we were trained to do, that is, move forward and then crouch and fire. One problem was we didn't quite know what to fire at. I saw some tracers coming from a concrete emplacement which, to me, looked mammoth. I never anticipated any gun emplacements being that big. I shot at it but there was no way I was going to knock out a German concrete emplacement with a .30-caliber rifle."

The tide was coming in, rapidly, and the men around Valance were getting hit. He found it difficult to stay on his feet—like most infantrymen, he was badly overloaded, soaking wet, exhausted, trying to struggle through wet sand and avoid the obstacles with mines attached to them. "I abandoned my equipment, which was dragging me down into the water.

"It became evident rather quickly that we weren't going to accomplish very much. I remember floundering in the water with my hand up in the air, trying to get my balance, when I was first shot through the palm of my hand, then through the knuckle.

"Pvt. Henry Witt was rolling over toward me. I remember him saying, 'Sergeant, they're leaving us here to die like rats. Just to die like rats.' "

Valance was hit again, in the left thigh by a bullet that broke his hip bone. He took two additional flesh wounds. His pack was hit twice, and the chin strap on his helmet was severed by a bullet. He crawled up the beach "and staggered up against the seawall and sort of collapsed there and, as a matter of fact, spent the whole day in that same position. Essentially my part in the invasion had ended by having been wiped out as most of my company was. The bodies of my buddies were washing ashore and I was the one live body in amongst so many of my friends, all of whom were dead, in many cases very severely blown to pieces."

On his boat, Lt. Edward Tidrick was first off. As he jumped from the ramp into the water he took a bullet through his throat. He staggered to the sand, flopped down near Pvt. Leo Nash, and raised himself up to gasp, "Advance with the wire cutters!" At that instant, machine-gun bullets ripped Tidrick from crown to pelvis.

By 0640 only one officer from A Company was alive, Lt. E. Ray Nance, and he had been hit in the heel and the belly. Every sergeant was either dead or wounded. On one boat, when the ramp was dropped every man in the thirty-man assault team was killed before any of them could get out.

Pvt. George Roach was an assistant flamethrower. He weighed 125 pounds. He carried over a hundred pounds of gear ashore, including his M-1 rifle, ammunition, hand grenades, a five-gallon drum of flamethrower fluid, and assorted wrenches and a cylinder of nitrogen.

"We went down the ramp and the casualty rate was very bad. We couldn't determine where the fire was coming from, whether from the top of the bluff or from the summer beach-type homes on the shore. I just dropped myself into the sand and took my rifle and fired it at this house and Sergeant Wilkes asked, 'What are you firing at?' and I said, 'I don't know.' "

The only other live member of his assault team Roach could see was Pvt. Gil Murdoch. The two men were lying together behind an obstacle. Murdoch had lost his glasses and could not see. "Can you swim?" Roach asked.

"No."

"Well, look, we can't stay here, there's nobody around here that seems to have any idea of what to do. Let's go back in the water and come in with the tide." They fell back and got behind a knocked-out tank. Both men were slightly wounded. The tide covered them and they hung onto the tank. Roach started to swim to shore; a coxswain from a Higgins boat picked him up about halfway in. "He pulled me on board, it was around 1030. And I promptly fell asleep."

Roach eventually got up to the seawall, where he helped the medics. The following day, he caught up with what remained of his company. "I met General [Norman] Cota and I had a brief conversation with him. He asked me what company I was with and I told him and he just shook his head. A Company was just out of action. When we got together, there were eight of us left from Company A ready for duty."

(Cota asked Roach what he was going to do when the war was over. "Someday I'd like to go to college and graduate," Roach replied. "I'd like to go to Fordham." Five years to the day later, Roach did graduate from Fordham. "Over the years," he said in 1990, "I don't think there has been a day that has gone by that I haven't thought of those men who didn't make it.")

Sgt. Lee Polek's landing craft was about to swamp as it approached the shore. Everyone was bailing with helmets. "We yelled to the crew to take us in, we would rather fight than drown. As the ramp dropped we were hit by machine-gun and rifle fire. I yelled to get ready to swim and fight. We were getting direct fire right into our craft. My three squad leaders in front and others were hit. Some men climbed over the side. Two sailors got hit. I got off in water only ankle deep, tried to run but the water was suddenly up to my hips. I crawled to hide behind a steel beach obstacle. Bullets hit off it, others hit more of my men. Got up to the beach to crawl behind the shingle and a few of my men joined me. I took a head count and there was only eleven of us left, from the thirty on the craft. As the tide came in we took turns running out to the water's edge to drag wounded men to cover. Some of the wounded were hit again while on the beach. More men crowding up and crowding up. More people being hit by shellfire. People trying to help each other.

"While we were huddled there, I told [Pvt.] Jim Hickey that I would like to live to be forty years old and work forty hours a week and make a dollar an hour (when I joined up I was making thirty-seven-and-a-half cents an hour). I felt, boy, I would really have it made at $40 a week.

"Jim Hickey still calls me from New York on June 6 to ask, 'Hey, Sarge, are you making forty bucks per yet?' "

A Company had hardly fired a weapon. Almost certainly it had not killed any Germans. It had expected to move up the Vierville draw and be on top of the bluff by 0730, but at 0730 its handful of survivors were huddled up against the seawall, virtually without weapons. It had lost 96 percent of its effective strength.

But its sacrifice was not in vain. The men had brought in rifles, BARs (Browning automatic rifles), grenades, TNT charges, machine guns, mortars and mortar rounds, flamethrowers, rations, and other equipment. This was now strewn across the sand at Dog Green. The weapons and equipment would make a life-or-death difference to the following waves of infantry, coming in at higher tide and having to abandon everything to make their way to shore.

F Company, 116th, supposed to come in at Dog Red, landed near its target, astride the boundary between Dog Red and Easy

Green. But G Company, supposed to be to the right of F at Dog White, drifted far left, so the two companies came in together, directly opposite the heavy fortifications at Les Moulins. There was a kilometer or so gap to each side of the intermixed companies, which allowed the German defenders to concentrate their fire.

For the men of F and G Companies, the two hundred meters or more journey from the Higgins boats to the shingle was the longest and most hazardous trip they had ever experienced, or ever would. The lieutenant commanding the assault team on Sgt. Harry Bare's boat was killed as the ramp went down. "As ranking noncom," Bare related, "I tried to get my men off the boat and make it somehow to get under the seawall. We waded to the sand and threw ourselves down and the men were frozen, unable to move. My radioman had his head blown off three yards from me. The beach was covered with bodies, men with no legs, no arms—God it was awful."

As what was left of A, F, G, and E Companies of the 116th huddled behind obstacles or the shingle, the following waves began to come in: B and H Companies at 0700; D at 0710; C, K, I, and M at 0720. Not one came in on target. The coxswains were trying to dodge obstacles and incoming shells, while the smoke drifted in and out and obscured the landmarks and what few marker flags there were on the beach.

On the command boat for B Company, the CO, Capt. Ettore Zappacosta, heard the British coxswain cry out, "We can't go in there. We can't see the landmarks. We must pull off."

Zappacosta pulled his Colt .45 and ordered, "By God, you'll take this boat straight in."

The coxswain did. When the ramp dropped, Zappacosta was first off. He was immediately hit. Medic Thomas Kenser saw him bleeding from hip and shoulder. Kenser, still on the ramp, shouted, "Try to make it in! I'm coming." But the captain was already dead. Before Kenser could jump off the ramp he was shot dead. Every man in the boat save one (Pvt. Robert Sales) was either killed or wounded before reaching the beach.

Nineteen-year-old Pvt. Harold Baumgarten of B Company got

a bullet through the top of his helmet while jumping from the ramp, then another hit the receiver of his M-1 as he carried it at port arms. He waded through the waist-deep water as his buddies fell alongside him.

"I saw Pvt. Robert Ditmar of Fairfield, Connecticut, hold his chest and heard him yell, 'I'm hit, I'm hit!' I hit the ground and watched him as he continued to go forward about ten more yards. He tripped over an obstacle and, as he fell, his body made a complete turn and he lay sprawled on the damp sand with his head facing the Germans, his face looking skyward. He was yelling, 'Mother, Mom.'

"Sgt. Clarence 'Pilgrim' Robertson had a gaping wound in the upper-right corner of his forehead. He was walking crazily in the water. Then I saw him get down on his knees and start praying with his rosary beads. At this moment, the Germans cut him in half with their deadly crossfire."

Baumgarten had drawn a Star of David on the back of his field jacket, with "The Bronx, New York" written on it—that would let Hitler know who he was. He was behind an obstacle. He saw the reflection from the helmet of one of the German riflemen on the bluff "and took aim and later on I found out I got a bull's-eye on him." That was the only shot he fired because his damaged rifle broke in two when he pulled the trigger.

Shells were bursting about him. "I raised my head to curse the Germans when an 88 shell exploded about twenty yards in front of me, hitting me in my left cheek. It felt like being hit with a baseball bat, only the results were much worse. My upper jaw was shattered, the left cheek blown open. My upper lip was cut in half. The roof of my mouth was cut up and teeth and gums were laying all over my mouth. Blood poured freely from the gaping wound."

The tide was coming in. Baumgarten washed his face with the cold, dirty Channel water and managed not to pass out. The water was rising about an inch a minute (between 0630 and 0800 the tide rose eight feet) so he had to get moving or drown. He took another hit, from a bullet, in the leg. He moved forward in a dead man's float with each wave of the incoming tide. He finally reached the seawall where a medic dressed his wounds. Mortars were coming in, "and I grabbed the medic by the shirt to pull him down. He hit my hand away and said, 'You're injured now. When I get hurt you can take care of me.' " *

Sgt. Benjamin McKinney was a combat engineer attached to C Company. When his ramp dropped, "I was so seasick I didn't care if a bullet hit me between the eyes and got me out of my misery." As he jumped off the ramp, "rifle and machine-gun fire hit it like rain falling." Ahead, "it looked as if all the first wave were dead on the beach." He got to the shingle. He and Sergeant Storms saw a pillbox holding a machine gun and a rifleman about thirty meters to the right, spraying the beach with their weapons. Storms and McKinney crawled toward the position. McKinney threw hand grenades as Storms put rifle fire into it. Two Germans jumped out; Storms killed them. The 116th was starting to fight back.

Capt. Robert Walker was on LCI (landing craft, infantry) 91. As it approached the beach, the craft began taking rifle and machine-gun fire. Maneuvering through the obstacles, the craft got caught on one of the pilings and set off the Teller mine. The explosion tore off the starboard landing ramp.

The skipper tried to back off. Walker moved to the port-side ramp, only to find it engulfed in flames. A man carrying a flame-thrower had been hit by a bullet; another bullet had set the jellied contents of his fuel tank on fire. Screaming in agony, he dove into the sea. "I could see that even the soles of his boots were on fire." Men around him also burned; Walker saw a couple of riflemen "with horrendous drooping face blisters."

The skipper came running to the front deck, waving his arms and yelling, "Everybody over the side." Walker jumped into water about eight feet deep. He was carrying so much equipment that despite two Mae Wests he could not stay afloat. He dropped his rifle, then his helmet, then his musette bag, which enabled him to swim to where he could touch bottom.

---

* Baumgarten was wounded five times that day, the last time by a bullet in his right knee as he was being carried on a stretcher to the beach for evacuation. He went on to medical school and became a practicing physician. He concluded his oral history, "Happily, in recent years when I've been back to Normandy, especially on Sept. 17, 1988, when we dedicated a monument to the 29th Division in Vierville, I noted that the French people really appreciated us freeing them from the Germans, so it made it all worthwhile."

"Here I was on Omaha Beach. Instead of being a fierce, well-trained, fighting infantry warrior, I was an exhausted, almost helpless, unarmed survivor of a shipwreck." When he got to waist-deep water he got on his knees and crawled the rest of the way. Working his way forward to the seawall, he saw the body of Captain Zappacosta. At the seawall, "I saw dozens of soldiers, mostly wounded. The wounds were ghastly to see."

(Forty-nine years later, Walker recorded that the scene brought to his mind Tennyson's lines in "The Charge of the Light Brigade," especially "Cannon to right of them/Cannon to left of them/Cannon in front of them/Volley'd and thunder'd." He added that so far as he could tell every GI knew the lines, "Theirs not to reason why/Theirs but to do and die," even if the soldiers did not know the source. Those on Omaha Beach who had committed the poem to memory surely muttered to themselves, "Some one had blunder'd.")

Walker came to Cota's conclusion. Anyplace was better than this; the plan was kaput; he couldn't go back; he set out on his own to climb the bluff. He picked up an M-1 and a helmet from a dead soldier and moved out. "I was alone and completely on my own."

Maj. Sidney Bingham (USMA 1940) was CO of 2nd Battalion, 116th. When he reached the shingle he was without radio, aide, or runner. His S-3 was dead, his HQ Company commander wounded, his E Company commander dead, his F Company commander wounded, his H Company commander killed, "and in E Company there were some fifty-five killed out of a total of something just over two hundred who landed."

Bingham was overwhelmed by a feeling of "complete futility. Here I was, the battalion commander, unable for the most part to influence action or do what I knew had to be done." He set out to organize a leaderless group from F Company and get it moving up the bluff.

By this time, around 0745, unknown others were doing the same, whether NCOs or junior officers or, in some cases, privates. Staying on the beach meant certain death; retreat was not possible; someone had to lead; men took the burden on themselves and did. Bingham put it this way: "The individual and small-unit initiative carried the day. Very little, if any, credit can be accorded company, battalion, or regimental commanders for their tactical prowess and/or their coordination of the action."

Bingham did an analysis of what went wrong for the first and second waves. Among other factors, he said, the men were in the Higgins boats far too long. "Seasickness occasioned by the three or four hours in LCVPs played havoc with any idealism that may have been present. It markedly decreased the combat effectiveness of the command."

In addition, "The individual loads carried were in my view greatly excessive, hindered mobility, and in some cases caused death by drowning." In his view, "If the enemy had shown any sort of enthusiasm and moved toward us, they could have run us right back into the Channel without any trouble."

From June 6, 1944, on to 1990, Bingham carried with him an unjustified self-criticism: "I've often felt very ashamed of the fact that I was so completely inadequate as a leader on the beach on that frightful day." That is the way a good battalion commander feels when he is leading not much more than a squad—but Bingham got that squad over the shingle and into an attack against the enemy, which was exactly the right thing to do, and the only thing he could do under the circumstances.

The Germans did not counterattack for a number of reasons, some of them good ones. First, they were not present in sufficient strength. Gen. Kraiss had but two of his infantry battalions and one artillery battalion on the scene, about two thousand men, or less than 250 per kilometer. Second, he was slow to react. Not until 0735 did he call up his division reserve, *Kampfgruppe Meyer* (named for the CO of the 915th Regiment of Kraiss's 352nd Division), and then he decided to commit only a single battalion, which did not arrive until midday. He was acting on a false assumption: that his men had stopped the invasion at Omaha. Third, the German infantrymen were not trained for assaults, only to hold their positions and keep firing.

One German private who was manning an MG 42 on top of the bluff put it this way in a 1964 radio interview: "It was the first time I shoot at living men. I don't remember exactly how it was: the only thing I know is that I went to my machine gun and I shoot, I shoot, I shoot."

□

The sacrifice of good men that morning was just appalling. Capt. Walter Schilling of D Company, who had given a magnificent briefing to his magnificently trained men, was in the lead boat in the third wave. He was as good a company CO as there was in the U.S. Army. The company was coming into a section of the beach that had no one on it; there was no fire; Schilling remarked to Pvt. George Kobe, "See, I told you it was going to be easy." Moments later, before the ramp went down, Schilling was killed by a shell.

Lt. William Gardner was the company executive officer, a West Point graduate described by Sgt. John R. Slaughter as "young, articulate, handsome, tough, and aggressive. He possessed all the qualities to become a high-ranking officer in the Army." The ramp went down on his boat some 150 meters from shore. The men got off without loss. Gardner ordered them to spread out and keep low. He was killed by machine-gun fire before he made the shore.

Sergeant Slaughter's boat was bracketed by German artillery fire. At 100 meters from shore, the British coxswain said he had to lower the ramp and everyone should get out quickly. Sgt. Willard Norfleet told him to keep going: "these men have heavy equipment and you *will* take them all the way in."

The coxswain begged, "But we'll *all* be killed!"

Norfleet unholstered his .45 Colt pistol, put it to the sailor's head, and ordered, "All the way in!" The coxswain proceeded.

Sergeant Slaughter, up at the front of the boat, was thinking, If this boat don't hurry up and get us in, I'm going to die from seasickness. The boat hit a sandbar and stopped.

"I watched the movie *The Longest Day*," Slaughter recalled, "and they came charging off those boats and across the beach like banshees, but that isn't the way it happened. You came off the craft, you hit the water, and if you didn't get down in it you were going to get shot."

The incoming fire was horrendous. "This turned the boys into men," Slaughter commented. "Some would be very brave men, others would soon be dead men, but all of those who survived would be frightened men. Some wet their britches, others cried unashamedly, and many just had to find it within themselves to get the job done." In a fine tribute to Captain Schilling, Slaughter concluded, "This is where the discipline and training took over."

Slaughter made his way toward shore. "There were dead men floating in the water and there were live men acting dead, letting the tide take them in." Most of D Company was in the water a full hour, working forward. Once he reached shore, for Slaughter "getting across the beach to the shingle became an obsession." He made it. "The first thing I did was to take off my assault jacket and spread my raincoat so I could clean my rifle. It was then I saw bullet holes in my raincoat. I lit my first cigarette [they were wrapped in plastic]. I had to rest and compose myself because I became weak in my knees.

"Colonel [Charles] Canham came by with his right arm in a sling and a .45 Colt in his left hand. He was yelling and screaming for the officers to get the men off the beach. 'Get the hell off this damn beach and go kill some Germans.' There was an officer taking refuge from an enemy mortar barrage in a pillbox. Right in front of me Colonel Canham screamed, 'Get your ass out of there and show some leadership.' " To another lieutenant he roared, "Get these men off their dead asses and over that wall."

This was the critical moment in the battle. It was an ultimate test: Could a democracy produce young men tough enough to take charge, to lead? As Pvt. Carl Weast put it, "It was simple fear that stopped us at that shingle and we lay there and we got butchered by rocket fire and by mortars for no damn reason other than the fact that there was nobody there to lead us off that goddamn beach. Like I say, hey man, I did my job, but somebody had to lead me."

Sgt. William Lewis remembered cowering behind the shingle. Pvt. Larry Rote piled in on top of Lewis. He asked, "Is that you shaking, Sarge?"

"Yeah, damn right!"

"My God," Rote said. "I thought it was me!" Lewis commented, "Rote was shaking all right."

They huddled together with some other men, "just trying to stay alive. There was nothing we could do except keep our butts down. Others took cover behind the wall."

All across Omaha the men who had made it to the shingle hid behind it. Then Cota, or Canham, or a captain here, a lieutenant there, a sergeant someplace else, began to lead. They would cry out, "Follow me!" and start moving up the bluff.

In Sergeant Lewis's case, "Lt. Leo Van de Voort said, 'Let's go, goddamn, there ain't no use staying here, we're all going to get killed!' The first thing he did was to run up to a gun emplacement and throw a grenade in the embrasure. He returned with five or six prisoners. So then we thought, hell, if he can do that, why can't we. That's how we got off the beach."

That was how most men got off the beach. Pvt. Raymond Howell, an engineer attached to D Company, described his thought process. He took some shrapnel in helmet and hand. "That's when I said, bullshit, if I'm going to die, to hell with it I'm not going to die here. The next bunch of guys that go over that goddamn wall, I'm going with them. If I'm gonna be infantry, I'm gonna be infantry. So I don't know who else, I guess all of us decided well, it is time to start."

The 16th Infantry Regiment of the 1st Division (the Big Red One) was the only first-wave assault unit on D-Day with combat experience. It didn't help much. Nothing the 16th had seen in the North Africa (1942) and Sicily (1943) landings compared to what it encountered at Easy Red, Fox Green, and Fox Red on June 6.

Like the 116th, the 16th landed in a state of confusion, off target, badly intermingled (except L Company, the only one of the eight assault companies that could be considered a unit as it hit the beach), under intense machine-gun, rifle, mortar, and artillery fire from both flanks and the front. Schedules were screwed up, paths through the obstacles were not cleared, most officers—the first men off the boats—were wounded or killed before they could take even one step on the beach.

The naval gunfire support lifted as the Higgins boats moved in and would not resume until the smoke and haze revealed definite targets or until navy fire-control officers ashore radioed back specific coordinates (few of those officers made it and those who did had no working radios). Most of the DD tanks had gone down in the Channel; the few that made it were disabled.

As a consequence, the German defenders were able to fire at pre-sited targets from behind their fortifications unimpeded by incoming fire. The American infantry struggled ashore with no support whatsoever. Casualties were extremely heavy, especially in the water and in the two hundred meters or so of open beach. As with the 116th to the right, for the 16th Regiment first and second waves D-Day was more reminiscent of an infantry charge across no-man's-land at the Somme in World War I than a typical World War II action.

"Our life expectancy was about zero," Pvt. John MacPhee declared. "We were burdened down with too much weight. We were just pack mules. I was very young, in excellent shape. I could walk for miles, endure a great deal of physical hardship, but I was so seasick I thought I would die. In fact, I wished I had. I was totally exhausted."

Jumping off the ramp into chest-deep water, MacPhee barely made it to the beach. There, "I fell and for what seemed an eternity I lay there." He was hit three times, once in the lower back, twice in the left leg. His arm was paralyzed. "That did it. I lost all my fear and knew I was about to die. I made peace with my Maker and was just waiting."

MacPhee was lucky. Two of his buddies dragged him to the shelter of the seawall; eventually he was evacuated. He was told he had a million-dollar wound. For him the war was over.

As the ramp on his Higgins boat went down, Sgt. Clayton Hanks had a flashback. When he was five years old he had seen a World War I photograph in a Boston newspaper. He had said to his mother, "I wish I could be a war soldier someday."

"Don't ever say that again," his mother had replied.

He didn't, but at age seventeen he joined the Regular Army. He had been in ten years when the ramp went down and he recalled his mother's words. "I volunteered," he said to himself. "I asked for this or whatever was to come." He leaped into the water and struggled forward.

Pvt. Warren Rulien came in with the second wave. Dead soldiers floated around in the water, which had risen past the first obstacles. He ducked behind a steel rail in waist-deep water. His platoon leader, a nineteen-year-old lieutenant, was behind another rail.

The lieutenant yelled, "Hey, Rulien, here I go!" and began attempting to run to the shore. A machine gun cut him down. Rulien grabbed one of the bodies floating in the water and pushed it in front of him as he made his way to the shore.

"I had only gone a short distance when three or four soldiers began lining up behind me. I shouted, "Don't bunch up!" and moved out, leaving them with the body. I got as low as I could in the water until I reached a sandbar and crossed it on my belly." On the inland side of the sandbar the water was up to his chest. He moved forward. "On the shore, there were officers sitting there, stunned. Nobody was taking command." He joined other survivors at the seawall.

The coxswain on Pvt. Charles Thomas's boat was killed by machine-gun fire as he was taking his craft in. A crew member took over. The platoon leader had his arm shot off trying to open the ramp. Finally the ramp dropped and the assault team leaped into the surf. Thomas had a bangalore torpedo to carry so he was last man in the team.

"As I was getting off I stopped to pick up a smoke grenade, as if I didn't have enough to carry. The guy running the boat yelled for me to get off. He was in a hurry, but I turned around and told him that I wasn't in any hurry."

Thomas jumped into chest-deep water. "My helmet fell back on my neck and the strap was choking me. My rifle sling was dragging under the water and I couldn't stand." He inflated his Mae West and finally made it to shore. "There I crawled in over wounded and dead but I couldn't tell who was who and we had orders not to stop for anyone on the edge of the beach, to keep going or we would be hit ourselves."

When he reached the seawall, "it was crowded with GIs all being wounded or killed. It was overcrowded with GIs. I laid on my side and opened my fly, I had to urinate. I don't know why I did that because I was soaking wet anyway and I was under fire, and I guess I was just being neat."

Thomas worked his way over to the left, where "I ran into a bunch of my buddies from the company. Most of them didn't even have a rifle. Some bummed cigarettes off of me because I had three cartons wrapped in waxed paper." Thomas was at the base of the bluff (just below the site of the American cemetery today). In his opinion, "The Germans could have swept us away with brooms if they knew how few we were and what condition we were in."

Capt. Fred Hall was in the LCVP carrying the 2nd Battalion

headquarters group (Lt. Col. Herb Hicks, CO). Hall was battalion S-3. His heart sank when he saw yellow life rafts holding men in life jackets and he realized they were the crews from the DD tanks. "That meant that we would not have tank support on the beach." The boat was in the E Company sector of Easy Red. E Company was supposed to be on the far right of the 16th, linking up with the 116th at the boundary between Easy Green and Easy Red, but it came in near the boundary between Easy Red and Fox Green, a full kilometer from the nearest 116th unit on its right (and with sections of the badly mislanded E Company of the 116th on its left).

There was nothing to be done about the mistake. The officers and men jumped into the water and "it was every man for himself crossing the open beach where we were under fire." Fourteen of the thirty failed to make it. Hall got up to the seawall with Hicks and "we opened our map case wrapped in canvas, containing our assault maps showing unit boundaries, phase lines, and objectives. I remember it seemed a bit incongruous under the circumstances."

The incoming fire was murderous. "And the noise—always the noise, naval gunfire, small arms, artillery, and mortar fire, aircraft overhead, engine noises, the shouting and the cries of the wounded, no wonder some people couldn't handle it." The assistant regimental commander and the forward artillery observer were killed by rifle fire. Lieutenant Colonel Hicks shouted to Hall to find the company commanders. To Hall, "It was a matter of survival. I was so busy trying to round up the COs to organize their men to move off the beach that there wasn't much time to think except to do what had to be done."

Hicks wanted to move his men to the right, where the battalion was supposed to be, opposite the draw that led up the bluff between St.-Laurent and Colleville, but movement was almost impossible. The tide was coming in rapidly, follow-up waves were landing, the beach was narrowing from the incoming tide, "it became very crowded and the confusion increased." So far as Hall could make out, "there was no movement off the beach."

In fact, one platoon from E Company, 16th Regiment, was making its way up to the top of the bluff. It was led by Lt. John Spaulding of E Company. He was one of the first junior officers to make it across the seawall, through the swamp and beach flat, and up the bluff.

G Company, 16th Regiment, 1st Division, came in at 0700. The CO, Capt. Joe Dawson, was first off his boat, followed by his communications sergeant and his company clerk. As they jumped, a shell hit the boat and destroyed it, killing thirty men, including the naval officer who was to control fire support from the warships.

Dawson expected to find a path up the bluff cleared out by F Company, but "as I landed I found nothing but men and bodies lying on the shore." He got to the shingle where survivors from other boats of G Company joined him. Among them was Sgt. Joe Pilck. He recalled, "We couldn't move forward because they had a double apron of barbed wire in front of us, and to our right it was a swampy area we couldn't cross and to the left they had minefields laid out so we couldn't go there."

"Utter chaos reigned," Dawson recalled, "because the Germans controlled the field of fire completely." He realized that "there was nothing I could do on the beach except die." To get through the barbed wire he had Pvts. Ed Tatara and Henry Peszek put two bangalore torpedoes together, shoved them under the wire, and blew a gap. They started through the minefield and up the bluff, engaging the enemy.

Dawson got to the top. How he got there is a story he tells best himself: "On landing I found total chaos as men and material were literally choking the sandbar just at the water's edge. A minefield lay in and around a path extending to my right and upward to the crest of the bluff. After blowing a gap in the concertina wire I led my men gingerly over the body of a soldier who had stepped on a mine in seeking to clear the path. I collected my company at the base of the bluff and proceeded on. Midway toward the crest I met Lieutenant Spaulding.

"I proceeded toward the crest, asking Spaulding to cover me. Near the crest the terrain became almost vertical. This afforded complete defilade from the entrenched enemy above. A machine-gun nest was busily firing at the beach, and one could hear rifle and mortar fire coming from the crest.

"I tossed two grenades aloft, and when they exploded the machine gun fell silent. I waved my men and Spaulding to proceed as rapidly as possible and I then proceeded to the crest where I saw the enemy moving out toward the E-3 exit and the dead Germans in the trenches.

"To my knowledge no one had penetrated the enemy defenses until that moment.

"As soon as my men reached me we debouched from that point, firing on the retreating enemy and moving toward a . . . wooded area, and this became a battleground extending all the way into town."

In an analysis of how he became the first American to reach the top of the bluff in this area, written in 1993, Dawson pointed out: "The Battle of Omaha Beach was 1st, Deadly enemy fire on an exposed beach where total fire control favored the defender and we were not given *any* direct fire support from the Navy or tanks. 2nd, the poor German marksmanship is the *only* way I could have made it across the exposed area because I could not engage the enemy nor even see him until I reached the machine gun. 3rd, the fortunate ability to control my command both in landing together and debouching up the bluff together as a fighting unit. 4th, our direct engagement of the enemy caused him to cease concerted small-arms, machine-gun and mortar fire with which he was sweeping the beach below." *

At the top, Dawson was experiencing difficulties in moving on Colleville. Dawson led by example and gave orders that were simple, direct, impossible not to understand: "I said, 'Men, there is the enemy. Let's go get them.' "

G Company worked its way to within a kilometer of Colleville. Dawson paused under a large oak tree. "There, a very friendly French woman welcomed us with open arms and said, 'Welcome to France.' "

Dawson advanced to the edge of Colleville. The dominant building, as always in the Normandy villages, was a Norman church, built of stone, its steeple stretching into the sky. "Sure enough," Dawson noted, "in the steeple of the church there was an artillery observer." He dashed inside the church with a sergeant and a private.

---

* Dawson's route to the top was approximately the same as the paved path that today leads from the beach to the lookout with the bronze panorama of Omaha Beach on the edge of the American cemetery.

"Immediately, three Germans inside the church opened fire. Fortunately, we were not hit by this burst. But as we made our way through the church the private was killed, shot by the observer in the tower. I turned and we secured the tower by eliminating him. My sergeant shot the other two Germans and thus we took care of the opposition at that point."

As Dawson ran out of the church, a German rifleman shot at him. Dawson fired back with his carbine, but not before the German got off a second shot. The bullet went through Dawson's carbine and shattered the stock. Fragments from the bullet went through his kneecap and leg, which "caused my knee to swell and caused me to be evacuated the next day."

Beyond the church, G Company ran into heavy fire from a full German company occupying the houses in Colleville. Built of stone, the positions were all but impregnable to small-arms fire. G Company got into what Dawson called "a very severe firefight," but could not advance.

It was shortly after noon. Maj. William Washington, executive officer of the 2nd Battalion, 16th Regiment, came up, arriving at about the same time as Spaulding's platoon. Washington set up a command post (CP) in a drainage ditch just west of Colleville. He sent the E Company platoon to the right (south) of the village. Spaulding moved out and got separated from Dawson. Germans moved into the gap; in forty minutes Spaulding's platoon was surrounded. Just that quickly, Spaulding realized that instead of attacking, he was being counterattacked. He set up a defensive position in the drainage ditches. Several squads of Germans came toward the platoon. Spaulding's men were able to beat them off.

Spaulding saw a runner coming from the battalion CP with a message from Major Washington. "The Germans opened fire on him. After he fell they fired at least a hundred rounds of machine-gun ammunition into him. It was terrible but we do the same thing when we want to stop a runner bearing information."

Spaulding's platoon spent the remainder of the day in the ditches, fighting a defensive action. By nightfall, Spaulding was down to six rounds of carbine ammunition; most of his men were down to their last clip. The platoon was still surrounded.

It had been the first platoon to take prisoners. It had eliminated several machine-gun posts on the bluff and the emplacement looking down the E-1 draw. It had landed with thirty men; by nightfall, two had been killed, seven wounded. Five men in the platoon were awarded DSCs, personally presented by General Eisenhower: they were Lt. John Spaulding, Kentucky; Sgt. Philip Streczyk, New Jersey; Pvt. Richard Gallagher, New York; Pvt. George Bowen, Kentucky; Sgt. Kenneth Peterson, New Jersey.

Spaulding's and Dawson's and the other small groups were like magnets to the men along the shingle embankment. If they can make it so can I, was the thought.

Simultaneously, the men were being urged forward by other junior officers and NCOs, and by the regimental commander, forty-seven-year-old Col. George Taylor. He landed about 0800. Pvt. Warren Rulien watched him come in. "He stepped across the sandbar and bullets began hitting the water around him. He laid down on his stomach and started crawling toward shore, his staff officers doing the same."

"He had a couple of tattered-ass second louies following him," according to Pvt. Paul Radzom, who was also watching. "They looked like they were scared to death."

When Taylor made it to the seawall, Rulien heard him say to the officers, "If we're going to die, let's die up there." To other groups of men, Taylor said, "There are only two kinds of people on this beach: the dead and those about to die. So let's get the hell out of here!"

Men got to work with the bangalores, blowing gaps in the barbed wire. Engineers with mine detectors moved through, then started laying out tape to show where they had cleared paths through the minefields. Others hit the pillboxes at the base of the bluff. "I went up with my flamethrower to button up the aperture of a pillbox," Pvt. Buddy Mazzara of C Company remembered, "and [Pvt.] Fred Erben came in with his dynamite charge. Soon some soldiers came out of the pillbox with their hands up saying, 'No shoot. No shoot. Me Pole.' "

Pvt. John Shroeder, his machine gun cleaned and ready to fire, watched as a rifleman moved out. "So the first man, he started out across, and running zigzag he made it to the bluff. So we all felt a little better to see that we had a chance, we were going to get off.

And the minefield was already full of dead and wounded. And finally it came my turn and I grabbed my heavy .30-cal and started up over the shingle and across the minefield, trying to keep low. Finally I got to the base of the bluff." There he ducked behind the old foundation of a house. Two others joined him. "It was just the three of us there, we couldn't find our platoon leaders or our platoon sergeants or anybody."

But they could see two heartening sights. One was Americans on the crest of the bluff. The other was a line of POWs, sent down by Captain Dawson under guard. The enemy prisoners "were really roughed up. Their hair was all full of cement, dirt, everything. They didn't look so tough. So we started up the bluff carrying our stuff with us, and the others started following us."

Lt. William Dillon gathered the survivors from his platoon, joined three bangalores together, shoved them under the barbed wire, blew a gap, dashed through, crossed the swamp, swam across an antitank ditch filled with water, and made it to the base of the bluff.

"I knew that the Germans had to have a path up the hill that was clear of mines. I looked around. When I was younger I'd been a good hunter and could trail a rabbit easily. I studied the ground and saw a faint path zigzagging to the left up the hill, so I walked the path very carefully. Something blew up behind me. I looked back and a young soldier had stepped on a mine and it had blown off his foot up to his knee. I brought the others up the path. At the top we saw the first and only Russian soldiers I have ever seen."

In his column for June 12, 1944, reporter Ernie Pyle wrote, "Now that it is over it seems to me a pure miracle that we ever took the beach at all. . . . As one officer said, the only way to take a beach is to face it and keep going. It is costly at first, but it's the only way. If the men are pinned down on the beach, dug in and out of action, they might as well not be there at all. They hold up the waves behind them, and nothing is being gained.

"Our men were pinned down for a while, but finally they stood up and went through, and so we took that beach and accomplished our landing. We did it with every advantage on the enemy's side and every disadvantage on ours. In the light of a couple of days of retrospection, we sit and talk and call it a miracle that our men ever got on at all or were able to stay on."

It was not a miracle. It was infantry. The plan had called for the air and naval bombardments, followed by tanks and dozers, to blast a path through the exits so that the infantry could march up the draws and engage the enemy, but the plan had failed, utterly and completely failed. As is almost always the case in war, it was up to the infantry. It became the infantry's job to open the exits so that the vehicles could drive up the draws and engage the enemy.

Exhortation and example, backed by two years of training, got the GIs from the 16th Regiment to overcome their exhaustion, confusion, and fear and get out from behind the shingle and start up the bluff. Colonel Taylor and many others pointed out the obvious, that to stay behind the "shelter" was to die. Retreat was not possible.

Captain Dawson, Lieutenants Spaulding and Dillon, and many others provided the example; their actions proved that it was possible to cross the swamp, the antitank ditch, the minefields, and find paths to the top of the bluff.

As they came onto the beach, the junior officers and NCOs saw at once that the intricate plan, the one they had studied so hard and committed to memory, bore no relationship whatsoever to the tactical problem they faced. They had expected to find ready-made craters on the beach, blasted by the bombs from the B-17s, to provide shelter in the unlikely event that they encountered any small-arms fire when they made the shoreline. They had expected to go up the draws, which they anticipated would have been cleared by the DD tanks and dozers, to begin fighting up on the high ground. They had expected fire support from tanks, half-tracks, artillery. Nothing they had expected had happened.

Yet their training had prepared them for this challenge. They sized up the situation, saw what had to be done, and did it. This was leadership of the highest order. It came from men who had been civilians three or even two years earlier.

Sgt. John Ellery of the 16th Regiment was one of those leaders. When he reached the shingle, "I had to peer through a haze of sweat, smoke, dust, and mist." There was a dead man beside him, another behind him. Survivors gathered around him; "I told them that we had to get off the beach and that I'd lead the way." He did. When he got to the base of the bluff, he started up, four or five men following. About halfway up, a machine gun opened up on them from the right.

"I scurried and scratched along until I got within ten meters of the gun position. Then I unloaded all four of my fragmentation grenades. When the last one went off, I made a dash for the top. The other kids were right behind me and we all made it. I don't know if I knocked out that gun crew but they stopped shooting. Those grenades were all the return fire I provided coming off that beach. I didn't fire a round from either my rifle or my pistol."

In giving his account Ellery spoke about leadership. "After the war," he said, "I read about a number of generals and colonels who are said to have wandered about exhorting the troops to advance. That must have been very inspirational! I suspect, however, that the men were more interested and more impressed by junior officers and NCOs who were willing to lead them rather than having some general pointing out the direction in which they should go."

Warming to the subject, Ellery went on: "I didn't see any generals in my area of the beach, but I did see a captain and two lieutenants who demonstrated courage beyond belief as they struggled to bring order to the chaos around them." Those officers managed to get some men organized and moving up the bluff. One of the lieutenants had a broken arm that hung limply at his side, but he led a group of seven to the top, even though he got hit again on the way. Another lieutenant carried one of his wounded men thirty meters before getting hit himself.

"When you talk about combat leadership under fire on the beach at Normandy," Ellery concluded, "I don't see how the credit can go to anyone other than the company-grade officers and senior NCOs who led the way. It is good to be reminded that there are such men, that there always have been and always will be. We sometimes forget, I think, that you can manufacture weapons, and you can purchase ammunition, but you can't buy valor and you can't pull heroes off an assembly line."

□

The next morning Pt. Robert Healey of the 149th Combat Engineers and a friend decided to go down the bluff to retrieve their packs. Healey had run out of cigarettes, but he had a carton in a waterproof bag in his pack.

"When we walked down to the beach, it was just an unbelievable sight. There was debris everywhere, and all kinds of equipment washing back and forth in the tide. Anything you could think of seemed to be there. We came across a tennis racquet, a guitar, assault jackets, packs, gas masks, everything. We found half a jar of olives which we ate with great relish. We found my pack but unfortunately the cigarettes were no longer there.

"On the way back I came across what was probably the most poignant memory I have of this whole episode. Lying on the beach was a young soldier, his arms outstretched. Near one of his hands, as if he had been reading it, was a pocketbook (what today would be called a paperback).

"It was *Our Hearts Were Young and Gay* by Cornelia Otis Skinner. This expressed the spirit of our ordeal. Our hearts were young and gay because we thought we were immortal, we believed we were doing a great thing, and we really believed in the crusade which we hoped would liberate the world from the heel of Nazism."

8

Pointe-du-Hoc

IT WAS A NEARLY 100-meter-high cliff, with perpendicular sides jutting out into the Channel. It looked down on Utah Beach to the left and Omaha Beach to the right. There were six 155mm cannon in heavily reinforced concrete bunkers that were capable of hitting either beach with their big shells. On the outermost edge of the cliff, the Germans had an elaborate, well-protected outpost, where the spotters had a perfect view and could call back coordinates to the gunners at the 155s. Those guns had to be neutralized.

The Allied bombardment of Pointe-du-Hoc had begun weeks before D-Day. Heavy bombers from the U.S. Eighth Air Force and British Bomber Command had repeatedly plastered the area, with a climax coming before dawn on June 6. Then the battleship *Texas* took up the action, sending dozens of 14-inch shells into the position. Altogether, Pointe-du-Hoc got hit by more than ten kilotons of high explosives, the equivalent of the explosive power of the atomic bomb used at Hiroshima. *Texas* lifted her fire at 0630, the moment the rangers were scheduled to touch down.

Col. James Earl Rudder was in the lead boat. He was not supposed to be there. Lt. Gen. Clarence Huebner, CO of the 1st Division and in overall command at Omaha Beach, had forbidden Rudder to lead D, E, and F Companies of the 2nd Rangers into

Pointe-du-Hoc, saying, "We're not going to risk getting you knocked out in the first round."

"I'm sorry to have to disobey you, sir," Rudder had replied, "but if I don't take it, it may not go." *

The rangers were in LCA boats manned by British seamen (the rangers had trained with British commandos and were therefore accustomed to working with British sailors). The LCA was built in England on the basic design of Andrew Higgins's boat, but the British added some light armor to the sides and gunwales. That made the LCA slower and heavier—the British were sacrificing mobility to increase security—which meant that the LCA rode lower in the water than the LCVP.

On D-Day morning all the LCAs carrying the rangers took on water as spray washed over the sides. One of the ten boats swamped shortly after leaving the transport area, taking the CO of D Company and twenty men with it. (They were picked up by an LCT a few hours later. "Give us some dry clothes, weapons and ammunition, and get us back in to the Pointe. We gotta get back!" Capt. "Duke" Slater said as he came out of the water. But his men were so numb from the cold water that the ship's physician ordered them back to England.) One of the two supply boats bringing in ammunition and other gear also swamped; the other supply boat had to jettison more than half its load to stay afloat.

That was but the beginning of the foul-ups. At 0630, as Rudder's lead LCA approached the beach, he saw with dismay that the coxswain was headed toward Pointe-de-la-Percee, about halfway between the Vierville draw and Pointe-du-Hoc. After some argument Rudder persuaded the coxswain to turn right to the objective. The flotilla had to fight the tidal current (the cause of the drift to the left) and proceeded only slowly parallel to the coast.

The error was costly. It caused the rangers to be thirty-five

* Lt. James W. Eikner, Rudder's communications officer on D-Day, comments in a letter of March 29, 1993, to the author: "The assault on the Pointe was supposed to be led by a recently promoted executive officer who unfortunately managed to get himself thoroughly drunk and unruly while still aboard his transport in Weymouth harbor. This was the situation that decided Col. Rudder to personally lead the Pointe-du-Hoc assault. The ex. ofc. was sent ashore and hospitalized—we never saw him again."

minutes late in touching down, which gave the German defenders time to recover from the bombardment, climb out of their dugouts, and man their positions. It also caused the flotilla to run a gauntlet of fire from German guns along four kilometers of coastline. One of the four DUKWs was sunk by a 20mm shell. Sgt. Frank South, a nineteen-year-old medic, recalled, "We were getting a lot of machine-gun fire from our left flank, alongside the cliff, and we could not, for the life of us, locate the fire." Lieutenant Eikner remembered "bailing water with our helmets, dodging bullets, and vomiting all at the same time."

USS *Satterlee* and HMS *Talybont,* destroyers, saw what was happening and came in close to fire with all guns at the Germans. That helped to drive some of the Germans back from the edge of the cliff. D Company had been scheduled to land on the west side of the point, but because of the error in navigation Rudder signaled by hand that the two LCAs carrying the remaining D Company troops join the other seven and land side by side along the east side.

Lt. George Kerchner, a platoon leader in D Company, recalled that when his LCA made its turn to head into the beach, "My thought was that this whole thing is a big mistake, that none of us were ever going to get up that cliff." But then the destroyers started firing and drove some of the Germans back from the edge of the cliff. Forty-eight years later, then retired Colonel Kerchner commented, "Some day I would love to meet up with somebody from *Satterlee* so I can shake his hand and thank him."

The beach at Pointe-du-Hoc was only ten meters in width as the flotilla approached, and shrinking rapidly as the tide was coming in (at high tide there would be virtually no beach). There was no sand, only shingle. The bombardment from air and sea had brought huge chunks of the clay soil from the point tumbling down, making the rocks slippery but also providing an eight-meter buildup at the base of the cliff that gave the rangers something of a head start in climbing the forty-meter cliff.

The rangers had a number of ingenious devices to help them get to the top. One was twenty-five-meter extension ladders mounted in the DUKWs, provided by the London Fire Department. But one DUKW was already sunk, and the other three could not get a footing on the shingle, which was covered with wet clay and thus rather like greased ball bearings. Only one ladder was extended.

Sgt. William Stivinson climbed to the top to fire his machine gun. He was swaying back and forth like a metronome, German tracers whipping about him. Lt. Elmer "Dutch" Vermeer described the scene: "The ladder was swaying at about a forty-five-degree angle—both ways. Stivinson would fire short bursts as he passed over the cliff at the top of the arch, but the DUKW floundered so badly that they had to bring the fire ladder back down."

The basic method of climbing was by rope. Each LCA carried three pairs of rocket guns, firing steel grapnels which pulled up plain three-quarter-inch ropes, toggle ropes, or rope ladders. The rockets were fired just before touchdown. Grapnels with attached ropes were an ancient technique for scaling a wall or cliff, tried and proven. But in this case, the ropes had been soaked by the spray and in many cases were too heavy. Rangers watched with sinking hearts as the grapnels arched in toward the cliff, only to fall short from the weight of the ropes. Still, at least one grapnel and rope from each LCA made it; the grapnels grabbed the earth, and the dangling ropes provided a way to climb the cliff.

To get to the ropes, the rangers had to disembark and cross the narrow strip of beach to the base of the cliff. To get there they had two problems to overcome. The first was a German machine gun on the rangers' left flank, firing across the beach. It killed or wounded fifteen men as it swept bullets back and forth across the beach.

Colonel Rudder was one of the first to make it to the beach. With him was Col. Travis Trevor, a British commando who had assisted in the training of the rangers. He began walking the beach, giving encouragement. Rudder described him as "a great big [six feet four inches], black-haired son of a gun—one of those staunch Britishers." Lieutenant Vermeer yelled at him, "How in the world can you do that when you are being fired at?"

"I take two short steps and three long ones," Trevor replied, "and they always miss me." Just then a bullet hit him in the helmet and drove him to the ground. He got up and shook his fist at the machine gunner, hollering, "You dirty son of a bitch." After that, Vermeer noted, "He crawled around like the rest of us."

The second problem for the disembarking rangers was craters, caused by bombs or shells that had fallen short of the cliff. They were underwater and could not be seen. "Getting off the ramp," Sergeant South recalled, "my pack and I went into a bomb crater and the world turned completely to water." He inflated his Mae West and made it to shore.

Lieutenant Kerchner was determined to be first off his boat. He thought he was going into a meter or so of water as he hollered "OK, let's go" and jumped. He went in over his head, losing his rifle. He started to swim in, furious with the British coxswain. The men behind him saw what had happened and jumped to the sides. They hardly got their feet wet. "So instead of being the first one ashore, I was one of the last ashore from my boat. I wanted to find somebody to help me cuss out the British navy, but everybody was busily engrossed in their own duties so I couldn't get any sympathy."

Two of his men were hit by the machine gun enfilading the beach. "This made me very angry because I figured he was shooting at me and I had nothing but a pistol." Kerchner picked up a dead ranger's rifle. "My first impulse was to go after this machine gun up there, but I immediately realized that this was rather stupid as our mission was to get to the top of the cliff and get on with destroying those guns.

"It wasn't necessary to tell this man to do this or that man to do that," Kerchner said. "They had been trained, they had the order in which they were supposed to climb the ropes and the men were all moving right in and starting to climb up the cliff." Kerchner went down the beach to report to Colonel Rudder that the D Company commander's LCA had sunk. He found Rudder starting to climb one of the rope ladders.

"He didn't seem particularly interested in me informing him that I was assuming command of the company. He told me to get the hell out of there and get up and climb my rope." Kerchner did as ordered. He found climbing the cliff "very easy," much easier than some of the practice climbs back in England.

The machine gun and the incoming tide gave Sgt. Gene Elder "a certain urgency" to get off the beach and up the cliff. He and his squad freeclimbed, as they were unable to touch the cliff. When they reached the top, "I told them, 'Boys, keep your heads down, because headquarters has fouled up again and has issued the enemy live ammunition.' "

Other rangers had trouble getting up the cliff. "I went up about, I don't know, forty, fifty feet," Pvt. Sigurd Sundby remembered. "The rope was wet and kind of muddy. My hands just couldn't hold, they were like grease, and I came sliding back down. As I was going down, I wrapped my foot around the rope and slowed myself up as much as I could, but still I burned my hands. If the rope hadn't been so wet, I wouldn't have been able to hang on for the burning.

"I landed right beside [Lt. Tod] Sweeney there, and he says, 'What's the matter, Sundby, chicken? Let me—I'll show you how to climb.' So he went up first and I was right up after him, and when I got to the top, Sweeney says, 'Hey, Sundby, don't forget to zigzag.' "

Sgt. William "L-Rod" Petty, who had the reputation of being one of the toughest of the rangers, a man short on temper and long on aggressiveness, also had trouble with a wet and muddy rope. As he slipped to the bottom, Capt. Walter Block, the medical officer, said to Petty, "Soldier, get up that rope to the top of the cliff." Petty turned to Block, stared him square in the face, and said, "I've been trying to get up this goddamned rope for five minutes and if you think you can do any better you can f——ing well do it yourself." Block turned away, trying to control his own temper.

Germans on the top managed to cut two or three of the ropes, while others tossed grenades over the cliff, but BAR men at the base and machine-gun fire from *Satterlee* kept most of them back from the edge. They had not anticipated an attack from the sea, so their defensive positions were inland. In addition, the rangers had tied pieces of fuse to the grapnels and lit them just before firing the rockets; the burning fuses made the Germans think that the grapnels were some kind of weapon about to explode, which kept them away.

Within five minutes rangers were at the top; within fifteen minutes most of the fighting men were up. One of the first to make it was a country preacher from Tennessee, Pvt. Ralph Davis, a dead shot with a rifle and cool under pressure. When he got up, he dropped his pants and took a crap. "The war had to stop for awhile until 'Preacher' could get organized," one of his buddies commented.

As the tide was reducing the beach to almost nothing, and because the attack from the sea—although less than two hundred rangers strong—was proceeding, Colonel Rudder told Lieutenant Eikner to send the code message "Tilt." That told the floating reserve of A and B Companies, 2nd Rangers, and the 5th Ranger Battalion to land at Omaha Beach instead of Pointe-du-Hoc. Rudder expected them to pass through Vierville and attack Pointe-du-Hoc from the eastern, landward side.

On the beach there were wounded who needed attention. Sergeant South had barely got ashore when "the first cry of 'Medic!' went out and I shrugged off my pack, grabbed my aid kit, and took off for the wounded man. He had been shot in the chest. I was able to drag him in closer to the cliff. I'd no sooner taken care of him than I had to go to another and another and another." Captain Block set up an aid station.

"As I got over the top of the cliff," Lieutenant Kerchner recalled, "it didn't look anything at all like what I thought it was going to look like." The rangers had studied aerial photos and maps and sketches and sand table mock-ups of the area, but the bombardment from air and sea had created a moonscape: "It was just one large shell crater after the other."

Fifty years later Pointe-du-Hoc remains an incredible, overwhelming sight. It is hardly possible to say which is more impressive, the amount of reinforced concrete the Germans poured to build their casemates or the damage done to them and the craters created by the bombs and shells. Huge chunks of concrete, as big as houses, are scattered over the kilometer-square area, as if the gods were playing dice. The tunnels and trenches were mostly obliterated, but enough of them still exist to give an idea of how much work went into building the fortifications. Some railroad tracks remain in the underground portions; they were for handcarts used to move ammunition. There is an enormous steel fixture that was a railroad turntable.

Surprisingly, the massive concrete observation post at the edge of the cliff remains intact. It was the key to the whole battery; from it one has a perfect view of both Utah and Omaha Beaches; German artillery observers in the post had radio and underground telephone communication with the casemates.

The craters are as big as ten meters across, a meter or two deep, some even deeper. They number in the hundreds. They were a godsend to the rangers, for they provided plenty of immediate cover. Once on top, rangers could get to a crater in seconds, then begin firing at the German defenders.

What most impresses tourists at Pointe-du-Hoc—who come today in the thousands, from all over the world—is the sheer cliff and the idea of climbing up it by rope. What most impresses military professionals is the way the rangers went to work once they got on top. Despite the initial disorientation they quickly recovered and went about their assigned tasks. Each platoon had a specific mission, to knock out a specific gun emplacement. The men got on it without being told.

Germans were firing sporadically from the trenches and regularly from the machine-gun position on the eastern edge of the fortified area and from a 20mm anti-aircraft gun on the western edge, but the rangers ignored them to get to the casemates.

When they got to the casemates, to their amazement they found that the "guns" were telephone poles. Tracks leading inland indicated that the 155mm cannon had been removed recently, almost certainly as a result of the preceding air bombardment. The rangers never paused. In small groups they began moving inland toward their next objective, the paved road that connected Grandcamp and Vierville, to set up roadblocks to prevent German reinforcements from moving to Omaha.

Lieutenant Kerchner moved forward and got separated from his men. "I remember landing in this zigzag trench. It was the deepest trench I'd ever seen. It was a narrow communications trench, two feet wide but eight feet deep. About every twenty-five yards it would go off on another angle. I was by myself and I never felt so lonesome before or since, because every time I came to an angle I didn't know whether I was going to come face-to-face with a German or not." He was filled with a sense of anxiety and hurried to get to the road to join his men "because I felt a whole lot better when there were other men around."

Kerchner followed the trench for 150 meters before it finally ran out near the ruins of a house on the edge of the fortified area. Here he discovered that Pointe-du-Hoc was a self-contained fort in itself, surrounded on the land side with minefields, barbed-wire entanglements, and machine-gun emplacements. "This is where we began running into most of the German defenders, on the perimeter."

Other rangers had made it to the road, fighting all the way, killing Germans, taking casualties. The losses were heavy. In Kerchner's D Company, only twenty men out of the seventy who had started out in the LCAs were on their feet. Two company commanders were casualties; lieutenants were now leading D and E. Capt. Otto Masny led F Company. Kerchner checked with the three COs and learned that all the guns were missing. "So at this stage we felt rather disappointed, not only disappointed but I felt awfully lonesome as I realized how few men we had there."

The lieutenants decided that there was no reason to go back to the fortified area and agreed to establish a perimeter around the road "and try to defend ourselves and wait for the invading force that had landed on Omaha Beach to come up."

At the base of the cliff at around 0730, Lieutenant Eikner sent out a message by radio: "Praise the Lord." It signified that the rangers were on top of the cliff.

At 0745, Colonel Rudder moved his command post up to the top, establishing it in a crater on the edge of the cliff. Captain Block also climbed a rope to the top and set up his aid station in a two-room concrete emplacement. It was pitch black and cold inside; Block worked by flashlight in one room, using the other to hold the dead.

Sergeant South remembered "the wounded coming in at a rapid rate, we could only keep them on litters stacked up pretty closely. It was just an endless, endless process. Periodically I would go out and bring in a wounded man from the field, leading one back, and ducking through the various shell craters. At one time, I went out to get someone and was carrying him back on my shoulders when he was hit by several other bullets and killed."

The fighting within the fortified area was confused and confusing. Germans would pop up here, there, everywhere, fire a few rounds, then disappear back underground. Rangers could not keep contact with each other. Movement meant crawling.* There was nothing resembling a front line. Germans were taken prisoner; so were some rangers. In the observation post a few Germans held out despite repeated attempts to overrun the position.

The worst problem was the machine gun on the eastern edge of the fortified area, the same gun that had caused so many casualties on the beach. Now it was sweeping back and forth over the battlefield whenever a ranger tried to move. Rudder told Lieutenant Vermeer to eliminate it.

Vermeer set out with a couple of men. "We moved through the shell craters and had just reached the open ground where the machine gun could cover us also when we ran into a patrol from F Company on the same mission. Once we ran out of shell holes and could see nothing but a flat 200–300 yards of open ground in front of us, I was overwhelmed with the sense that it would be impossible to reach our objective without heavy losses." The heaviest weapon the rangers had was a BAR, hardly effective over that distance.

Fortunately, orders came from Rudder to hold up a moment. An attempt was going to be made to shoot the machine gun off the edge of that cliff with guns from a destroyer. That had not been tried earlier because the shore-fire-control party, headed by Capt. Jonathan Harwood from the artillery and Navy Lt. Kenneth Norton, had been put out of action by a short shell. But by now Lieutenant Eikner was on top and he had brought with him an old World War I signal lamp with shutters on it. He thought he could contact the *Satterlee* with it. Rudder told him to try.

Eikner had trained his men in the international Morse code on the signal lamp "with the idea that we might just have a need for them. I can recall some of the boys fussing about having to lug this old, outmoded equipment on D-Day. It was tripod-mounted, a dandy piece of equipment with a telescopic sight and a tracking device to stay lined up with a ship. We set it up in the middle of the shell-hole command post and found enough dry-cell batteries to get it going. We established communications and used the signal

* Pvt. Robert Fruling said he spent two and a half days at Pointe-du-Hoc, all of it crawling on his stomach. He returned on the twenty-fifth anniversary of D-Day "to see what the place looked like standing up" (Louis Lisko interview, Eisenhower Center).

lamp to adjust the naval gunfire. It was really a lifesaver for us at a very critical moment."

Satterlee banged away at the machine-gun position. After a couple of adjustments *Satterlee*'s five-inch guns blew it off the cliff-side. Eikner then used the lamp to ask for help in evacuating the wounded; a whaleboat came in but could not make it due to intense German fire.

The rangers were cut off from the sea. With the Vierville draw still firmly in German hands, they were getting no help from the land side. With the radios out of commission, they had no idea how the invasion elsewhere was going. The rangers on Pointe-du-Hoc were isolated. They had taken about 50 percent casualties.

A short shell from British cruiser *Glasgow* had hit next to Rudder's command post. It killed Captain Harwood, wounded Lieutenant Norton, and knocked Colonel Rudder off his feet. Lieutenant Vermeer was returning to the CP when the shell burst. What he saw he never forgot: "The hit turned the men completely yellow. It was as though they had been stricken with jaundice. It wasn't only their faces and hands, but the skin beneath their clothes and the clothes which were yellow from the smoke of that shell—it was probably a colored marker shell."

Rudder recovered quickly. Angry, he went out hunting for snipers, only to get shot in the leg. Captain Block treated the wound; thereafter Rudder stayed in his CP, more or less, doing what he could to direct the battle. Vermeer remarked that "the biggest thing that saved our day was seeing Colonel Rudder controlling the operation. It still makes me cringe to recall the pain he must have endured trying to operate with a wound through the leg and the concussive force he must have felt from the close hit by the yellow-colored shell. He was the strength of the whole operation."

On his return trip in 1954, Rudder pointed to a buried block-house next to his CP. "We got our first German prisoner right here," he told his son. "He was a little freckle-faced kid who looked like an American. . . . I had a feeling there were more of them around, and I told the rangers to lead this kid ahead of them. They just started him around this corner when the Germans opened up out of the entrance and he fell dead, right here, face down with his hands still clasped on the top of his head."

□

Out by the paved road, the fighting went on. It was close quarters, so close that when two Germans who had been hiding in a deep shelter hole jumped to their feet, rifles ready to fire, Sergeant Petty was right between them. He threw himself to the ground, firing his BAR as he did so—but the bullets went between the Germans, who were literally at his side. The experience so un-nerved them they threw their rifles down, put their hands in the air, and called out *"Kamerad, Kamerad."* A buddy of Petty's who was behind him commented dryly, "Hell, L-Rod, that's a good way to save ammunition—just scare 'em to death."

In another of the countless incidents of that battle, Lt. Jacob Hill spotted a German machine gun behind a hedgerow just beyond the road. It was firing in the general direction of some hidden rangers. Hill studied the position for a few moments, then stood up and shouted, "You bastard sons of bitches, you couldn't hit a bull in the ass with a bass fiddle!" As the startled Germans spun their gun around, Hill lobbed a grenade into the position and put the gun out of action.

The primary purpose of the rangers was not to kill Germans or take prisoners, but to get those 155mm cannon. The tracks leading out of the casemates and the effort the Germans were mak-ing to dislodge the rangers indicated that they had to be around somewhere.

By 0815 there were about thirty-five rangers from D and E Companies at the perimeter roadblock. Within fifteen minutes an-other group of twelve from F Company joined up. Excellent sol-diers, those rangers—they immediately began patrolling.

There was a dirt road leading south (inland). It had heavy tracks. Sgts. Leonard Lomell and Jack Kuhn thought the missing guns might have made the tracks. They set out to investigate. At about 250 meters (one kilometer inland), Lomell abruptly stopped. He held his hand out to stop Kuhn, turned, and half whispered, "Jack, here they are. We've found 'em. Here are the goddamned guns."

Unbelievably, the well-camouflaged guns were set up in bat-tery, ready to fire in the direction of Utah Beach, with piles of ammunition around them, but no Germans. Lomell spotted about a hundred Germans a hundred meters or so across an open field, apparently forming up. Evidently they had pulled back during the bombardment, for fear of a stray shell setting off the amunition dump, and were now preparing to man their guns, but they were in no hurry, for until their infantry drove off the rangers and reoccupied the observation post they could not fire with any accuracy.

Lomell never hesitated. "Give me your grenades, Jack," he said to Kuhn. "Cover me. I'm gonna fix 'em." He ran to the guns and set off thermite grenades in the recoil and traversing mechanisms of two of the guns, disabling them. He bashed in the sights of the third gun.

"Jack, we gotta get some more thermite grenades." He and Kuhn ran back to the highway, collected all of the thermite grenades from the rangers in the immediate area, returned to the battery, and disabled the other three guns.

Meanwhile Sgt. Frank Rupinski, leading a patrol of his own, had discovered a huge ammunition dump some distance south of the battery. It too was unguarded. Using high-explosive charges, the rangers detonated it. A tremendous explosion occurred as the shells and powder charges blew up, showering rocks, sand, leaves, and debris on Lomell and Kuhn. Unaware of Rupinski's patrol, Lomell and Kuhn assumed that a stray shell had hit the ammo dump. They withdrew as quickly as they could and sent word back to Rudder by runner that the guns had been found and destroyed.

And with that the rangers had completed their offensive mission. It was 0900. Just that quickly they were now on the defensive, isolated, with nothing heavier than 60mm mortars and BARs to defend themselves.

In the afternoon Rudder had Eikner send a message—by his signal lamp and homing pigeon—via the *Satterlee:* "Located Pointe-du-Hoc—mission accomplished—need ammunition and reinforcement—many casualties."

An hour later *Satterlee* relayed a brief message from General Huebner: "No reinforcements available—all rangers have landed [at Omaha]." The only reinforcements Rudder's men received in the next forty-eight hours were three paratroopers from the 101st who had been misdropped and who somehow made it through German lines to join the rangers, and two platoons of rangers from

Omaha. The first arrived at 2100. It was a force of twenty-three men led by Lt. Charles Parker. On the afternoon of June 7, Maj. Jack Street brought in a landing craft and took off wounded and prisoners. After putting them aboard an LST he took the craft to Omaha Beach and rounded up about twenty men from the 5th Ranger Battalion and brought them to Pointe-du-Hoc.

The Germans were as furious as disturbed hornets; they counterattacked the fortified area throughout the day, again that night, and through the next day. The rangers were, in fact, under siege, their situation desperate. But as Sgt. Gene Elder recalled, they stayed calm and beat off every attack. "This was due to our rigorous training. We were ready. For example, Sgt. Bill Stivinson [who had started D-Day morning swaying back and forth on the London Fire Department ladder] was sitting with Sgt. Guy Shoff behind some rock or rubble when Guy started to swear and Bill asked him why. Guy replied, 'They are shooting at me.' Stivinson asked how he knew. Guy's answer was, 'Because they are hitting me.' "

Pvt. Salva Maimone recalled that on D-Day night "one of the boys spotted some cows. He went up and milked one. The milk was bitter, like quinine. The cows had been eating onions."

Lieutenant Vermeer said he could "still distinctly remember when it got to be twelve o'clock that night, because the 7th of June was my birthday. I felt that if I made it until midnight, I would survive the rest of the ordeal. It seemed like some of the fear left at that time."

The rangers took heavy casualties. A number of them were taken prisoner. By the end of the battle only fifty of the more than two hundred rangers who had landed were still capable of fighting. But they never lost Pointe-du-Hoc.

Later, writers commented that it had all been a waste, since the guns had been withdrawn from the fortified area around Pointe-du-Hoc. That is wrong. Those guns were in working condition before Sergeant Lomell got to them. They had an abundance of ammunition. They were in range (they could lob their huge shells 25,000 meters) of the biggest targets in the world, the 5,000-plus ships in the Channel and the thousands of troops and equipment on Utah and Omaha Beaches.

Lieutenant Eikner was absolutely correct when he concluded

his oral history, "Had we not been there we felt quite sure that those guns would have been put into operation and they would have brought much death and destruction down on our men on the beaches and our ships at sea. But by 0900 on D-Day morning the big guns had been put out of commission and the paved highway had been cut and we had roadblocks denying its use to the enemy. So by 0900 our mission was accomplished. The rangers at Pointe-du-Hoc were the first American forces on D-Day to accomplish their mission and we are proud of that."

9

The British
and Canadian Beaches

FOR THE BRITISH 3rd Infantry Division at Sword Beach, the critical point was five kilometers inland, at the Orne Canal and Orne River bridges. The British 6th Airborne Division had landed during the night to the east of the Orne waterways; the landings at Sword Beach extended only to the mouth of the river; if there were to be contact between the 3rd and 6th Divisions, it had to be over the Orne bridges. Maj. John Howard's Ox and Bucks had captured both bridges right after midnight. By 0026, his concern shifted from the offense to the defense. He could expect a German counterattack at any time. He was not concerned about the safety of the river bridge because British paratroopers were scheduled to begin landing around Ranville within a half hour, and they could take care of protecting that bridge. But to the front of the canal bridge, toward the west, he had no help at all—and a countryside jammed with German troops, German tanks, German trucks. Howard sent a runner over to the river bridge, with orders for Lt. Dennis Fox to bring his platoon over to the canal bridge. When Fox arrived, Howard intended to push his platoon forward to the T-junction, as the lead platoon.

Howard knew that it would take Fox some time to call his men in from their firing positions, for Lt. Tod Sweeney to take over, and for Fox to march the quarter mile from one bridge to the other.

But he could already hear tanks starting up in Le Port. They headed south along the road to Benouville. To Howard's immense relief, the tanks did not turn at the T-junction and come down toward the bridge, but instead continued on into Benouville. He surmised that the commanders of the garrisons in the two villages were conferring. Howard knew that the tanks would be back.

Tanks coming down the T-junction were by far his greatest worry. With their machine guns and cannon, German tanks could easily drive D Company away from the bridges. To stop tanks, he had only the Piat guns, one per platoon, and the Gammon bombs. Pvt. Wally Parr came back to the CP from the west end of the bridge to report that he had heard tanks, and to announce that he was going back to the glider for the Piat. "Good man," Howard said.

Parr went down the embankment, climbed into the glider, and "I couldn't see a bloody thing, could I? There was no flashlight. I started scrambling around and at last I found the Piat." Parr picked it up, tripped over some ammunition, sprawled, got up again, and discovered the barrel of the Piat had bent. The gun was useless. Parr threw it down, grabbed some ammunition, and returned to the CP to tell Howard that the Piat was kaput.

Howard yelled at one of Lt. Sandy Smith's men to go to his glider and get that Piat. S. Sgt. Jim Wallwork trudged by, loaded like a packhorse, carrying ammunition up to the forward platoons. Howard looked at Wallwork's blood-covered face and thought, That's a strange color camouflage to be wearing at night. To Wallwork, he said, "You look like a bloody red Indian." Wallwork explained about his cuts—by this time, Wallwork thought he had lost his eye—and went about his business.

At 0130, Howard could hear tanks approaching. He was desperate to establish radio communication with Fox, but could not. Then he saw a tank swing slowly, ever so slowly, toward the bridge, its great cannon sniffing the air like the trunk of some prehistoric monster. "And it wasn't long before we could see a couple of them about twenty-five yards apart moving very, very slowly, quite obviously not knowing what to expect when they got down to the bridges."

Everything was now at stake and hung in the balance. If the Germans retook the canal bridge they would then drive on to overwhelm Sweeney's platoon at the river bridge. There they could set up a defensive perimeter, bolstered by tanks, so strong that the 6th Airborne Division would find it difficult, perhaps impossible, to break through. In that case, the division would be isolated, without antitank weapons to fight off Luck's armor. It sounds overly dramatic to say that the fate of the more than ten thousand fighting men of the 6th Airborne depended on the outcome of the forthcoming battle at the bridge, but we know from what happened to the 1st Airborne that September at Arnhem that this was in fact exactly the case.

Beyond the possible loss of the 6th Airborne, it stretches matters only slightly to state that the fate of the invasion as a whole was at risk on John Howard's bridge. We have the testimony of Luck himself on this subject. He contends that if those bridges had been available to him, he could have crossed the Orne waterways and thrown his regiment into the late-afternoon D-Day counterattack. That attack, by the 192nd Regiment of 21st Panzer, almost reached the beaches. Luck feels that had his regiment also been in that attack, 21st Panzer would have surely driven to the beaches. A panzer division loose on the beaches, amidst all the unloading going on, could have produced havoc with unimaginable results.

Enough speculation. The point has been made—a great deal was at stake up there at the T-junction. Fittingly, as so much was at stake, the battle at the bridge at 0130 on D-Day provided a fair test of the British and German armies of World War II. Each side had advantages and disadvanatages. Howard's opponents were the company commanders in Benouville and Le Port. Like Howard, they had been training for more than a year for this moment. They had been caught by surprise, but the troops at the bridge had been their worst troops, not much of a loss. In Benouville, the 1st Panzer Engineering Company of the 716th Infantry Division, and in Le Port, the 2nd Engineers, were slightly better quality troops. The whole German military tradition, reinforced by orders, compelled them to launch an immediate counterattack. They had the platoons to do it with and the armored vehicles. What they did not have was a sure sense of the situation because they kept getting conflicting reports.

Howard was commanding British troops, every one of them from the United Kingdom and every man among them a volunteer who was superbly trained. They were vastly superior to their opponents. Except for Fox and the crippled Smith, Howard was without officers, but he personally enjoyed one great advantage over the German commanders. He was in his element in the middle of the night—fresh, alert, capable of making snap decisions, getting accurate reports from his equally fresh and alert men. The German commanders were confused, getting conflicting reports, tired, and sleepy. Howard had placed his platoons exactly where he had planned to put them, with three on the west side to meet the first attacks, two in reserve on the east side (including the sappers), and one at the river bridge. Howard had seen to it that his antitank capability was exactly where he had planned to put it, right up at the T-junction. By way of contrast, the German commanders were groping, hardly sure of where their own platoons were, unable to decide what to do.

But, as noted, the Germans had the great advantage of badly outgunning Howard. They had a half-dozen tanks to his zero. They had two dozen trucks, and a platoon to fill each one, to Howard's six platoons and no trucks. They had artillery, a battery of 88mms, while Howard had none. Howard did not even have Gammon bombs. Hand-thrown grenades were of little or no use against a tank because they usually bounced off and exploded harmlessly in the air. Bren and Sten guns were absolutely useless against a buttoned-down tank. The only weapon Howard had to stop those tanks was Sgt. Wagger Thornton's Piat gun. That gun, and the fact that he had trained D Company for precisely this moment, the first contact with tanks. He felt confident that Thornton was at the top of his form, totally alert, not the least bothered by the darkness or the hour, and that Thornton was fully proficient in the use of a Piat, that he knew precisely where he should hit the lead tank to knock it out.

Others were not quite so confident. Sandy Smith recalled "hearing this bloody thing, feeling a sense of absolute terror, saying, 'My God, what the hell am I going to do with these tanks coming down the road?' " Billy Gray, who had taken up a position in an unoccupied German gun pit, remembered: "Then the tank came down the road. We thought that was it, you know, no way were we going to stop a tank. It was about twenty yards away from us, because we were up on this little hillock, but it did give a sort of field of fire straight up the road. We fired up the road at anything we could see moving."

Gray was tempted to fire at the tank. Most men in their first hour of combat would have done so. But, Gray said, paying a tribute to his training, "I didn't fire at the tank." Gray, along with all Howard's men on the west side of the bridge, held fire. They did not, in short, reveal their positions, thus luring the tanks into the killing zone.

Howard had expected the tanks to be preceded by an infantry reconnaissance patrol—that was the way he would have done it—but the Germans had neglected to do so. Their infantry platoons were following the two tanks. So the tanks rolled forward, ever so slowly, the tankers unaware that they had already crossed the front line.

The first Allied company in the invasion was about to meet the first German counterattack. It all came down to Thornton and the German tankers. The tankers' visibility was such that they could not see Thornton, half buried as he was under that pile of equipment. Thornton was about thirty yards from the T-junction, and, he says today, "I don't mind admitting it, I was shaking like a bloody leaf!" He could hear the tank coming toward him. He fingered his Piat.

"The Piat actually is a load of rubbish, really," Thornton says. "The range is around about fifty yards and no more. You're a dead loss if you try to go farther. Even fifty yards is stretching it, very much so. Another thing is that you must never, never miss. If you do, you've had it, because by the time you reload the thing and cock it, which is a bloody chore on its own, everything's gone, you're done. It's indoctrinated into your brain that you mustn't miss."

Thornton had taken his position as close to the T-junction as he could get because he wanted to shoot at the shortest possible distance. "And sure enough, in about three minutes, this bloody great thing appears. I was more hearing it than seeing it, in the dark; it was rattling away there, and it turned out to be a Mark IV tank coming along pretty slowly, and they hung around for a few seconds to figure out where they were. Only had two of the bombs with me. Told myself, 'You mustn't miss.' Anyhow, although I was shaking, I took an aim and bang, off it went."

The tank had just turned at the T-junction. "I hit him round about right bang in the middle. I made sure I had him right in the middle. I was so excited and so shaking I had to move back a bit."

Then all hell broke loose. The explosion from the Piat bomb penetrated the tank, setting off the machine-gun clips, which started setting off grenades, which started setting off shells. As Glenn Gray points out in his book *The Warriors,* one of the great appeals of war is the visual display of a battlefield, with red, green, or orange tracers skimming about, explosions going off here and there, flares lighting up portions of the sky. But few warriors have ever had the opportunity to see such a display as that at the T-junction on D-Day.

The din, the light show, could be heard and seen by paratroopers many kilometers from the bridge. Indeed, it provided an orientation and thus got them moving in the right direction.

When the tank went off, Fox took protection behind a wall. He explained, "You couldn't go very far because whizbang a bullet or shell went straight past you, but finally it died down, and incredibly we heard this man crying out. Ole Tommy Klare couldn't stand it any longer and he went straight out up to the tank and it was blazing away and he found the driver had got out of the tank still conscious, was laying beside it, but both legs were gone. He had been hit in the knees getting out, and Klare, who was always kind, he was an immensely strong fellow—back in barracks he once broke a man's jaws by just one blow for getting on his nerves—and Tommy hunched this poor old German on his back and took him to the first-aid post. I thought it was useless of course, but, in fact, I believe the man lived." He did, but only for a few more hours. He turned out to be the commander of the 1st Panzer Engineering Company.

The fireworks show went on and on—all told it lasted for more than an hour—and it helped convince the German company commanders that the British were present in great strength. Indeed, the lieutenant in the second tank withdrew to Benouville, where he reported that the British had six-pounder antitank guns at the bridge. The German officers decided that they would have to wait until dawn and a clarification of the situation before launching another counterattack. John Howard had won the battle of the night.

Through the night the lead tank smoldered, right across the T-junction, thus blocking movement between Benouville and Le Port, and between Caen and the coast. An argument can therefore be made that Sergeant Thornton had pulled off the single most important shot of D-Day because the Germans badly needed that road. Thornton himself is impatient with any such talk. When I had completed my interview with him, and had shut off the tape recorder, he remarked: "Whatever you do in this book, don't go making me into a bloody hero." To which I could only think to reply, "Sergeant Thornton, I don't make heroes. I only write about them."

With the position secure for the moment, the Ox and Bucks waited for dawn and the linkup with seaborne troops.

At Gold Beach, the UDT (Underwater Demolition Team) men and the Royal Engineers began to touch down at 0735, followed immediately by the first wave of LCTs carrying tanks and LCAs bringing in infantry assault teams. It was an hour later than the American landings because the tide moved from west to east and low tide came later on the British beaches. But the wind at Gold was coming almost straight in from the northwest, piling up the water to such a depth that the outer line of obstacles was underwater before the UDT men could get to them.

The later time of the attack was fortunate in that it gave the bombers and battleships longer to work over the beach defenses. Many of the Germans were in the resort houses that dotted the coast, concentrated at Le Hamel (right-center of Gold Beach) and La Riviere (left flank boundary with Juno Beach). Unlike the concrete emplacements, the houses could be set on fire by naval shells and air-dropped bombs.

The official British observer described the initial action: "Just as it was getting light, a tremendous bombing attack was delivered inland and fires which appeared to come from Ver-sur-Mer and La Riviere could be clearly seen. Apart from some flak, there was no enemy opposition of any sort, although it was broad daylight and the ships must have been clearly visible from the beaches. It was not until the first flight of assaulting troops were away and the cruiser HMS *Belfast* opened fire that the enemy appeared to realize that something out of the ordinary was afoot. For some time after this the anchorage was ineffectually shelled by the enemy coastal battery situated about three-quarters of a mile inland. Shooting was very desultory, and inaccurate, and the guns of only 6- to 8-inch calibre."

As Lt. Pat Blamey's LCT moved toward shore, shells from naval guns ranging from five-inch to fourteen-inch whistled overhead. Blamey commanded a Sherman tank with a twenty-five-pounder cannon mounted on it; behind him in the LCT were four twenty-five-pounder field-artillery pieces that he would be towing ashore. The battery commenced firing when it was twelve kilometers from shore, and continued to fire a steady three rounds per minute until down to three kilometers.

"This was a period of furious activity," Blamey remembered. "Ammo boxes and shell cases jettisoned overboard as I called out the ranges received from the control craft. The noise was terrific, but nothing compared with the blast from the rocket ships when they opened up as our assault craft closed the beach."

The beach obstacles proved to be more dangerous than German infantry or artillery. German snipers concentrated their fire on UDT teams, so almost no clearing of lanes had been completed. LCTs landed first, near Asnelles, where they disgorged two companies of Hobart's Funnies.* Twenty of the LCTs hit mined obstacles, suffering moderate to severe damage, losing some tanks and some men.

This "damn the torpedoes, full speed ahead" approach by the LCTs was in accord with the rules for guidance handed out to the coxswains by the Royal Navy. *"Hedgehogs, stakes or tetrahedra will not prevent your beaching provided you go flat out,"* those instructions read. "Your craft will crunch over them, bend them and squash them into the sand and the damage to your outer bottom can be accepted. So drive on.

* Special tanks named after Gen. Percy Hobart of the 79th Armoured Division— they included swimming tanks and tanks that carried their own bridges

"Do not worry too much about how you are to get out again. The first and primary object is to get in and land without drowning the vehicles."

Once the ramp went down, the men and vehicles rushed off the craft. A commando explained why: "The reason we stormed Normandy like we did was because the soldiers would rather have fought the whole German Army than go back on the ships and be as seasick as they were going over. My God! Those soldiers couldn't wait to get on dry land. Nothing would have got in their way . . . they would have torn tanks to pieces with their bare hands."

They didn't have to because there were no German tanks on the beach. Even the infantry resistance was ineffective. When Blamey drove off his LCT, towing the artillery pieces, he found that "local strong points had been neutralized by the bombardment. Shelling and mortaring from inland was slight and inaccurate. Except for some dozen Jerries, the beach was deserted of enemy. The ones I saw were completely shattered by the bombardment. They appeared to be Mongolians."

To Blamey, it seemed like "an ordinary exercise. The only difference that there was were the LCTs blowing up on the beach obstacles and swinging about." He went to work, laying out the line for his guns, putting up flags where he wanted the twenty-five-pounders to position themselves (the British landed some two hundred of these excellent antitank guns on D-Day, a much better record than the American artillery achieved).

"One wasn't conscious of being in the middle of a hurly-burly," Blamey said. "Everything was very well ordered. Things were arriving, being unloaded. All those nice little French villas just inland had been set on fire and almost all were destroyed. I was more frightened of making a cock-off of my job and letting the side down than anything else."

Asked if the organization was better than he had expected, Blamey replied, "It was absolutely like clockwork. We knew it would be. We had every confidence. We had rehearsed it so often, we knew our equipment, we knew it worked, we knew given reasonable conditions we would get off the craft." He gave the credit to the navy and the RAF; in his opinion, "they made our landing a pushover."

As the second wave began to arrive and the tide reduced the width of the beach, Blamey had his gunners cease fire and prepare to move inland. He hooked the pieces up to his tank and drove to the outskirts of Asnelles, where he stopped to brew up some tea before proceeding on to just west of Meuvaines, where he began to take fire from German 88s on a ridge ahead. Blamey lined up his cannon and replied; soon enough the German fire was silenced.

The sectors at Gold were, from west to east, Item, Jig, King, and Love. The attackers from the Northumbrian (50th) Division were the Devonshire, Hampshire, Dorsetsire, and East Yorkshire Regiments, accompanied by the Green Howards and Durham Light Infantry, plus engineer, communication, and artillery units, followed by the 7th Armoured Division, the famous "Desert Rats."

Blamey had landed at Jig; Seaman Ronald Seaborne, a forward observer for the *Belfast,* landed to his left at Love. Everyone on Seaborne's LCM (landing craft, medium) was seasick: "We had had a fried egg breakfast, washed down by a tot of rum (not my choice but mandatory for all those going ashore)."

The LCM ran aground two hundred meters or more from the waterline, but Seaborne—carrying his radio—was as eager as everyone else to "run down the ramp and into the water—anything to abandon that instrument of torture."

LCAs passed Seaborne as he struggled through the chest-deep water. "By the time I was on the beach there were 200 or so troops already there effectively dealing with the straggling rifle fire coming from the defenses of La Riviere." After the bombardment the Germans had taken, Seaborne was surprised that any of them were still alive, much less firing back.

Seaborne's party consisted of a Royal Artillery captain, a bombardier, and a leading telegraphist. They crossed the seawall and the coastal road. The captain told Seaborne to report to *Belfast* that the beachhead was secure and that the party was going inland, then begin hiking toward Crepon.

Seaborne was unable to raise *Belfast.* After a quarter of an hour of frustration, he decided to follow the captain. "As I walked along a lane in the direction of Crepon, I could not see another person.

"Suddenly, from a field ahead, three men in German uniforms

emerged. I thought this was the end of the war for me, but they raised their hands about their heads and by a mixture of French, German and English, I learned that they were Russians. I pointed the way to the beach and proceeded on. Before long I came to a small church. After halfway through the graveyard a shot whistled by me. I dropped to the ground amid a mass of poppies, then moved slowly toward a stone tombstone for safer shelter. Another shot rang out. I hid behind the tombstone, peered round it, and spotted a German helmet. I fired back and for the next few minutes it was real cowboys and Indians stuff. With the last of my ammunition, I got a lucky ricochet on my enemy, who slumped from his hiding place into my full view. I went over and looked at him and found I was gazing at a young boy, presumably one of the Hitler *Jugend.* I felt sick—sicker even than I had done on the LCM an hour or so previously."

Mlle Genget was a resident of St.-Côme-de-Fresne, where the Royal Marines landed. On the evening of June 6 she wrote in her diary, "What seemed impossible has really happened! The English have landed on the French coast and our little village has become famous in a few hours! Not one civilian killed or wounded. How can we express our surprise after such long years of waiting in wonderment and fear?"

In the morning she and a friend went to the edge of the cliff to see what was happening. "From there what a sight met our eyes! As far as we could see there were ships of all kinds and sizes and above floated big balloons silvery in the sun. Big bombers were passing and repassing in the sky. As far as Courseulles one could see nothing but ships."

Mlle Genget returned to St.-Côme, where she encountered British soldiers. "The English had thought that all civilians had been evacuated from the coast and were very surprised to find the inhabitants had stayed in their homes. Our little church had received a direct hit on the roof and fire broke out, but with the help of the villagers it was soon overcome. Guns were firing. What a noise everywhere and smell of burning!"

She wondered if she were dreaming. "Is it all really true?" she wrote. "We are at last liberated. The enormous strength that all this war material represents is fantastic, and the way it has been handled with such precision is marvelous. . . . A group of Tommies pass and ask us for water. We fill their bottles, say a few words, and, having given chocolate and sweets to the children, they continue on their way."

On the beach, Lt. Comdr. Brian T. Whinney noted that as night came on "all was quiet. An eerie feeling remained. There was not a soul in sight." He went to a farmhouse, which backed onto the pillbox that had given so much trouble at Le Hamel in the forenoon, and was surprised to hear a noise inside. He knocked on the door "and to my astonishment an old lady appeared. She seemed quite unconcerned. She had apparently been there all day, carrying out her household chores as usual."

By nightfall on June 6 the British at Gold Beach had penetrated some ten kilometers inland and hooked up with the Canadians at Creully on their left. They were on the cliff looking down on Arromanches. They had not taken Bayeux or crossed the N-13, but they were in position to do so the next day. They had put 25,000 men ashore at a cost of four hundred casualties. It was a good start.

Courseulles-sur-Mer, in the center of Juno Beach, was the most heavily defended point in the long stretch from Arromanches on the far right of the British beaches to Ouistreham on the far left. St.-Aubin and Langrune, to the left (east) of Courseulles, were well defended also. Gen. Wilhelm Richter's 716th Division had eleven heavy batteries of 155mm guns and nine medium batteries, mainly 75s. All were supposed to be in fortified bunkers, but only two bunkers were complete. Elsewhere the crews were protected by unroofed bunkers or earthen gun pits in open fields.

There were *Widerstandnester* (strong points) at Vaux, Courseulles, Bernieres, and St.-Aubin, each heavily fortified with reinforced concrete. The *Widerstandnester* were supported by trenches and gun pits, surrounded by barbed wire and minefields. All weapons were sighted to fire along the beach in enfilade, not out to sea; the zones of fire were calculated to interlock on the formidable array of beach obstacles situated just below the high-water mark. To the Germans, as historian John Keegan noted, "The combination of fixed obstacles and enfilading fire from the resistance nests was deemed to guarantee the destruction of any landing force."

But General Richter had some serious problems. His *Widerstandnester* were a kilometer apart. His mobility was practically nonexistent—the 716th used horses to move its artillery and supplies, while its men moved by foot. Their weapons were a hodgepodge of captured rifles and cannon. The men were under eighteen or over thirty-five years of age, or veterans of the Eastern Front in their mid-twenties who had suffered more or less disabling wounds, or *Ost* battalion troops from Russia and Poland. Their orders were to stand fast. Giving an inch of ground was forbidden, and German NCOs were there to enforce those orders (in any case, the encircling minefields and barbed wire would keep them in just as much as they would keep the Canadians out). Man for man, they were hardly a match for the young, tough, magnificently trained Canadians, and they were outnumbered by the Canadians in the first wave at a ratio of six to one (2,400 Canadians, 400 Germans).

The Canadian 3rd Division contained lumberjacks, fishermen, miners, farmers, all tough outdoorsmen and all volunteers (Canada had conscription in World War II, but only volunteers were sent into combat zones). Sapper Josh Honan "volunteered" in a way familiar to all veterans. He was a surveyor in an engineer company in Canada in late 1943 when a colonel called him to headquarters.

"You're Irish," the colonel declared.

"Yes, sir."

"An Irishman always likes a good scrap, doesn't he? We got a job we'd like you to do."

Honan replied that he would just as soon stay with his company. "We're all together, sir, we're going overseas and I don't want to get separated from my mates."

"Never mind about all that, you may meet them again in England."

Honan asked what the job was; the colonel replied that he could not say. "The only thing I can tell you about it is that there are many men in England today who would gladly change places with you."

"Just one will do," Honan responded.

"Well, you Irish will have your little joke. I can promise you that you will be totally pleased that you took this job."

"Will I?"

"Oh, yes, I know you Irish, you enjoy a good scrap, don't you?"

In his interview, Honan commented, "I wasn't too keen on this jolly-good-scrap business talk," but there it was. A few days later he was on his way to England, where he discovered that the job was just about the worst imaginable—he was to precede the first wave and blow up beach obstacles.

On the night crossing on his LST, Honan noted that the men he was with (the Regina Rifle Regiment, headed toward Mike sector of Juno) spent their time alternating between using their whetstones to sharpen knives, daggers, and bayonets and playing poker. He saw one man who had a knife with a wooden haft covered with leatherwork with a big diamond-like gem inserted into it "sharpening it like mad." Others were "playing poker like nothing I'd ever seen before. There was no use in holding back, nothing made any difference, bet the lot. When officers came around they would sort of cover the money with the blankets they were playing on."

Asked if the officers didn't try to stop the men from gambling, Honan said matter-of-factly, "You couldn't stop anybody from doing anything at that stage."

Honan saw a single ship steaming through his convoy, between the rows of ships, "and as it passed we could see on the prow the solitary piper silhouetted against the evening sky and the thin lament coming across, 'We No' Come Back Again.' It was very touching and everybody was hushed and everybody just stood there watching, not a sound from anyone, and then gradually it passed by and faded away in the distance. And we often thought that we no' come back again."

The Canadians were scheduled to land at 0745, but rough seas made them ten minutes and more late, and extremely seasick ("Death would be better than this," Pvt. Gerald Henry of the Royal Winnipeg Rifles moaned to one of his mates). They had been told in the final briefings that all the pillboxes, machine guns, and artillery pieces would be kaput as a result of the air and naval bombardments, but things did not work out that way.

The midnight June 5–6 air bombardment by RAF Bomber Command was heavy enough—the 5,268 tons of bombs dropped was the heaviest raid the British had yet mounted in the war—but it was woefully inaccurate. American B-17s came over at first light, but as at Omaha they delayed dropping their bombs up to thirty seconds after crossing the aiming point. As a result, the bombs fell well inland. Very few of the fortifications were hit, none on Juno.

Royal Navy cruisers and battleships began firing at 0600. The destroyers went into action at 0619. At 0710 the tanks and twenty-five-pounders on LCTs joined in, followed by the rockets from the LCT(R)s. It was the heaviest bombardment ever fired from ship to shore. But the smoke and haze was such that very few of the shells actually hit their targets (a target-analysis team later calculated that only about 14 percent of the bunkers were destroyed).

The smoke was so thick that for the most part the German defenders could not see out to sea. At 0645, Seventh Army's routine morning report read: "Purpose of naval bombardment not yet apparent. It appears to be a covering action in conjunction with attacks to be made at other points later." Occasionally the wind would sweep away the smoke; when it did, the Germans could see "countless ships, ships big and small, beyond comprehension."

The bombardment lifted at 0730, when the first wave was supposed to be landing. This gave the Germans time to recover and man their guns. "All the softening up did was alert the enemy of the landing," Pvt. Henry remarked, "and give them the chance to be settled in for our guys to run into." Another soldier in the Royal Winnipeg Rifles commented, "The bombardment had failed to kill a single German or silence one weapon."

Yet as the Canadian landing craft approached the beach obstacles, mostly underwater due to the strong northwest wind, there was an eerie silence. The Germans were not firing, which the Canadians found encouraging; they did not yet realize the reason was all the German guns were sighted to fire down the beach.

Josh Honan was on an LST, waiting to be off-loaded onto an LCA for the final run of five kilometers or so to the beach. One of his mates asked, "Do you think this might just be a rehearsal?"

"It looks a bit elaborate for that," Honan replied.

Honan had his own fantasy, that his demolition team would be forgotten by the officer in charge. "It was like being called for the dentist," Honan said. "I was hoping that I wouldn't be next, that maybe somebody else would go before me. But then this fellow with the bullhorn called out, 'Sapper assault team, report to your boat stations on number six deck, NOW!' "

Safely loaded, Honan's LCA joined five others and began to circle. He went to the ramp to watch the action. He noted that all the Canadian soldiers had deeply suntanned faces, while the British coxswains and crews were moon white. He looked for landmarks but could not see any through the smoke. The LCA was pitching and bucking in the waves. "The rougher it got," Honan said, "the less I looked around me to see what was happening to anybody else."

The craft started closing up on each other, but not in an organized fashion. The LCAs began losing way and losing steerage, bumping into each other and into beach obstacles.

When the leading craft—mostly carrying engineers and UDT teams—reached the outer line of obstacles, a quarter or more of them set off Teller mines. The mines were not big enough to blow the craft out of the water or otherwise destroy them (the open tops allowed most of the explosive power to escape into the air), but they made holes in the bottoms or damaged the ramps.

Honan's LCA came in opposite Bernieres-sur-Mer. Honan tried to give the coxswain directions to avoid obstacles, "but he hadn't enough steerage for the boat to answer. So we finished up by running on top of one of the obstacles with the ramp up against it. We could see the mine just beside us; one bump and bang.

"So Major Stone [Honan's CO] said, 'I'm going over.' I said, 'Bloody good luck to you,' but my orders were to try to keep Stonie alive so I had to go over after him."

Honan dumped all his equipment overboard—rifle, explosives, walkie-talkie, the works—and dove into the water after his major.

"And Stonie was starting to swim for the front of the boat, and I said, 'Bugger it, I've got to do that too,' so I swam to the front and the obstacle was wired onto two adjacent tetrahedrons and the major had cutting pliers and he said, 'I'll cut the wires,' and I said, 'OK, I'll take out the detonators.'

"So I got astride the tetrahedron, wrapped my legs around it, and started to unscrew the detonators. Stonie shouted to get a dozen men off the craft and for the others to go to the stern to help lift the prow off the obstacle. So a dozen soldiers dove in and we all got our shoulders to the prow and pushed."

It was about 0800. The leading LCAs carrying assault teams were dropping their ramps. Canadians were making their way on foot through the obstacles up onto the beach.

The Germans commenced firing. Snipers and mortar crews were aiming at the landing craft as machine guns concentrated on the first wave of infantry. Bullets were creating miniature geysers around Honan. He, Major Stone, and the men managed to free the LCA. Its ramp went down and the infantry made toward shore as Honan moved to the next obstacle to remove the detonator on its mine.

"My mates were attacking the pillboxes; that was their business and I was doing my business. I was a sitting duck, I didn't have anything to work with except my bare hands." The rising tide covered the obstacles faster than Honan could unscrew the detonators. Honan remarked, "I could do my job only by wrapping my legs around the obstacles to keep from being floated away, and I could only use one hand."

At about 0815 he decided, "Bugger this lark, I'm going ashore." He swam for the shore. There he saw a headless corpse. The man had apparently been wounded in the water and then run over by an LCA. The propeller had cut his head off. He was clutching in his hand the knife with a diamond-like gem inserted into the leather wrapped around the handle that Honan had noticed during the night.

When Honan reached the seawall, a couple of the chaps hauled him up and over. One of them pulled out a flask of whiskey and offered Honan a drink.

"No thanks," Honan said.

The soldier took a slug himself and asked, "Why not? You're not an 'effin teetotaler are you?"

"I'm not," Honan replied, "but I'm afraid that stuff will make me feel brave or some bloody thing like that."

Honan moved into the village, where he took shelter until the German machine-gun fire was suppressed. "I had done my bit," he explained. "I was watching the others get on with it." Until the tide receded, he could do no more demolition of obstacles.

Soon the guns fell silent and the people began coming out into the street, waving for the liberators, throwing bouquets of roses. The village priest appeared.

"Monsieur le cure," Honan said in his best high-school French, "I hope that you are pleased that we have arrived."

"Yes," the priest replied, "but I will be better pleased when you are gone again," as he pointed sadly to the hole in the top of his seventeenth-century church.

The barber came out and asked Honan if he would like a cognac. No, Honan replied, "but I could do with a shave." The barber was happy to comply, "so I went in and sat in the chair in my wringing-wet battle dress, the water squelching in my shoes, and he gave me a shave."

Refreshed and rested, Honan returned to the beach to go back to work. "I was in time to see the DD tanks coming ashore. Two of them came out of the water, I had never seen nor heard of them before. So this was like sea monsters for me coming out of the deep. Those two tanks pulled up their skirts and ducked around the village with the other girls."

The Canadian infantry moved across the seawall and into the street fighting in the villages, or against pillboxes, with a fury that had to be seen to be believed. One who saw it happen was Private Henry. His company of the Royal Winnipegs was scheduled to land at 0800, but it was late, so he was an observer for the initial action. His comment was to the point: "It took a great deal of heroics and casualties to silence the concrete emplacements and the various machine-gun nests."

Sgt. Sigie Johnson saw one of the bravest acts possible in war. A pioneer platoon was held up by barbed wire. It was supposed to use a bangalore torpedo to blow a gap, but the torpedo failed to explode. A soldier, unknown to Johnson, threw himself over the wire so that others could cross on his back. Johnson saw others crawl through barbed wire and minefields to get close enough to the embrasures of pillboxes to toss in grenades. He concluded his interview with these words: "Very few publications ever get the truth of what our Winnipeg infantry faced and did."

Sword Beach ran from Lion-sur-Mer to Ouistreham at the mouth of the Oran Canal.* In most areas there were vacation homes and tourist establishments just inland from the paved promenade that ran behind the seawall. There were the usual beach obstacles and emplacements in the sand dunes, with mortar crews and medium and heavy artillery pieces inland. Primarily, however, the Germans intended to defend Sword Beach with the 75mm guns of the Merville battery and the 155mm guns at Le Havre.

But Lt. Col. T. B. H. Otway's 6th Airborne Division men had taken and destroyed the Merville battery, and the big guns at Le Havre proved to be ineffective against the beach for two reasons. First, the British laid down smoke screens to prevent the Germans' ranging. Second, the Le Havre battery spent the morning in a duel with HMS *Warspite* (which it never hit), a big mistake on the Germans' part as the targets on the beach were much more lucrative.

Nevertheless, the 88mms on the first rise, a couple of kilometers inland, were able to put a steady fire on the beach to supplement the mortars and the machine-gun fire coming from the windows of the seaside villas and from pillboxes scattered among the dunes. In addition, there were antitank ditches and mines to impede progress inland, as well as massive concrete walls blocking the streets. These defenses would cause considerable casualties and delay the assault.

The infantry assault teams consisted of companies from the South Lancashire Regiment (Peter sector, on the right), the Suffolk Regiment (Queen sector, in the middle), and the East Yorkshire Regiment (Roger sector, on the left), supported by DD tanks. Their job was to open exits through which the immediate follow-up wave, consisting of troops of commandos and more tanks, could pass inland to their objectives. Meanwhile, UDT units and engineers

* The eight-kilometer stretch from the left flank at Juno (St.-Aubin) and the right flank of Sword (Lion-sur-Mer) was too shallow and rocky to permit an assault. Ironically, at Ouistreham there was a monument to the successful repulse of a British landing attempted on July 12, 1792.

would deal with the obstacles. Other regiments from the British
3rd Division scheduled to land later in the morning included the
Lincolnshire, the King's Own Scottish Borderers, the Royal Ulster
Rifles, the Royal Warwickshire, the Royal Norfolk, and the King's
Shropshire Light Infantry. H-Hour was fixed for 0725.

On the run-in to the beach, Brigadier Lord Lovat, CO of the
commando brigade, had his piper, Bill Millin, playing Highland
reels on the fo'c'sle on his LCI (landing craft, infantry). Maj.
C. K. King of the 2nd Battalion, the East Yorkshire Regiment,
riding in an LCA, read to his men the lines from Shakespeare's
Henry V: "On, on, you noble English! whose blood is fet from
fathers of war-proof. . . . Be copy now to men of grosser blood and
teach them how to war! The game's afoot: Follow your spirit."

Lovat was with Comdr. Rupert Curtis, commander of the
200th Flotilla (LCIs). As the LCIs were coming in, Curtis recalled,
"a lumbering LCT passed close, having discharged her tanks. Lord
Lovat asked me to hail her and through my megaphone I spoke to
a sailor on her quarterdeck. 'How did it go?' He grinned cheerfully,
raised his fingers in the familiar V-for-Victory sign, and said with
relish, 'It was a piece of cake.' This was encouraging, but I had
reason to doubt his optimistic report because the enemy was obviously recovering from the shock of the initial bombardment and
hitting back."

Going in, Curtis raised the flag that meant "Assume arrowhead
formation," and each craft fanned out to port or starboard, forming
a V that presented less of a target for the Germans. To his left, on
the beach, Curtis could see an LCT on fire and stranded. "Judging
from the wounded at the edge of the waves the German mortar fire
was laid accurately on the water's edge.

"Now was the moment. I increased engine revolutions to full
ahead and thrust in hard between the stakes. As we grounded I kept
the engines moving at half ahead to hold the craft in position on
the beach and ordered 'Out ramps.' The commandos proceeded to
land quite calmly. Every minute detail of that scene seemed to take
on a microscopic intensity, and stamped in my memory is the sight
of Shimi Lovat's tall, immaculate figure striding through the water,
rifle in hand, and his men moving with him up the beach to the
skirl of Bill Millin's bagpipes."

☐

Amid all the carnage, exploding shells, smoke, and noise on Sword Beach, some of the chaps with Pvt. Harold Pickersgill claimed that they saw a most remarkable sight, an absolutely stunningly beautiful eighteen-year-old French girl who was wearing a Red Cross armband and who had ridden her bicycle down to the beaches to help with the wounded.

Pickersgill himself met a French girl inland later that day; she had high school English, he had high school French; they took one look at each other and fell in love; they were married at the end of the war and are still together today, living in the little village of Matheiu, midway between the Channel and Caen. But he never believed the story of the Red Cross girl on the beach.

"Oh, you're just hallucinating," he protested to his buddies. "That just can't be, the Germans wouldn't have allowed civilians to come through their lines and we didn't want any civilians messing about. It just didn't happen."

But in 1964, when he was working as a shipping agent in Ouistreham for a British steamship line, Pickersgill met John Thornton, who introduced him to his wife, Jacqueline. Her maiden name was Noel; she had met Thornton on D plus four; they fell in love and married after the war; he too worked as a shipping agent in Ouistreham. It was Jacqueline who had been on the beach, and the story was true.

Pickersgill arranged an interview for me with Jacqueline for this book. "Well," she said, "I was on the beach for a silly reason. My twin sister had been killed in an air raid a fortnight before in Caen, and she had given me a bathing costume for my birthday, and I had left it on the beach, because we were allowed about once a week to remove the fences so we could pass to go swimming, and I had left the costume in a small hut on the beach, and I just wanted to go and pick it up. I didn't want anybody to take it.

"So I got on my bicycle and rode to the beach."

I asked, "Didn't the Germans try to stop you?"

"No, my Red Cross armband evidently made them think it was OK."

"There was quite a bit of activity," she went on in a grand understatement, "and I saw a few dead bodies. And of course once

I got to the beach I couldn't go back, the English wouldn't let me. They were whistling at me, you know. But mostly they were surprised to see me. I mean, it was a ridiculous thing to do. So I stayed on the beach to help with the wounded. I didn't go back to the house until two days after. There was a lot to do." She changed bandages, helped haul wounded and dead out of the water, and otherwise made herself useful.

"I remember one thing horrible which made me realize how stupid I was. I was on top of the dune and there was a trunk, completely bare, no head on it. I never knew if it was a German or an Englishman. Just burned completely."

When asked what her most vivid lingering memory of D-Day was, she replied, "The sea with all the boats on it. All the boats and planes. It was something which you just can't imagine if you have not seen it. It was boats, boats, boats and more boats, boats everywhere. If I had been a German, I would have looked at this, put my weapon down, and said, 'That's it. Finished.' "

The British had put 29,000 men ashore at Sword. They had taken 630 casualties, inflicted far more, and had many prisoners in cages. Lovett's Commandos had linked up with Howard's Ox and Bucks. At no point had the British reached their far-too-optimistic D-Day objectives—they were still five kilometers short of the outskirts of Caen—but they had an enormous follow-up force waiting in the transport area in the Channel to come in as reinforcements on D plus one. The 21st Panzer Division had lost its best opportunity to hurl them into the sea, and the bulk of the German armor in France was still in place in the pas-de-Calais area, waiting for the real invasion.

Toward dusk Commander Curtis had his LCI make a run along the coast. "We set off on a westerly course parallel to the shore," he later reported, "and we now had a grandstand view of the invasion beaches for which many would have paid thousands. Past Luc-sur-Mer, St.-Aubin, Bernieres, and Courseulles in the Canadian sector, past La Riviere lighthouse and Le Hamel and so to Arromanches. It was all an unforgettable sight. Through the smoke and haze I could see craft after craft which had been driven onto the beach with relentless determination in order to give the troops as dry a landing as possible. Many of these craft were now helplessly stranded on obstacles and I could not help feeling a sense of pride at the spirit which their officers and crews had shown.

"We anchored off Arromanches and stood by for air attack that night. Already parts of the prefabricated Mulberry harbors were under tow from England to be placed in position off Arromanches and St.-Laurent. It was clear that the battle for the foothold in the British and Canadian sectors had gone well enough."

10

The End of the Day

GENERAL EISENHOWER had been scheduled to give the graduation address at Kelly Field in Texas on December 12, 1941, but, as noted, he had been ordered to report to the War Department and left by train for Washington that morning. He had prepared his speech, but never got to deliver it. His first and second drafts are at the Eisenhower Library in Abilene, Kansas.

The speech stands the test of time, and is especially appropriate when thinking of the junior officers on D-Day. The exemplary manner in which they had seized their opportunity, their dash, boldness, initiative, teamwork, and tactical skills were outstanding beyond praise. These were exactly the qualities the army had hoped for—and spent two years training its civilians-turned-soldiers to achieve.

Here is what Eisenhower intended to say:

> You are ready, now, to take your places as efficient lieutenants in the Army of the United States and what we need —now—is efficient lieutenants.
>
> The lieutenant is the commissioned officer closest to the enlisted man. The lieutenant is the only officer charged with direct training of the individual fighting man, all other officers are charged, normally, with training junior officers.

On the lieutenant falls the burden of producing the small fighting units that, in the main, make up the army, no matter how large.

It is the lieutenant's privilege to live close to his men, to be their example in conduct, in courage, and in devotion to duty. He is in position to learn them intimately, to help them when in trouble, often to keep them out of trouble. No matter how young he may be nor how old and hard boiled his men he must become their counsellor, their leader, their friend, their old-man. This opportunity—that of becoming a real leader of fighting men—is one that you are yet to master. It is the part of soldiering that challenges the best that's in the officer, and it's the one part in which he must not fail! To gain the respect, the esteem, the affection, the readiness to follow into danger, the unswerving and undying loyalty of the American enlisted man. That is the privilege and the opportunity of the lieutenant, and it is his high and almost divine duty. It is the challenge to his talents, his patriotism, his very soul!

In an earlier draft of this speech, Eisenhower had spoken to a broader theme:

In military dictatorships the required unity of effort is always insured by the authority resting in one man's hands. Every individual must conform to the dictator's orders, the alternative is the firing squad. So, from the beginning, the necessary mechanical coordination is automatic.

In democracy this result is achieved more slowly. The overwhelming majority of its citizens must first come to realize that a common danger threatens, that collective and individual self-preservation demands the submission of self-interest to the nation's welfare. Because this realization and this unification come about so slowly, often only after disaster and loss of battles have rudely awakened a population, democracy is frequently condemned by unthinking critics as the least efficient form of government. Such criticism deals with the obvious factors only, it fails to throw into the balance the moral fibre, the staying qualities of a population. A

Democracy resorts to war only when the vast majority of its people become convinced that there is no other way out. The crisis they have entered is of their own choosing, and in the long, cruel ordeal of war this difference is likely to become decisive. The unification and coordination achieved in this way is lasting. The people work together because they have a common belief in the justice of their cause and a common readiness to sacrifice for attainment of national success. It was in appreciation of the great strength arising from this truth that Woodrow Wilson said "The highest form of efficiency is the spontaneous cooperation of a free people."

How right Wilson was the Allies demonstrated on D-Day. The Germans' tactical and strategic mistakes were serious, but their political blunders were the greatest of all. Their occupation policies in Poland and Russia precluded any enthusiasm whatsoever by their *Ost* battalions for their cause—even though nearly every one of the conscripted *Ost* troops hated the communists. Although German behavior in France was immeasurably better than in Poland and Russia, even in France the Germans failed to generate enthusiasm for their cause, and thus the Germans were unable to profit from the great potential of conquered France. What should have been an asset for Germany, the young men of France, became an asset for the Allies, either as saboteurs in the factories or as members of the Resistance.

What Hitler regarded as the greatest German assets—the leadership principle in the Third Reich, the unquestioning obedience expected of Wehrmacht personnel from field marshal down to private—all worked against the Germans on D-Day.

The truth is that despite individual acts of great bravery and the fanaticism of some Wehrmacht troops, the performance of the Wehrmacht's high command, middle-ranking officers, and junior officers was just pathetic. The cause is simply put: They were afraid to take the initiative. They allowed themselves to be paralyzed by stupid orders coming from far away that bore no relation to the situation on the battlefield. Tank commanders who knew where the enemy was and how and when he should be attacked sat in their headquarters through the day, waiting for the high command in Berchtesgaden to tell them what to do.

In adjusting and reacting to unexpected situations, the contrast between men like Generals Roosevelt and Cota, Colonels Canham and Otway, Major Howard, Captain Dawson, Lieutenants Spaulding and Winters, and their German counterparts could not have been greater. The men fighting for democracy were able to make quick, on-site decisions and act on them; the men fighting for the totalitarian regime were not. Except for a captain here, a lieutenant there, not one German officer reacted appropriately to the challenge of D-Day.

As for the Allies, Pvt. Carl Weast of the rangers has an answer to the question of how they did it. In his oral history he related a story about his company commander, Capt. George Whittington.

"He was a hell of a man," Weast said. "He led people. I recall the time a week or so after D-Day when we shot a cow and cut off some beef and were cooking it over a fire on sticks. Captain Whittington came up and threw a German boot next to the fire and said, 'I'll bet some son of a bitch misses that.' We looked at the boot. The German's leg was still inside of it. I'll bet by God he did miss it."

That same day Weast heard the executive officer of the 5th Ranger Battalion, Maj. Richard Sullivan, criticizing Captain Whittington for unnecessarily exposing himself.

"Whittington said to Sully, 'You saw it happen back on that goddamn beach. Now you tell me how the hell you lead men from behind.' "

Weast's introduction to combat came on D-Day. He fought with the rangers through the next eleven months. He concluded that the Allied high command had been right to insist that "there be practically no experienced troops in the initial waves that hit that beach, because an experienced infantryman is a terrified infantryman, and they wanted guys like me who were more amazed than they were frozen with fear, because the longer you fight a war the more you figure your number's coming up tomorrow, and it really gets to be God-awful."

Weast made a final point: "In war, the best rank is either private or colonel or better, but those ranks in between, hey, those people have got to be leaders."

At Omaha Beach they were.

At the end of the day Lt. John Reville of F Company, 5th Ranger Battalion, was on top of the bluff at Omaha. As the light faded he called his runner, Pvt. Rex Low, pointed out to the six thousand vessels in the Channel, and said, "Rex, take a look at this. You'll never see a sight like this again in your life."

Pvt. Robert Zafft, a twenty-year-old infantryman in the 115th Regiment, 29th Division, Omaha Beach, put his feelings and experience this way: "I made it up the hill, I made it all the way to where the Germans had stopped us for the night, and I guess I made it up the hill of manhood."

Pvt. Felix Branham was a member of K Company, 116th Infantry, the regiment that took the heaviest casualties of all the Allied regiments on D-Day. "I have gone through lots of tragedies since D-Day," he concluded his oral history. "But to me, D-Day will live with me till the day I die, and I'll take it to heaven with me. It was the longest, most miserable, horrible day that I or anyone else ever went through.

"I would not take a million dollars for my experiences, but I surely wouldn't want to go through that again for a million dollars."

Sgt. John Ellery, 16th Regiment, 1st Division, Easy Red sector of Omaha, recalled: "The first night in France I spent in a ditch beside a hedgerow wrapped in a damp shelter-half and thoroughly exhausted. But I felt elated. It had been the greatest experience of my life. I was ten feet tall. No matter what happened, I had made it off the beach and reached the high ground. I was king of the hill, at least in my own mind, for a moment. My contribution to the heroic tradition of the United States Army might have been the smallest achievement in the history of courage, but at least, for a time, I had walked in the company of very brave men."

Adm. Bertram Ramsay ended his June 6 diary with this entry: "We have still to establish ourselves on land. The navy has done its

part well. News continued satisfactory throughout the day from
E.T.F. [Eastern Task Force, the British beaches] and good progress
was made. Very little news was rec[eived] from W.T.F. [Western
Task Forces, the American beaches] & anxiety exists as to the position on shore.

"Still on the whole we have very much to thank God for this
day."

One soldier who did not forget to thank God was Lt. Richard
Winters, 506th PIR, 101st Airborne. At 0001 on June 6, he had
been in a C-47 headed to Normandy. He had prayed the whole way
over, prayed to live through the day, prayed that he wouldn't fail.

He didn't fail. He won the DSC that morning.

At 2400 on June 6, before bedding down at Ste.-Marie-du-
Mont, Winters (as he later wrote in his diary) "did not forget to get
on my knees and thank God for helping me to live through this day
and ask for help on D plus one." And he made a promise to himself:
if he lived through the war, he was going to find an isolated farm
somewhere and spend the remainder of his life in peace and quiet.
In 1951 he got the farm, in south-central Pennsylvania, where he
lives today.

"When can their glory fade?" Tennyson asked about the Light
Brigade, and so ask I about the men of D-Day.

> *O the wild charge they made!*
> *All the world wondered.*
> *Honor the charge they made!*

General Eisenhower, who started it all with his "OK, let's go"
order, gets the last word. In 1964, on D-Day plus twenty years, he
was interviewed on Omaha Beach by Walter Cronkite.

Looking out at the Channel, Eisenhower said, "You see these
people out here swimming and sailing their little pleasure boats and
taking advantage of the nice weather and the lovely beach, Walter,
and it is almost unreal to look at it today and remember what
it was.

"But it's a wonderful thing to remember what those fellows
twenty years ago were fighting for and sacrificing for, what they did

to preserve our way of life. Not to conquer any territory, not for any ambitions of our own. But to make sure that Hitler could not destroy freedom in the world.

"I think it's just overwhelming. To think of the lives that were given for that principle, paying a terrible price on this beach alone, on that one day, 2,000 casualties. But they did it so that the world could be free. It just shows what free men will do rather than be slaves."

11

Hedgerows

SOME 90,000 GIs ENTERED FRANCE on June 6, coming by air or by sea. More than two million would follow. Most of those who landed on D-Day had been in the army for two or even three years. There were some teenagers among them, but the average age was more like twenty-two or twenty-three among the enlisted men, in the mid-twenties or older for the junior officers. The divisions that entered France after D-Day, from June until September, were similar in age and time in the army. But those who came in as replacements, or in new divisions after September, had been overwhelmingly high school or college students when America got into the war. They had been drafted or enlisted voluntarily in late 1942, 1943, and 1944. From June 7 to September they came in over Omaha and Utah Beaches; from September to the spring of 1945 they came in at Cherbourg and Le Havre. Whenever they entered the Continent, they came as liberators, not conquerors. Only a tiny percentage of them wanted to be there, but only a small percentage failed to do their duty.

None of them, not even the D-Day veterans, had been trained for what they were about to encounter. For all its thoroughness, intelligence-gathering capacity, and astonishing achievements in logistics, the army had failed to tell its men about Norman hedgerows. They were going to have to find out for themselves, and then figure out a way to launch a successful attack in hedgerow country.

First light came to Ste.-Mere-Eglise around 0510. Twenty-four hours earlier it had been just another Norman village, with more than a millennium behind it. By nightfall of June 6 it was a name known around the world, the village where the invasion began and now headquarters for the 82nd Airborne Division.

At dawn on June 7, Lt. Waverly Wray, executive officer in Company D, 505th PIR, who had jumped into the night sky over Normandy twenty-eight hours earlier, was on the northwestern outskirts of the village. He peered intently into the lifting gloom. What he couldn't see, he could sense. From the sounds of the movement of personnel and vehicles to the north of Ste.-Mere-Eglise, he could feel and figure that the major German counter-attack, the one the Germans counted on to drive the Americans into the sea and the one the paratroopers had been expecting, was coming at Ste.-Mere-Eglise.

It was indeed. Six thousand German soldiers were on the move, with infantry, artillery, tanks, and self-propelled guns—more than a match for the six hundred or so lightly armed paratroopers in Ste.-Mere-Eglise. A German breakthrough to the beaches seemed imminent. And Lieutenant Wray was at the point of attack.

Wray was a big man, 250 pounds with "legs like tree trunks." The standard-issue army parachute wasn't large enough for his weight and he dropped too fast on his jumps, but the men said hell, with his legs he didn't need a chute. He was from Bates-ville, Mississippi, and was an avid woodsman, skilled with rifles and shotguns. He claimed he had never missed a shot in his life. A veteran of the Sicily and Italy campaigns, Wray was—in the words of Col. Ben Vandervoort, commanding the 505th—"as experienced and skilled as an infantry soldier can get and still be alive."

Wray had Deep South religious convictions. A Baptist, each month he sent half his pay home to help build a new church. He never swore. His exclamation when exasperated was, "John Brown!" meaning abolitionist John Brown of Harpers Ferry. He didn't drink, smoke, or chase girls. Some troopers called him "The Deacon," but in an admiring rather than critical way. Vandervoort had something of a father-son relationship with Wray, always calling him by his first name, Waverly.

On June 7, shortly after dawn, Wray reported to Vandervoort —whose leg, broken in the jump, was now in a cast—on the movements he had spotted, the things he had sensed, and where he expected the Germans to attack and in what strength.

Vandervoort took all this in, then ordered Wray to return to the company and have it attack the German flank before the Germans could get their attack started.

"He said 'Yes Sir,' " Vandervoort later wrote, "saluted, about-faced, and moved out like a parade ground Sergeant Major."

Back in the company area, Wray passed on the order. As the company prepared to attack, he took up his M-1, grabbed a half-dozen grenades, and strode out, his Colt .45 on his hip and a silver-plated .38 revolver stuck in his jump boot. He was going to do a one-man reconnaissance to formulate a plan of attack.

Wray was going out into the unknown. He had spent half a year preparing for this moment but he was not trained for it. In one of the greatest intelligence failures of all time, neither G-2 (intelligence) at U.S. First Army, nor SHAEF G-2, nor any division S-2 had ever thought to tell the men who were going to fight the battle that the dominant physical feature of the battlefield was the maze of hedgerows that covered the western half of Normandy.

One hundred years before Lieutenant Wray came to Normandy, Honore de Balzac had described the hedges: "The peasants from time immemorial, have raised a bank of earth about each field, forming a flat-topped ridge, two meters in height, with beeches, oaks, and chestnut trees growing upon the summit. The ridge or mound, planted in this wise, is called a hedge; and as the long branches of the trees which grow upon it almost always project across the road, they make a great arbor overhead. The roads themselves, shut in by clay banks in this melancholy way, are not unlike the moats of fortresses."

How could the various G-2s have missed such an obvious feature, especially as aerial reconnaissance clearly revealed the hedges? Because the photo interpreters, looking only straight down at them, thought that they were like English hedges, the kind the fox hunters jump over, and they had missed the sunken nature of the roads entirely. "We had been neither informed of them or trained to overcome them," was Capt. John Colby's brief comment. The GIs would have to learn by doing, as Wray was doing on the morning of June 7.

Wray and his fellow paratroopers, like the men from the 1st and 29th Divisions at Omaha and the 4th Division at Utah, and all the support groups, had been magnificently trained to launch an amphibious assault. By nightfall of June 6, they had done the real thing successfully, thanks to their training, courage, and dash. But beginning at dawn, June 7, they were fighting in a terrain completely unexpected and unfamiliar to them.

The Germans, meanwhile, had been going through specialized training for fighting in hedgerows. "Coming within thirty meters of the enemy was what we meant by close combat," Pvt. Adolf Rogosch of the 353rd Division recalled. "We trained hard, throwing hand grenades, getting to know the ground. The lines of hedges crisscrossing one another played tricks on your eyes. We trained to fight as individuals; we knew when the attack came we'd probably be cut off from one another. We let them come forward and cross the hedge, then we blew them apart. That was our tactic, to wait until they crossed over the hedge and then shoot."

The Germans also pre-sited mortars and artillery on the single gaps that provided the only entrances into the fields. Behind the hedgerows, they dug rifle pits and tunneled openings for machine-gun positions in each corner.

Wray moved up sunken lanes, crossed an orchard, pushed his way through hedgerows, crawled through a ditch. Along the way he noted concentrations of Germans in fields and lanes. A man without his woodsman's sense of direction would have gotten lost. He reached a point near the N-13, the main highway coming into Ste.-Mere-Eglise from Cherbourg.

The N-13 was the axis of the German attacks. Wray, "moving like the deer stalker he was" (Vandervoort's words), got to a place where he could hear guttural voices on the other side of a hedgerow. They sounded like officers talking about map coordinates. Wray rose up, burst through the obstacle, swung his M-1 to a ready position, and barked in his strong command voice, *"Hande hoch!"* to the eight German officers gathered around a radio.

Seven instinctively raised their hands. The eighth tried to pull a pistol from his holster; Wray shot him instantly between the eyes. Two Germans in a slit trench one hundred meters to Wray's rear fired bursts from their Schmeisser machine pistols at him. Bullets cut through his jacket; one cut off half of his right ear.

Wray dropped to his knee and began shooting the other seven officers, one at a time as they attempted to run away. When he had used up his clip, Wray jumped into a ditch, put another clip into his M-1, and dropped the German soldiers with the Schmeissers with one shot each.

Wray made his way back to the company area to report on what he had seen. At the command post he came in with blood down his jacket, a big chunk of his ear gone, holes in his clothing. "Who's got more grenades?" he demanded. He wanted more grenades.

Then he started leading. He put a 60mm mortar crew on the German flank and directed fire into the lanes and hedgerows most densely packed with the enemy. Next he sent D Company into an attack down one of the lanes. The Germans broke and ran. By mid-morning Ste.-Mere-Eglise was secure, and the potential for a German breakthrough to the beaches was much diminished.

The next day Vandervoort, Wray, and Sgt. John Rabig went to the spot to examine the German officers Wray had shot. Unforgettably, their bodies were sprinkled with pink and white apple blossom petals from an adjacent orchard. It turned out that they were the commanding officer and his staff of the 1st Battalion, 158th Grenadier Infantry Regiment. The maps showed that it was leading the way for the counterattack. The German confusion and subsequent retreat were in part due to having been rendered leaderless by Wray.

Vandervoort later recalled that when he saw the blood on Wray's jacket and the missing half-ear, he had remarked, "They've been getting kind of close to you, haven't they Waverly?"

With just a trace of a grin, Wray had replied, "Not as close as I've been getting to them, sir."

At the scene of the action Vandervoort noted that every one of the dead Germans, including the two Schmeisser-armed Grenadiers more than a hundred meters away, had been killed with a single shot in the head. Wray insisted on burying the bodies. He said he had killed them, and they deserved a decent burial, and it was his responsibility.

Later that day Sergeant Rabig commented to Vandervoort, "Colonel, aren't you glad Waverly's on our side?"

The next day Rabig wasn't so sure. He and Wray were crouched behind a hedgerow. American artillery was falling into the next field. "I could hear these Germans screaming as they were getting hit. Lieutenant Wray said, 'John, I wish that artillery would stop so we can go in after them.'

"Jesus! I thought, the artillery is doing good enough."

Before the battle was joined, Hitler had been sure his young men would outfight the young Americans. He was certain that the spoiled sons of democracy couldn't stand up to the solid sons of dictatorship. If he had seen Lieutenant Wray in action in the early morning of D-Day plus one, he might have had some doubts.

Of course, Wray was special. You don't get more than one Wray to a division, or even to an army. Vandervoort compared Wray to a sergeant in the 82nd Division in World War I, also a Southern boy, named Alvin York. Yet if the qualities Wray possessed were unique, others could aspire to them without hoping or expecting to match his spectacular performance. Indeed, they would have to if the United States was going to win the war. Victory depended on the junior officers and NCOs on the front lines. That is the spine of this book.

Among other elite German outfits in Normandy, there were paratroopers. They were a different proposition altogether from the Polish or Russian troops. The 3rd *Fallschirmjager* Division came into battle in Normandy on June 10, arriving by truck after night drives from Brittany. It was a full-strength division, 15,976 men in its ranks, mostly young German volunteers. It was new to combat but it had been organized and trained by a veteran paratroop battalion from the Italian campaign. Training had been rigorous and emphasized initiative and improvisation. The equipment was outstanding.

Indeed, the *Fallschirmjager* were perhaps the best-armed infantrymen in the world in 1944. The 3rd FJ had 930 light machine guns, eleven times as many as its chief opponent, the U.S. 29th Division. Rifle companies in the FJ had twenty MG 42s and forty-three submachine guns; rifle companies in the 29th had two machine guns and nine BARs. At the squad level, the GIs had a single BAR; the German parachute squad had two MG 42s and three submachine guns. The Germans had three times as many mortars as the Americans, and heavier ones. So in any encounter between equal numbers of Americans and *Fallschirmjager,* the Germans had from six to twenty times as much firepower.

And these German soldiers were ready to fight. A battalion commander in the 29th remarked to an unbelieving counterpart from another regiment, "Those Germans are the best soldiers I ever saw. They're smart and they don't know what the word 'fear' means. They come in and they keep coming until they get their job done or you kill 'em."

These were the men who had to be rooted out of the hedgerows. One by one. There were, on average, fourteen hedgerows to the kilometer in Normandy. The enervating, costly process of gearing up for an attack, making the attack, carrying the attack home, mopping up after the attack, took half a day or more. And at the end of the action there was the next hedgerow, fifty to a hundred meters or so away. All through the Cotentin Peninsula, from June 7 on, GIs labored at the task. They heaved and pushed and punched and died doing it, for two hedgerows a day.

No terrain in the world was better suited for defensive action with the weapons of the fourth decade of the twentieth century than the Norman hedgerows, and only the lava and coral, caves and tunnels of Iwo Jima and Okinawa were as favorable.

The Norman hedgerows dated back to Roman times. They were mounds of earth to keep cattle in and to mark boundaries. Typically there was only one entry into the small field enclosed by the hedgerows, which were irregular in length as well as height and set at odd angles. On the sunken roads the brush often met overhead, giving the GIs a feeling of being trapped in a leafy tunnel. Wherever they looked the view was blocked by walls of vegetation.

Undertaking an offensive in the hedgerows was risky, costly, time-consuming, fraught with frustration. It was like fighting in a maze. Platoons found themselves completely lost a few minutes after launching an attack. Squads got separated. Just as often, two platoons from the same company could occupy adjacent fields for hours before discovering each other's presence. The small fields limited deployment possibilities; seldom during the first week of battle did a unit as large as a company go into an attack intact.

Where the Americans got lost, the Germans were at home. The 352nd Division had been in Normandy for months, training for this battle. Further, the Germans were geniuses at utilizing the fortification possibilities of the hedgerows. In the early days of the battle, many GIs were killed or wounded because they dashed through the opening into a field, just the kind of aggressive tactics they had been taught, only to be cut down by pre-sited machine-gun fire or mortars (mortars caused three-quarters of American casualties in Normandy).

American army tactical manuals stressed the need for tank-infantry cooperation. But in Normandy, the tankers didn't want to get down on the sunken roads because of insufficient room to traverse the turret and insufficient visibility to use the long-range firepower of the cannon and machine guns. But staying on the main roads proved impossible; the Germans held the high ground inland and had their 88mm cannon sited to provide long fields of fire along highways. So into the lanes the tanks perforce went. But there they were restricted; they wanted to get out into the fields. But they couldn't. When they appeared at the gap leading into a field, presited mortar fire, plus panzerfausts (handheld antitank weapons), disabled them. Often, in fact, it caused them to "brew up," or start burning—the tankers were discovering that their tanks had a distressing propensity for catching fire.

So tankers tried going over or through the embankments, but the hedgerows were proving to be almost impassable obstacles to the American M4 Sherman tank. Countless attempts were made to break through or climb over, but the Sherman wasn't powerful enough to break through the cement-like base, and when it climbed up the embankment, at the apex it exposed its unarmored belly to German panzerfausts. Further, coordination between tankers and infantry was almost impossible under battle conditions, as they had no easy or reliable way to communicate with one another.

Lt. Sidney Salomon of the 2nd Ranger Battalion, one of the D-Day heroes, found that out on June 7. He was leading the remnants of his battalion, which had come ashore on the right flank at Omaha and been involved in a day-long firefight on D-Day, westward along the coastal road that led to Pointe-du-Hoc. Three companies of the 2nd Rangers had taken the German emplacement there, and destroyed the coastal guns, but they were under severe attack and had taken severe casualties. Salomon was in a hurry to get to them.

But his column, marching in combat formation, began taking well-placed artillery shells. To his right, Salomon could see a Norman church, its steeple the only high point around. He was certain the Germans had an observer spotting for their artillery in that steeple. Behind Salomon a Sherman tank chugged up, the only American tank to be seen. It was buttoned up. Salomon wanted it to elevate its 75mm cannon and blast that steeple, but he couldn't get the crew's attention, not even when he knocked on the side of the tank with the butt of his carbine. "So I ultimately stood in the middle of the road directly in front of the tank, waving my arms and pointing in the direction of the church. That produced results. After a couple of shots from the cannon and several bursts from the .50-caliber machine gun, the artillery spotter was no more."

Salomon's daring feat notwithstanding, it was obvious that the army was going to have to work out a better system for tank-infantry communication than having junior officers jump up and down in front of American tanks. Until that was done, the tanks would play a minor supporting role to the infantry, following the GIs into the next field as the infantry overran it.

The U.S. First Army had not produced anything approaching a doctrine for offensive action in the hedgerows. It had expended enormous energy to get tanks by the score into Normandy, but it had no doctrine for the role of tanks in the hedgerows. In peacetime, the army would have dealt with the problem by setting up commissions and boards, experimenting in maneuvers, testing ideas, before establishing a doctrine. But in Normandy time was a luxury the army didn't have. So as the infantry lurched forward in the Cotentin, following frontal assaults straight into the enemy's kill zones, the tankers began experimenting with ways to utilize their weapons in the hedgerows.

Beginning at daylight on June 7, each side had begun to rush reinforcements to the front. The Americans came in on a tight schedule, long since worked out, with fresh divisions almost daily. Sgt. Edward "Buddy" Gianelloni, a medic in the 79th Division, came ashore on D-Day plus six on Utah Beach. The men marched inland; when they reached Ste.-Mere-Eglise, a paratrooper called out to Gianelloni, "Hey, what outfit is that?"

"This is the 79th Infantry Division," Gianelloni replied.

"Well, that's good," the paratrooper said. "Now if you guys are around this time tomorrow you can consider yourselves veterans."

The Germans came in by bits and pieces because they were improvising, having been caught with no plans for reinforcing Normandy. Further, the Allied air forces had badly hampered German movement from the start.

At dawn, all along the plateau above the bluff at Omaha, GIs shook themselves awake, did their business, ate some rations, smoked a cigarette, got into some kind of formation, and prepared to move out to broaden the beachhead. But in the hedgerows, individuals got lost, squads got lost. German sniper fire came from all directions. The Norman farm homes, made of stone and surrounded by stone walls and a stone barn, made excellent fortresses. Probing attacks brought forth a stream of bullets from the Germans, pretty much discouraging further probes.

Brig. Gen. Norman "Dutch" Cota, assistant division commander of the 29th, came on a group of infantry pinned down by some Germans in a farmhouse. He asked the captain in command why his men were making no effort to take the building.

"Sir, the Germans are in there, shooting at us," the captain replied.

"Well, I'll tell you what, Captain," said Cota, unbuckling two grenades from his jacket. "You and your men start shooting at them.

I'll take a squad of men and you and your men watch carefully. I'll show you how to take a house with Germans in it."

Cota led his squad around a hedge to get as close as possible to the house. Suddenly, he gave a whoop and raced forward, the squad following, yelling like wild men. As they tossed grenades into the windows, Cota and another man kicked in the front door, tossed a couple of grenades inside, waited for the explosions, then dashed into the house. The surviving Germans inside were streaming out the back door, running for their lives.

Cota returned to the captain. "You've seen how to take a house," said the general, still out of breath. "Do you understand? Do you know how to do it now?"

"Yes, sir."

"Well, I won't be around to do it for you again," Cota said. "I can't do it for everybody."

That little story speaks to the training of the U.S. Army for the Battle of Normandy. At first glance, Cota's bravery stands out, along with his sense of the dramatic and his knowledge of tactics. He could be sure the story would get around the division. A lesson would be learned. His own reputation would go even higher, the men would be even more willing to follow him.

But after that first glance, a question emerges. Where had that captain been the last six months? He had been in training to fight the German army. He had been committed to offensive action, trained to it, inspired to it. But no one had thought to show him how to take an occupied house. He knew all about getting ashore from an LCVP, about beach obstacles, about paths up the bluff, about ravines, about amphibious assault techniques. But no one had shown him how to take a house because there were no standing houses on Omaha Beach, so that wasn't one of his problems.

Not on June 6. But on June 7 it became his number one problem. The same was true for the two hundred or so company commanders already ashore and would be for the hundreds of others waiting to enter the battle. As Cota said, he couldn't be there to teach all of them how to take a house. They were going to have to figure it out for themselves.

□

Normandy was a soldier's battle. It belonged to the riflemen, machine gunners, mortarmen, tankers, and artillerymen who were on the front lines. There was no room for maneuver. There was no opportunity for subtlety. There was a simplicity to the fighting: for the Germans, to hold; for the Americans, to attack.

Where they would hold or attack required no decision-making: it was always the next village or field. The real decision-making came at the battalion, company, and platoon levels: where to place the mines, the barbed wire, machine-gun pits, where to dig the foxholes—or where and how to attack them.

Throughout First Army, young men made many discoveries in the first few days of combat, about war, about themselves, about others. They quickly learned such basics as to keep down or die—to dig deep and stay quiet—to distinguish incoming from outgoing artillery—to judge when and where a shell or a mortar barrage was going to hit—to recognize that fear is inevitable but can be managed—and many more things they had been told in training but that can only be truly learned by doing. Putting it another way, after a week in combat, infantrymen agreed that there was no way training could have prepared them for the reality of combat.

Capt. John Colby caught one of the essences of combat, the sense of total immediacy: "At this point we had been in combat six days. It seemed like a year. In combat, one lives in the now and does not think much about yesterday or tomorrow."

Colby discovered that there was no telling who would break or when. His regimental CO was "grossly incompetent," his battalion commander had run away from combat in his first day of action, and his company CO was a complete bust. On June 12 the company got caught in a combined mortar-artillery barrage. The men couldn't move forward, they couldn't fall back, and they couldn't stay where they were—or so it appeared to the CO, who therefore had no orders to give, and was speechless.

Colby went up to his CO to ask for orders. The CO shook his head and pointed to his throat. Colby asked him if he could make it back to the aid station on his own, "and he leaped to his feet and took off. I never saw him again."

Another thing Colby learned in his first week in combat was:

"Artillery does not fire forever. It just seems like that when you get caught in it. The guns overheat or the ammunition runs low, and it stops. It stops for a while, anyway."

He was amazed to discover how small he could make his body. If you get caught in the open in a shelling, he advised, "the best thing to do is drop to the ground and crawl into your steel helmet. One's body tends to shrink a great deal when shells come in. I am sure I have gotten as much as eighty percent of my body under my helmet when caught under shellfire."

Colby learned about hedgerows. Once he got into a situation where "I had to push through a hedgerow. A submachine-gun emitted a long burst right in front of my face. The gun was a Schmeisser, which had a very high rate of fire that sounded like a piece of cloth being ripped loudly. The bullets went over my head. I fell backward and passed out cold from fright."

About themselves, the most important thing a majority of the GIs discovered was that they were not cowards. They hadn't thought so, they had fervently hoped it would not be so, but they couldn't be sure until tested. After a few days in combat, most of them knew they were good soldiers. They had neither run away nor collapsed into a pathetic mass of quivering Jell-O (their worst fear, even greater than the fear of being afraid).

They were learning about others. A common experience: the guy who talked toughest, bragged most, excelled in maneuvers, everyone's pick to be the top soldier in the company, was the first to break, while the soft-talking kid who was hardly noticed in camp was the standout in combat. These are the cliches of war novels precisely because they are true. They also learned that while combat brought out the best in some men, it unleashed the worst in others —and a further lesson, that the distinction between best and worst wasn't clear.

On June 9, Pvt. Dutch Schultz of the 82nd Airborne was outside Montebourg. That morning he was part of an attack on the town. "I ran by a wounded German soldier lying alongside of a hedgerow. He was obviously in a great deal of pain and crying for help. I stopped running and turned around. A close friend of mine put the muzzle of his rifle between the German's still crying eyes and pulled the trigger. There was no change in my friend's facial expression. I don't believe he even blinked an eye."

Schultz was simultaneously appalled and awed by what he had seen. "There was a part of me that wanted to be just as ruthless as my friend," he commented. Later, he came to realize that "there but for the grace of God go I."

By June 12, Easy Company, 501st PIR, had been fighting since shortly after midnight, June 6. Mostly its engagements were small firefights in the fields and tiny villages. But on June 12 it was ordered to make an all-out attack in the town of Carentan. It would spearhead the drive to link up the men from Omaha Beach with those from Utah. Street fighting was a new experience for the company, and it showed.

The objective was a T-junction defended by a company of German parachutists—elite troops. The last hundred or so meters of the road leading to the T-junction was straight, with a gentle downward slope. There were shallow ditches on both sides, then sidewalks and behind them houses. Lt. Richard Winters put the 1st platoon, under Lt. Harry Welsh, on the left side of a road, just past where the road curved then straightened out, with 2nd platoon on the right and 3rd platoon in reserve. The men lay down in the ditches by the side of the road, awaiting orders. The German defenders had not revealed their machine-gun position or fired any mortars. Everything was quiet.

At 0600 Winters ordered, "Move out." Welsh kicked off the advance, running down the road toward the T-junction some fifty meters away, his platoon following. The German machine gun opened fire, straight down the road. It was in a perfect position, at the perfect time, to wipe out the company.

The fire split the platoon. The seventh man behind Welsh stayed in the ditch. So did the rest of the platoon, almost thirty men. They were facedown in the ditches on both sides of the road, trying to snuggle in as close as they could.

Winters jumped into the middle of the road, highly agitated, yelling, "Move out! Move out!" It did no good; the men remained in place, heads down in the ditch.

From his rear, Winters could hear Lt. Col. Robert Strayer,

Lts. Clarence Hester and Louis Nixon, and other members of the battalion HQ hollering at him to "get them moving, Winters, get them moving."

Winters threw away his gear, holding onto his M-1, and ran over to the left side, "hollering like a madman, 'Get going!' " He started kicking the men in the butt. He crossed to the other side and repeated the order, again kicking the men.

"I was possessed," Winters recalled. "Nobody'd ever seen me like that." He ran back to the other side, machine-gun bullets zinging down the street. He thought to himself, My God, I'm leading a blessed life. I'm charmed.

He was also desperate. His best friend, Harry Welsh, was up ahead, trying to deal with that machine gun. If I don't do something, Winters thought to himself, he's dead. No question about it.

But the men wouldn't move. They did look up. Winters recalled, "I will never forget the surprise and fear on those faces looking up at me." The German machine gun seemed to be zeroing in on him, and he was a wide open target. "The bullets kept snapping by and glancing off the road all around me."

"Everybody had froze," Pvt. Rod Strohl remembered. "Nobody could move. And Winters got up in the middle of the road and screamed, 'Come on! Move out! Now!' "

That did it. No man in the company had ever before heard Winters shout. "It was so out of character," Strohl said, "we moved out as one man."

According to Winters, "Here is where the discipline paid off. The men got the message, and they moved out."

As Sgt. Floyd Talbert passed Winters, he called out, "Which way when we hit the intersection?"

"Turn right," Winters ordered.

(In 1981, Talbert wrote Winters: "I'll never forget seeing you in the middle of that road. You were my total inspiration. All my boys felt the same way.")

Welsh, meanwhile, was neutralizing the machine gun. "We were all alone," he remembered, "and I couldn't understand where the hell everybody was." Thanks to the distraction caused by Winters running back and forth, the machine gunner had lost track of Welsh and his six men. Welsh tossed some grenades at the gun, followed by bursts from his carbine. The men with him did the same. The machine gun fell silent.*

The remainder of Easy Company drove into the intersection at a full run and secured it. Winters sent the 1st platoon to the left, the 2nd to the right, clearing out the houses, one man throwing grenades through windows while another waited outside the door. Immediately after the explosion, the second man kicked in the door to look for and shoot any survivors.

Pvts. Ed Tipper and Joe Liebgott cleared out a house. As Tipper was passing out the front door, "A locomotive hit me, driving me far back inside the house. I heard no noise, felt no pain, and was somehow unsteadily standing and in possession of my M-1." The German rear guard was bringing its pre-positioned mortars into play. Liebgott grabbed Tipper and helped him to a sitting position, called for a medic, and tried to reassure Tipper that he would be OK.

Welsh came up and got some morphine into Tipper, who was insisting that he could walk. That was nonsense; both his legs were broken, and he had a serious head wound. Welsh and Liebgott half dragged him into the street, where "I remember lying at the base of the wall with explosions in the street and shrapnel zinging against the wall above my head." Welsh got Tipper back to the aid station being set up in a barn about twenty meters to the rear.

Mortars continued coming in, along with sniper fire. Pvt. Carwood Lipton led 3rd platoon to the intersection and peeled off to the right. There were explosions on the street; he huddled against a wall and yelled to his men to follow him. A mortar shell dropped about two meters in front of him, putting shell fragments in his left cheek, right wrist, and right leg at the crotch. His rifle clattered to the street. He dropped to the ground, put his left hand to his cheek and felt a large hole, but his biggest concern was his right hand, as

---

* Winters wrote in 1990: "Later in the war, in recalling this action with Major [Clarence] Hester, he made a comment that has always left me feeling proud of Company E's action that day. As S-3, Hester had been in a position to see another company in a similar position caught in M.G. [machine-gun] fire. It froze and then got severely cut up. E Company, on the other hand, had moved out, got the job done, and had not been cut up by that M.G."

blood was pumping out in spurts. Sergeant Talbert got to him and put a tourniquet on his arm.

Only then did Lipton feel the pain in his crotch. He reached down for a feel, and his left hand came away bloody.

"Talbert, I may be hit bad," he said. Talbert slit his pants leg with his knife, took a look, and said, "You're OK."

"What a relief that was," Lipton remembered. The two shell fragments had gone into the top of his leg and "missed everything important."

Talbert threw Lipton over his shoulder and carried him to the aid station. The medics gave Lipton a shot of morphine and bandaged him up.

Sgt. Don Malarkey recalled that during "this tremendous period of fire I could hear someone reciting a Hail Mary. I glanced up and saw Father John Maloney holding his rosary and walking down the center of the road to administer last rites to the dying at the road juncture." (Maloney was awarded the DSC.)

Winters got hit by a ricochet bullet that went through his boot and into his leg. He stayed in action long enough to check the ammunition supply and consult with Welsh (who tried to remove the bullet with his knife but gave it up) to set up a defensive position in the event of a counterattack.

By this time it was 0700, and the area was secured. F Company, meanwhile, had hooked up with the 327th. Carentan had been captured. Lieutenant Colonel Strayer came into town, where he met the commander of the 3rd Battalion of the 327th. They went into a wine shop and opened a bottle to drink to the victory.

Winters went back to the battalion aid station. Ten of his men were there receiving first aid. A doctor poked around Winters's leg with a tweezers, pulled the bullet, cleaned out the wound, put some sulfa powder on it and a bandage.

Winters circulated among the wounded. One of them was Pvt. Albert Blithe.

"How're you doing, Blithe? What's the matter?"

"I can't see, sir. I can't see."

"Take it easy, relax. You've got a ticket out of here, we'll get you out of here in a hurry. You'll be going back to England. You'll be OK. Relax," Winters said, and started to move on.

Blithe began to get up. "Take it easy," Winters told him. "Stay still."

"I can see, I can see, sir! I can see you!"

Blithe got up and rejoined the company. "Never saw anything like it," Winters said. "He was that scared he blacked out. Spooky. This kid just completely could not see, and all he needed was somebody to talk to him for a minute and calm him down."

The company went into defensive position south of Carentan. The second day in this static situation, someone came down the hedgerow line asking for Pvts. Don Malarkey and Skip Muck. It was Fritz Niland. He found Muck, talked to him, then found Malarkey, and had only enough time to say good-bye; he was flying home.

A few minutes after Niland left, Muck came to Malarkey, "his impish Irish smile replaced by a frown." Had Niland explained to Malarkey why he was going home? No. Muck told the story.

The previous day Niland had gone to the 82nd to see his brother Bob, who had told Malarkey in London that if he wanted to be a hero, the Germans would see to it, fast, which had led Malarkey to conclude that Bob Niland had lost his nerve. Fritz Niland had just learned that his brother had been killed on D-Day. Bob's platoon had been surrounded, and he manned a machine gun, hitting the Germans with harassing fire until the platoon broke through the encirclement. He had used up several boxes of ammunition before getting killed.

Fritz Niland next hitched a ride to the 4th Infantry Division position, to see another brother who was a platoon leader. He too had been killed on D-Day, on Utah Beach. By the time Fritz returned to Easy Company, Father Francis Sampson was looking for him, to tell him that a third brother, a pilot in the China–Burma–India theater, had been killed that same week. Fritz was the sole surviving son, and the army wanted to remove him from the combat zone as soon as possible.

Fritz's mother had received all three telegrams from the War Department on the same day.

Father Sampson escorted Fritz to Utah Beach, where a plane flew him to London on the first leg of his return to the States.

With Carentan captured, the Americans had linked up and established a continuous line. Attention now shifted to the drive inland, through the hedgerows. It wasn't going well. Less than two weeks after the exultation over the success of D-Day came the letdown. On the left, Montgomery had promised to take Caen on D-Day, but he still didn't have it and showed no great urgency in going after it. His reluctance to attack (as the Americans saw it) led to a severe strain on the Alliance, and on the relations between Eisenhower and Montgomery specifically.

That the two men would have difficulty in dealing with each other was almost inevitable, given the contrasts between them. Eisenhower was gregarious, while Montgomery lived in isolation. Eisenhower mixed easily with his staff and discussed all decisions with his subordinates; Montgomery set himself up in a lonely camp, where he slept and ate in a wood-paneled trailer he had captured from Rommel in the desert. Montgomery wrote his directives by hand and handed them down from on high, while Eisenhower waited for general agreement among his staff and usually had his operations officer write the final directive. Montgomery had shunned the company of women after his wife's death and did not smoke or drink. Eisenhower was modest, Montgomery conceited. "I became completely dedicated to my profession," Montgomery once said of himself.

He had indeed made an intensive study of how to command. What he had not studied was how to get his ideas across. He always seemed to be talking down to people, and his condescension became more marked the more intensely he felt about a subject. Montgomery's arrogance offended even British officers, while most Americans found him insufferable. What one American called "his sharp beagle-like nose, the small grey eyes that dart about quickly like rabbits in a Thurber cartoon," his self-satisfaction, all irritated.

The personality differences were significant factors in the always strained Eisenhower-Montgomery relationship, but what mattered more was fundamental disagreement over strategy and tactics, and their different structural positions. Eisenhower's military theory was straightforward and aggressive. Like Grant in the Virginia Wilderness in 1864, he favored constant attack, all along the line. He was an advocate of the direct approach and put his faith in the sheer smashing power of great armies. He was once accused of having a mass-production mentality, which was true but beside the point. He came from a mass-production society, and like any good general he wanted to use his nation's strengths on the battlefield.

To Montgomery, "it was always very clear . . . that Ike and I were poles apart when it came to the conduct of the war." Montgomery believed in "unbalancing the enemy while keeping well-balanced myself." He wanted to attack on a narrow front, cut through the German lines, and dash on to his objective.

Further, Eisenhower was responsible to the Combined Chiefs of Staff, and beyond that body to the two governments. Montgomery was in theory responsible to Eisenhower, but in reality he looked to Field Marshal Alan Brooke, not Eisenhower, for guidance. Montgomery was the senior British officer on the Continent, and as such saw himself as responsible for his nation's interests. The British had neither the manpower nor the material resources to overwhelm the Germans, and they had learned from 1914 to 1918 that it was near suicidal for them to attempt to do so. The British strength was brains, not brawn. Montgomery proposed to defeat the Germans in France by outthinking and outmaneuvering them; Eisenhower wanted to outfight them.

The initial difficulty centered around the taking of Caen. Montgomery had promised it, did not have it, would not attack it. By mid-June, he was claiming that he had never intended to break out of the beachhead at Caen, on the direct road to Paris; rather, his strategy was to hold on the left while Bradley broke out on the right. His critics charge that he changed his plan because of his failure at Caen; Montgomery himself insisted that he had all along planned to pin the German panzers down in front of Caen while Gen. Omar Bradley outflanked them. There is a fierce, continuing, and unresolvable controversy among military experts on this point.

On July 1, Eisenhower went to Normandy to see what he could do to galvanize his commanders. He told Bradley he was bringing "nothing but a bedroll, one aide and an orderly" and wanted "nothing but a trench with a piece of canvas over it." He stayed five days visiting with troops, inspecting the battlefield, talking with Bradley and the American corps and division commanders.

None of them liked having Eisenhower around because their various headquarters were all subject to sporadic German artillery fire. Eisenhower's old friend Lt. Gen. Wade Haislip, commanding the XV Corps, told him flatly to get out. "Don't think I'm worrying about your possible demise," he added. "I just don't want it said that I allowed the Supreme Commander to get killed in my corps area. Now if you want to get killed, go into some other area."

At one point Eisenhower commandeered a jeep and, accompanied by his British aide, Col. James Gault, and an orderly, with no other escort, personally drove around the countryside, and even managed to wander behind the German lines. No startling events occurred, and he did not know he had been in danger until he reached 90th Division headquarters and was told where he had been. The GIs were delighted to see Eisenhower driving the jeep and shouted and whistled as he drove past.

On July 4, Eisenhower went to a fighter airfield; while there, he learned that a mission was about to be flown. Eisenhower said he wanted to go along in order to see the hedgerow country from the air. Bradley, who was with him, demurred, but Eisenhower insisted. His last words, as he climbed into a Mustang, were, "All right, Brad, I am not going to fly to Berlin."

When he got back to his headquarters, disappointed at the lack of progress in the hedgerows, despairing of ever breaking out in that awful country, British Air Marshal Arthur Tedder and Chief of Staff Walter Smith both told him that it was all Montgomery's fault. They insisted that Eisenhower had to force him to act. Tedder complained that Montgomery was unjustly blaming the air forces for his own failure and said that "the Army did not seem prepared to fight its own battles."

Eisenhower wrote a letter to Montgomery, but it was too weak —more a statement of desired objectives than a firm order—to impel action. On July 12, Patton commented in his diary, "Ike is bound hand and foot by the British and does not know it. Poor fool. We actually have no Supreme Commander—no one who can take hold and say that this shall be done and that shall not be done." There was a general uneasy feeling around SHAEF that Eisenhower would never take hold of Montgomery. Gossips at SHAEF were speculating on "who would succeed Monty if sacked."

'For you the war is over,' and these German POWs – officers and enlisted men on board an LST headed away from Normandy toward England – couldn't be happier.
Below: Old men and boys made up much of the German army manning the Atlantic Wall. These kids look as if they have not even reached their teens. They should have been spanked, not shot.

THREE PHOTOS: U.S. ARMY SIGNAL CORPS

The end of the day at Omaha Beach. American men and equipment coming ashore in staggering numbers. One pilot thought, as he looked down on this scene on June 6, that Hitler must have been mad to think he could beat the United States.

U.S. COAST GUARD

OPPOSITE:
Middle: A German soldier lies dead outside a machine-gun emplacement he so vainly defended at Les Dunes de Madeleine, Utah Beach, June 6. He was almost surely running from the emplacement when he got shot; he was probably trying to surrender; whether a GI or his German sergeant shot him cannot be said.
Bottom: A young GI wants to see the papers of two even younger Germans, Utah Beach, June 7. Hitler was certain that his youngsters, raised in the Hitler Youth, would outfight the American kids raised in the Boy Scouts. Hitler was wrong.

Easy Company, 506th PIR, hams it up for the cameras on June 7 in the village square of Ste. Marie-du-Mont, which the company liberated on June 6, in the process knocking out a battery of German 105mm cannon.

Right: Pvt. Forrest Guth in a captured German helmet; *below:* Pvts. John Eubanks and Walter Gordon display the Nazi flag they seized as a souvenir; *bottom;* Pvts. Guth, Frank Mellet, David Morris, Daniel West, Floyd Talbert and C.T. Smith of Easy Company pose with three infantrymen from the 4th Division *(back row)* who had come in from Utah Beach.

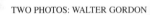

TWO PHOTOS: WALTER GORDON

FORREST GUTH

U.S. COAST GUARD

A part of the continuous stream of men and equipment sailing from England to France, June 7. In the background, a rhino ferry loaded with ambulances eases toward the beach. They kept coming, without pause, for eleven months.

Below: The men of Easy Company in the square at Ste. Marie-du-Mont meet some local belles; the girls have eyes only for the GIs, while the older residents of the village pose for the cameraman.

U.S. ARMY SIGNAL CORPS

Normandy, July 6. A captured German sits on the side of his vehicle, practically ignored by the GIs, who are more interested in the intricacies of his machine pistol. The hedge growing out of the stone wall gives some idea of what superb defensive positions the Germans had available to them.

Below: Unidentified American troops moving into the battle in the hedgerow country. This is not particularly heavy growth; in many cases the treetops met over the sunken lanes.

FIVE PHOTOS: U.S. ARMY SIGNAL CORPS

The first lesson for infantry-men is to learn to love the ground.

Above: As his buddies keep watch, a GI takes a break to wolf down his K-rations – biscuits and cheese.

Right: Two GIs from the 4th Division, in combat since D-Day, catch some rest. They have the necessities of war surrounding their foxhole: ammo clips, hand grenades, water, rations and bandages in their musette bags.

Bottom: A mortar crew from the 35th Infantry Division at work. The GI on the phone is calling out the adjustments from a forward observer.

Normany suffered terribly. This is the village of Cerisy-la-Salle, July 25. Sgt. David Weiss appears to be telling the little girl – the only person alive in the village – that it is going to be OK. I love this photo, which seems to me to sum up the essential quality of the GI. He came to liberate, not to terrorize.

OPPOSITE:

Top: Sgt. Curtis Culin, of Cranford, New Jersey, in Normandy, July 30. Culin exemplified the citizen soldier: a prewar mechanic, he was one of the men responsible for the rhino, equipment that, when welded to the front of his Sherman tank, made it possible for armor to break through the hedgerows and provide fire support for attaching infantry.

Bottom: GIs outside the German placement office in Argentan, France, August 20, celebrate putting it out of business.

Paris, August 26. Sgt Kenneth Averill of 4th Division gets a welcome. The old folks beam their approval. The liberation of the city set off one of the great parties of all time. Unfortunately for the men of the 4th Division, they didn't get to participate – they marched through the city and back into battle the same day. *Below:* Hotel Majestic, Paris, August 26. The hotel had been a German occupation headquarters; now it was a temporary POW cage.

FOUR PHOTOS: U.S. ARMY SIGNAL CORPS

The Hurtgen in 1944 had a marked resemblance to the wilderness in Virginia in 1864 – a terrible place to be, much less to have to mount an infantry offensive. Here Pvt. Maurice Berzon, Sgt. Bernard Spurr, and Sgt. Harold Glessler take a break.

Below: The Hurtgen was also a terrible place to have to defend, as the face of this German POW, captured on December 12, reveals. An unidentified GI from the 9th Division is doing the interrogation.

The Third Platoon, Easy Company, 506th PIR, loads into ten-ton trailers at Mourmelon, France, on the afternoon of December 18. The Germans had broken through the American lines in the Ardennes. Short on food, ammunition, and winter clothing, Easy still had to get to Bastogne before the Germans.

FORREST GUTH

Above: Sgt. Carwood Lipton in his foxhole outside Bastogne. Easy Company was in this position for nearly a month, fighting on the defensive, hurling back everything the SS Panzer divisions could throw at them, enduring the prevailing cold.

Left: Capt. Ronald Speirs, who took command of Easy in mid-January and led it on an offensive into the village of Foy. Speirs was even tougher than he looks, an outstanding rifle company commander, highly respected by the men.

FOUR PHOTOS: U.S. ARMY SIGNAL CORPS

Sgt. Carl Butler, 1st Division, Belgium, December 22, peers out from his armored car.

Bottom: Two teenage boys a long way from home. The German soldier is better dressed for the conditions than his American guard. He was also luckier – he had made it safely into POW status and was headed toward the rear, and eventually to the United States, where he would do farm labor until the war was over. His guard had to carry on.

Right: Two unidentified GIs ham it up with their cold rations for the photographer, Soy, Belgium December 26.

Below: Sgt. Joseph Arnaldo, an infantry squad leader, comes off the line after ten days in the Ardennes, December 30. He has what the soldiers called the thousand-yard stare.

Below: Sgt. William Howard, 79th Division, in the Scheibenhardt area, January 2.

The January cold was intense. By February, mud was the problem. The tension was always there.

Right: Sgt. Joseph Holmes, 35th Division, Belgium, January 10.

Below: Pvt. Morton Frenberg, 8th Division, February 24.

FIVE PHOTOS: U.S. ARMY SIGNAL CORPS

TWO PHOTOS: U.S. ARMY SIGNAL CORPS

Above: Medics at work on an unidentified wounded GI. In training camp, the medics were derided. In combat they were called Doc and universally praised.

Left: Medics helping an unidentified GI to the aid station. The GIs were convinced there was an army regulation against dying if you made it alive to the aid station. The GI on the left has all the look of a just-arrived replacement, including new boots.

To Eisenhower, this simple solution was out of the question because of Montgomery's popularity with the British troops, Brooke, and the British public. Further, Eisenhower had no right to remove the senior British command. The Supreme Commander seems to have been the only man at SHAEF to recognize these obvious truths, and they provide the answer to the nagging question, Why did Eisenhower put up with Montgomery? He had no choice. He had to cooperate with the difficult and exasperating British general, for Montgomery's place in the command structure was secure.

The real threat to Montgomery's position was Tedder's recommendation that Eisenhower move his headquarters to Normandy and take personal control of the land battle. Montgomery knew that he needed to buy time, not so much to protect his position as to keep Eisenhower in England so that he could run the land battle.

On July 18, Montgomery finally launched an attack, code name Goodwood. In its initial stages, assisted by the tremendous air bombardment, it went well. But after Montgomery lost 401 tanks and suffered 2,600 casualties, he called it off. The British Second Army had taken Caen, gained a few square miles, and inflicted heavy casualties on the Germans, but there had been nothing like a breakthrough. Montgomery announced that he was satisfied with the results.

Eisenhower was angry. He thundered that it had taken more than seven thousand tons of bombs to gain seven miles and that the Allies could hardly hope to go through France paying a price of a thousand tons of bombs per mile. Tedder blamed Montgomery for "the Army's failure," and SHAEF officers wondered aloud whether Montgomery should be made a peer and sent to the House of Lords or given the governorship of Malta.

This was all wild and irresponsible talk. After the war Eisenhower said he felt the powers of a supreme commander should be greater, that he should have the right to dismiss any subordinate, whatever his nationality. But even had Eisenhower had that power in 1944, he would not have exercised it. Sensitive to the morale factor and keenly aware of Montgomery's great popularity, he would not consider asking for Montgomery's removal.

At Smith's and Tedder's urging, Eisenhower sent a letter to Montgomery. *"Time is vital,"* he said, and he urged Montgomery to resume the attack. Many American officers thought that Montgomery hesitated because of the critical British manpower situation. The United Kingdom could no longer make good the losses in the Second Army, so it could not afford the cost in casualties of an all-out attack. Eisenhower argued that an attack now would save lives in the long run.

Everyone was depressed and irritable. After seven weeks of fighting, the deepest Allied penetrations were some twenty-five to thirty miles inland, on a front of only eighty miles, hardly enough room to maneuver or to bring in the American forces waiting in England for deployment. The Americans were still struggling in the hedgerow country, measuring their advance in yards rather than miles. Goodwood had failed and Montgomery refused to mount another attack. The newspapers were full of the ugly word "stalemate."

There were two bright spots. Ultra radio intercepts revealed that the Germans were stretched to the limit, and Bradley was working on a plan, code name Cobra, to break out on the right. As Eisenhower noted in his letter to Montgomery, "Now we are pinning our hopes on Bradley."

By July 23, the Americans had landed a total of 770,000 troops in Normandy. First Army had suffered 73,000 casualties. The British and Canadians had landed 591,000 troops and suffered 49,000 casualties. There was a large, immediately available reserve of American divisions in England waiting to enter the battle. The Germans in Normandy, meanwhile, had twenty-six divisions in place, six of them armored, to face the AEF's thirty-four divisions. As the Allies were on the offensive, their superiority on the ground was only marginal; in addition, the German Fifteenth Army was still intact in the Pas de Calais, which meant that the German ability to reinforce was greater than that of the Allies.

Eisenhower's great advantage continued to be control of the air. Bradley planned to use it in Operation Cobra to break through the German lines; once he was through, Eisenhower intended to rush divisions over from England, activate Patton's Third Army, and send it racing for Brittany to open the ports there.

The problem with air power was weather; it was a weapon that could be used only under suitable conditions. Cobra was scheduled to begin on July 21. That day Eisenhower flew over to Normandy to witness the beginning. The sky was overcast and his B-25 was the only plane in the air. By the time he arrived it was raining hard. Bradley told him the attack had been called off and dressed him down for flying in such weather. Eisenhower tossed away his soggy cigarette, smiled, and said his only pleasure in being Supreme Commander was that nobody could ground him.

"When I die," he added, looking at the steady rain, "they ought to hold my body for a rainy day and then bury me out in the middle of a storm. This damned weather is going to be the death of me yet."

The next day, as the rains continued, he flew back to London; on the twenty-fourth, still waiting for a clear day, he wired Bradley, urging him to an all-out effort when the weather permitted. "A break through at this juncture will minimize the total cost," he said, and added that he wanted First Army to "pursue every advantage with an ardor verging on recklessness." If it broke through, "the results will be incalculable."

Bradley hardly needed urging, but Montgomery did. Eisenhower wanted Second Army to attack when Cobra began—indeed he had promised Bradley he would see to it—so after sending his message to Bradley, Eisenhower flew to Montgomery's headquarters. What he wanted, as Smith noted, was "an all-out co-ordinated attack by the entire Allied line, which would at last put our forces in decisive motion. He was up and down the line like a football coach, exhorting everyone to aggressive action."

All this was highly irritating to Montgomery and Brooke. "It is quite clear that Ike considers that [General Miles] Dempsey [commanding Second Army] should be doing more than he does," Brooke wrote to Montgomery. "It is equally clear that Ike has the very vaguest conception of war." The British officers agreed that Eisenhower had no notion of balance. If everybody was to attack, Montgomery argued, nobody would have the strength to make a decisive breakthrough or to exploit it. Eisenhower "evidently . . . has some conception of attacking on the whole front," Brooke complained, "which must be an American doctrine."

Tedder too was unhappy with Eisenhower, but as usual he disagreed with Montgomery and Brooke. Cobra got started on the morning of July 25; that day Tedder called Eisenhower on the telephone, demanding to know why Montgomery was not doing more and what Eisenhower was doing about it. Eisenhower said he had talked with Churchill and that they were satisfied that this time Montgomery's attack would be in earnest. Tedder "rather uh-huhed, being not at all satisfied, and implying the PM must have sold Ike a bill of goods." Eisenhower told his aide Capt. Harry Butcher of the conversation and said he thought he could work things out satisfactorily, for "there's nothing so wrong a good victory won't cure."

To get that victory, to get through the hedgerows, junior officers in the tank units had been experimenting with various techniques and methods. One idea that worked was to bring to the front the specially equipped dozer tanks (tanks with a blade mounted on the front similar to those on commercial bulldozers) used on the beaches on D-Day. They could cut through a hedgerow well enough, but there were too few of them—four per division—to have much impact. A rush order back to the States for 278 bulldozer blades was put in, but it would take weeks to fill.

In the 747th Tank Battalion, attached to the 29th Division, someone—name unknown—suggested using demolitions to blow gaps in the hedgerows. After some experimenting the tankers discovered that two fifty-pound explosive charges laid against the bank would blow a hole in a hedgerow big enough for a Sherman tank to drive through. Once on the other side, the tank could fire its cannon into the far corners, using white phosphorous shells, guaranteed to burn out the Germans at the machine-gun pits, and hose down the hedgerow itself with its .50-caliber machine gun. Infantry could follow the tank into the field and mop up what remained when the tanker got done firing.

Good enough, excellent even. But when the planners turned to the logistics of getting the necessary explosives to the tanks, they discovered that each tank company would need seventeen tons of explosives to advance a mile and a half. The explosives were not available in such quantities, and even had they been the transport problems involved in getting them to the front were too great.

An engineer suggested drilling holes in the embankment and placing smaller charges in them. That worked, too—except that it took forever to dig holes large enough and deep enough in the bank because of the vines and roots, and the men doing the digging were exposed to German mortar fire.

A tanker in the 747th suggested welding two pipes of four feet in length and six inches in diameter to the front of a tank, reinforced by angle irons. The tank could ram into the hedgerow and back off leaving two sizable holes for explosives. The engineers learned to pack their explosives into expended 105mm artillery shell casings, which greatly increased the efficiency of the charges and made transport and handling much easier. Some tankers discovered that if the pipes were bigger, sometimes that was enough to allow a Sherman to plow right on through, at least with the smaller hedge-rows. Other experiments were going on all across Normandy. The U.S. First Army was starting to get a grip on the problem.

One major part of the problem, as the tankers saw it, was the Sherman tank. It was universally denounced by anyone who had to fight in one against a German Panther or Tiger. The Sherman was a thirty-two-ton tank; the Panther was forty-three tons; the Tiger was fifty-six tons. The Sherman's 75mm cannon could not pene-trate the heavy armor of the German tanks, while the Panther's 75, and of course the Tiger's 88, easily penetrated the Sherman. But one thing about the Shermans—there were a lot more of them than there were Panthers or Tigers. In 1944, German industry produced 24,630 tanks, only a handful of them Tigers. The British built 24,843. But the Americans turned out the staggering total of 88,410, mainly Shermans, and then managed to ship most of them to Europe, a few thousand to the Pacific.

For all their shortcomings, the Shermans were a triumph of American mass-production techniques. First of all, they were won-derfully reliable, in sharp contrast to the Panthers and Tigers. In addition, GIs were far more experienced in the workings of the internal combustion engine than were their opposite numbers. The Americans were also infinitely better at recovering damaged tanks and patching them up to go back into action; the Germans had nothing like the American maintenance battalions.

Indeed no army in the world had such a capability. Within two days of being put out of action by German shells, about half the damaged Shermans had been repaired by maintenance battalions and were back on the line. Kids who had been working at gas stations and body shops two years earlier had brought their mechanical skills to Normandy, where they replaced damaged tank tracks, welded patches on the armor, and repaired engines. Even the tanks beyond repair were dragged back to the maintenance depot by the Americans and stripped for parts. The Germans just left theirs where they were.

The Red Army had its own tanks, the T-34s (American-designed, and perhaps the best tank of the war). What it needed was trucks. The American Lend-Lease program supplied thousands of Studebaker trucks (surely a capitalist plot!). When the spark plugs clogged, as they quickly did on the dirt roads, the Russians just walked away from the trucks. The American armored division maintenance crews had men who worked day and night sand-blasting plugs. When they ran out of blasting sand they sent men to the beach to get more. It had to be dried and sifted before it could be used, but it did the job.

Nearly all this work was done as if the crews were back in the States, rebuilding damaged cars and trucks—that is, the men on the shop floor made their own decisions, got out their tools, and got after the job. One of their officers, Capt. Belton Cooper, commented, "I began to realize something about the American Army I had never thought possible before. Although it is highly regimented and bureaucratic under garrison conditions, when the Army gets in the field, it relaxes and the individual initiative comes forward and does what has to be done. This type of flexibility was one of the great strengths of the American Army in World War II."

Thanks to American productivity and ingenuity, there were many more Shermans in action than Panthers or Tigers (in fact, about half the Wehrmacht's tanks in Normandy were Mark IVs, twenty-six tons). Besides numbers, the Shermans had other advantages. They used less than half the gasoline of the larger tanks. They were faster and more maneuverable, with double and more the range. A Sherman's tracks lasted for 2,500 miles; the Panther's and Tiger's more like 500. The Sherman's turret turned much faster than that of the Panther or Tiger. In addition, the narrower track of the Sherman made it a much superior road vehicle. But the wider track of the Panther and Tiger made them more suited to soft terrain.

And so it went. For every advantage of the German heavy tanks, there was a disadvantage, as for the American medium tanks. The trouble in Normandy was that the German tanks were better designed for hedgerow fighting. If and when the battle ever became a mobile one, the situation would reverse. Then the much-despised Sherman could show its stuff.

American transport and utility vehicles were far superior to the German counterpart. For example, the jeep and the deuce-and-a-half (two-and-a-half-ton) truck had four-wheel-drive capability, and they were more reliable than the German vehicles. But again like the Sherman, their advantages did not show in the hedgerows, where squad-size actions predominated and the mass movement of large numbers of troops over long distances was irrelevant.

With any weapon, design differences lead to losses as well as gains. The German potato masher, for example, could be thrown farther in part because it was lighter. It had less than half the explosive power of the American grenade. The GIs said it made more noise than damage.

One other point about weapons. Over four decades of interviewing former GIs, I've been struck by how often they tell stories about duds, generally about shells falling near their foxholes and failing to explode. Lt. George Wilson of the 4th Division said that after one shelling near St.-Lo, "I counted eight duds sticking in the ground within thrity yards of my foxhole." There are no statistics available on this phenomenon, nor is there any evidence on why, but I've never heard a German talk about American duds. The shells fired by the GIs were made by free American labor; the shells fired by the Wehrmacht were made by slave labor from Poland, France, and throughout the German empire. And at least some of the slaves must have mastered the art of turning out shells that passed examination but were nevertheless sabotaged effectively.

(In 1998, I received a letter from a man who identified himself as a Jewish slave laborer in a German factory making panzerfaust shells. He said he and his fellow slaves had discovered that if they mixed sand in with the sulfur they could render the explosive inoperable, and that they could do it when the German inspectors' heads were turned. He said only German soldiers put on the final touch, the trigger mechanism. But those German soldiers liked to take breaks. When they did, the slaves speeded up their output but in the process screwed up the mechanism. The German soldiers were glad to have a higher output and never inspected the shells that had been produced while they were on break. That, he said proudly, was his contribution, and he was glad to see from the story about German duds in *Citizen Soldiers* that the GIs had noticed and lives had been saved.)

A major shortcoming of the Sherman for hedgerow fighting was its unarmored underbelly, which made it particularly vulnerable to the panzerfaust when it tried to climb a hedgerow. British tanks without infantry support had been unable to make significant progress at Caen; American infantry without tank support were unable to take St.-Lo, the key crossroads city in lower Normandy. Lt. Col. Fritz Ziegelmann of the 352nd Division attributed the German success in holding St.-Lo to "the surprising lack of tanks. Had tanks supported the American infantry on June 16, St. Lo would not have been in German hands any longer that evening."

Another reason St.-Lo wasn't in American hands: Normandy had its wettest July in forty years. One Marauder unit, the 323rd Group, had seventeen straight missions scrubbed during the first two and a half weeks of July. Others fared little better. Perhaps more than any other single factor, this bad weather explains the relative German success in Normandy in the early summer of 1944. Rain and fog made it possible for them to move reinforcements and supplies to the front.

There was nothing the Americans could do about the weather, but they could go after their problems in getting tanks into the hedgerow fighting. In so doing, they showed their mechanical ability and talents, and their ingenuity and resourcefulness. Rommel was impressed by the effort and results, saying that he thought the Americans "showed themselves to be very advanced in the tactical handling of their forces" and that they "profited much more than the British from their experiences."

Experiments involved welding pipes or steel teeth onto the front of the Sherman tank. Lt. Charles Green, a tanker in the 29th Division, devised a bumper that was made from salvaged railroad tracks that Rommel had used as beach obstacles. It was incredibly strong and permitted the Shermans to bull their way through the thickest hedgerows. In the 2nd Armored Division, Sgt. Curtis Culin designed and supervised the construction of a hedgerow-cutting device made from scrap iron pulled from a German roadblock. The blades gave the tank a resemblance to a rhinoceros, so Shermans equipped with Culin's invention were known as rhino tanks.

Another big improvement was in communications. After a series of experiments with telephones placed on the back of the tank, the solution that worked best was to have an interphone box on the tank, into which the infantryman could plug a radio handset. The handset's long cord permitted the GI to lie down behind or underneath the tank while talking to the tank crew, which, when buttoned down, was all but blind. Many, perhaps a majority, of the tank commanders killed in action had been standing in the open turret, so as to see. Now, at least in some situations, the tank could stay buttoned up while the GI on the phone acted as a forward artillery observer.

These improvements, and others, have prompted Michael Doubler to write in his prize-winning *Closing with the Enemy: How GIs Fought the War in Europe*, "In its search for solutions to the difficulties of hedgerow combat, the American army encouraged the free flow of ideas and the entrepreneurial spirit. Coming from a wide variety of sources, ideas generally flowed upward from the men actually engaged in battle."

They were learning by doing.

THE DEFEAT OF GERMANY
AUGUST 1944 - MAY 1945

———— Front Line Sept.14/44 ▪▬▪▬▪ Front Line Dec.16/44
- - - - Front Line Mar.28/45 ▲▲▲▲▲ Front Line May 7/45

⊽ Operation Market-Garden, Sept.17 - Dec.16/44
① Battle of the Bulge Dec.16/44 - Feb.7/45
② U.S. First Army Rhine Crossing (Remagen Bridge)
   Mar.7/45
③ U.S. Third Army Rhine Crossing Mar.22/45
④ Br. Second Army Rhine Crossing Mar.23/45
⑤ Link-up of Twelfth Army Group and Sixth Army Group
⑥ U.S.-Russia Official Link-up (Torgau)

MILES 100
KM 100

GREAT BRITAIN

London

ENGLISH CHANNEL

Dover

Dieppe

Le Havre

Caen

Falaise

Argentan

Alençon

Le Mans

Angers

Tours

Orléans

LOIRE R.

F   R   A   N   C   E

Chartres

Mantes

Paris

Melun

SEINE R.

AG 21
MONTGOMERY

AG 12
BRADLEY

Rouen

Amiens

U.S.
XIX

U.S. V

U.S. VII

CAN. FIRST
CRERAR

BR. SECOND
DEMPSEY

U.S. FIRST
HODGES

U.S. THIRD
PATTON

Boulogne

Calais

Dunkirk

Ostend

SCHELDT ESTUARY

Antwerp

BELGIUM

Brussels

Namur

Dinant

Liège

Aachen

Colog

Amsterdam

Rotterdam

NETHERLANDS

Arnhem

RHINE R.

Nijmegen

Eindhoven

Wes

4/18

CAN. FIR

CAN. I

VII

XVIII

①
Bastogne

LUX.

VIII

101st AB

XII

III

Metz

Reims

MARNE R.

U.S. XX

Verdun

St.Mihiel

MEUSE R.

U.S. XII

Troyes

U.S. XV

Épina

C   E

U.S. SEVENTH

AG 6
DEVERS

9/11/44
FR. II

⑤

Dijon

FR. FIR

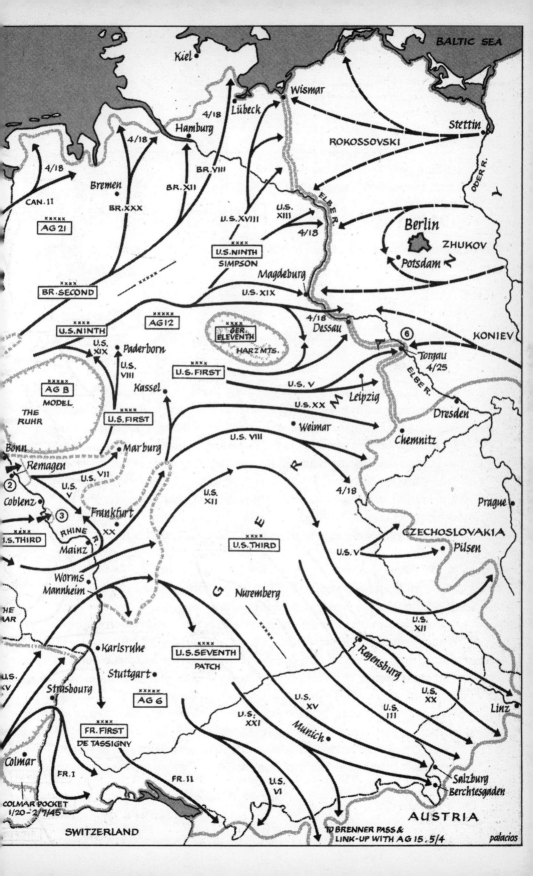

BALTIC SEA

Kiel

Wismar

Lübeck
4/18
Hamburg

Stettin

ROKOSSOVSKI

ODER R.

4/18

Bremen

BR. VIII
BR. XII
BR. XXX

CAN. II

Berlin
ZHUKOV

ELBE R.

U.S.
XIII

U.S. XVIII

4/18

AG 21

Potsdam

U.S. NINTH
SIMPSON

Magdeburg

BR. SECOND

U.S. XIX

KONIEV

AG 12

Dessau
4/18

U.S. NINTH

Paderborn

GER.
ELEVENTH

HARZ MTS.

Torgau
4/25

U.S.
XIX

U.S.
VIII

ELBE R.

(6)

U.S. FIRST

AG B

Kassel

MODEL

THE
RUHR

U.S. FIRST

U.S. V

Leipzig

Dresden

U.S. XX

Bonn

Remagen

Marburg

U.S. VII

Weimar

Chemnitz

(2)

U.S.
V

U.S. VIII

R

Coblenz

(3)

Frankfurt

U.S.
XII

Prague

U.S. THIRD

RHINE

XX

E

Mainz

CZECHOSLOVAKIA

Worms

U.S. THIRD

U.S. V

Pilsen

Mannheim

G

Nuremberg

U.S.
XII

Karlsruhe

U.S. SEVENTH

Regensburg

Stuttgart

PATCH

U.S.
XX

Strasbourg

AG 6

U.S.
XV

U.S.
III

Linz

U.S.
XXI

FR. FIRST

DE TASSIGNY

Munich

Colmar

FR. I

FR. II

U.S.
VI

Salzburg
Berchtesgaden

COLMAR POCKET
1/20 - 2/7/45

AUSTRIA

SWITZERLAND

TO BRENNER PASS &
LINK-UP WITH AG 15. 5/4

palacios

12

Breakout and Pursuit

From the high command down to the lowliest private, the Americans in Normandy applied everything they had learned to the mounting of Operation Cobra, including a massive air bombardment, forward observers in small planes and at the front lines calling in artillery fire, tanks slicing through hedgerows with their rhinos, and infantry moving forward before the smoke cleared, not pausing to help a wounded buddy or ducking behind a bit of shelter and letting the others go ahead. The shock of the bombardment and the elan of the infantry were sufficient to drive the Germans from their positions.

The breakthrough was a great feat of arms. First Army had accomplished something that had been nearly impossible in 1914–1918, and not achieved by the British in front of Caen in June–July 1944. First Army had accomplished something that it had not been trained or equipped to do, in the process developing an air-ground team unmatched in the world. Now, along with Third Army, it was finally going to get into a campaign for which it had been trained and equipped.

The dean of American military historians, Russell Weigley, referring to the flow of GIs that poured around the German open flank, writes in his classic study *Eisenhower's Lieutenants,* "This virtual road march was war such as the American army was designed for, especially the American armored divisions. Appealing also to the passion for moving on that is so much a part of the American character and heritage, it brought out the best in the troops, their energy and mechanical resourcefulness. . . .

"Now that Cobra had achieved the breakout, the most mobile army in the world for the first time since D-Day could capitalize on its mobility." Weigley further notes that with the hard-won mobility, "the issues confronting the army became for the first time in Europe strategic rather than tactical. The soldiers' battle of Normandy was about to become the generals' battle of France."

With the German left flank in the air, and the Allies facing an open road to Paris, Patton was activated and all his pent-up energy turned loose. He had come over in time for Cobra, to familiarize himself with the situation and to set up Third Army headquarters. He took command of one of the corps already in Normandy and had other divisions coming in from England.* By August 1, he had divisions attacking in four directions. Meanwhile First Army pressed forward to the south as German resistance collapsed.

As the general German retreat began, the American air-ground team pounded the enemy. The Wehrmacht was out of the hedge-rows, out in the open, trying desperately to move by day to get away. Patton's tanks mauled them, the Jabos (the German term for the Allied fighter-bombers) terrorized them.

"I had seen the first retreat from Moscow," Sgt. Helmut Gunther of the 17th Panzer Grenadiers recalled, "which was terrible enough, but at least units were still intact. Here, we had become a cluster of individuals. We were not a battleworthy company any longer. All that we had going for us was that we knew each other very well."

The P-47s responded to calls from the tankers and infantry over the radio, descended on their targets, and hit them with napalm, 500-pound bombs, rockets, and .50-caliber machine-gun fire. Destroyed German tanks, trucks, scout cars, wagons, and artillery pieces, along with dead and wounded horses and men, covered the landscape.

---

* When Third Army was activated, Gen. Courtney Hodges succeeded Bradley as First Army commander while Bradley moved up to command Twelfth Army Group (First and Third Armies).

Capt. Belton Cooper described the Allied teamwork. When two Panther tanks threatened his maintenance company from across a hedgerow, the liaison officer in a Sherman got on its radio to give the coordinates to any Jabos in the area. "Within less than 45 seconds, two P-47's appeared right over the tree tops traveling like hell at 300 feet." They let go their bombs a thousand feet short of Cooper's location: "It seemed like the bombs were going to land square in the middle of our area." He and his men dove into their foxholes.

The bombs went screaming over. The P-47s came screaming in right behind them, firing their eight .50-caliber machine guns. The bombs hit a German ammunition dump. "The blast was awesome; flames and debris shot some 500 ft. into the air. There were bogie wheels, tank tracks, helmets, backpacks and rifles flying in all directions. The hedgerow between us and the German tanks protected us from the major direct effects of the blast, however, the tops of trees were sheared off and a tremendous amount of debris came down on us."

"I have been to two church socials and a county fair," said one P-47 pilot, "but I never saw anything like this before!"

The Jabos were merciless. The constant attacks inevitably broke up German units, which had a terrible effect on morale. A theme that always comes up when interviewing German veterans is comradeship. So, too, with American veterans, of course, but there is an intensity about the Germans on the subject that is unique. One reason is that generally German squads were made up of men from the same town or region, so the men had known each other as children. Another is the experience of being caught in a debacle —Jabos overhead, artillery raining down, tanks firing from the rear.

Corp. Friedrich Bertenrath of the 2nd Panzer Division spoke to the point: "The worst thing that could happen to a soldier was to be thrown into some group in which he knew no one. In our unit, we would never abandon each other. We had fought in Russia together. We were comrades, and always came to the rescue. We protected our comrades so they could go home to their wives, children, and parents. That was our motivation. The idea that we would conquer the world had fallen long ago."

Lt. Walter Padberg of Grenadier Regiment 959 was appalled: "Everything was chaos. Allied artillery and airplanes were everywhere." Then, the worst possible happened: "I did not know any of the people around me." Padberg continued fleeing, essentially on his own even though in the midst of others. The retreat was turning into a rout.

A historic opportunity presented itself. As the British and Canadians picked up the attack on their front, Patton had open roads ahead of him, inviting his fast-moving armored columns to cut across the rear of the Germans—whose horse-drawn artillery and transport precluded rapid movement—encircle them and destroy the German army in France, then end the war with a triumphal unopposed march across the Rhine and on to Berlin.

Patton lusted to seize that opportunity. He had trained and equipped Third Army for just this moment. Straight east to Paris, then northwest along the Seine to seize the crossings, and the Allies would complete an encirclement that would lead to a bag of prisoners bigger than North Africa or Stalingrad. More important, it would leave the Germans defenseless in the west because Patton could cut off the German divisions in northern France, Belgium, and Holland as he drove for the Rhine.

That was the big solution. Obviously risky, if successful it promised the kind of big encirclements the Wehrmacht had achieved in 1940 in France and 1941 in the Soviet Union. But neither Eisenhower nor Bradley was bold enough to take it. They worried about Patton's flanks—he insisted that the Jabos could protect them. They worried about Patton's fuel and other supply— he insisted that in an emergency they could be airlifted to him.

Arguing over the merits of different generals is a favorite pastime of many military history buffs. It is harmless and often instructive. And we all have the right to pass judgment; that right comes from the act of participation. The American people had provided Generals Eisenhower and Bradley with a fabulous amount of weaponry and equipment, and some two million of their young men. There has to be an accounting of how well they used these assets to bring about the common goal. And how well means, Did they achieve the victory at the lowest cost in the shortest time? Were they prudent where prudence was appropriate? More important, given their superiority over the enemy, did they take appropriate risks that utilized the greatest assets their country had given them, air power and mobility?

In Normandy, in August, the answer is no. Ike and Bradley picked the safer alternative, the small solution. Thus was a great opportunity missed. But of course we know now that the risk was worth taking because we know the cost of finally overrunning Germany; in July 1944, Eisenhower and Bradley didn't.

They were also responding to their obsession with ports. They wanted the small ports of Brittany, such as St.-Malo, and the one big port, Brest. So they insisted that Patton stay with the pre-D-Day plan, with modifications. It had called for Patton to turn the whole of Third Army into Brittany; when he protested that being wedded to plans was a mistake and insisted that he wanted to attack toward Germany, not away from it, Eisenhower and Bradley relented to the extent that they gave him permission to reduce the Brittany attack to one corps, leaving two corps to head east.

Eisenhower had often said that in war, plans are everything before the battle begins, but once the shooting started plans were worthless. And back in 1926, when he had graduated first in his class at the Command and General Staff School at Fort Leavenworth, Patton had written to congratulate him, then to warn him to put all that Leavenworth stuff out of his mind from now on. "Victory in the next war," Patton had declared, "will depend on EXECUTION not PLANS."

To Patton, it was outrageous that his superiors wouldn't turn him loose. "I am so nauseated," he grumbled, "by the fact that Hodges and Bradley state that all human virtue depends on knowing infantry tactics." Patton thought that "Omar the tent maker," as he called Bradley, was never audacious enough. "Bradley and Hodges are such nothings," he wrote. "Their one virtue is that they get along by doing nothing. . . . They try to push all along the front and have no power anywhere."

Monty agreed with Patton. He, too, wanted to abandon the plan to overrun Brittany. He pointed out the obvious: "The main business lies to the East." He pointed out the not-so-obvious: if the Allies seized the opportunity before them, Brest and St.-Malo would not be needed. And indeed, in the event, St.-Malo held out to the end of the war—Hitler's orders—and Brest until late September. German destruction of the port facilities was so effective that it never made a significant contribution to the supply situation.

An entire corps of well-trained, well-equipped tankers, infantrymen, and artillery had been wasted at a critical moment. In the boxing analogy, Patton wanted to throw a roundhouse right and get the bout over; his superiors ordered him to throw a short right hook to knock the enemy off balance. But the enemy already was staggering. He should have been knocked out.

Instead of allowing Patton to go for the big solution, Eisenhower had him turn away from Paris and toward Falaise, where he wanted U.S. Third Army to join with the Canadians coming from Caen to encircle the German army in Normandy. This was accomplished, and although many thousands of individual Germans escaped, hardly any of them had any equipment or got out as part of an organized unit. Meanwhile the American and Canadian artillery and infantry and the Allied air force pounded the Germans inside the pocket.

For sheer ghastliness in World War II, nothing exceeded the experience of the Germans caught in the Falaise gap. Feelings of helplessness waved over them. They were in a state of total fear day and night. They seldom slept. They dodged from bomb crater to bomb crater. "It was complete chaos," Pvt. Herbert Meier remembered. "That's when I thought, This is the end of the world."

The word "chaos" was used by every survivor of the retreat interviewed for *Citizen Soldiers*. German army, corps, and division headquarters got out first and were on the far side of the Seine, headed toward the Siegfried Line. In the pocket, most junior officers felt like the enlisted men, it was every man for himself.

The farmhouses were abandoned; rations consisted of whatever one could find in the cellars. "It was terrible," Lt. Gunter Materne recalled, "especially for those lying there in pain. It was terrible to see men screaming, 'Mother!' or 'Take me with you, don't leave me here! I have a wife and child at home. I'm bleeding to death!' "

Lieutenant Padberg explained: "Honestly said, you did not

stop to consider whether you could help this person when you were running for your life. One thought only of oneself."

Private Meier recalled "one of the officers from the occupation, who had had a nice life in France, tried to get through in a troop truck filled with goodies and his French girlfriend. With wounded men lying right there. So we stopped him, threw him and his girlfriend out, along with all of their things, and laid the wounded in the truck.

"It was terrible," Meier went on. "I began to think everyone was crazy. I came across an airfield, the Luftwaffe had long since gone, all of the ground troops there were drunk."

"All shared a single idea," according to Corporal Bertenrath: "Out! Out! Out!"

All this time the 1,000-pound bombs, the 500-pound bombs, the rockets, the 105s and the 155s, the 75s on the Shermans, the mortars, and the .50-caliber machine-gun fire came down on the Germans. Along the roads and in the fields, dead cows, horses, and soldiers swelled in the hot August sun, their mouths agape, filled with flies. Maggots crawled through their wounds. Tanks drove over men in the way—dead or alive. Human and animal intestines made the roads slippery. Maj. William Falvey of the 90th Division recalled seeing "six horses hitched to a large artillery gun. Four horse were dead and two were still alive. The driver was dead but still had the reins in his hands." Those few men, German or American, who had not thrown away their gas masks had them on, to the envy of all the others. The stench was such that even pilots in the Piper Cubs threw up.

Lt. George Wilson of the 4th Division saw "dead German soldiers and dead and wounded horses and wrecked wagons scattered all along the road." He was astonished to discover that the Wehrmacht was a horse-drawn army, but impressed by the equipment. He had been raised on a farm and "I was amazed at such superb draft horses and accouterments. The harness work was by far the finest I had ever seen. The leather was highly polished, and all the brass rivets and hardware shone brightly. The horses had been groomed, with tails bobbed, as though for a parade." His men mercifully shot the wounded animals.

□

By August 18, a week after the lead American elements had reached Argentan, the 1st Polish Armored Division moved south, almost to the point of linking up with the U.S. 90th Division, finally released for a northward drive to close the gap. Still Germans escaped. One of them was Maj. Heinz Guderian, who recalled driving past the Poles, only a hundred meters away, in the rain, in the night, out of the pocket. He and his driver would go for two or three minutes, then stop for ten to listen. They made it out.

Lieutenant Padberg did, too. "When we made it out of the pocket," he recalled, "we were of the opinion that we had left hell behind us." He quickly discovered that the boundaries of hell were not so constricted. Once beyond the gap, Padberg ran into an SS colonel.

"Line up!" he bellowed. "Everyone is now under my command! We are going to launch a counterattack." There were twenty or so men in the area, none known to Padberg. He had a pistol only. The others shuffled into something like a line, Padberg said, "but unfortunately, I had to go behind a bush to relieve myself and missed joining the group behind the colonel."

Lt. Walter Kaspers got out, thanks to some unexpected help. "I moved only at night," he remembered. "By myself. I became dog tired. I came to a small farmhouse. I knocked and asked the girl if I could sleep in the barn. I pointed to the east and said that I was heading that way. She told me not to worry, allowed me to stay and even brought me a jug of milk and a few pieces of bread. I thanked her and pushed on the next day."

After telling the little story, Lieutenant Kaspers smiled and added, "Women are always better in these situations in war. They have a feeling for people in need."

Three German soldiers who got out had similar experiences. French farm wives fed them. In each case, the women explained that their sons were POWs in Germany and that they hoped some German mother was feeding their boys.

Even in the bloody chaos of Falaise, a humane spirit could come over these young men so far from home. Lt. Hans-Heinrich Dibbern, of Panzer Grenadier Regiment 902, set up a roadblock outside Argentan. "From the direction of the American line came an ambulance driving toward us," he remembered. "The driver was obviously lost. When he noticed that he was behind German lines, he slammed on the brakes." Dibbern went to the ambulance. "The driver's face was completely white. He had wounded men he was responsible for. But we told him, 'Back out of here and get going— we don't attack the Red Cross.' He quickly disappeared."

An hour or so later, "here comes another Red Cross truck. It pulls up right in front of us. The driver got out, opened the back, and took out a crate. He set it down on the street and drove away. We feared a bomb, but nothing happened and we were curious. We opened the box and it was filled with Chesterfield cigarettes."

The Battle of Normandy was over. It had lasted seventy-five days. It had cost the Allies 209,672 casualties, 39,976 dead. Two-thirds of the losses were American. It cost the Germans around 450,000 men, 240,000 of them killed or wounded. Of the approximately 1,500 tanks committed to Normandy by the Wehrmacht, a total of sixty-seven got out, and only twenty-four of these got across the Seine. The Germans left behind 3,500 artillery pieces and 20,000 vehicles.

But between 20,000 and 40,000 Wehrmacht and SS soldiers got out. They had but a single thought: get home. Home meant Germany, prepared defensive positions in the Siegfried Line, fresh supplies, reinforcements, a chance to sort out the badly mixed troops into fighting units. They had taken a terrible pounding, but they were not as sure as SHAEF G-2 that they had "had it."

The German rout was so complete that not only did the retreating troops not carry supplies out with them, they didn't even take the time to destroy the supply dumps. Elements of Patton's Third Army captured tons of grain, flour, sugar, and rice, along with hundreds of carloads of coal, all of which the GIs distributed to the French civilian population. At another dump Patton's men captured 2.6 million pounds of frozen beef and 500,000 pounds of canned beef, which were distributed to the troops.

The GIs were getting all mixed up in their pell-mell pursuit. Sgt. Buddy Gianelloni remembered trucks going up and down the road, jeeps, tanks, half-tracks, and other combat vehicles headed toward the front. He came up on a battalion of African-American soldiers. "What outfit are you?" he asked.

"Artillery," was the reply. "What outfit are you guys?"

"The 79th Infantry."

According to Gianelloni, "This black guy, he almost turned white. He said, 'The boss done fucked up, he has got us here ahead of the infantry.' They had so many artillery battalions lined up there they was gun to gun."

In the 4th Infantry Division, Lt. George Wilson felt he was engaging in "a wild, mad, exciting race to see which army could gain the most ground in a single day." To the men of the 743rd Tank Battalion, 2nd Armored Division, it was "holiday warfare." There was a little shooting at occasional crossroads, but no casualties. Mainly this was because they had warning of trouble ahead— if the villages were bedecked with flowers and the people were lining the streets, holding out food and bottles of wine, the Germans had pulled out; if there was no reception committee, the Germans were still there.

At dusk on September 2, Shermans from the 743rd got to the crest of a hill overlooking Tournai, Belgium. They sat there looking, instead of moving down to be the first to cross the border, because they were out of gasoline. More Shermans came up; they had just enough fuel to get into town. Then they too were immobilized. The great supply crisis in ETO had hit the 743rd.

The crisis was inevitable. It had been foreseen. It could not have been avoided. Too many vehicles were driving too far away from the ports and beaches. The Red Ball Express, an improvised truck transport system that got started in late August, made every effort to get the fuel, food, and ammunition to the front lines. Drivers, mainly blacks in the Service of Supply, were on the road twenty hours a day, driving without lights at night. The deuce-and-a-half trucks were bumper-to-bumper on the one-way roads. Between August 29 and September 15, 6,000 trucks carried 135,000 tons of supplies on two highways running from St.-Lo to a supply dump near Chartres. At the dump the supplies were picked up by other drivers and taken to the front. But the front line continued to move east and north, and the system just couldn't keep up. From Le Havre and the Normandy beaches it was getting close to five hundred kilometers to the front. It took a lot of gasoline just to get the trucks back and forth.

To ease the burden, SHAEF was putting into place an extension onto PLUTO ("pipe line under the ocean," running from England to Omaha Beach), to move gasoline forward by pipe to Chartres. But it didn't get into operation until September 13. Even then it didn't help much. At Chartres, gasoline was put into jerry cans, which were loaded onto trucks that carried the fuel forward to the front-line vehicles. But among other crises in supply, ETO was short on the five-gallon jerry cans because so many GIs just threw them away after filling their tanks instead of putting them back on the truck.*

In the case of the 743rd, the battalion stayed in Tournai for four days, waiting for fuel. On September 7 the battalion filled its vehicles and took off. In one day it made 105 kilometers. On September 9, a day-long pause to wait for fuel. On September 10, another leap forward, to Fort Eben Emael close to the Dutch border. According to the battalion history, "it was a swashbuckling, almost skylarking campaign. There was no fighting and the job was to keep moving, looking for a fight."

The GIs got a wild welcome in the Belgian villages. "They cheered, and waved, and risked their lives to crowd up to the tanks in motion and in all the demonstrative ways of a happy people they showed their enthusiastic thanks." On September 12 the leading platoon of Charlie Company in the 743rd crossed the border into Holland, the first Americans to reach that country. The German border was but a few kilometers away.

Now there was opposition. German artillery boomed. Panzerfaust shells disabled a couple of Shermans. The other Shermans could still fire, but not move. Their fuel tanks were empty. And the Germans had gotten into the Siegfried Line. They had fuel problems, too, but as they were on the defensive they could dig their tanks in and use them as fortified batteries. Their supply lines had grown shorter—Aachen was just to the south, Dusseldorf and Cologne were just to the east.

They had reached home. Men who saw no point to fighting to retain Hitler's conquests in France were ready to fight to defend the homeland. The German officer corps began taking the terrified

---

* All across France today, those jerry cans are still there, serving innumerable purposes.

survivors of the rout in France and organizing them into squads, platoons, companies, battalions, divisions—and suddenly what had been a chaotic mob became an army again. Slave labor, meanwhile, worked on improving the neglected Siegfried Line. The Germans later called the transformation in their army and in the defensive works the Miracle of the West.

On August 19 Eisenhower told Montgomery and Bradley that it was his intention to take personal control of the land battle as soon as SHAEF could set up in France a forward command post with adequate communication facilities. He also outlined a plan of campaign that would send 21st Army Group northeast, toward Antwerp and the Ruhr, with 12th Army Group heading straight east from Paris toward Metz.

Now it was Montgomery's turn for anger. On August 22 he sent his chief of staff, Freddie de Guingand, to see Eisenhower and protest against both decisions. Montgomery argued that the quickest way to end the war was to hold Patton in Paris, give control of U.S. First Army and all incoming supplies to 21st Army Group, and send it to Antwerp and beyond to the Ruhr.

This force had to operate as a single unit under single control, which was "a WHOLE TIME job for one man." Montgomery warned that "to change the system of command now, after having won a great victory, would be to prolong the war." De Guingand pressed these points in a two-hour meeting with Eisenhower, but Eisenhower refused to change his mind. Montgomery then invited Eisenhower to come to his tactical headquarters at Conde for lunch the next day, August 23, to discuss future operations.

Eisenhower drove to Conde for the meeting. His chief of staff, Walter Smith, was with him, but when they arrived Montgomery abruptly announced that he wanted to see Eisenhower alone and thus Smith would have to stay outside. Eisenhower meekly accepted Montgomery's really quite insulting demand that Smith be locked out, even though de Guingand was with Montgomery.

Once inside the trailer, Montgomery tried his best to be tactful, but his idea of tact was to deliver a patronizing lecture on elementary strategy that a Sandhurst or West Point cadet would have found insulting. Standing before the map, his feet spread, hands behind his back, head up, eyes darting about, Montgomery outlined the situation, said the immediate need was for a firm plan, discussed logistics, told Eisenhower what the plans should be (a single thrust to the Ruhr by 21st Army Group, with First Army in support), declared that if Eisenhower's plan was followed the result would be failure, and told Eisenhower that he "should not descend into the land battle and become a ground C-in-C." He said that the Supreme Commander "must sit on a very lofty perch in order to be able to take a detached view of the whole intricate problem" and that someone must run the land battle for him. Eisenhower replied that he would not change his mind and intended to take control on September 1.

Unable to move Eisenhower on the question of command, Montgomery shifted to the real issue, the nature of the advance into Germany. He wanted Patton stopped where he was; he wanted the Airborne Army and First Army assigned to him; he wanted all available supplies; he wanted a directive that would send him through the Pas de Calais, on to Antwerp and Brussels, and beyond to the Ruhr.

Eisenhower, after an hour's argument, made some concessions, of which the most important were to give Montgomery control of the Airborne Army and the "authority to effect the necessary operational coordination" between the right flank of 21st Army Group and Bradley's left (i.e., First Army). In addition, 21st Army Group would have "priority" in supplies. Still, Eisenhower insisted, to Montgomery's dissatisfaction, "on building up . . . the necessary strength to advance eastward from Paris toward Metz." After the meeting Montgomery reported to Brooke that "it has been a very exhausting day," but overall he was pleased, as he felt he had won the main points, "operational control" over the Airborne and the First Armies, plus priority in supplies.

Eisenhower's attempt to appease Montgomery made both Bradley and Patton furious. The two American generals met; Patton recorded in his diary that Bradley "feels that Ike won't go against Monty . . . Bradley was madder than I have ever seen him and wondered aloud 'what the Supreme Commander amounted to.' " Patton felt that the southern advance offered much better tank terrain than the water-logged country to the north, but noted in disgust that Montgomery "has some way of talking Ike into his own way of thinking." He suggested to Bradley that they threaten to resign. "I feel that in such a showdown we would win, as Ike would not dare to relieve us."

Bradley would not go so far, but he did spend two days with Eisenhower, arguing against giving First Army to Montgomery. Tedder agreed with Bradley, as did Eisenhower's operations officer (G-3), Maj. Gen. Harold Bull, and his G-2, Gen. Kenneth Strong. Eisenhower yielded to their pressure. When he issued his directive, on August 29, he did not give operational control of First Army to Montgomery; instead, Montgomery was only "authorized to effect" —through Bradley—"any necessary coordination between his own forces" and First Army. That decision, and its sequel, strengthened Montgomery's and Brooke's—and Bradley's and Patton's—conviction that Eisenhower always agreed with the last man he talked to.

It was a most serious charge, but a bit off the mark. Montgomery tended to hear what he wanted to hear, read what he wanted to read; Eisenhower tended to seek out words or phrases that would appease. There was, consequently, a consistent misunderstanding between the two men. Nevertheless, Eisenhower never yielded on the two main points, command and single thrust, not in August and September 1944, nor again when they were raised in January and March 1945. He took—and kept—control of the land battle, just as he said he would. And he never wavered, from the moment he first saw the SHAEF plans for a two-front advance into Germany to the last month of the war, on the question of the so-called broad front.

He did waver, sometimes badly, on some important issues, primarily the relative importance of Arnhem and Antwerp, and the meaning of the word "priority." But he never told Montgomery anything that a reasonable man could have construed as a promise that Patton would be stopped in Paris and 21st Army Group be sent on to Berlin. Nor did he ever encourage Patton to believe that he would be sent to Berlin alone. He always insisted on invading Germany from both north and south of the Ardennes.

His reasons were manifold. His analysis of German morale and geography played a large role. Even after the Allies got through the

West Wall, there was still a major barrier between them and the German heartland, the Rhine River. A single thrust, especially beyond the Rhine, would be subject to counterattacks on the flanks. Eisenhower believed that the counterattacks might be powerful enough to sever the supply lines and then destroy the leading armies. Currently, with the Allies' limited port capacity, the Allies could not bring forward adequate supplies to sustain an army beyond the Rhine. Every mile that the advancing troops moved away from the Normandy ports added to the problems. For example, forward airfields had to be constructed to provide fighter support for the troops. But to construct them it was necessary to move engineers and building materials forward at the expense of weapons and gasoline. One senior engineer involved pointed out that if Patton had gone across the Rhine in September, he would have done so without any logistical or air support at all. "A good task force of panzerfaust, manned by Hitler Youth, could have finished them off before they reached Kassel."

As for 21st Army Group, de Guingand pointed out that when (and if) it reached the Rhine, bridging material would have to be brought forward, at the expense of other supplies. Like Eisenhower, de Guingand doubted that there would be a collapse of German morale; he expected the enemy to fight to the bitter end.

As, of course, the Germans did; it took the combined efforts of 160 Russian divisions *and* the entire AEF *and* Gen. Harold Alexander's Italian offensive *and* eight additional months of devastating air attack to force a German capitulation. After the war de Guingand remarked, a bit dryly, that he had to doubt that Montgomery could have brought about the same result with 21st Army Group alone. "My conclusion, is, therefore," de Guingand wrote, "that Eisenhower was right."

The personality and political factors in Eisenhower's decision are obvious: Patton pulling one way, Montgomery the other; each man insistent; each certain of his own military genius; each accustomed to having his own way. Behind them, there were the adulating publics, who had made Patton and Montgomery into symbols of their nation's military prowess. In Eisenhower's view, to give one or the other the glory would have serious repercussions, not just the howls of agony from the press and public of the nation left behind, but in the very fabric of the Alliance itself. Eisenhower feared it could not survive the resulting uproar. It was too big a chance to take, especially on such a risky operation. Eisenhower never considered taking it.

Montgomery and Patton showed no appreciation of the pressures on Eisenhower when they argued so persistently for their plans, but then Eisenhower's worries were not their responsibility. Montgomery wanted a quick end to the war, he wanted the British to bring it about, and he wanted to lead the charge into Berlin personally. Patton would have given anything to beat him to it. Had Eisenhower been in their positions, he almost surely would have felt as they did, and he wanted his subordinates to be aggressive and to believe in themselves and their troops.

Eisenhower's great weakness in this situation was not that he wavered on the broad-front question, but rather his eagerness to be well liked, coupled with his desire to keep everyone happy. Because of these characteristics, he would not end a meeting until at least verbal agreement had been found. Thus he appeared to be always shifting, "inclining first one way, then the other," according to the views and wishes of the last man with whom he had talked. Eisenhower, as Brooke put it, seemed to be "an arbiter balancing the requirements of competing allies and subordinates rather than a master of the field making a decisive choice." Everyone who talked to him left the meeting feeling that Eisenhower had agreed with him, only to find out later that he had not. Thus Montgomery, Bradley, and Patton filled their diaries and letters and conversations with denunciations of Eisenhower (Bradley less so than the others).

The real price that had to be paid for Eisenhower's desire to be well liked was not, however, animosity toward him from Montgomery and Patton. It was, rather, on the battlefield. In his attempts to appease Montgomery and Patton, Eisenhower gave them great tactical leeway, to the point of allowing them to choose their own objectives. The result was one of the great mistakes of the war, the failure to take and open Antwerp promptly, which represented the only real chance the Allies had to end the war in 1944. The man both immediately and ultimately responsible for that failure was Eisenhower.

□

From the Rhone to the Channel, the armies of the AEF were coming to a halt. On September 2, Third Army requested 750,000 gallons of gasoline and got 25,390. The next day, it was 590,000 with 49,930 received. For the following two days Patton got about half the quantity he demanded; after September 7 he got a trickle only. A handful of advance patrols had gotten across the Moselle River north and south of Nancy, but Third Army was caught up in a terrible battle for the ancient fortresses of Metz, which were practically impervious to artillery shells or bombs. Patton's men were still far short of the Rhine River and the Siegfried Line protecting it.

On September 12 the 4th Division, First Army, to the north, managed to get through the Siegfried Line. Lt. George Wilson led a reconnaissance platoon into the defenses. He saw a German soldier emerge from a mound of earth not a hundred meters away. "I got a slight chill as I realized I might well be the first American to set eyes on a pillbox in the famous Siegfried Line." He was east of St.-Vith in the Ardennes.

13

At the German Border

CAPT. JOSEPH DAWSON, G Company, 16th Infantry, 1st Division, had been the first company commander to get his men up the bluff at Omaha on D-Day. By mid-September he had been in battle for a hundred days. He had learned to fight in the hedgerows, how to work with tanks and planes in the attack on St.-Lo, how to pursue a defeated enemy in the dash across France. He was thirty-one years old, son of a Waco, Texas, Baptist preacher. He had lost twenty-five pounds off his already thin six-foot-two-inch frame.

On September 14 Dawson led his company into the border town of Eilendorf, southeast of Aachen. Although it was inside the Siegfried Line, the town was deserted, the fortifications unoccupied. The town was on a ridge, 300 meters high, 130 meters long, which gave it excellent observation to the east and north. Dawson's company was on the far side of a railroad embankment that divided the town, with access only through a tunnel under the railroad. Dawson had his men dig in and mount outposts. The expected German counterattack came after midnight and was repulsed.

In the morning Dawson looked east. He could see Germans moving up in the woods in one direction, in an orchard in another, and digging in. In the afternoon a shelling from artillery and mortars hit G Company, followed by a two-company attack. "The intensity of the attack carried the enemy into my positions," Dawson later told reporter W. C. Heinz of the *New York Sun.* "I lost men. They weren't wounded. They weren't taken prisoners. They were killed. But we piled up the Krauts."

But it was the Germans who were attacking, the Americans who were dug in. Dawson was short on ammunition, out of food. His supporting tanks were out of gasoline. The artillery behind him was limited to a few shells a day. If he was going to go anywhere, it would be to the rear. The U.S. Army's days of all-out pursuit were over.

There was one more punch left to the Allies, the Airborne Army, consisting of the British 1st Airborne and the U.S. 82nd and 101st Airborne, which had been refitting and recuperating in England since early July. From Eisenhower on down, everyone had been eager to use this asset, but although a number of operations were laid on, the troops on the ground always overran the drop zones before the operations could be mounted. In early September, however, Montgomery came up with a daring plan that called for dropping the paratroopers along the main north-south road through Belgium, to seize the bridges and thus open a way through the Netherlands for the British Second Army. The final objective was Arnhem. Once across the bridge there, the British would be beyond the Rhine River, with open country between them and Berlin. Code name for the operation was Market-Garden.

September 17 was a beautiful end-of-summer day, with a bright blue sky and no wind. No resident of the British Isles who was below the line of flight of the hundreds of C-47s carrying three divisions into combat ever forgot the sight. Nor did the paratroopers. Pvt. Dutch Schultz of the 82nd was jumpmaster for his stick; he stood in the open door as his plane formed up and headed east. "In spite of my anxiety about the jump and subsequent danger," he recalled, "it was exhilarating to see thousands of people on the ground waving to us as we flew over the British villages and towns." It was even more reassuring to see the fighter planes join the formation.

When the air armada got over Holland, Schultz could see a tranquil countryside. It was Sunday. Not many people were on the roads. Cows grazed in the fields. The Luftwaffe wasn't to be seen. There was some anti-aircraft fire, which intensified five minutes from the DZ (Drop Zone), but there was no breaking of formation or evasive action by the pilots as there had been over Normandy. The jump was a dream. A sunny midday. Little or no opposition on the ground. Plowed fields that were "soft as a mattress."

Gen. James Gavin led the way for the 82nd. His landing wasn't so soft; he hit a pavement and damaged his back. Some days later a doctor checked him out, looked Gavin in the eye, and said, "There is nothing wrong with your back." Five years later at Walter Reed Hospital, Gavin was told that he had two broken disks. It was too late to do anything; Gavin's comment was, "Now I have one heel higher than the other to account for the curvation in my back."

To indulge in a generalization, one based on four decades of interviewing former GIs but supported by no statistical data, Jim Gavin was the most beloved division commander in ETO. Some veterans can't remember their division commanders' names because there were so many of them, or because they never saw them; others don't want to remember. But veterans of the 82nd get tongue-tied when I ask them how they feel about General Gavin, then burst into a torrent of words—bold, courageous, fair, smart as hell, a man's man, trusted, a leader, beloved.

Gavin (USMA 1929) was thirty-seven years old, the youngest general in the U.S. Army since George Custer's day. His athletic grace and build combined with his boyish looks to earn him the affectionate nickname of "Slim Jim."

Dutch Schultz wasn't necessarily the best soldier in the 82nd, but he was one of the most insightful. After landing in Holland, Schultz saw Gavin come down, struggle to his feet in obvious pain, sling his M-1, and move out for his command post. "From my perspective," Schultz wrote, "it was crucial to my development as a combat soldier seeing my Commanding General carrying his rifle right up on the front line. This concept of leadership was displayed by our regiment, battalion, and company grade officers so often that we normally expected this hands-on leadership from all our officers. It not only inspired us but saved many lives."

□

There were but a handful of enemy troops in the DZ area. Lt. James Coyle recalled, "I saw a single German soldier on the spot where I thought I was going to land. I drew my .45 pistol and tried to get a shot at him but my parachute was oscillating. I was aiming at the sky as often as I was aiming at the ground. When I landed I struggled to my knees and aimed my pistol. The German was no more than 15 feet away, running. Just as I was about to shoot him he threw away his rifle, then his helmet and I saw he was a kid of about seventeen years old, and completely panicked. He just ran past me without looking at me. I didn't have the heart to shoot him."

Sgt. D. Zane Schlemmer of the 82nd had developed a "soft spot in my heart" for the cows of Normandy because whenever he saw them grazing in a hedgerow-enclosed field, he knew there were no land mines in it. In Holland, he had another bovine experience. His landing was good, right where he wanted to be. He gathered up his men and after recovering the 81mm mortars, ammunition, and equipment, set out for his objective in Nijmegen. He spotted two cows. He had plenty of rope. So "we commandeered the cows and hung our mortars and equipment on them. They were very docile and plodded right along with us.

"As we neared Nijmegen, the Dutch people welcomed us. But while pleased and happy to be liberated, they were quite shocked to see paratroopers leading two cows. The first questions were, 'Where are your tanks?' We were not their idea of American military invincibility, mobility and power. We could only tell them, 'The tanks are coming.' We hoped it was true."

The Germans had been caught by surprise, but were waking up. They got units to the various bridges, to defend them or blow them if necessary. The GIs, moving into Nijmegen and Eindhoven and their other objectives, started taking casualties.

Sgt. Ben Popilski of Coyle's platoon, who had just lost his British girlfriend, was shot in the head. A trooper reported it to Sgt. Otis Sampson. "I just happened to be looking his way," the trooper told Sampson. "He turned white before he was hit, as if he knew it was coming." Sampson recalled Popilski's last words back in England, "I hope this jump straightens it all out," and thought, He got his wish.

As the troopers moved toward their assigned objectives, gliders bearing soldiers and equipment began coming into the DZs.

One crash-landed on the edge of a wooded area and was under German small-arms fire coming from the tree line. Capt. Anthony Stefanich (Captain Stef to the men) called out to Private Schultz and others to follow him, and headed toward the German positions.

Stefanich was one of those officers brought up by General Gavin. Schultz remembered him as a man "who led through example rather than virtue of rank. He was what I wanted to be when I finally grew up."

Stefanich got hit in the upper torso by rifle fire, which set afire a smoke grenade he was carrying. Lt. Gerald Johnson jumped on him to put the fire out, then carried the wounded captain back to the assembly point, where an aid station had been set up. As he bent over his captain, Schultz's mind went back to his mother. She had taught him that if he said three Hail Marys daily he would never go to hell. Then he thought of his teachers, all nuns, "who taught me about the power of the rosary, and that if I really wanted something from Jesus Christ I should use our Blessed Mother as my emissary. That made sense, because more than once I had used my mother as an intermediary in trying to get my Dad to change his mind."

So he prayed to the Blessed Mother for Captain Stef's life.

But it was too late. Just before he died, Stefanich whispered to Lieutenant Johnson, "We have come a long way—tell the boys to do a good job." The medic, a Polish boy from Chicago, stood up beside the body. He was crying and calling out, "He's gone, he's gone. I couldn't help him." It was, Schultz said, "a devastating loss. It was the only time in combat that I broke down and wept."

On September 19, Lt. Waverly Wray, the man who had broken up the German counterattack on the morning of June 7 at Ste.-Mere-Eglise, and killed ten Germans with a single shot to the head of each, led an assault on the bridge. "The last I saw of him," one trooper reported, "he was headed for the Germans with a grenade in one hand and a tommy gun in the other." As Wray raised his head over the railroad track embankment, a German sniper firing from a signal tower killed him with a single shot in the middle of his head.

☐

On the afternoon of September 19, Gavin met with Lt. Gen. Brian Horrocks, commanding the Guards Armored Division. Horrocks said he could provide tank support for an attack on the Nijmegen bridges, and that he could have trucks bring forward assault boats for a crossing of the river downstream from the bridges. Gavin decided to hit the western ends with Lt. Col. Ben Vandervoort's 2nd Battalion, 505th PIR, and to give the task of crossing the river in the boats to Maj. Julian Cook's 3rd Battalion, 504th PIR.

Cook wanted to cross under cover of darkness, but he was helpless until the trucks carrying the boats came up. They were promised for late that afternoon, but were delayed because the Germans were putting heavy fire on the single road running back to the start point in Belgium. So effective were these attacks that the GIs were calling the road "Hell's Highway." Bulldozers and tanks were assigned to roam its length, pushing wrecks out of the way. Traffic jams ran for miles and took hours to unsnag. Hitler authorized one of the Luftwaffe's final mass raids on the clogged road—two hundred bombers hit Eindhoven, while another two hundred fighter-bombers went after the troops and vehicles jamming Hell's Highway—Jabos in reverse.

At 1530 of September 19, Gavin flung Vandervoort's battalion at the bridges. The boats had not come up, but Gavin hoped the combination of British tanks (all Shermans) and parachute infantry could break through Nijmegen and take the bridges.

Vandervoort's men rode into the attack on the backs of more than forty British armored vehicles. They got to the center of the city without much difficulty. There Vandervoort split the regiment, sending half for the railroad bridge and the other half for the highway span. Both attacks met fierce opposition from 88s, self-propelled guns, mortars, and well-placed machine guns.

Lieutenant Coyle and Sergeant Sampson's platoon led the assault. "On approaching the last houses before the open area in front of the railway bridge," Coyle recalled, "the lead tank began firing its cannon. The roar was deafening. I was moving up alongside the third tank in the column. When I cleared the last house and could see the bridge, I got quite a shock. I didn't expect it to be so large.

I learnt after the war that it was the largest single-span bridge in Europe."

As the two Shermans in front of Coyle moved across the traffic circle, two hidden 57mm antitank guns fired. The tanks shook, stopped, began to flare up. The tank beside Coyle went into reverse and backed into a street leading to the traffic circle. Coyle had his platoon retreat into houses on the outer ring, then take up positions on the second floor.

From there, the GIs could see Germans on foot and bicycles coming across the bridge. The men wanted to set up their machine guns in the windows and fire at the enemy, but Coyle ordered them to stay back, because he didn't want the Germans to know he was there, at least not until those antitank guns had been found and knocked out. He was passing this order on to Sergeant Sampson when Sampson saw a German running through the street not twenty yards away. Instinctively, Sampson raised his tommy gun and stepped toward the window. Coyle pushed the weapon aside.

"Not yet," Coyle whispered.

Looking out, he saw the Germans manhandling an antitank gun from behind some bushes in the park and bringing it forward to a spot ten meters in front, pointing it up the street. The Germans were unaware of his presence.

Just at that moment Vandervoort came into the room. Coyle explained the situation, showed him the German gun, and said he wanted to coordinate an attack with the British tanks. Vandervoort agreed. He told Coyle to open up in five minutes; then he dashed downstairs to find the British tanks and put them into the attack. But before Vandervoort could get the tankers organized, someone opened fire from a building adjacent to Coyle. The Germans started firing back. Coyle motioned Pvt. John Keller forward. He fired a rifle grenade at the antitank gun in the street and knocked it out.

"Kla-boom!" as Coyle remembered it. There was a terrific explosion in the room. Another 57mm had fired; the shell went through one wall and exploded against the other. Then another, and another. Coyle pulled his platoon out of the house and occupied the cellar of another. By now dark had come on. Coyle got orders to button down and wait for morning.

□

Dawn, September 20. One mile downstream from the bridges, Major Cook's battalion waited. The men were ready to go but the assault boats had not arrived. Through the morning, they waited. Vandervoort's battalion, meanwhile, was unable to drive the Germans out of the park, despite great effort (Sergeant Sampson was badly wounded that morning by shell fire).

Vandervoort described the fighting: "The troopers fought over roof tops, in the attics, up alleys, out of bedroom windows, through a maze of backyards and buildings. . . . Where feasible, tanks served as bulldozers, smashing through garden walls, etc. A tank cannon thrust through a kitchen door really stimulates exodus. In the labyrinth of houses and brick-walled gardens, the fighting deteriorated into confusing face-to-face, kill or be killed show downs."

Meanwhile, Cook's battalion waited for the boats. Cook went to the top of a tower at a nearby power station to survey the opposite bank of the Waal. A young captain with Cook, Henry Keep, wrote a letter home, "We had a glimpse of a scene which is indelibly imprinted on my mind. What greeted our eyes was a broad flat plain void of all cover or concealment . . . some 300 meters, where there was a built-up highway [where] we would get our first opportunity to get some protection and be able to reorganize. . . . We could see all along the Kraut side of the river strong defensive positions, a formidable line both in length as well as in depth—pillboxes, machine gun emplacements. . . ."

Cook had support; ten British tanks and an artillery battery were lined up along the river to give covering fire when he crossed. But not until 1500 did the trucks arrive. What they brought wasn't much. There were only twenty-six assault boats, instead of the thirty-three that had been promised. And they were the frailest of tiny craft, six meters long, of canvas with a reinforced plywood bottom. And there were only three paddles per boat. The Waal was almost four hundred meters wide, with a swift current of about ten kilometers an hour.

The paratroopers dragged the boats to the shore, pushed off into deep water, climbed in (thirteen men to a boat, plus three British engineers with the paddles) and tried to use their rifle butts as paddles. But as they got out into the current, some of the boats started whirling in circles. The tanks and artillery fired away. A smoke screen was laid down—but the wind blew it away. As the boats got straightened out and headed for the bank, the Germans opened fire.

Cook and Keep were in the first boat. That was not where the battalion commander ought to have been, but Cook had been brought up by Gavin.

"It was a horrible picture, this river crossing," Captain Keep wrote his mother, "set to the deafening roar of omnipresent firing. It was fiendish and dreadful. . . . Defenseless, frail canvas boats jammed to overflowing with humanity, all striving desperately to cross the Waal as quickly as possible, and get to a place where at least they could fight."

Some boats took direct hits, leaving nothing but flotsam. Small-arms fire ripped through the boats. The flotilla seemed to scatter. Yet it came on. Only eleven of the twenty-six boats made it to the far shore, but when they did the paratroopers who had survived the ordeal had their blood up. They were not going to be denied.

"Nobody paused," a British tank officer wrote. "Men got out and began running toward the embankment. My God what a courageous sight it was!"

Cook led the way. Captain Keep commented, "Many times I have seen troops who are driven to fever pitch—troops who, for a brief interval of combat, are lifted out of themselves—fanatics rendered crazy by rage and the lust for killing—men who forget temporarily the meaning of fear. However, I have never witnessed this human metamorphosis so acutely displayed as on this day. The men were beside themselves. They continued to cross that field in spite of all the Kraut could do, cursing savagely, their guns spitting fire."

In less than a half hour Cook and his men had reached the top of the highway embankment and driven the Germans out. The engineers, meanwhile, had paddled back to the west bank and returned with a second wave. Altogether it took six crossings to get Cook's battalion over.

As those crossings were being made, Cook led the first wave in an assault on the bridges. His men came on fast. Meanwhile Vandervoort's people on the west side had finally overrun the park and were starting onto the bridges. The Germans scrambled frantically for the plungers to set off the explosives in place on the bridges, but Cook's men did what they had been trained to do—wherever they saw wires on the ground they cut them. The German engineers hit the plungers, and nothing happened.

Cook's men set up defensive positions at the bridges, facing east. As the British tanks with Vandervoort started across the highway bridge, their crews saw the Stars and Stripes go up on the other end. Cook had lost forty men killed, a hundred wounded, but he had the bridges. There were 267 German dead on the railroad bridge alone, plus many hundreds wounded and captured, plus no one could guess how many had fallen into the river. It was one of the great feats of arms of World War II. Lt. Gen. Miles Dempsey, commanding the British Second Army, came up to shake Gavin's hand. "I am proud to meet the commander of the greatest division in the world today," he said.

It was 1910 hours. Darkness was descending. Arnhem was but eleven kilometers away. Lt. Col. John Frost's battalion was still holding the eastern end of the bridge, but barely. General Horrocks decided to get up defensive positions for the night. When that was done, the guards began to brew up their tea.

Cook's men were enraged. They yelled and swore at the Brits, told them those were their countrymen in Arnhem and they needed help now. Horrocks commented, "This operation of Cook's was the best and most gallant attack I have ever seen carried out in my life. No wonder the leading paratroopers were furious that we did not push straight on for Arnhem. They felt they had risked their lives for nothing, but it was impossible, owing to the confusion which existed in Nijmegen, with houses burning and the British and U.S. forces all mixed up."

In the morning (September 21) the tanks moved out, only to be stopped halfway to Arnhem by two enemy battalions, including one of SS troopers, with tanks and 88s. There were Jabos overhead, but the radio sets in the RAF ground liaison car would not work (neither would the radios with the British 6th Airborne in Arnhem). That afternoon the 9th Panzer Division in Arnhem overwhelmed the last survivors of Frost's battalion. Some days later the survivors of 1st Airborne crossed the Rhine to safety. The division had gone into Arnhem 10,005 men strong. It came out with 2,163 live soldiers.

Lieutenant Colonel Frost put the blame on the Guards Armored Division. Standing on the bridge on the fortieth anniversary of the event, he looked west, as he had so often, so fruitlessly, four decades earlier, and got to talking about the guards brewing up their tea, and then on to the relatively light casualties the guards suffered as compared to the 1st Airborne, and on to the magnificent performance of the 82nd.

His face blackened. As I watched, mesmerized, he shook his fist and roared a question into the air, a question for the guards: "Do you call that fighting?"

Market-Garden was a high-risk operation that failed. It was undertaken at the expense of two other possible offensives that had to be postponed because Eisenhower diverted supplies to Market-Garden. The first was the Canadian attack on the approaches to Antwerp, Europe's greatest port and essential to the support of any Allied offensive across the Rhine. In the event, Antwerp was not opened and operating until the end of 1944, which meant that through the fall the AEF fought with inadequate supplies. The second postponed offensive was that of Patton's Third Army, south of the Ardennes. Patton believed that if *he* had gotten the supplies that Monty got for Market-Garden, he could have crossed the Rhine that fall and then had an unopposed path open to Berlin. That seems doubtful, but we will never know because it was never tried.

To the end of his life Eisenhower insisted that Market-Garden was a risk that had to be run. In my interviews with him, between 1964 and 1969, we discussed the operation innumerable times. He always came back to this: The first rule in the pursuit of a defeated enemy is to keep after him, stay in contact, press him, exploit every opportunity. The northern approach to Germany was the shortest, over the terrain most suitable to offensive operations (once the Rhine had been crossed). Eisenhower felt that, given how close Market-Garden came to succeeding, it would have been criminal for him not to have tried.

The trouble with Market-Garden was that it was an offensive

on much too narrow a front. The pencil-like thrust over the Rhine was vulnerable to attacks on the flanks. The Germans saw and took advantage of that vulnerability with furious counterattacks all along the length of the line, hitting it from all sides.

In retrospect, the idea that a force of several divisions, consisting of British, American, and Polish troops, could be supplied by one highway could only have been accepted by leaders guilty of overconfidence.

14

Metz, Aachen, and the Hurtgen

PATTON'S THIRD ARMY had been stopped in its thrust through France not by the Germans but by a shortage of gasoline. But when the supply line caught up with Patton's lead tanks, he discovered another problem, the mighty fortress system around Metz. The initial key to the system was Fort Driant, built in 1902 and strengthened almost every year since, either by the French or the Germans after 1940. In size, thickness, and firepower it was a monster, with clear fields of fire up and down the Moselle River. Patton could not cross that river until he held Driant.

Driant was surrounded by a deep moat, which in turn was surrounded by a twenty-meter band of barbed wire. It had living quarters for a garrison of two thousand, with sufficient supplies for a month or more of battle. Its big guns rose from the earth on hydraulic mounts, sniffed around, fired, and disappeared back into the earth. There were four outlying casement batteries, and concealed machine-gun pillboxes were scattered through the area. The only way in was over a causeway.

On September 27, Third Army had made its first attempt to take Driant. The Americans had assumed that the fort would be lightly garrisoned by inferior troops. Although they had only a vague idea of the fort's works and surrounding terrain, they figured that a pre–World War I fortress system couldn't possibly stand up to the pounding of modern artillery, much less air-dropped bombs of 500 to 1,000 pounds, not to mention napalm. From dawn to 1415 hours, the Americans hit the fort with all the high explosives in their arsenal. The men of the 11th Infantry Regiment, who led the assault, were confident that nothing could have survived inside the fort.

At 1415 the infantry began to move in on the fort. To their astonishment, when they reached the barbed wire surrounding the moat, Germans rose up from pillboxes to their front, sides, and rear and opened fire. Shermans came forward to blast the pillboxes, but their 75mm shells hardly chipped or scarred the thick concrete. The infantry went to the ground, and ignominiously withdrew under cover of darkness.

With that withdrawal Third Army's advance came to a halt. It now faced a new problem in its experience, but the oldest tactical/ engineering problem in warfare, how to overcome a fortified position. Like First Army to the north, Third Army began thinking and got started on the challenge of Driant by adopting some new techniques and weapons. It helped considerably that the Americans finally got their hands on the blueprints of the fort, which showed a warren's den of tunnels.

No amount of high explosive was going to knock it down. Infantry would have to get inside the fort, kill the German defenders who resisted, and take possession. To do that, the 11th Regiment would have to get over the causeway. To do that, there were a few new weapons. One was the tankdozer, another was a "snake," a longer version of the bangalore torpedo. The dozer would clear away rubble, the snake would blast a path through the barbed wire. A third new weapon was the flamethrower. A Company got four of them.

On October 3 the second assault on Driant began. The snakes got shoved under the wire, but they broke and were useless. The tankdozers had mechanical failures. Only one of the four flamethrowers worked. B Company, nevertheless, was able to get into the fort. Capt. Harry Anderson led the way, tossing grenades into German bunkers as he ran across the causeway, inspiring his men to follow him into Driant, where he established a position alongside one of the casements.

An intense firefight ensued. Germans popped out of their holes like prairie dogs, fired, and dropped back. They called in their own artillery from other forts in the area. Some American engineers got forward with TNT, to blast a hole in the casement so that the GIs could enter the fortress system. But the heavy walls were as impervious to TNT as to shells and bombs.

On top of the casement, Pvt. Robert Holmlund found a ventilator shaft. Despite enemy fire he managed to open the shaft's cover and dropped several bangalore torpedoes down the opening. Germans who survived evacuated the area, and Captain Anderson led the first Americans inside the fort. The room they had taken turned out to be a barracks. They quickly took an adjacent one.

The Germans counterattacked. The ensuing firefight was a new dimension of combat. It shattered nerves, ears, and lives. One small firecracker set off in the bowels of one of the old forts is guaranteed to startle a tour group, and cause ringing ears; no one who had not been there can imagine the assault on the ears by machine-gun fire and hand-grenade explosions reverberating in the tunnels enclosed by the thick, dripping masonry walls.

The air was virtually unbreathable; men in the barracks room had to take turns at gulping some fresh air from firing slits. The stench was a mixture of gunpowder, gas fumes, and excrement. Wounded could not be treated properly. Fresh water was nonexistent.

B Company was stuck there. It had neither the equipment nor the manpower to fight its way through the maze of tunnels. It couldn't go back; being on top of the fort was more dangerous than being in it. At dark American reinforcements, accompanied by a half-dozen Shermans, crossed the causeway and assaulted another casement, but they were badly shot up and forced to withdraw when the Germans came up from the tunnels and filtered into their rear. These small, local counterattacks could be devastating. Four of the Shermans were knocked out by panzerfaust shells.

Capt. Jack Gerrie, CO of G Company, 11th Infantry, led the reinforcements. He had no illusions about the enemy. He had been in on the September 27 attack. "Watch out for these birds," he had told another company commander. "They are plenty tough. I've never run across guys like these before, they are new, something you read about."

On October 4 Gerrie tried to knock down the steel doors at the rear of the fort. Direct cannon fire couldn't do it, and protruding grillwork made it impossible to put TNT charges against the doors themselves. The Germans again called down fire on Driant, which forced G Company to scatter to abandoned pillboxes, ditches, shell holes, and open bunkers, anywhere they could find shelter. That evening Gerrie tried to reorganize his company, but his efforts were hampered by the Germans, who came out of the underground tunnels, here, there, everywhere, fired and retreated, causing confusion and further disorganization in G Company. Gerrie could count about half the men he had led to the fort the previous evening.

At dawn on October 5, German artillery commenced firing at Driant. After hours of this, Gerrie wrote a report for his battalion commander: "The situation is critical[;] a couple more barrages and another counterattack and we are sunk. We have no men, our equipment is shot and we just can't go on. . . . We cannot advance. We may be able to hold till dark but if anything happens this afternoon I can make no predictions. The enemy artillery is butchering these troops. . . . We cannot get out to get our wounded and there is a hell of a lot of dead and missing. . . . There is only one answer the way things stand. First either to withdraw and saturate it with heavy bombers or reinforce with a hell of a strong force, but eventually they'll get it by artillery too. They have all of these places zeroed in by artillery. . . . This is just a suggestion but if we want this damned fort let's get the stuff required to take it and then go. Right now you haven't got it."

Written from a shell hole, under fire, by a man who hadn't slept in two days, nor had a hot meal, it is a remarkable report, accurate, precise, and rightly critical of the fools who had got him into this predicament. It was so compelling it moved right up to the corps commander, who showed it to Patton and said the battalion commander wanted to withdraw.

Never, Patton replied. He ordered that Driant be seized "if it took every man in the XX Corps, but he could not allow an attack by this Army to fail."

Over the next three days Third Army ignored Gerrie's advice. It threw one more regiment into the attack, with similar ghastly results. The men on top of the fort were the ones under siege. The lowliest private among them could see perfectly clearly what Patton could not, that this fort had to be bypassed and neutralized because it was never going to be taken.

Patton finally relented. Still, not until October 13 were the GIs withdrawn. About half as many returned as went up. This was Third Army's first defeat in battle.

The only good thing about a defeat is that it teaches lessons. The Driant debacle caused a badly needed deflation of Patton's—and Third Army's—hubris. That led to a recognition of the need to plan more thoroughly, to get proper equipment, to take units out of the line to integrate their replacements, and to conduct courses and exercises on the use of explosives in an assault on a fortress. The next time, Third Army was going to get it right.

North of Luxembourg, at Eilendorf, just outside Aachen, Captain Dawson's G Company was holding its position on the ridge astride the Siegfried Line. The Germans needed to restore the integrity of their line, so they kept counterattacking. By October 4, G Company had repulsed three German counterattacks, and endured five hundred shells per day from 105s. Then the Germans came on in division strength, but again Dawson's company beat them back, with help from the artillery and air. "We had constant shelling for eight hours," Dawson remembered. "We had twelve direct hits on what was our command post." Then the German infantry came on. "When they stopped coming we could count 350 that we ourselves had killed—not those killed by our artillery or planes, but just by the one lousy little old company all by itself."

An officer in headquarters company in Dawson's battalion, Lt. Fred Hall, wrote his mother on October 6, "This action is as rough as I have seen. Still the hardships are borne with little complaint." Back at 12th Army Group HQ, Bradley might be circling Berlin on the map, but outside Aachen there was more realism. Hall told his mother, "In the lower echelons of command, faced with the realities of the situation, the feeling is that the war will not be over before the spring of 1945 at the earliest."

☐

Eisenhower continued to urge his subordinates to offensive action. All responded to the best of their ability. It was a war of attrition. Like Grant in 1864–65, Eisenhower could afford to continue to attack because his overall resources were superior to those of the Germans. In his memoirs, he writes that attrition "was profitable to us only where the daily calculations showed that enemy losses were double our own." But calculations were seldom as favorable as two to one—they were more like one to one. Eisenhower kept attacking. At no other time in the war did he so resemble Haig or Joffre in World War I, or Grant in the Wilderness.

Like Grant, Eisenhower justified what many critics considered a sterile, cold-blooded strategy on the grounds that in the long run "this policy would result in shortening the war and therefore in the saving of thousands of Allied lives." And he was quite cold-blooded about the need to kill Germans. "People of the strength and warlike tendencies of the Germans do not give in," he told a critic. "They must be beaten to the ground."

The campaign that resulted was the least glamorous, yet one of the toughest, of the war. There wasn't much strategy involved: The idea was just to attack to the east. The terrain in the center of the American line—the Eifel Mountains and the rugged Ardennes and Hurtgen Forests—dictated that the main efforts would take place to the north and south of these obstacles. To the north, First and Ninth Armies would head toward the Rhine River along the axis Maastricht–Aachen–Cologne. The major obstacles were the Siegfried Line, the city of Aachen, and the northern part of the Hurtgen. To the south, Third Army would continue to attack around Metz.

To carry out those missions, the American army needed to learn new forms of warfare, 1944-style. These would be set-piece attacks, like D-Day but in different terrain—cities, villages, forts, and forests. As in the Norman hedgerows, the army would have to develop new tactics to overcome the enemy.

Problems there were aplenty. For the first time since early August, when they had fled the hedgerow country, the Germans had prepared positions to defend. One of the first tasks they accomplished as they manned the Siegfried Line was to put S-mines, Bouncing Betties, that sprang when triggered by a trip wire or foot pressure a meter or so into the air before exploding, in front of their positions. Thousands of them. The canister contained 360 steel balls or small pieces of scrap steel. They were capable of tearing off a leg above the knee, or inflicting the wound that above all others terrified the soldiers.

Lt. George Wilson had joined the 4th Division as a replacement at the time of St.-Lo. By early October he had been in combat for nine weeks, but he had not yet seen an S-mine. On October 10, when he led a reconnaissance platoon into the Siegfried Line straight east of Malmedy, Belgium, suddenly they were everywhere. "By now I had gone through aerial bombing, artillery and mortar shelling, open combat, direct rifle and machine-gun firing, night patrolling and ambush. Against all of this we had some kind of chance; against mines we had none. The only defense was to not move at all."

Engineers came forward to clear the mines and use white tape to mark paths through the fields. They took every precaution, but one of the engineers lost his leg at the knee to an S-mine, so they set to probing every inch of ground with trench knives, gently working the knives in at an angle, hoping to hit only the sides of the mines. They began uncovering—and sometimes exploding— devilish little handmade mines, in pottery crocks, set just below the ground. The only metal was the detonator, too small to be picked up by mine detectors. They blew off hands.

A squad to Wilson's right got caught in a minefield. The lieutenant leading it had a leg blown off. Four men who came to help him set off mines; each lost a leg. Wilson started over to help, but the lieutenant yelled at him to stay back. Then the lieutenant began talking, calmly, to the wounded men around him. One by one, he directed them back over the path they had taken into the minefield. One by one, on hands and knee, dragging a stump, they got out. Then the lieutenant dragged himself out.

Wilson had seen a lot, but this was "horribly gruesome. Five young men lying there each missing a leg." Wilson stayed in the war to the end. He saw every weapon the Wehrmacht had, in action. After the war, he flatly declared that the S-mine was "the most frightening weapon of the war, the one that made us sick with fear."

□

Behind the minefields were the dragon's teeth. They rested on a concrete mat between ten and thirty meters wide, sunk a meter or two into the ground (to prevent any attempt to tunnel underneath them and place explosive charges). On top of the mat were the teeth themselves, truncated pyramids of reinforced concrete about a meter in height in the front row, to two meters high in the back. They were staggered and spaced in such a manner that a tank could not drive through. Interspersed among the teeth were minefields, barbed wire, and pillboxes that were virtually impenetrable by artillery and set in such a way as to give the Germans crossing fire across the entire front. The only way to take those pillboxes was for infantry to get behind them and attack the rear entry. But behind the first row of pillboxes and dragon's teeth, there was a second, and often a third, sometimes a fourth.

"The Siegfried Line was undoubtedly the most formidable man-made defense ever contrived," according to Capt. Belton Cooper. "Its intricate series of dragon's teeth, pillboxes, interconnected communication trenches, gun pits and foxholes in depth supported by an excellent road net and backed up by a major autobahn system that ran back to Cologne, Dusseldorf and other manufacturing sites less than 50 kilometers to the east, provided the Germans with not only an excellent defense system but also a base from which to launch a major offensive."

Cooper was describing the Siegfried Line as it faced Belgium. Farther south, on the Franco-German border, it was more formidable, with major fortifications holding heavy artillery. The pillboxes were more numerous and better constructed. They were half underground, with cannon and machine guns and ammunition storage rooms and living quarters for the defenders, typically about fifteen soldiers. Throughout the length of the Siegfried Line, villages along the border were incorporated into the system. The houses, churches, and public buildings in these villages were built of stone and rock. The second floors of the buildings and the belfries on the churches provided excellent observation.

For Captain Dawson and G Company outside Aachen, the task wasn't to attack but defend. This too was new. State-side training had emphasized offensive tactics, while in France the GIs had done far more attacking than defending. But Dawson and his men were holding high ground east of Aachen, which gave them observation posts to call in targets to the gunners and pilots. The Germans were desperate to get him off that ridge, which reporter W. C. Heinz of the *New York Sun* had taken to calling in his dateline "Dawson Ridge, Germany." The Germans needed the ridge to restore their line and relieve the pressure on Aachen. So Dawson was going to have to defend.

At 2300 hours, October 15, an SS panzer division hit G Company. The first shots came as a surprise because the leading tank in the column was a captured Sherman, with American markings on it. The battle that was thus joined went on for forty-eight hours. There was hand-to-hand fighting, with rifle butts and bayonets. It was surreal, almost slow-motion, because the mud was ankle deep. Dawson called in artillery to within ten meters of his position. At one foxhole a German toppled dead over the barrel of an American machine gun, while in another a wounded American waited until the German who had shot him came up and looked down on him, then emptied his tommy gun in the German's face. The two men died, at the bottom of the hole, in a macabre embrace.

The American battalion commander cracked. He all but disappeared, or as Lieutenant Hall put it, "he became less and less interested in the conduct of the war." The officers conferred among themselves, then persuaded the battalion executive officer to talk to the regimental commander. He did, and the CO was reassigned. The battalion held its position.

On October 17 a German attack overran Dawson's antitank gun position. He set out to retake it. Lieutenant Hall, battalion S-3, sent a report to regimental S-3 that evening: "I just talked to Dawson and he says that he has position restored where gun was. The gun was knocked out. He was not able to take the house. Said he would get it tomorrow. . . . Dawson's men killed 17 Jerries including five from the crew of a tank which was in back of the house. . . . His men have had no food for 24 hours. Their last hot meal was the night before last. Possibly we can get them a hot meal tomorrow."

Inside Aachen the battle raged. The Germans fell back to the center of the city, charging a price for every building abandoned.

The rubble in the streets grew to monstrous proportions. In the center, the old buildings, made of masonry and stone, were almost impervious to tank cannon fire, so Col. Derrill Daniel brought a self-propelled 155mm artillery piece into the city, using a bulldozer to clear a path. Daniel reported that its effects were "quite spectacular and satisfying."

On October 16 the battalion ran into a strong German position in the city's main theater building. Daniel brought the 155 forward and wheeled it into the line side by side with the infantry. It fired more than a dozen shells, point-blank, into the theater. The theater survived but its defenders, dazed, surrendered.

Still the fighting continued. For another four days and nights the Germans and Americans pounded each other while they destroyed Aachen. Finally, on October 21, Daniel's men secured the downtown area. Col. Gerhard Wilck dared to disobey Hitler and surrendered his 3,473 survivors. At his interrogation he protested bitterly against the use of the 155 in Aachen, calling it "barbarous" and claiming it should be outlawed.

American losses were heavy, over 5,000. The 30th and 1st Divisions were badly depleted, exhausted, used up. They were in no condition to make a dash to the Rhine. German losses were heavier, 5,000 casualties and 5,600 prisoners of war. Aachen was destroyed, with the exception of the cathedral, which housed Charlemagne's coronation chair. It escaped major damage.*

Outside Aachen, Dawson's company continued to hold. After Aachen fell there were fewer, less vigorous German attacks. On October 22 reporter W. C. Heinz got to Dawson's headquarters to do an interview. Dawson summarized the action simply, directly: "This is the worst I've ever seen. Nobody will ever know what this has been like up here."

Heintz wanted to know, as best he could, and arranged to stay with Dawson for a few days to find out. The dispatches he filed

---

* The standing cathedral surrounded by ruin and rubble was common after World War II. Five and more decades later, you can see the phenomenon in London, where St. Paul's stands surrounded by post-1945 buildings, or in Cologne, Aachen, Reims, and elsewhere. Thank God—and thank those medieval craftsmen and architects.

beginning October 24 give a vivid portrait of a rifle company commander in action in World War II. Of course Dawson was special,
but not so special that what he was going through was that much
different from what his fellow COs were experiencing. Of them it
can be truly said that they held the most dangerous and difficult job
in the world.

Dawson's HQ was in a cellar in the village. There were a
candle and a kerosene lamp, a table and some chairs, a radio playing
classical music. There were a couple of lieutenants in the room, and
a radioman, and Dawson's dachshund, Freda. Heinz got Dawson
talking about what it had been like.

"And the kid says to me," Dawson related, " 'I'll take that
water to that platoon.' And he starts out. He is about fifty yards
from this doorway and I'm watching him. He is running fast; then
I can see this 88 hit right where he is, and, in front of my eyes, he
is blown apart."

Dawson spoke of other strains. "I had a kid come up and say,
'I can't take it anymore.' What could I do? If I lose that man, I lose
a squad. So I grab him by the shirt, and I say: 'You will, you will.
There ain't any going back from this hill except dead.' And he goes
back and he is dead."

Dawson sighed. "He doesn't know why, and I don't know why,
and you don't know why. But I have got to answer those guys."

He looked Heinz in the eye. "But I have got to answer those
guys," he repeated, "because I wear bars. I've got the responsibility
and I don't know whether I'm big enough for the job." He continued to fix his eyes on Heinz. "But I can't break now. I've taken this
for the thirty-nine days we've held this ridge and I'm in the middle
of the Siegfried Line and you want to know what I think? I think it
stinks."

Dawson began to shed tears. Then he jerked his head up.
"Turn it up," he said to a lieutenant by the radio. "That's Puccini. I
want to hear it."

Two GIs came into the room. They were apprehensive because
Captain Dawson had sent for them. But it was good news. "I'm
sending you to Paris," Dawson announced. "For six days. How do
you like that?"

"Thanks," one replied, reluctantly.

"Well, you had better like it," Dawson said, "and you had better stay out of trouble, but have a good time and bless your hearts." The men mumbled thanks and left.

"Two of the best boys I've got," Dawson told Heinz. "Wire boys. They've had to run new lines every day because the old ones get chopped up. One day they laid heavy wire for 200 yards and by the time they got to the end and worked back, the wire had been cut in three places by shellfire."

Dawson told Heinz that he had men who had been wounded in mid-September, when he first occupied the ridge, who returned four weeks later. They had gone AWOL from the field hospital and made their way back "and the first thing I know they show up again here and they're grinning from ear to ear. I know it must sound absolutely crazy that anyone would want to come back to this, but it is true."

The following morning one of the lieutenants told Dawson, "Captain, those wire men, they say they don't want to go to Paris."

"All right," Dawson sighed. "Get two other guys—if you can."

The Battle of Aachen benefited no one. The Americans never should have attacked. The Germans never should have defended. Neither side had a choice. This was war at its worst, wanton destruction for no purpose.

Still the Americans continued to attack. A steady flow of replacements coming from England allowed the generals to build companies up to full strength after a few days on the line, even when casualties had run as high as 90 percent.

This replacement flow added to the sense of strength—surely the Germans couldn't keep up. At higher headquarters the feeling was, just one more push here, or another there, and we'll be through the Siegfried Line and up to and across the Rhine.

In addition to individual replacements, new divisions were coming onto the line in a steady stream. These high-number divisions were made up of the high school classes of 1942, 1943, and 1944. The training these young men had gone through at Fort Benning and the other State-side posts was rigorous physically but severely short on the tactical and leadership challenges the junior officers would have to meet.

Paul Fussell was a twenty-year-old lieutenant in command of a

rifle platoon in the 103rd Division. He found the six months' training period in the States to be repetitious and unrealistic. He was
struck by "the futility and waste of training and re-training and
finding some work to do for the expendables awaiting their moment
to be expended." In the field, "Our stock-in-trade was the elementary fire-and-flank maneuver hammered into us over and over at
Benning. It was very simple. With half your platoon, you establish
a firing line to keep your enemy's heads down while you lead the
other half around to the enemy's flank for a sudden surprise assault,
preferably with bayonets and shouting."

Fire-and-movement had been the doctrine developed by General Marshall when he was at Benning in the 1920s. Marshall had
reasoned that in the next war, the army would expand rapidly and
therefore needed to "develop a technique and methods so simple
and so brief that the citizen officer of good common sense can
readily grasp the idea."

"We all did grasp the idea," Fussell remembered, "but in combat it had one signal defect, namely the difficulty, usually the impos-
sibility, of knowing where your enemy's flank *is*. If you get up and
go looking for it, you'll be killed." Nevertheless, Fussell saw the
positive benefit to doing fire-and-movement over and over: "Perhaps its function was rather to raise our morale and confidence than
to work as defined. It did have the effect of persuading us that such
an attack could be led successfully and that we were the people who
could do it. That was good for our self-respect and our courage,
and perhaps that was the point." This was distressingly close to the
Duke of Wellington's sole requirement for his lieutenants, that they
be brave.

Fussell was a rich kid from southern California who had a
couple of years of college and some professional journalism behind
him. He had blown the lid off the IQ test. Had he been born two
years earlier and brought into the army in 1941 or 1942, he would
have gone into the Army Air Force, or intelligence, or onto somebody's staff, or been sent back to college for more education. But
he was one of those American males born in 1924 or 1925 to whom
fell the duty, as rifle platoon leaders, to bear the brunt of the Battle
of Northwest Europe, after their older brothers and friends, born
in 1922 or 1923, had driven the enemy back to his border.

There were hundreds of young officers like Fussell, lieutenants who came into Europe in the fall of 1944 to take up the fighting. Rich kids. Bright kids. The quarterback on the championship high-school football team. The president of his class. The chess champion. The lead in the class play. The solo in the spring concert. The wizard in the chemistry class. America was throwing its finest young men at the Germans.

It was bad enough being an untrained infantry replacement; it could be worse going into armor untrained. Yet many did. One tank commander remembered that in the Bulge "I spent long hours in the turret when I was literally showing men how to feed bullets to the gun. Could they shoot straight? They couldn't even hold the gun right! In the midst of the toughest fighting of the Third Army's campaign I was teaching men what I had learned in basic training."

Sgt. Raymond Janus of the 1st Armored Division got a new three-man crew for his light tank. They were all eighteen years of age. Only one had driven a car, and that only to church on Sundays. He became driver. Neither of the other two had any experience firing a machine gun or a 37mm tank gun. Janus gave them a two-hour demonstration. Then they moved out on a mission.

The tank had hardly proceeded a half kilometer when the driver panicked and rolled the tank down a hill. The crash threw Janus out of the turret and on his head, causing a severe concussion that cost him his hearing.

The replacements paid the price for a criminally wasteful Replacement System that chose to put quantity ahead of quality. Its criterion was the flow of bodies. Whose fault was this?

Eisenhower's first. He was the boss. And Bradley's. And Patton's. They demanded an ever greater flow of replacements while doing precious little to insist on improving the training, and got what they demanded. In no other way did the American high command in ETO show such disengagement as Eisenhower, Bradley, et al. did in failing to look at the source of their replacements and then to force some obvious and relatively easy improvements in the Repple Depples* and in the assignment methods. It can only be

* Replacement Depots

that Eisenhower, Bradley, et al. had no clear conception of life on the front line. They didn't listen to foxhole GIs often enough. So they threw the eighteen-year-olds and the former ASTPers* into the battle, untrained, alone.

The American army approaching Germany in the fall of 1944 was in part a children's crusade. It had hundreds of thousands of eighteen- to twenty-year-old soldiers, most of them at the cutting edge of the general offensive and almost none of them properly trained for combat. Capt. Charles Roland remembered receiving replacements in January, "a number of whom had eaten Christmas dinner at home with their families, who were killed in action before they had an opportunity to learn the names of the soldiers in the foxholes with them."

Eisenhower said that in war everything is expendable—even generals' lives—in pursuit of victory. If victory required replacements, some of them would have to be expended. One had to be tough. The problem here is that the Replacement System was guilty of the worst sin of all in war, inefficiency. It was paying lives but getting no return. It was just pure waste and the commanders should have done something about it.

Example: In January 1945, Captain Cooper of the 3rd Armored Division got thirty-five replacements to help crew the seventeen new tanks the division had received. "These men had just unloaded from the boat in Antwerp a few hours earlier," Cooper said. "They had received no previous indoctrination on what they were to do." Not one had any previous experience with tanks. "Most of them had never even been in a tank or even close to one."

Cooper gave them a brief verbal orientation. Then his mechanics took small groups into tanks, where each recruit got to fire the main gun three times. "This was all the training time permitted," Cooper remembered, because the guides came to take the tanks to their assignments to the various units.

The previous night, the thirty-five replacements had been in Antwerp. At 1500 they lumbered off in a convoy of seventeen tanks headed for the front. Two hours later fifteen of the seventeen were knocked out by German panzers firing 88s.

* Army Specialist Training Program, for the brightest enlisted men. Broken up in 1943

It often happened that more than half the replacements sent directly into combat became casualties in the first few days.

At Metz, Patton continued to attack the forts—although not Driant, which he was by now content to bypass. Finally, on November 22, Metz was secured—except that six forts around the city were still defiant. The Americans made no attempt to overrun them, and soon enough they began to surrender. The last to give up was Fort Driant, which finally capitulated on December 8.

In August, Third Army had advanced almost six hundred kilometers, from Normandy to the Moselle River. From September 1 to mid-December it advanced thirty-five kilometers east of the Moselle. The Siegfried Line, which Patton had said he would reach on November 10, was still a dozen or so kilometers to the east. In crossing the Moselle and taking Metz, Third Army had suffered 47,039 battle casualties.

Up north of Aachen, the Americans continued to attack, side by side with the British. Gen. Brian Horrocks surprised the GIs by showing up on the front lines to see conditions. He was a sympathetic yet critical observer. The 84th Division struck him as "an impressive product of American training methods which turned out division after division complete, fully equipped." The division "was composed of splendid, very brave, tough young men." But he thought it a bit much to ask of a green division that it penetrate the Siegfried Line, then stand up to counterattacks from two first-class divisions, the 15th Panzer and the 10th SS. And he was disturbed by the failure of American division and corps commanders and their staffs to *ever* visit the front lines. He was greatly concerned to find that the men were not getting hot meals brought up from the rear, in contrast to the forward units in the British line. He gave the GIs "my most experienced armoured regiment, the Sherwood Rangers Yeomanry," told the American battalion and division commanders to get up front, and returned to his headquarters.

The problem Horrocks saw was becoming endemic in the U.S. Army in ETO. Not even battalion commanders were going to the front. From the Swiss border north to Geilenkirchen, the Americans were attacking. SHAEF put the pressure on Twelfth Army

Group; Bradley passed it on to First, Third, and Ninth Armies; Hodges, Patton, and Lt. Gen. William Simpson told their corps commanders to get results; by the time the pressure reached the battalion COs, it was intense. They raised it even higher as they set objectives for the rifle company COs. The trouble with all this pressure was that the senior officers and their staffs didn't know what they were ordering the rifle companies to do. They had seen neither the terrain nor the enemy. They did their work from maps and over radios and telephones. And unlike the company and platoon leaders, who had to be replaced every few weeks at best, and every few days at worst, the staff officers took few casualties, so the same men stayed at the same job, doing it badly.

In the First World War, a British staff officer from Gen. Douglas Haig's headquarters visited the Somme battlefield a week or so after the battle. The orders had been to attack, with objectives drawn up back at headquarters. The attacks had gone forward, through barbed wire, mud, mines, mortar, and machine-gun fire, fallen back with appalling loss, only to be ordered forward again. This had gone on for weeks. And the officer looked at the sea of mud and was shocked by his own ignorance. He cried out, "My God! Did we really send men to fight in this?"

In the Second World War, the U.S. Army in ETO was getting disturbingly close to the British model of the earlier war. When the chase across France was on, senior commanders (although seldom their staffs) were often at the front, urging the men forward. But when the line became stationary, headquarters personnel from battalion on up to corps and army found themselves good billets and seldom strayed. Of course there were notable exceptions, but in general the American officers handing down the orders to attack and assigning the objective had no idea what it was like at the front. Any answer to why this happened would have to be a guess, and I have no statistics on front-line visits, but from what combat veterans from the fall campaigns have told me, it was only on the rarest of occasions that any officer above the rank of captain or officer from the staff was seen by them.

This was inexcusable. It was humiliating that a British general would have to order American staff officers and their COs to go see for themselves. It was costly to a heartbreaking degree. Tens of thousands of young Americans and Germans died in battles that November, battles that did little to hasten the end of the war and should have been avoided. If there was anything positive to these battles, it was that they gave the American commanders, from Eisenhower on down, the feeling that with all this pressure coming down on them, the Germans surely didn't have the resources to build a reserve for an offensive thrust.

Just south of Aachen lies the Hurtgen Forest. Roughly fifty square miles, it sits along the German-Belgian border, within a triangle outlined by Aachen, Monschau, and Duren. It is densely wooded, with fir trees twenty to thirty meters tall. They block the sun, so the forest floor is dark, damp, devoid of underbrush. The firs interlock their lower limbs at less than two meters, so everyone has to stoop all the time. It is like a green cave, always dripping water, low-roofed and forbidding. The terrain is rugged, a series of ridges and deep gorges formed by the numerous streams and rivers.

The Roer River runs along the eastern edge of the Hurtgen. Beyond it is the Rhine. First Army wanted to close to the Rhine, which General Hodges decided required driving the Germans out of the forest. Neither he nor his staff noted the obvious point that the Germans controlled the dams upstream on the Roer. If the Americans ever got down into the river valley, the Germans could release the dammed-up water and flood the valley. The forest could have been bypassed to the south, with the dams as the objective. The forest without the dams was worthless; the dams without the forest were priceless. But the generals got it backward, and went for the forest. Thus did the Battle of Hurtgen get started on the basis of a plan that was grossly, even criminally stupid.

It was fought under conditions as bad as American soldiers ever had to face, even including the Wilderness and the Meuse-Argonne. Sgt. George Morgan of the 4th Division described it: "The forest was a helluva eerie place to fight. You can't get protection. You can't see. You can't get fields of fire. Artillery slashes the trees like a scythe. Everything is tangled. You can scarcely walk. Everybody is cold and wet, and the mixture of cold rain and sleet keeps falling. They jump off again, and soon there is only a handful of the old men left."

On September 19 the 3rd Armored Division and the 9th Infantry Division began the attack. The lieutenants and captains quickly learned that control of formations larger than platoons was nearly impossible. Troops more than a few feet apart couldn't see each other. There were no clearings, only narrow firebreaks and trails. Maps were almost useless. When the Germans, secure in their bunkers, saw the GIs coming forward, they called down pre-sited artillery fire, using shells with fuses designed to explode on contact with the treetops. When men dove to the ground for cover, as they had been trained to do and as instinct dictated, they exposed themselves to a rain of hot metal and wood splinters. They learned that to survive a shelling in the Hurtgen, hug a tree. That way they exposed only their steel helmets.

Tanks could barely move on the few roads, which were too muddy, too heavily mined, too narrow. The tanks could not move at all off the roads. Airplanes couldn't fly. The artillery could shoot, but not very effectively, as forward observers (FOs) couldn't see ten meters to the front. The Americans could not use their assets—air, artillery, mobility. They were committed to a fight of mud and mines, carried out by infantry skirmish lines plunging ever deeper into the forest, with machine guns and light mortars their only support.

For the Germans, it was equally horrible. One enemy commander, Gen. Hans Schmidt of the 275th Infantry Division, called the forest a "weird and wild" place, where "the dark pine trees and the dense tree-tops give the forest even in the daytime a somber appearance which is apt to cast gloom upon sensitive people." Gen. Paul Mahlmann, commanding the 353rd Infantry Division, said his troops "were fighting in deplorable conditions, exposed to incessant enemy fire, fighting daily without relief, receiving little support from their own artillery, drenched by frequent rain, and without the possibility of changing clothes." He went on, "Forsaken as they were they had no choice but to hold out in hopeless resignation."

For the GIs, it was a calamity. In their September action, the 9th and 2nd Armored lost up to 80 percent of their front-line troops and gained almost nothing. In October the 9th—reinforced —tried again, but by mid-month it was dead in the water and had suffered terribly. Casualties were around 4,500 for an advance of 3,000 meters. German losses were somewhat less, around 3,300.

Staff officers were learning, if slowly. On the last day of October the staff of the 9th Division issued a five-page report, "Notes on Woods Fighting." Troops already in the line and still alive knew what the lessons were, but the report was valuable to new units and replacements being fed into the forest. It advised training in forest fighting prior to commitment, pressing against a tree when the shelling began, fighting during the day because night operations were physically impossible, never traveling in the woods without a compass, and never sending reinforcements forward in the midst of a battle or shelling.

Call it off! That's what the GIs wanted to tell the generals, but the generals shook their heads and said, Attack. On November 2 the 28th Infantry Division took it up. Maj. Gen. Norman Cota, one of the heroes of D-Day, was the CO. The 28th was the Pennsylvania National Guard and was called the Keystone Division. Referring to the red keystone shoulder patch, the Germans took to calling it the Bloody Bucket Division.

It tried to move forward, but it was like walking into hell. From their bunkers the Germans sent forth a hail of machine-gun and rifle fire, and mortars. The GIs were caught in thick minefields. Everything was mud and fir trees. The attack stalled.

"The days were so terrible that I would pray for darkness," Pvt. Clarence Blakeslee recalled, "and the nights were so bad I would pray for daylight." Lt. John Forsell, K Company, 110th Infantry, 28th Division, had a macabre day-night experience. He was outside the village of Schmidt, which was no-man's-land. "Daily we would check the houses," he explained. "The Germans patrolled the same town at night. One morning our patrol came into town and found a G.I. hung on the Crucifixion Cross. We cut him down. We stayed in town and hid in a few houses waiting for the Germans. A German patrol came in, we had a gunfight, they were caught by surprise. A few of the patrol got away but we took three Germans and hung them on three crosses. That ended that little fanfare for both sides in Schmidt."

For two weeks the 28th kept attacking, as ordered. On November 5 division sent down orders to move tanks down a road called the Kall trail. But no staff officer had gone forward to assess the situation in person, and in fact the "trail" was all mud and anyway blocked by felled trees and disabled tanks. The attack led only to loss.

There were men who broke under the strain, and there were heroes. On November 5 the Germans counterattacked. An unknown GI dashed out of his foxhole, took a bazooka from a dead soldier, and engaged two German tanks. He fired from a range of twenty-five meters and put one tank out of action. He was never seen again.

On November 6 an entire company passed the breaking point. An all-night shelling had caused numerous casualties. At dawn a German counterattack began. When the small-arms fire erupted from the woods, the men could endure no more. First one, then another, then two and three together, began to run to the rear. Capt. Joe Pruden was sympathetic: "They had just had too much. Their endurance could stand no more." But he knew he had to stop them, get them to turn and face the enemy. Along with other officers at the command post, he tried. But the men were "pushing, shoving, throwing away equipment, trying to outrun the artillery and each other in a frantic effort to escape. They were all scared." He saw badly wounded men lying where they fell, crying out for medics, being ignored.

The 28th's lieutenants kept leading. By November 13 all the officers in the rifle companies had been killed or wounded. Most of them were within a year of their twentieth birthday. Overall in the Hurtgen, the 28th Division suffered 6,184 combat casualties, plus 738 cases of trench foot and 620 battle fatigue cases. Those figures mean that virtually every front-line soldier was a casualty.

Col. Ralph Ingersoll, the creator of the "Talk of the Town" for the *New Yorker* magazine, was an intelligence officer with First Army. He met with lieutenants who had just come out of the Hurtgen: "They did not talk; they just sat across the table or on the edge of your cot and looked at you very straight and unblinking with absolutely no expression in their faces, which were neither tense nor relaxed but completely apathetic. They looked, unblinking."

Bradley and Hodges remained resolute to take the Hurtgen. They put in the 4th Infantry Division. It had led the way onto Utah Beach on June 6, and gone through a score of battles since. Not many D-Day veterans were still with the division—most were dead or badly wounded. In the Hurtgen, the division poured out its lifeblood once again.

First Army put the 8th Infantry Division into the attack. On November 27 it closed to the town of Hurtgen, the original objective of the offensive when it began in mid-September. It fell to Lt. Paul Boesch, G Company, 121st Infantry, to take the town. At dawn on November 28, Boesch put one of his lieutenants to the left side of the road leading to town, while he took the other platoon to the other side. Boesch ran from man to man, explaining what the company was about to do. When he gave the signal, they charged. "It was sheer pandemonium," he recalled. Once out of that damned forest, the men went mad with battle lust.

Boesch described it as "a wild, terrible, awe-inspiring thing. We dashed, struggled from one building to another shooting, bayoneting, clubbing. Hand grenades roared, fires cracked, buildings to the left and right burned with acrid smoke. Dust, smoke, and powder filled our lungs, making us cough, spit. Automatic weapons chattered while heavier throats of mortars and artillery disgorged deafening explosions. The wounded and dead—men in the uniforms of both sides—lay in grotesque positions at every turn."

American tanks supported Boesch's company. He remembered that they would first spray the buildings with their .50-calibers, then use their 75s to blow holes for the infantry. "We hurled ourselves through the holes or through windows or splintered doors. Then it became a battle from floor to floor—from room to room." The company took nearly three hundred prisoners.

As the battle sputtered to a close, Boesch "started to shake, and it wasn't the cold. I realized that I had not been afraid during that whole day. Not once did I feel afraid. I was busy as hell, and that occupied my mind. But when I shook, visibly, on that floor with a roof at least two feet thick over my head, I was hoping that I would not forget to be afraid because that was the best way to stay alive, to not make careless moves." He was wounded later that night by a German shell and was sent to a hospital in the States.

The 8th Division didn't get far beyond Hurtgen. By December 3, it was used up. A staff officer from the regiment was shocked when he visited the front that day. He reported, "The men of this battalion are physically exhausted. The spirit and will to fight are there; the ability to continue is gone. These men have been fighting without rest or sleep for four days and last night had to lie unprotected from the weather in an open field. They are shivering with cold, and their hands are so numb that they have to help one another on with their equipment. I firmly believe that every man up there should be evacuated through medical channels." Many had trench foot; all had bad colds or worse, plus diarrhea.

15

The Battle of the Bulge

THROUGH THE FALL, the great offensive continued. The only place the Allies were not on the attack was in the Ardennes itself, which was thinly held by Lt. Gen. Troy Middleton's corps. On a drive to Maastricht on December 7, Eisenhower had noted how spread out the troops in the Ardennes were, and he questioned Bradley about the vulnerability of this sector of the front. Bradley said he could not strengthen the Ardennes area without weakening Patton's and Hodges's offensives, and that if the Germans counterattacked in the Ardennes they could be hit on either flank and stopped long before they reached the Meuse River. Although he did not expect a German counterattack, he said he had taken the precaution of not placing any major supply installations in the Ardennes. Eisenhower was satisfied by Bradley's explanation.

December 16 was a day of celebration at SHAEF main headquarters in Versailles, featuring a wedding, a promotion, and a medal. In the morning, Eisenhower aide Sgt. Mickey McKeogh married one of the WAC sergeants. Eisenhower hosted a champagne reception in his house in Saint-Germain. He had something else to celebrate: the U.S. Senate had just announced his promotion to the newly created rank of General of the Army, which made him equal in rank to Marshall, MacArthur—and Montgomery.

Late in the afternoon Bradley arrived to complain about the replacement situation. The United States now had all but one of its divisions committed, the flow of replacements was not keeping pace with the casualty rate, and because of the general offensive that Eisenhower insisted on conducting, SHAEF had few men in reserve.

While they talked in Eisenhower's office, British Gen. Kenneth Strong interrupted to inform them that a German attack had been launched that morning in the Ardennes. Bradley's initial reaction was to dismiss it as a mere spoiling attack, designed to draw Patton's forces out of the Saar offensive. But Eisenhower immediately sensed something bigger. "That's no spoiling attack," he said, explaining that since the Ardennes itself offered no worthwhile objective, the Germans must be after some strategic gain. "I think you had better send Middleton some help," he told Bradley. Studying the operations map with Strong, Eisenhower noticed that the 7th Armored Division was out of the line, in First Army sector, and that the 10th Armored Division, a part of Third Army, was currently uncommitted. He told Bradley to send the two divisions to Middleton, in the Ardennes. Bradley hesitated; he knew that both Hodges and Patton would be upset at losing the divisions, Patton especially, as the 10th Armored was one of his favorites. With a touch of impatience, Eisenhower overruled Bradley.

In the morning, the news Strong brought, based on identification of German divisions in the Ardennes and on captured documents, was about as bad as it could have been. Eisenhower's rapid and intuitive judgment had been right—the Germans were engaged in a counteroffensive, not just a counterattack. Two German panzer armies of twenty-four divisions had struck Middleton's corps of three divisions. The Germans had managed to achieve both complete surprise and overwhelming local superiority, an eight-to-one advantage in infantrymen and a four-to-one advantage in tanks.

Eisenhower accepted the blame for the surprise, and he was right to do so, as he had failed to read correctly the mind of the enemy. Eisenhower failed to see that Hitler would take desperate chances, and Eisenhower was the man responsible for the weakness of Middleton's line in the Ardennes because he was the one who had insisted on maintaining a general offensive.

But despite his mistakes, Eisenhower was the first to grasp the full import of the offensive, the first to be able to readjust his thinking, the first to realize that, although the surprise and the initial Allied losses were painful, in fact Hitler had given the Allies a great opportunity. On the morning of December 17, Eisenhower showed that he saw the opportunity immediately, when he wrote the War Department that "if things go well we should not only stop the thrust but should be able to profit from it."

After dictating that letter Eisenhower held a conference with Smith, Gen. J. F. M. Whiteley, and Strong. SHAEF now had only two divisions in reserve, the 82nd and 101st Airborne, which were refitting from the battles around Arnhem. The SHAEF generals anticipated that the Germans would attempt to cross the Meuse River, thus splitting 21st and 12th Army Groups, and take the huge Allied supply dumps at Liege. The dumps were crucial to the Germans, as they contained the fuel Hitler counted on to sustain a drive to Antwerp.

Whiteley put his finger on the small Belgian town of Bastogne and declared that the crossroads there was the key to the battle. Bastogne was surrounded by rolling countryside, unusually gentle in the rough Ardennes country, and had an excellent road network. Without it the Germans would not be able to cross the Ardennes to the Meuse. Eisenhower decided to concentrate his reserves at Bastogne. He ordered a combat command of the 10th Airborne to proceed immediately to the town, and told the 101st to get there as soon as possible. He also sent the 82nd Airborne to the northern edge of the penetration, where it could lead a counterattack against the German right flank. Finally the Supreme Commander ordered the cessation of all offensives by the AEF "and the gathering up of every possible reserve to strike the penetration on both flanks."

The following morning, December 18, Ike called Smith, Bradley, and Patton to a conference. The generals met in a cold, damp squad room in a Verdun barracks, on the site of the greatest battle ever fought. There was only one lone potbellied stove to ease the bitter cold. Eisenhower's subordinates entered the room glum, depressed, embarrassed. Noting this, he opened by saying, "The present situation is to be regarded as one of opportunity for us and not of disaster. There will be only cheerful faces at this conference table." Patton quickly picked up on the theme. "Hell, let's have the guts to let the ―――― ―――― ―――― go all the way to Paris," he said. "Then we'll really cut 'em off and chew 'em up."

Eisenhower said he was not *that* optimistic: the line of the Meuse had to be held. But he was not thinking defensively. He informed his commanders that he was not going to let the Germans get away with emerging from the West Wall without punishing them. He asked Patton how long it would take him to change the direction of his offensive, from east to north, to counterattack the Germans' left, or southern, flank.

Patton replied, "Two days." The others chuckled at this typical Patton bravado; Eisenhower advised him to take an extra day and make the attack stronger. He told Patton to cancel his offensive in the Saar, change directions, and organize a major counterblow toward Bastogne by December 23. He was going to have Montgomery organize an attack in the north, against the German right flank. In short, by December 18, on the third day of the Bulge, well before the issue was settled at Bastogne or on the Meuse. Eisenhower had already put in motion a counterattack designed to destroy the German panzer armies in the Ardennes.

That Eisenhower was able to react so positively to news that had other generals shaking spoke well of him. But the real heroes of the day were the junior officers, the NCOs, and the enlisted men in the Ardennes. They were the ones who stood up to what should have been an overwhelming German attack. Hitler had managed to gather in the Eifel, across from the Ardennes, a force greater than the one that had attacked through the same area in May 1940. At the point of attack, the Germans had as much as a ten-to-one superiority. In such circumstances it was to be expected that the untried American troops in the Ardennes would cut and run, and some of them did, or surrender in mass, and some of them did. But at crossroads, on hilltops, in villages, individuals stood to their guns and did their duty, holding up the German onslaught, disrupting Hitler's timetable, giving Eisenhower a chance to gather reinforcements and rush them to the battlefield. Not least of these was Lt. Lyle Bouck.

Lieutenant Bouck commanded the intelligence and reconnaissance (I&R) platoon of the 394th Regiment, 99th Division. He had enlisted before the war, lying about his age. He was commissioned a second lieutenant at age eighteen. Informal in manner, he was sharp, incisive, determined, a leader. The only man younger than he in the platoon was Pvt. William James. The platoon was near Lanzerath. Bouck kept his men up all night December 15–16, sensing that something was stirring somewhere.

Shortly before dawn, December 16, the sleepy-eyed men saw the sky lit up from the muzzle flashes of a hundred pieces of German artillery. In the light of those flashes, Bouck could see great numbers of tanks, self-propelled guns, and other vehicles on the German skyline. He and his men were in deep, covered foxholes, so they survived the hour-long shelling without casualties. Bouck sent a patrol forward to Lanzerath, with orders to climb to a second story and observe. The men came back to report a German infantry column coming toward the village.

Bouck tried to telephone battalion headquarters, but the lines had been cut by the shelling. He got through on the radio. When he reported, the officer at the other end was incredulous.

"Damn it," Bouck hollered. "Don't tell me what I don't see! I have twenty-twenty vision. Bring down some artillery, all the artillery you can, on the road south of Lanzerath. There's a Kraut column coming up from that direction!"

No artillery came. A couple of tanks that had been supporting the I&R platoon had pulled out when the shelling began. The men told Bouck it was time for them to retreat; after all, they had gathered and reported the intelligence, which was their job.

Bouck said no. He started pushing men into their foxholes. Including Bouck, there were eighteen of them. They were on the edge of a wood, looking down on the road leading into Lanzerath. Bouck, Sgt. Bill Slape, and Private James had their foxhole in the edge of the village. They were in a perfect position to ambush the enemy, and they had plenty of firepower—a couple of .30-caliber machine guns, a .50-caliber on the jeep, a half-dozen BARs, and a number of submachine guns.

The German columns came marching on, one on each side of the road, in close order, weapons slung, no security on either flank. They were teenage paratroopers. The men of the I&R platoon were fingering the triggers of their weapons. Sergeant Slape took aim on the lead German. "Your mother's going to get a telegram for Christmas," he mumbled.

Bouck knocked the rifle aside. "Maybe they don't send telegrams," he said. Then he explained that he wanted to let the lead units pass so as to spring the ambush on the main body. He waited until about three hundred men had passed his position and gone into the village. Then he saw his target. Separated from the others, three officers came along, carrying maps and binoculars, with a radioman just behind—obviously the battalion CO and his staff. James rested his M-1 on the edge of his foxhole and took careful aim.

A little blond girl dashed out of the house just down the street. She made a vivid impression on James—later he recalled the red ribbons in her hair—and he held his fire. The girl pointed quickly at the I&R position and ran back inside. James tightened his finger on the trigger. In that split second the German officer shouted an order and dove into the ditch. So did his men, on each side of the road.

The ambush ruined, the firefight began. Bouck's men had the Germans pinned down. Through the morning they fired their weapons, including the .50-caliber mounted on the jeep. Without armored support, the German infantry couldn't get at the jeep, nor fire with much effect on the men in the foxholes. By noon, the I&R had taken some casualties but no fatalities.

Private James kept screaming at Bouck to bring in artillery with the new proximity fuse.* Bouck in turn was screaming over the radio. Battalion replied that there were no guns available.

"What shall we do then?" Bouck demanded.

"Hold at all costs."

A second later a bullet hit and destroyed the radio Bouck had been holding. He was unhurt and passed on the order to hold.

Private James was amazed at the German tactics. Their paratroopers kept coming straight down the road, easy targets. "Who-

* A fuse that incorporated a tiny transceiver that emitted radio waves after firing, which exploded on the reflection back from the waves when the shell was near the target. Initially it was used only for anti-aircraft fire, but by late 1944 it was being used for bombardment by artillery against Germans caught in the open.

ever's ordering that attack," James said, "must be frantic. Nobody in his right mind would send troops into something like this without more fire support." He kept firing his BAR. The Germans kept coming. He felt a certain sickness as he cut down the tall, good-looking "kids." The range was so close James could see their faces. He tried to imagine himself firing at movement, not at men.

As the Germans, despite their loses, threatened to overrun the position, James dashed on to the jeep and got behind the .50-caliber. Three Germans crawled up close enough to toss grenades at Pvt. Risto Milosevich, who was firing his .30-caliber at men in front of him. Unable to swing the .50-caliber fast enough, James brought up the submachine gun he had slung around his neck and cut the three Germans down. In a frenzy he ran to the bodies and emptied an entire magazine of nineteen rounds into the corpses.

By mid-afternoon there were four hundred to five hundred bodies in front of the I&R platoon. Only one American had been killed, although half the eighteen men of the platoon were wounded. There was a lull. Bouck said to James, "I want you to take the men who want to go and get out."

"Are you coming?"

"No, I have orders to hold at all costs. I'm staying."

"Then we'll all stay."

An hour later they were both wounded, the platoon out of ammunition. They surrendered and were taken into a cafe set up as a first-aid post. James thought he was dying. He thought of the mothers of the boys he had mowed down and of his own mother. He passed out, was treated by a German doctor. When he came to, a German officer tried to interrogate him but gave it up, leaned over James's stretcher, and whispered in English, "*Ami,* you and your comrades are brave men."

At midnight, the cuckoo clock in the cafe struck. Lt. Lyle Bouck, on his stretcher on the floor, had turned twenty-one years old. "What a hell of a way to become a man," he mumbled to himself.

On the third day of the attack, December 19, German armor began to acquire momentum; the greatest gains made by the armored spearhead columns were achieved that day. The U.S. Army, meanwhile, was in an apparent rout, reminiscent of First Bull Run eighty-three years earlier. As the Germans straightened out their traffic jams behind the front, the Americans in retreat were colliding with the reinforcements Eisenhower had sent to the battle, causing a monumental traffic jam of their own.

The U.S. Army in retreat was a sad spectacle. When the 101st Airborne got to Bastogne on December 19, the columns marched down both sides of the road, toward the front. Down the middle of the road came the defeated American troops, fleeing the front in disarray, moblike. Many had thrown away their rifles, their coats, all encumbrances. Some were in a panic, staggering, exhausted, shouting, "Run! Run! They'll murder you! They'll kill you! They've got everything, tanks, machine guns, air power, everything!"

"They were just babbling," Maj. Richard Winters of the 506th PIR recalled. "It was pathetic. We felt ashamed."

The 101st had packed and left Mourmelon in a hurry. The troopers were short of everything, including ammunition. "Where's the ammo? We can't fight without ammo," the men were calling out as they marched through Bastogne to the sound of the guns. The retreating horde supplied some. "Got any ammo?" the paratroopers would ask those who were not victims of panic.

"Sure, buddy, glad to let you have it."

Cpl. Walter Gordon noted sardonically that by giving away their ammo, the retreating men relieved themselves of any further obligation to stand and fight. They had long since left behind partly damaged or perfectly good artillery pieces, tanks, half-tracks, trucks, jeeps, food, rations, and more.

Abandonment of equipment was sometimes unavoidable, but often it was inexcusable. Panic was the cause. Guns that should have been towed out of danger were not. When a convoy stalled, drivers and passengers jumped out of their vehicles and headed west on foot.

Panic was costly in every way. Pvt. Ralph Hill of the 99th Division remembered a platoon of infantry who were occupying a deep dugout with a heavy wooden cover. An antitank gun was set up at the nearest crossroads. At 0530, December 16, heavy artillery shells began falling around the position. The gun crew, with no cover, dashed for the dugout. "When they tore off the cover, the 99th Division infantry opened fire from the dugout, thinking they were German. All of the gun crew was killed so the gun was abandoned."

Major Winters was not alone in feeling ashamed. Pvt. Kurt Vonnegut was a recently arrived replacement in the 106th Division. He was caught up in the retreat before he could be assigned. To his eyes, it was just rout, pure and simple.

His unit surrendered. Vonnegut decided he would take his chances and bolted into the woods, without a rifle or rations, or proper winter clothing. He hooked up with three others who wouldn't surrender and set off hoping to find American lines.

Every man for himself. It was reminiscent of the German retreat through the Falaise Gap. But there were two critical differences. All along the front, scattered groups of men stuck to their guns at crossroads and in villages. They cut the German infantry columns down as a scythe cuts through a wheat field. German losses were catastrophic. The GIs were appalled at how the enemy infantry came on, marching down the middle of the road, their weapons slung, without outposts or reconnaissance of any sort, without armor support, with no idea of where the American strong points were located. The German soldiers scarcely knew how to march or fire their weapons, and knew nothing of infantry tactics.

In launching an offensive, the German army in the first year of the Great War had been better than the German army in the last year of the Second World War. What was happening at the front was exactly what Eisenhower had predicted—the Volkssturm divisions were not capable of effective action outside their bunkers. In far too many cases, however, they were attacking eighteen- and nineteen-year-old barely trained Americans. Both sides had been forced to turn to their children to fight the war to a conclusion. In this last winter of World War II, neither army could be said to be a veteran army.

Another difference between the German retreat in August and the American retreat in December was that as the beaten, terrified GIs fled west down the middle of the roads, there were combat troops on each side headed east, reinforcements marching to the sound of the guns.

☐

In this crisis the men of the U.S. Army in Northwest Europe shook themselves and made this a defining moment in their own lives and in the history of the army. They didn't like retreating, they didn't like getting kicked around, and as individuals, squads, and companies as well as at SHAEF, they decided they were going to make the enemy pay.

That they had the time to adjust and prepare to pound the Germans was thanks to a relatively small number of front-line GIs. The first days of the Battle of the Bulge were a triumph of the soldiers of democracy, marked by innumerable examples of men seizing the initiative, making decisions, leading. Captain Roland of the 99th put it best: "Our accomplishments in this action were largely the result of small, virtually independent and isolated units fighting desperately for survival. They present an almost-unprecedented example of courage, resourcefulness, and tenacity on the part of the enlisted men, noncommissioned officers, and junior-grade commissioned officers of the line companies."

By midday, December 20, Charlie Company, 395th Infantry Regiment, 99th Division, had been retreating for three and a half days, mostly without sleep and water and not enough food, through daytime mud "that was knee deep, so deep that men carrying heavy weapons frequently mired in mud so others had to take their weapons and pull them out. In one area it took 1½ hours to cover a hundred meters." Sgt. Vernon Swanson said that when word came down at 1700 hours that the regiment was withdrawing to Elsenborn Ridge, where it would dig in beside the 2nd Division and where more reinforcements were headed, "It was certainly good news. We felt it was the equivalent of saying we were returning to the United States."

The journey to Elsenborn, however, Swanson remembered "as the worst march of that week" because of the combination of mud, ice, frozen ground, and snow, seemingly all at once and all along the route. A high-pressure system had moved in from the Atlantic on December 18, temporarily opening the skies so the Allied air forces could fly a few support missions and starting a daytime thaw that slowed German tanks as much as American infantry. After darkness fell on the twentieth the ground began to freeze again; on the twenty-first there was a hodgepodge of snow, blizzards, fog, and sleet. Through this miserable weather Charlie Company marched.

"We left most of our supplies behind," Swanson said, "but our weapons were always ready. Throughout this entire journey our men made their way, cold, tired, miserable, stumbling, cursing the Army, the weather and the Germans, yet none gave up."

They arrived on the ridge around midnight, and although "we were beyond exhaustion," the men dug in. A good thing, because at dawn a German artillery shelling came down on them. Too late, the Germans had realized the critical importance of Elsenborn. Swanson's company was well dug in, but nevertheless took seven casualties. Four of them were sergeants, "which opened up the field for promotions." One of those hit was Swanson, who got wounded in the neck by shrapnel. "I couldn't make a sound because blood was pouring down my throat." Litter bearers brought him to an aid station, where a chaplain bent over him. "I could dimly make out his collar ornament which was a Star of David. He, in turn, misread my dogtag, thought I was a Catholic and gave me last rites. I remember thinking that I really had all bases covered."

Elsenborn was the Little Round Top of the Battle of the Bulge. Lt. Col. Jochen Peiper, commander of the 1st Panzer Division, could have taken it without difficulty on the seventeenth or eighteenth, but he stuck with Hitler's orders and moved west rather than north once through the American line. The low ridge lay across the direct line from the Eifel to Antwerp and should have been the main objective of the Germans on the northern flank. But the Americans got there first and dug in. Only a direct frontal assault could oust them from the position.

The Germans tried. "The first night at Elsenborn is unforgettable," Captain Roland of the 99th wrote fifty years later. "The flash and roar of exploding shells was incessant. In all directions the landscape was a Dante's inferno of burning towns and villages." The men of his regiment, the 394th Infantry, dug furiously throughout the night. "We distributed ammunition and field rations, cleaned and oiled weapons, dug foxholes and gun emplacements in the frozen earth, planted antitank mines, strung barbed wire, studied maps and aerial photographs by shielded flashlights, plotted fire zones for machine guns, mortars, and artillery, put in field telephone lines to the various command posts, and set up an aid station to receive a fresh harvest of casualties.

"Everyone was aware that there would be no further withdrawal, whatever the cost. Moreover, I could sense in the demeanor of the troops at all ranks that this resolution was written in their hearts."

Enemy mortar and artillery fire hit the 99th. American artillery fired continuously. At night the temperature fell well below zero on the Fahrenheit scale. No GI had winter clothing. "The wind blew in a gale that drove the pellets of snow almost like shot into our faces. Providing hot food on the front line became impossible, and we were obliged to live exclusively on K rations. Remaining stationary in damp, cold foxholes, with physical activity extremely limited, we began to suffer casualties from trenchfoot. . . . In time the combination of extreme cold, fatigue, boredom, and hazard became maddening. A few men broke under the strain, wetting themselves repeatedly, weeping, vomiting, or showing other physical symptoms." But there was no more retreating.

The fighting was at its most furious in the twin villages of Rocherath and Krinkelt, on the eastern edge of the ridge. There a battalion from the 2nd Infantry Division engaged a German armored division. The Germans and Americans were intermingled in a wild melee that included hand-to-hand combat. American tank crews knew they could not take on the big German tanks toe-to-toe, so they allowed the Panthers and Tigers to close on their positions for an intricate game of cat and mouse among the twin villages' streets and alleys. Shermans remained hidden and quiet behind walls, buildings, and hedgerows, waiting for a German tank to cross their sights. Most engagements took place at ranges of less than twenty-five meters. The 741st Tank Battalion knocked out twenty-seven panzers at a cost of eleven Shermans. The 644th Tank Destroyer Battalion destroyed seventeen enemy tanks at a cost of two of their own vehicles.

On December 21 Eisenhower expressed his mood and perception of the enemy in a rare Order of the Day. "We cannot be content with his mere repulse," he said of the Germans. "By rushing out from his fixed defenses the enemy may give us the chance to turn his great gamble into his worst defeat. . . . Let everyone hold before him a single thought—to destroy the enemy on the ground, in the air, everywhere—destroy him!"

His confidence was great because his basic situation was so good. He was rushing reinforcements to the battle to take advantage of the German audacity, men and equipment in great numbers. Maj. John Harrison, at First Army headquarters, wrote his wife on December 22: "There is something quite thrilling about seeing all of the troops and armour moving in on the Kraut. There has been a steady stream for days and tho the Belgians are mighty worried I am sure they are amazed at the sights they see. The armor moves about 25 miles an hour in and out of towns and to see and hear a tank roar thru a fair sized town, turn on one tread and never slow down is quite a sight. The Belgians still line the streets and tho they are not as joyous as when we first moved in, they still wave and show their appreciation."

In the middle of the Bulge, the Germans had been unable to exploit the breakthrough because the 101st Airborne and elements of the 10th Armored Division got to Bastogne before they did. Although the Germans surrounded the Americans they were denied the use of the roads, and flowing around Bastogne was time-consuming. So from December 19 on they tried to overrun the place, with apparently overwhelming strength. Altogether they launched fifteen divisions at Bastogne, four of them armored, supported by heavy artillery.

Inside the perimeter, casualties piled up in the aid stations. Most went untreated because on December 19 a German party had captured the division's medical supplies and doctors. Nevertheless, spirits stayed strong. Cpl. Gordon Carson took some shrapnel in his leg and was brought into town. At the aid station "I looked around and never saw so many wounded men. I called a medic over and said, 'Hey, how come you got so many wounded people around here? Aren't we evacuating anybody?' "

"Haven't you heard?" the medic replied.

"I haven't heard a damn thing."

"They've got us surrounded—the poor bastards."

As the battle for Bastogne raged, it caught the attention of the world. The inherent drama, the circled-wagons image, the heroic resistance, the daily front-page maps showing Bastogne surrounded, the early identification of the division by PR men in the War Department, combined to make the 101st the most famous American division of the war. As the division history put it, the legend of the 101st was aided by those maps "showing one spot holding out inside the rolling tide of the worst American military debacle of modern times."

At Bastogne, the encircled 101st Airborne won its head-to-head battles with a dozen crack German armored and infantry divisions. The Americans went through a much more miserable month than the Germans, who had an open and bountiful supply line. For the 101st, surrounded, there were no supplies in the first week and insufficient supplies thereafter. Those were the weeks that tried the souls of men who were inadequately fed, clothed, and armed. This was war at its harshest, horrible to experience. The 101st, hungry, cold, underarmed, fought the finest units Nazi Germany could produce at this stage of the war. Those Wehrmacht and SS troops were well fed, warm, and fully armed, and they heavily outnumbered the 101st.

It was a test of arms, will, and national systems, matching the best the Nazis had against the best the Americans had, with all the advantages on the German side. The 101st not only endured, it prevailed. It is an epic tale as much for what it revealed as what happened. The defeat of the Germans in their biggest offensive in the West in World War II, and the turning of that defeat into a major opportunity "to kill Germans west of the Rhine," as Eisenhower put it, was a superb feat of arms. The Americans established a moral superiority over the Germans. It was based not on equipment or quantity of arms but on teamwork, coordination, leadership, and mutual trust in a line that ran straight from Ike's HQ right on down to the companies. The Germans had little in the way of such qualities. The moral superiority was based on better training methods, better selection methods for command positions, ultimately on a more open army reflecting a more open society. Democracy proved better able to produce young men who could be made into superb soldiers than Nazi Germany.

☐

Still, there were Germans of high quality in the battle. Lt. Gottfried Kischkel, an infantry officer outside Bastogne, was in his foxhole on the afternoon of December 22. An American tank was hit and began burning. Kischkel heard cries for help from the tank. "So I crawled to it. An American was hanging out of the hatch, badly wounded. I pulled him out and dragged him to a ditch, where I applied first aid."

Kischkel looked up from his bandaging and saw several Americans staring down with their M-1s pointed at him. An American lieutenant asked, in German, "What are you doing?"

"He cried for help and I helped," Kischkel replied. The Americans put their heads together. Then the lieutenant asked, "Do you want to be taken prisoner, or do you want to go back to your comrades?"

"I must return to my comrades."

"I expected no other answer," the American said. He told Kischkel to take off.

The scenery was like a Christmas card. It drew oohs and ahs from even the most hardened warrior. One lieutenant said later, "If it hadn't been for the fighting, that would have been . . . the most beautiful Christmas. . . . The rolling hills, the snow-covered fields and mountains, and the tall, majestic pines and firs really made it a Christmas I'll never forget in spite of the fighting."

The towns evoked memories. In Arlon, Belgium, on December 20, Sgt. Bruce Egger of the 26th was amazed: "This area seemed to be untouched by the war, as the city and stores were bedecked with decorations and Christmas trees." Lt. Lee Otts, who was with Egger, remarked that "the streets were crowded with shoppers and people going home from work. . . . Everything had a holiday look about it. It really made us homesick."

Nearly every one of those four million men on the Western Front was homesick. Loneliness was their most shared emotion. Christmas meant family, and reminders of Christmas were all around these men at war. Family and home meant life. The yearning for home was overpowering. Beyond thinking of loved ones, the men in the holes thought of the most ordinary day-to-day activities of civilian life—being able to flick a switch to light a room, no need for blackout curtains, able to smoke at night, hot food on dishes served at a table, cold beer, a bed!, clean sheets, regular showers, changes of clothes, nobody shooting at you!—they thought of these things and could have cried for missing them.

One of the loneliest GIs on the Western Front on Christmas Day was Pvt. Donald Chumley, a replacement assigned to the 90th Division. "I was nineteen, just out of high school—a farm boy with little experience in anything." He was led to his one-man foxhole and told to get in and watch for Germans. Chumley didn't catch the sergeant's name. He couldn't see the men to his right and left. He didn't know what squad, platoon, company, or battalion he was in.

For Pvt. Bill Butler of the 106th it was a day of "fog, rain, snow, freezing sleet combined with someone trying to kill you. I was in a fox hole alone. I had no one to wish me a Merry Christmas." For Pvt. Wesley Peyton of the 99th Division, it was a turning-point day. He was on Elsenborn Ridge. "Christmas Day dawned clear, bright and cold." American planes were in the air, hot food came forward, along with ammunition and replacements. "I began to believe I might celebrate my 20th birthday after all."

Many men were in houses. That is where most rear-echelon people lived and slept. Sometimes front-line men, too, but only when the line ran down the middle of a village. But if the houses were within the enemy's artillery range the GIs were staying in the cellars. In many cases the second and first floors had been blown away anyway, and if they weren't they made inviting targets. So even in town men lived below ground level.

Almost any civilian walking into one of those cellars would have immediately declared it uninhabitable. The air was a mixture of sweat, brick dust, soot, and cigarette smoke. It could not be breathed. It was too dark to see much more than outlines. It was either too hot or too cold and it had no running water.

Every front-line soldier who walked into one of those cellars thought it the most desirable place in his entire world. The cellars were secure from all but a direct hit. They were dry. There was coffee on the stove. The cooks provided hot food. Sometimes there was a radio and "Axis Sally" playing American music. The exhausted GI could push some straw into a corner, lie down, and plunge into a deep sleep, completely relaxed because he felt secure.

Usually, he was right—he was secure. Even during heavy shellings, direct hits on cellars were rare. Still, they happened. Capt. Gunter Materne of the German artillery was in Belgium. "On Christmas Eve of 1944, my men and I were lying in the basement of a corner house. I was lying near the back on some straw. At about 2200 a shell exploded in our cellar. It came through the wall before it exploded." Materne's two radiomen were killed instantly. His sergeant was badly wounded and he had shrapnel in his back. As he was being pulled out the house burned down with the others still inside.

Pvt. Phillip Stark was a nineteen-year-old machine gunner in the 84th Division. He arrived on Christmas Eve at a position outside the Belgian village of Verdenne on the northern shoulder of the Bulge. His company had been on the offensive for a month and as a result lost 175 out of the original 200 men. Replacements had brought it back to strength. "Upon arrival in this sector," Stark wrote three years later, recording his experiences on paper for fear of forgetting details, "we were told no prisoners. They didn't say, 'Shoot any German who surrenders,' but there was no alternative. Our forces were spread thin. We had no one to take care of those who surrendered or were wounded. Few people back home were aware of or could understand the necessity of the thing."

At twilight the German troops in Verdenne began to celebrate. "Sounds and songs carried well across the cold clear air." Too well for Stark's safety—officers at regimental level heard the songs and decided to give the Germans a reminder of Washington crossing the Delaware to attack the Hessian troops on Christmas Eve 1776. Stark's platoon was ordered to attack and drive the Germans from the town. That meant going up a hill. In the dark the company got to the top, only to be shelled by American artillery. Stark and his buddy Wib tried to dig in, but below the frozen earth there was rock. They were digging from the prone position, and despite frantic efforts, when dawn came "our hole was only about a foot deep and six feet long. Wib was 6'2" and I'm 6'6", but at least we were able to keep ourselves below the all important ground level.

"This is how we spent Christmas Eve in 1944."

Christmas morning, Stark got to talking to Wib about the stories he had heard or read from the First World War, when on Christmas the front-line soldiers would declare a truce. "We longed for a lull, for a day of peace and safety." Instead they got a German barrage, intended to cover the retreat of German vehicles from Verdenne. Stark began cutting down fleeing enemy infantry: "Only on this Christmas Day did I ever find combat to be as pictured in the movies. We blazed away ruthlessly. This action could not be understood or accepted by persons not having combat experience."

At dawn the following day, German infantry and tanks counterattacked. The remainder of the platoon retreated, but Stark stayed with his machine gun, even when Wib took a bullet in the middle of his forehead. "Now I was alone and for the first time I was sure that I too was going to die. But I kept on firing, hoping to keep them off. By now three enemy tanks were very close and firing their machine guns and cannon directly at my position. I was nearing the end of my second box of ammunition." A German bullet ricocheted off his machine gun, broke into bits, and slammed into his left cheek, blinding him in the left eye. He ran to the rear only to bump up against a burning German tank. Then over the hill and back to where he had started three days ago, on Christmas Eve. He had lost an eye and won a Silver Star. In his sector, nothing had been gained by either side in this series of attacks and counterattacks.

Through the first weeks of January, the battle continued. Eisenhower insisted on an offensive that was effective but terribly costly. The total toll of American casualties in the Bulge was 80,987. More than half the killed or wounded came in January. For the period December 16 to January, the defensive phase of the battle for the Americans, the figures were 4,138 killed in action, 20,231 wounded in action, and 16,946 missing. For the period January 3 through 28, when the Americans were on the offensive, the losses were 6,138 killed, 27,262 wounded, and 6,272 missing. Thus January 1945 was the costliest month of the campaign in Northwest Europe for the U.S. Army.

Such figures boggle the mind. Bringing them down to the individual level helps comprehension. Easy Company, 506th PIR, was in the Bastogne battle from December 18 to January 17. Easy's losses were heavy. Exact figures are impossible to come by; in the hurry-up movement out of Mourmelon the company roster was not completed; replacements came in as individuals or in small groups and were not properly accounted for on the roster; wounded men dropped out of the line only to come back a few days later. An estimate is that Easy went into Belgium with 121 officers and men, received about two dozen replacements, and came out with 63. The Easy men killed in action in Belgium were Sgt. Warren Muck, Cpl. Francis Mellett, and Pvts. A. P. Herron, Kenneth Webb, Harold Webb, Carl Sowosko, John Shindell, Don Hoobler, Harold Hayes, Alex Penkala, and John Julian.

The best description of the cost of the Battle of the Bulge to Easy Company comes from Pvt. Ken Webster, who rejoined the company during the truck ride to Alsace. He had been wounded in early October; now it was mid-January. He wrote, "When I saw what remained of the 1st platoon, I could have cried; eleven men were left out of forty. Nine of them were old soldiers who had jumped in either Holland or Normandy or both: McCreary, Liebgott, Marsh, Cobb, Wiseman, Lyall, Martin, Rader, and Sholty. Although the other two platoons were more heavily stocked than the 1st, they were so understrength that, added to the 1st, they wouldn't have made a normal platoon, much less a company."

Beyond the wounded and killed, every man at Bastogne suffered. Men unhit by shrapnel or bullets were nevertheless casualties. There were no unwounded men at Bastogne. As Winters put it, "I'm not sure that anybody who lived through that one hasn't carried with him, in some hidden way, the scars. Perhaps that is the factor that helps keep Easy men bonded so unusually close together."

They knew each other at a level only those who have fought together in a variety of tactical situations can achieve, as only those who endured together the extreme suffering of combined cold, not enough food, and little sleep while living in constant tension could attain.

They knew fear together. Not only the fear of death or wound, but the fear that all this was for nothing. Glenn Gray wrote, "The deepest fear of my war years, one still with me, is that these happenings had no real purpose. . . . How often I wrote in my war journals that unless that day had some positive significance for my future life, it could not possibly be worth the pain it cost."

They got through the Bulge because they had become a band of brothers. The company had held together at the critical moments in the snow outside Bastogne because 1st Sgt. Carwood Lipton and his fellow NCOs, nearly all Toccoa men, provided leadership, continuity, and cohesiveness. Despite a new CO and new officers and enlisted recruits, the spirit of E Company was alive, thanks to the sergeants.

That spirit was well described by Webster. By this time Webster had been wounded twice and returned to combat after each occasion. He would not allow his parents to use their influence to get him out of the front lines. He would not accept any position of responsibility within E Company. He was a Harvard intellectual who had made his decision on what his point of view of World War II would be, and stuck to it.

He was a man of books and libraries, a reader and a writer, sensitive, level-headed, keenly observant, thoughtful, well educated. Here he was thrown into the most intimate contact (pressed together on an open truck on icy roads in hilly country, sleeping in a foxhole with other enlisted men) with ill-educated hillbillies, Southern farmers, coal miners, lumbermen, fishermen, and so on among most of the enlisted men in the company. Of those who had been to college, most were business or education majors. In short, Webster was thrown in with a group of men with whom he had nothing in common. He would not have particularly liked or disliked them in civilian life, he just would not have known them.

Yet it was among this unlikely group of men that Webster found his closest friendships and enjoyed most thoroughly the sense of identification with others.

His description of his truck ride with his platoon to Alsace deserves to be quoted at length:

"We squished through the mud to our trucks and climbed in. McCreary and Marsh lit cigarettes. Martin made a wisecrack about a passing officer. I asked what had happened to Hoobler. Killed at

Bastogne. Poor Hoobler, who got such a kick out of war, dead in the snow. And the others? Muck and his buddy Penkala, who had the deepest hole in one position, had been killed by a direct hit. Sowosko was shot through the head attacking Foy. And so on. Some replacements who had come in after Holland had also died. A lot of men had been evacuated for trench foot, too many, McCreary thought. The platoon wasn't what it used to be."

Webster thought that it was. He had followed a long and complicated route through the Replacement Depots to rejoin the company, a time of frustration and loneliness for him among that host of khaki-clad look-alike soldiers. Now he was home, back with 1st platoon, back with Easy Company.

"It was good to be back with fellows I knew and could trust," he wrote. "Listening to the chatter in the truck, I felt warm and relaxed inside, like a lost child who had returned to a bright home full of love after wandering in a cold black forest."

There were missing chairs at home. They belonged to the men who had been killed, badly wounded, or had broken. But as Webster's reaction indicates, although Easy had lost many members, and gained others, thanks to the former E Company officers now on battalion or regimental staff and to the noncoms, it remained an organic whole.

Not all did. The 29th Division's saying—We are three divisions, one in the grave, one in the hospital, one at the front—could be applied to more than two dozen U.S. divisions in ETO, including the 101st. And the one at the front consisted of replacements who did not know what to do and war-weary veterans whose fatalistic attitudes suggested that it did not matter what they did. Fortunately, there was that core of veterans who could teach as well as fight. It was critical to the victory because by the end of the war men who had been State-side on D-Day made up virtually the whole of the fighting army.

The army was always learning. After the war it conducted surveys among the ETO veterans, including detailed material on their training, rightly figuring that it was the combat veterans who could best judge its effectiveness. A majority of the men surveyed had their training in 1944 and fought in the last six to eight months of the war. Perhaps half of them had been through Repple Depples.

Every combat veteran I've interviewed, when asked about training, starts with some version of, "Nothing can prepare you for combat." Virtually all the men surveyed agreed. The paratroopers commented that they thought they had been put through a training regime so tough that "combat can't be worse than this," only to discover it was. There was a consensus among the GIs that training should be tougher, with more live ammunition, and the best way to prepare a soldier for combat was to improve his stamina and physical strength.

The veterans pointed to many additional shortcomings in their training. About 80 percent said they did not know enough about German weapons, how to defend against them or how to attack them. They further felt their knowledge of German tactics was deficient. They wished they had been taught more aircraft identification. Ninety percent were unprepared for mine warfare. No one had said to them one word about trench foot, much less how to prevent it.

No surprise: They felt all those hours spent doing close order drill and learning military courtesy were wasted. They felt their weapons training had been good. But they had not been taught to follow close behind supporting artillery fire, they tended to slow down on making contact, they allowed German indirect fire to pin them down, their noise and light discipline at night was poor, they bunched together when fired on. Those that survived the first few days learned how to do better, but they could have been taught at far less cost back in the States.

Captain Roland remarked, "The marvel is that the draftee divisions were able to generate and maintain any esprit de corps at all. Formed originally by mixing men indiscriminately from throughout the nation, thus severing all personal, social, community, and regional bonds, identified by anonymous numbers and replenished through the notorious Repple Depples, their only source of morale, other than the shared experience of hazard and hardship, was the character and patriotism of the soldiers. Fortunately, that proved to be sufficient."

In an article in *Army History,* published by the U.S. Army's Center of Military History in 1994, Professor Francis Steckel indicts the army for two reasons: "First, the replacement system rushed men into combat without adequate preparation and created an unnecessarily arduous challenge of adjustment on the field of battle. Second, the small number of divisions required units to remain in the front lines without rest and beyond the limits of individual human endurance, thus causing an earlier than necessary breakdown of veterans whose invaluable combat experience and skills were lost prematurely."

I'd add a third indictment: failure to pass on even rudimentary information. It was not the job of the front-line machine gunner or tanker to train replacements. The army was supposed to do that and it failed.

16

Night on the Line

IN THE WINTER CAMPS of 1864–65, Civil War soldiers drilled, marched in closed ranks, built log shelters, repaired equipment, foraged for food. On outpost duty they swapped tobacco, coffee, and insults with the enemy. At night they cooked and ate, sang around the campfire, and retired to bunks. Night was the best time for Johnny Reb and Billy Yank.

It wasn't like that at all in the winter of 1944–45 in Belgium, France, or Luxembourg. Night was the worst time.

The difference between 1864–65 and 1944–45 came about because of technological improvements. Civil War cannon seldom if ever fired at night, as the main body of the enemy was out of range and anyway Civil War gunners could only fire at what they could see—and then inaccurately. World War II gunners could fire much farther, arching high-trajectory shells in with precise accuracy to hit targets on the other side of the ridge, using a variety of exploding shells. Civil War soldiers had only limited, crude mortars. World War II soldiers had a variety of relatively accurate mortars and their small arms were much more accurate, with much greater range and rate of fire. Civil War soldiers at night could light their pipes, cigars, or cigarettes, and gather around a campfire with total security. World War II soldiers hardly dared to have even the smallest fire at the bottom of their foxhole or smoke a cigarette.

In the Civil War, communications between the front line and headquarters were by runner only. World War II communications were by handheld radio and, much better, telephone lines running from the front to the command post. Only the most primitive flares, and only a few of them, were available in the Civil War. In World War II, excellent flares and illuminating shells were readily available. In 1944 small, handheld bombs—grenades—unavailable in any quantity or sophistication in the Civil War, could be thrown across no-man's-land, which was in most cases narrower in 1944–1945 than in 1864–65.

The internal combustion engine gave armies a nighttime mobility that was not possible with horses. Tanks and self-propelled artillery provided a nighttime firepower far in excess of anything possible eighty years earlier. Combined, the changes in weapons and equipment made World War II commanders far more aggressive at night than Civil War commanders. The people who paid the price for this aggressiveness were the front-line soldiers.

In this chapter I attempt to give some sense of how it was for those who endured and prevailed in the dangerous environment that was life on the front line at night in World War II.

The only visitors to the front lines were sometimes a major or a lieutenant colonel commanding the battalion, less often a colonel commanding the regiment, very occasionally a brigadier general commanding the division. Reporters didn't go there, nor did the two-star generals and above. Neither did the traveling entertainers. "I never saw a USO show," Pvt. William Craft of the 314th Regiment remarked. "I heard they were good, but they didn't come to the front where I was."

The front line belonged to the men who worked there— riflemen and machine gunners, mortarmen, forward artillery observers, communications men, and medics. Its depth varied, depending on the terrain, but generally it was about one half a kilometer. Company CPs were 250 meters or so back from the main line of foxholes and were not considered front-line by the riflemen. Pvt. J. A. "Strawberry" Craft of the 84th Division defined a member of the rear echelon as "any son of a bitch behind my foxhole."

Outposts were anywhere from ten to fifty meters in front of the line of foxholes. The enemy outposts were sometimes almost within touching distance, more often up to fifty meters away. The friendly observation posts (OPs) were the edge of the known world.

Most of the time, the principal characteristic of the front line was how quiet it was. Artillery boomed in the distance and the "thump" of mortars sounded sporadically, but otherwise unless the enemy was shelling or attacking there was little noise.

Nor was there much movement. It was as if the earth had swallowed up all the human beings—as indeed it had, because on the front line men lived most of the time below the surface. Life-threatening violence was always present. Thousands of eyes searched their perimeters. Thousands of fingers were ready to pull triggers, thousands of hands were prepared to throw grenades or fire mortars at the slightest motion, or at night at the least noise or the light of a burning cigarette.

In early December the 84th Division was just inside Germany, near the border with Belgium, at Lindern. Pvt. Chalmers Davis, a mortarman, found an OP on top of a wrecked house. From it he spotted a haystack moving across an open field. He got on the phone to tell the CP that there was a camouflaged tank out there. Just then a German soldier jumped out of one foxhole and ran to another.

Davis decided to have some fun. "He never should have been out in the daytime," he told his crew, down below behind the house. "He made a mistake."

The crew fired two mortar shells and got a bracket on the foxhole. The third shell was a direct hit. A combination of luck and skill was involved, but whatever the cause the German paid for his mistake with his life. American artillery, meanwhile, got a bracket on the haystack, then knocked out the tank inside.

(Reading this story in *Citizen Soldiers* prompted one of the gunners on the 105s that did all the shooting to write. He said the gun crew thought it was all a joke and for the remainder of the war, and at postwar reunions, they would get a laugh from remembering the time they shot at a moving haystack. Not until fifty-three years later did they discover there really was a target and they had knocked out a German tank.)

□

The first rule of life on the front line: Don't move around because someone is watching. Stay in your hole whenever you can.

Depending on the length of the line a rifle company was holding, the foxholes were anywhere from a few to a hundred meters apart, occasionally even more. In this, World War II was markedly different from World War I. In the 1914–18 conflict, the trench line was continuous. You could walk from the Swiss border to the English Channel without ever showing your head above the earth's surface. The walls were lined with logs. Zigzag trenches ran back from the front to deep in the rear, so food, ammunition, and messages could be brought forward without exposure.

To man those extensive trenches, however, took hundreds of thousands of men, indeed millions. In November 1918 Marshal Foch had commanded three times more men than Eisenhower did in November 1944, on a front of approximately the same length. Hindenburg had commanded three to four times more men than Rundstedt. Necessarily, foxholes replaced trenches.

Soldiers in the Great War didn't know what a foxhole was. For all the terror of their daily existence, they at least had the comfort of being with comrades, seeing men around them, sensing their own power. World War II soldiers didn't know what trenches were. In their foxholes they had one, at most two companions. Otherwise they felt isolated—as in fact in a spread-out company they were.

Compounding the isolation was the unnatural situation of living below the surface of the earth plus the physical misery of digging a hole big enough for your coffin at the end of an exhausting day. But it had to be done, a lesson quickly learned.

Digging the hole was often arduous, sometimes exhausting. A typical position would be in or on the edge of a wood, which meant many roots, as most of the trees in Belgium were planted in rows, close together. During the second half of December, when the nighttime thermometer began to go down to near or below zero, the ground was frozen to the depth of a foot or more. Pickaxes were hard to come by on the front and even when available they weren't much help. Sometimes it took hours to chip away enough frozen earth to get to unfrozen ground. Men used grenades or satchel charges to blow away the frozen earth.

Often it was just impossible. On the night of December 18–19, near Echternach, Sgt. John Sweeney of the 10th Armored Division tried to dig in, "but the ground was made up of heavy wet clay and our entrenching shovel couldn't dig into it." After penetrating a few inches, he and his buddies gave up. "It was so cold that the rear echelon brought up some overcoats (2 for every 3 soldiers). We placed one overcoat on the ground and three of us lay on it and covered ourselves with the second overcoat. The only one who was warm was the middle guy so we changed places every twenty minutes or so."

The holes were usually rectangular, under the best conditions four or five feet deep, two or three feet wide by six feet long. When the men were in them for more than one night, or if they were veterans, they got them covered.

Sgt. Leo Lick of the 1st Division, a veteran of Sicily (where he won a Silver Star) and the Normandy invasion, moved into the line near Butgenbach at twilight of December 17. He and two buddies worked on their hole for a week. They got some logs which "we put over the hole and then put branches over the logs and then covered that layer with soil and camouflaged the top with snow. We also put six inches of evergreen needles on the bottom of the hole for comfortable sleeping. The opening to the foxhole also served as a warfare trench from which we could shoot or stand guard."

Just one night in a foxhole in Belgium in December 1944 was memorable. Ten, twenty, thirty nights was hell. To begin with, night lasted so long in those northern latitudes. Dusk began to come on around 1600 or 1615. By 1645 it was full dark. First light didn't come up for sixteen hours. It was bitterly cold, even for the GIs from Montana or North Dakota. It was frequently below zero and generally damp, with low clouds blowing in from the North Sea and a fog that penetrated everywhere—when it wasn't snowing. Then the wind blew like a gale, driving the pellets of snow into their faces. It was Northern Europe's coldest winter in forty years.

Col. Ralph Ingersoll described the cold: "Riding [in a jeep] through the Ardennes, I wore woolen underwear, a woolen uniform, armored force combat overalls, a sweater, an armored force field jacket with elastic cuffs, a muffler, a heavy lined trenchcoat, two pairs of heavy woolen socks, and combat boots with galoshes over them—and I cannot remember ever being warm."

Ingersoll was lucky. Although it was windy in the open jeep, it was dry, and he was much better dressed for the cold than any GI on the line. The infantrymen's clothing was woefully, even criminally inadequate, because of a command decision General Bradley had made in September. He had decided to keep weapons, ammunitions, food, and replacements moving forward at the expense of winter clothing, betting that the campaign would be over before December. As a consequence, the men in the holes had few of the items Ingersoll wore. Their footwear—leather combat boots—was almost worse than useless. Whenever the temperature went above freezing, they were standing in two to twenty inches of water, which the leather soaked up.

There were good boots available in Europe, of the type made popular by L. L. Bean after the war—well insulated, with leather uppers but rubber bottoms—but to the everlasting disgrace of the quartermasters and all other rear-echelon personnel, who were nearly all wearing them by mid-December, not until late January did the boots get to where they were needed. Maj. Gen. Paul Hawley, the chief surgeon for ETO, commented bluntly, "The plain truth is that the footwear furnished U.S. troops is lousy."

Three days before the Bulge began, Col. Ken Reimers of the 90th Division noted that "every day more men are falling out due to trench foot. Some men are so bad they can't wear shoes and are wearing overshoes over their socks. These men can't walk and are being carried from sheltered pillbox positions at night to firing positions in the day time."

In place of boots, the men got directives on how to prevent trench foot. They were ordered to massage their feet and change their socks every day. Sergeant Lick recalled, "We would remove our wet socks, hang them around our neck to dry, massage our feet and then put on the dry socks from around our neck that we had put there the day before. Then a directive came down stating that anyone getting trench foot would be tried by court martial."

Senior officers threatened court-martial to men who got trench foot, or took disciplinary action against junior officers whose units had a high incidence of the malady because they suspected the foxhole dwellers were getting it deliberately. They thought it was almost the equivalent of a self-inflicted wound.

The best way to avoid trench foot was to lace the boots lightly and take them off at night before climbing into the sleeping bag or covering yourself with a blanket. But, Lick said, "we couldn't take our boots off when we slept because they would freeze solid and we couldn't get them on again in the morning." The obvious solution, quickly learned by thousands of men, was to take the boots off but keep them inside the sleeping bag. Still there was another reason for keeping the boots on, the possible need for instant action.

Men wrapped their feet in burlap sacks, when available, but the burlap soaked up the snow, so the boots got soggy, the socks got wet. Sergeant Lick lost all his toenails, but through regular massages and a rotation of his socks he avoided trench foot. Thousands of others got it. Trench foot put more men out of action than German 88s, mortars, or machine-gun fire. During the winter of 1944–45, some 45,000 men had to be pulled out of the front line because of trench foot—the equivalent of three full infantry divisions.

First a man lost his toenails. His feet turned white, then purple, finally black. A serious case of trench foot made walking impossible. Many men lost their toes; some had to have their feet amputated. If gangrene set in, the doctors had to amputate the lower leg. It has to be doubted that many men did this deliberately. A shot in the foot was much quicker, less dangerous, and nearly impossible to prove that it hadn't been an accident.

One private in Lt. Lee Otts's platoon shot himself in the foot and there was no question of accident. The man had been talking all night to his mate, Pvt. Penrose LeCrone, about doing it. Le-Crone had the flu and was so depressed he just wanted the guy to shut up, so he told him to go ahead and do it. Otts commented: "It was three miles by trail to the aid station. The two medics who went with him made him walk all the way—there was no free ride for those with self-inflicted wounds."

During those long nights it was impossible to keep out of the mind the thought of how easy it would be to shoot a round into the foot. Sgt. Bruce Egger considered it, but "I did not have the nerve to shoot myself. . . . I thought about dropping a case of rations on my foot, but I did not want to live the rest of my life with that on my mind. I decided to stick it out and trust in the Lord." A man in Lt. Harold Leinbaugh's platoon begged his squad leader, "Do me a favor, sergeant, shoot me in the leg."

Captain Roland of the 99th Division recalled, "Men began to wound themselves one way or another in order to get away from the front. Sometimes this was intentional. Sometimes it occurred through a gross negligence born of fear, exhaustion, and misery."

"There were two things in front of you always," Cpl. Clair Galdonik of the 90th Division remarked: "the enemy and death. . . . Sometimes morale was so low that you preferred death instead of a day-by-day agonizing existence. When you were wet, cold, hungry, lonely, Death looked very inviting. It was always close at hand and I found myself being envious of a dead comrade. At least he suffered no more physically or mentally."

Pvt. Bert Morphis of the 1st Division remembered that on Christmas Eve he was "on an outpost right in front of the German lines where the choice seemed to be between moving and being shot, or lying perfectly still and freezing to death."

Most of them stuck it out. Pvt. Dutch Schultz of the 82nd Airborne was one of hundreds who refused to be evacuated because of trench foot. But when he also came down with dysentery and the flu, his CO ordered him to the rear. He commented, "I secretly experienced a great deal of guilt about going to the hospital for anything other than a bona fide wound. Anemia, bronchitis, dysentery, and trench foot seemed to be an easy way out. In hindsight, I understand that if you are sick you don't belong on a battlefield, but when you are an immature kid trying to be a hero it is something of a problem, particularly when you are trying to prove your courage to no one other than yourself."

Getting out of there honorably was every man's dream—thus the expression "million-dollar wound." Sgt. John Sabia took five machine-gun bullets in his right thigh. His CO asked if he could make it back to the aid station on his own, as the company couldn't spare a man.

"Hell, yes, I can do it."

Sabia took a tree limb to use as a crutch and began hopping awkwardly in the snow. After ten meters he stopped, turned around, waved his limb in a gesture of defiance and exuberance, and bellowed to his buddies in their holes, "Hey, you bastards! Clean sheets! Clean sheets!"

Pvt. Donald Schoo of the 80th Infantry Division recalled seeing one of his buddies, named Steehhourst, take a hit from an 88 that blew off his right hand. "He was crying and running around yelling, 'I'm going home! Thank you God, I'm going home!' "

Steehhourst was lucky, at least according to the standards of the men of the Bulge and specifically to Sgt. Richard Wallace of the 90th Division. After one shelling Wallace told his squad, "Boys, I'd give my right arm up to here"—holding it at his elbow—"if this war would end right now." The shelling resumed. Shrapnel tore into Wallace's face.

"I can't see!" he cried out. "I can't see! Oh, my God, I'm blind." He never saw again and the war was a long way from over.

Sleep deprivation was a universal experience. Two, three, at the most four hours of fitful sleep was about it. But no matter how sleepy a man was, he lived in constant tension. The men in the front line shivered in their foxholes, attempting to stay alert, straining to see, straining to hear, straining to stay awake. They would chew gum or tobacco. Pvt. Ken Russell of the 82nd Airborne remembered chewing one or the other "very slowly. I didn't want to finish too quickly and have nothing to do but think of the precarious position I was in."

Lt. Glenn Gray calls this "the tyranny of the present." In a foxhole, the past and, more important, the future do not exist. The only thing in the world that matters is the moment. Gray says that there is "more time for thinking and more loneliness in foxholes than [anywhere else] and time is measured in other ways than by clocks and calendars."

Pvt. Dave Nutt of the 99th Division recalled, "The cold, the snow, and the darkness were enough to set young nerves on edge. The thud of something as innocuous as snow plopping to the ground from a tree branch could be terrifying. Was it snow? Was it maybe a German patrol? Should you fire at the sound and risk giving away your position, or worse hitting one of your own men? But did the Germans have us surrounded?"

Lieutenant Otts heard a "thud" one night and went out to investigate in the morning. He found a dying German soldier who murmured over and over, "Oh God, I meant no harm, I meant no harm." The boy was unarmed and wore no helmet, so he may well have been coming in to surrender when he set off the booby trap. But the Germans often went on patrols unarmed so if they were captured they could say they were coming in to give up. Otts commented, "I imagine quite a few [Germans] would have surrendered but it was impossible in the daytime, as their own men would shoot them, and at night they were afraid to try and run our gauntlet of booby traps and machine guns."

An experience shared by many foxhole soldiers was the screaming of a wounded man in front of the outposts. Otts recalled "a helluva night. . . . Someone out in front of us was screaming, 'Help! Help! Can't anyone hear me? For God's sake help!' This went on all night. You can't imagine what it does to you to be sitting in a foxhole with the black night all around and someone yelling for help in a mournful voice." Otts knew that there were American wounded out in front, but he also knew that the Germans used such calls to trick the GIs and would ambush anyone going out to give aid, so he ordered his platoon to stay put.

Tension was at its most pronounced when changing guard. Every two hours the platoon sergeants would get two men from a foxhole and lead them to the outpost position, to relieve the men on duty. "The trip out to the OP was always eerie," Sgt. Burton Christenson of the 101st Airborne remembered of his nights outside Bastogne. "You eyed all silhouettes suspiciously, skeptical of any sound. Reluctantly, you approach the OP. The silhouettes of the men in their positions are not clear. . . . Are they Germans? The suspense is always the same . . . then finally you recognize an American helmet. Feeling a little ridiculous, yet also relieved, you change the guard, turn around and return to the main line, only to repeat the entire process in another two hours."

"You always slept with one eye open," Pvt. Arnold Lindblad of the 104th Medical Battalion recalled. "Unless you were on duty, you hit the hole when it got dark and stayed there till full light. There was no walking around in the dark, no talking from hole to hole. You never got used to it."

At Istres Airport near Marseilles, July 15, 1944, three crewmen pose beside 'Rum Dum', a B-17 that had the record for combat missions at 101. The plane was then put to work flying the wounded to England. The B-17 – plane, pilots, and crew – had a reputation for toughness and durability.

Below: The payoff for air superiority. Whenever a German soldier heard a plane overhead, he ducked. When a GI heard one, he looked up and smiled.

The 9th Infantry Division, afoot and riding the back of a tankdozer, passes through the dragons' teeth in the Siegfried Line, September 1944.
Below: Two American paratroopers on the attack, despite the German barrage, in Operation Market-Garden, Holland, September 1944.

FOUR PHOTOS: U.S. ARMY SIGNAL CORPS

A Replacement Depot, or Repple Depple, in Luneville, Fance, October 12. Boredom and a sense of isolation were the dominant mood in these depots, which the GIs hated, with good cause.

Below: Aachen, Germany, October 15. In a battle that did precious little good for either side, the ancient city was all but destroyed.

Sgt. Mike Ala, 4th Infantry Division, on the radio in the Hurtgen Forest, November 18. Communication by telephone was more secure, but less dependable, because the wire (in the spool behind Ala) kept getting cut by the shells.
Below: In the Hurtgen, December 9, German prisoners are being escorted to the rear by a GI from the 9th Division. The photo has the Bill Mauldin quality of sheer misery, for both sides.

More Willie and Joe photographs from the god-awful Hurtgen. Here GIs from the 9th Division move up for an attack later that day.

Below: Jungersdorf, Germany, December 12. GIs from the 9th Division with a bag of captured Germans. You can distinguish the victors from the vanquished by the smiles on the victors' faces.

On December 16, 1944, the German army struck out in its last great offensive of the war – an offensive on a greater scale than the one it had launched in the same area in May 1940. The Germans had been retreating since July. Going over to the offensive raised morale, as these captured German photographs, taken on December 17, the second day of the Battle of the Bulge, demonstrate.

OPPOSITE:

Top: Belgium, December 25. The urge to attend services and pray was overwhelming. Every man in the battle, German or American, who could went to church, to sing the same song, 'Silent Night'.

Bottom: Christmas 1944. In a manger six hundred meters from the German lines, men from the 94th Division dry out and count their blessings.

FOUR PHOTOS: U.S. ARMY SIGNAL CORPS

The GIs were surprised. Some were shocked. Some surrendered. Some ran. But enough stayed to do their duty. On December 17, GIs from the 2nd Infantry Division crouch in a ditch during a German shelling, ready to fight back when the German infantry began to attack.

Below: Men of the 90th Infantry Division wait out a shelling in Wiltz, Luxembourg, January 9.

For the GIs the way home led east. They couldn't get back to the States until Germany quit. So they sucked it up and moved out. Here men of I Company, 84th Division, get on with it.

Below: Belgium, January 5. Two 2nd Infantry Division men get ready for whatever might come.

FOUR PHOTOS: U.S. ARMY SIGNAL CORPS

To get a look at the enemy you had to expose yourself – but you kept the exposure to a minimum. Here Cpl. Irvin Kruger, 4th Cavalry Reconnaissance Squadron, Beffe, Belgium, spots German snipers.

Below: Pvts. James Acosta and Kenneth Horgan, 3rd Armored Division, in the Ardennes, January 14. They have their bazooka handy in the event of a German armored attack. Clear days with sunshine meant colder nights, but they also meant the U.S. Army Air Force could fly, a blessing to the ground troops.

Whatever the conditions, the GIs had to have foxholes. Here Pvt. Joe Fink digs his with a pickax, January 30, Wirtzfeld, Belgium.
Below: Horsbach, France, February 2. Pvt. Vincent Wenge, 70th Division, bails out his foxhole after a thaw.

FOUR PHOTOS: U.S. ARMY SIGNAL CORPS

FOUR PHOTOS: U.S. ARMY SIGNAL CORPS

Kerpen, Germany, February 28. Mortar crews fire in close support of advancing infantry. By this time, the GIs were attacking all along the line.

Below: Men from the 1st Infantry Division in Gladbach, Germany, March 1. The Big Red One had been in combat since D-Day – and before that it had fought in North Africa and Sicily. Virtually all the men in this photograph were replacements, most of them coming in during and after the Battle of the Bulge.

By March, the U.S. Army in Northwest Europe was made up of a handful of veterans in their early twenties and lots of replacements who were eighteen and nineteen years old. They either got wounded or killed, or they matured in veterans in a hurry.

Above: Two GIs who look to be 1944 high school graduates work at their 105mm cannon outside Erp, Germany, March 6.

Below: GIs in action in street fighting in Koblenz, March 18.

The look of victory. Gens. Eisenhower, Patton, Bradley, and Hodges at Hodges's First Army HQ near Remagen, Germany, March 25, 1945. The previous day American troops had broken out of their bridgeheads to begin the final drive through Germany.

Below: German officers wait along the autobahn near Giessen, Germany, watching vehicles of the U.S. 6th Armored Division moving up to the front. As one captured German officer put it, 'We had never seen how a rich man makes war before.'

The most welcome sight in the world for these prisoners in Dachau was the appearance of GIs. They ran up a homemade American flag to welcome their liberators, men of the 45th Infantry Division.

Below: Cpl. Larry Mutinsk, 45th Division, hands out his last pack of cigarettes to prisoners in Dachau.

By March 29, 1945, the U.S. Army was pouring across Germany. These German POWs, marching west to their POW camps along the Rhine River, were astonished at the number of trucks, tanks, half-tracks, and vehicles of all kinds their enemy possessed. But in the end, what beat the German army was not so much equipment as men. The GIs had proved themselves; here was the fruit of their victory.

On his first night in a foxhole, Pvt. Richard Heuer, a replacement with the 84th Division, was suffering with dysentery. "I didn't want to crap in my helmet," he related, "so I decided I'd crawl outside at night." As he wore two pair of long johns beneath his wool pants, "it was a real chore getting down to the point where I could do my duty. As I was doing my duty I heard some noises behind me. I thought they were Germans. I jumped into the hole without pulling my drawers up. That really startled my foxhole buddy. I had crapped in the first pair of drawers, so I had to stand there in the middle of the foxhole and cut it out. This wasn't easy, because I had to do the cutting with my bayonet."

Shelling made foxhole living worse. Mortars and artillery could come in at any time. The Germans would watch the GIs take up a position at the end of a day, mark it on their maps, and shell it at night. Pvt. Arnold "Ben" Parish of the 2nd Infantry Division remembered a night during the Bulge when he and a buddy had dug a hole long and wide enough to accommodate both men, but only about eight inches deep. As they worked on it, shelling began. "It was raining shells and they were exploding all around our hole. The air was full of shrapnel and spent pieces were hitting us as we laid on our backs with our helmets over our faces. The noise was unbearable and the ground was shaking and we were shaking from fright and cold. We didn't dare raise our heads. It would have been impossible to survive outside of the hole."

Cries of "Medic!" Tree limbs hurtling through the air. The smell of powder. The bangs and flashes and booms and screams, red-hot bits of metal zooming through the air. The only movement you could make was to press ever closer to the ground. Those who endured such a cataclysm were forever scarred by it, even if untouched by shrapnel.

"We were helpless and all alone and there was nothing we could do, so I prayed to God. . . . The time went by very slow. I tried to keep warm but that wasn't possible. I thought about my mother and hoped she didn't know where I was or what I was doing. . . . Maybe this is the end of the world, I thought."

Feelings of helplessness were universal. Cpl. Stanley Kalberer, a college student at the beginning of 1944, was by December a replacement in the 84th Division. During the Bulge he, too, got caught in a shelling and described his experience: "I never felt so alone, frightened, forgotten, abused and degraded. . . . I truly believed I would never survive, or if I did I would be maimed by the weather or killed by the enemy, or both."

When men got out of the holes, they looked like slaves coming up from a coal-mine shaft. In February 1945, C Company of the 395th Regiment "was relieved in position by the 69th Division after living in holes in the ground for almost three months," recalled Pvt. Vernon Swanson, 99th Division. "When we popped out of the ground, some of the green 69th Division troops passing by were convinced that they were relieving an all black infantry battalion."

God-awful though the conditions were, men endured and prevailed. How they did so differed with each individual. But all had a sense of fatalism. Pvt. Ken Webster expressed his feelings and insights in a letter to his mother: "I am living on borrowed time. . . . If I don't come back, try not to take it too hard. I wish I could persuade you to regard death as casually as we do over here. In the heat of battle you expect casualties, you expect somebody to be killed and you are not surprised when a friend is machine-gunned in the face. You have to keep going. It's not like civilian life, where sudden death is so unexpected." ("There was no time to mourn the dead," Capt. John Colby remarked, "even if they were good friends.")

When his mother wrote to express her considerable alarm at this attitude, Webster replied, "Would you prefer for somebody else's son to die in the mud? . . . Somebody has to get in and kill the enemy. Somebody has to be in the infantry and the paratroops. If the country all had your attitude, nobody would fight, everybody would be in the Quartermaster. And what kind of a country would that be?"

Carwood Lipton was a sergeant in the 101st Airborne on D-Day, a lieutenant with a battlefield commission during the Bulge. By the end of the war he had been involved in many different kinds of combat. Asked to comment on how he managed to cope with the challenges of combat, and insofar as he felt he could to speak for others in his answer, Lipton said, "When men are in combat, the inevitability of it takes over. They are there, there is nothing they can do to change that, so they accept it. They immediately become calloused to the smell of death, the bodies, the destruction, the killing, the danger. Enemy bodies and wounded don't affect them.

"Their own wounded and the bodies of their dead friends make only a brief impression, and in that impression is a fleeting feeling of triumph or accomplishment that it was not them. There is still work to be done, a war to be won, and they think about that."

According to Lipton, it was only later, when a man got off the front line, that he had time to think about how buddies were killed or wounded, or about the times when he personally was inches from death. Out of the line, far from combat, "death and destruction are no longer inevitable—the war might end, the missions might be canceled." Such thoughts made men nervous about going back into the line. But, Lipton insisted, once back in it, all doubts and nervousness disappear. "The callousness, the cold-bloodedness, the calmness return."

Fifty years later I remarked to Lipton that in December 1944 the stockade was preferable to a foxhole. He turned on me and snapped, "Come on, Steve. No man would choose disgrace. If the stockade was preferable the stockades would have been full, the foxholes empty, and we would have lost the war."

Just there is the point. In the face of conditions scarcely equaled anywhere for fear, degradation, and misery, the great majority of front-line soldiers in ETO in 1944–45 stayed in the line and did their duty, and prevailed.

There are no unwounded foxhole veterans. Sgt. Ed Stewart of the 84th Division commented decades after the war that he had "never known a combat soldier who did not show a residue of war." Stewart's mother told him that he "left Europe but never arrived home." Sgt. George Thompson said that when he came home the sounds of war came with him. Decades later, "when I'm home by myself, at nighttime, it all comes back. I'll hear the noise, the shells exploding. I stay awake thinking about it. I guess it comes from being in a foxhole—the long hours of nighttime."

17

The Rhineland Battles

THE GERMAN RETREAT out of the Bulge was slow, stubborn, and costly to the Americans—but to the Germans also. Hitler, always insistent on holding captured ground, refused to consider pulling out of the Bulge and returning to the Siegfried Line, as his generals urged him to do. Instead, he ordered a "hold to the last man" policy in the Ardennes, and an offensive in Alsace with the idea of preventing further American reinforcements from moving north to the Ardennes.

Operation Northwind, starting January 1, hit Lt. Gen. Alexander Patch's U.S. Seventh Army. Eventually a total of fifteen U.S. divisions with 250,000 men were involved in the fighting, which took place along a front that ran almost 150 kilometers from Saarbrucken in the north to a point on the west bank of the Rhine south of Strasbourg. This was a natural salient along the bend of the Rhine, so the battle was something of a mirror image of the one going on to the north in the Ardennes.

Behind the salient, the Alsatian Plain stretched westward from the Rhine to the foothills of the Vosges Mountains. It was unsuitable to the defense. The textbook response to the Northwind attack would have been to fall back on the rough country and leave the plain to the Germans. That was what Eisenhower wanted to do, but politics intervened. French leader Charles de Gaulle told the

Supreme Commander that if they were cadets at military school he would agree with Eisenhower's opinion, but as the French leader he absolutely could not accept abandoning Strasbourg, not only for reasons of national pride but also because of the fearful reprisals the Gestapo was sure to take on the citizens of Strasbourg. Eisenhower reluctantly agreed and the order went out to Seventh Army: hold your ground. As a result, bitter battles were waged through January at Wingen, Philippsbourg, Herrlisheim, Rittershoffen, and elsewhere.

Col. Hans von Luck's 125th Regiment of the 21st Panzer Division had the mission of breaking through the American lines on this northwestern base of the salient, cutting across the eastern foothills of the Vosges, and thus severing the American supply line to Strasbourg. That required, of all things, breaking through the Maginot Line. It ran east–west in this area, following the Rhine River bend. The Maginot Line, built at such great expense, had seen no fighting to speak of in 1940—the Germans went around it —but in January 1945 a part of the line was used for the purpose it had been designed for and showed what a superb fortification it was.

On January 7, Luck approached the line south of Wissembourg, at Rittershoffen. "Suddenly we could make out the first bunker, which received us with heavy fire. Our leading men and the accompanying SPV landed in thick minefields; the artillery stepped up its barrage of fire." The Americans, composed of men from the 79th Infantry Division, the 14th Armored Division, and elements of the 42nd Infantry Division, utilized the firing points, trenches, retractable cannon, and other features of the line to the fullest. They stopped the Germans cold.

Over the next two days the Germans reinforced the attack, with new 88s and some tanks, along with the 25th Panzer Division. They again assaulted the line. At one point they managed to drive the Americans out by getting close enough to throw grenades into the embrasures, but they were immediately driven back by heavy artillery fire.

Still the Germans came on. At times the battle raged inside the bunkers, a nerve-shattering experience made worse by the ear-shattering noise of explosives. Eventually Luck got through. On

January 10 he moved his regiment forward for an attack on Rittershoffen, preparatory to assaulting another part of the Maginot Line
from the rear (the French defenses were all pointed east), in order
to widen the breach. That night he got into the village but was not
able to drive the Americans out. They held one end, Luck's men
held the other. The situation in nearby Hatten village was similar.
There then developed a two-week-long battle that Luck, a veteran
of Poland, France, Russia, North Africa, and Normandy, characterized as "one of the hardest and most costly battles that ever raged."

Both sides used their artillery nonstop, firing 10,000 rounds
per day. The shelling was a curse to both sides, as the lines were
never more than one street apart, and sometimes they were on the
same side of the street, occasionally in the same house. Pvt. Pat
Reilly of the 79th recalled, "It was a weird battle. One time you
were surrounded, the next you weren't. Often we took refuge in
houses where the Germans were upstairs. We heard them and could
see them and vice versa. If they didn't make a move we left and if
we didn't make a move they left." Flamethrowers were used to set
houses afire. Adding to the horror, the civilian population had hidden when the battle began and now the women, children, and old
folks huddled in the cellars. There was no electricity. The pipes had
frozen so there was no water. The soldiers, on both sides, did what
they could to feed and care for the civilians.

Individual movement by day was dangerous. At night trucks
rolled up, on both sides, bringing ammunition and food, carrying
out wounded. The houses, public buildings, and the church were in
ruins. The dead, including some hundred civilians, lay in the
streets. There was hand-to-hand fighting with knives, room-to-
room fighting with pistols, rifles, and bazookas. Attacks and counterattacks took place regularly.

On January 21, Seventh Army ordered the much depleted 79th
and 14th Armored Divisions to retreat from Rittershoffen. The
Americans abandoned the Maginot Line and fell back on new positions along the Moder River. Luck only realized they had gone in
the morning. He walked around the village, unbelieving. At the
church, he crawled through the wreckage to the altar, which lay in
ruins. But in its place behind the altar, the organ was undamaged.
Luck directed one of his men to tread the bellows, sat down at the

organ, and played Bach's chorale *Danket Alle Gott.* The sound resounded through the village. German soldiers and the civilians of Rittershoffen gathered, knelt, prayed, sang.

Fifty years later I was in Rittershoffen with Luck and a half-dozen of his men, along with some American veterans of the battle. The mayor invited Luck to the new church, sat him down at the organ, and once again he played Bach.

Overall, the Northwind offensive was a failure. The Germans never got near Strasbourg, nor could they cut American supply lines. It was costly to both sides: Seventh Army's losses in January were 11,609 battle casualties plus 2,836 cases of trench foot. German losses were around 23,000 killed, wounded, or missing (Seventh Army processed some 5,985 German POWs).

For the front-line infantry, armor, and artillery of U.S. First and Third Armies, it was one of the most god-awful offensives of this or any other war. All but forgotten today, the battle that raged through January was for the GIs among the worst of the war, if possible even more miserable than Hurtgen or Metz. There was no glamour, little drama, zero maneuver. It was just straight-ahead attack, designed to eliminate the Bulge and then return to the German border. It was fought in conditions so terrible that they can only be marveled at, not really imagined. Only those who were there can know. More than once in interviewing veterans of the January fighting, when I ask them to describe the cold, men have involuntarily shivered.

These were the combat soldiers of ETO. At this time they numbered about 300,000. Perhaps half the enlisted were veterans, including replacements or men in divisions who had come into the battle in November or December and many who had been wounded once or twice. In the junior officer ranks, the turnover had been even greater, almost three-quarters. Still there was a corps of veterans in most of the divisions, including junior officers who had won battlefield promotions—the highest honor a soldier can receive, and the source of outstanding junior officers—and sergeants, most of whom by this stage were the privates of Normandy, St.-Lo, Falaise, Holland, and the Bulge, survivors who had moved up when the original NCOs were killed or wounded. These newly made lieutenants and sergeants, some of them teenage boys, most of them in their early twenties, provided the core leadership that got the U.S. Army through that terrible January.

Two themes dominate the memories of the men who fought these battles: the cold and American artillery. Every veteran I've ever interviewed, from whatever side, agrees that this was the coldest they had ever been, but disagrees on firepower: Each man insists that the other guy had more artillery. GIs can remember shellings that never seemed to have an end; so can the British troops. The GIs and their division, army, and army group commanders complained of a shortage of artillery shells (to which complaint the War Department answered, you are shooting too often), but in fact the Americans had twice as much and more artillery ammunition than the Germans.

This was a triumph of American industry and of the American way of war. This battle was raging along Germany's border. German shells had to travel from a hundred to only a couple of dozen kilometers to reach German guns on the front line. American shells had to travel thousands of kilometers to get there. But such was American productivity, many more American than German shells were arriving. The German attempt to cut Allied supply lines with their submarines had failed; the Allied attempt to cut German supply lines with their Jabos had great success. So the Americans banged away, confident that more shells were on the way. The Germans husbanded their shells, uncertain if any more would ever arrive.

As to the cold, all suffered equally. How cold was it? So cold that if a man didn't do his business in a hurry he risked a frostbitten penis. So cold that Pvt. Don Schoo, an anti-aircraft gunner attached to the 4th Armored Division, recalled, "I was due on guard and went out to my half track to relieve the man on guard. He couldn't get out of the gun turret. His overcoat was wet when he got in and it froze so he couldn't get out." It was so cold the oil in the engines froze. Weapons froze. Men pissed on them to get them working again, a good temporary solution but one that played hell with the weapon.

Sgt. D. Zane Schlemmer of the 82nd Airborne wore layers of

wool sweaters and overcoats and cut holes in his mummy-type sleeping bag so he could wear that, too. He had modified his wool gloves by slitting the fingers and sewing them together, except for the thumb and trigger finger, thus making them modified mittens. "Even with all this damn clothing, I never was warm," he recalled. Good luck: He acquired a long-haired German dog from a company of German soldiers his platoon had ambushed in a railroad cut. Schlemmer named the dog Adolph. He was Schlemmer's sleeping companion: "We'd curl up against each other wherever we could find a place to sleep."

Nights ranged from zero degrees Fahrenheit to minus ten and lower. Men without shelter—other than a foxhole—or heat either stayed awake, stomping their feet, through the fourteen-hour night, or they froze. Maj. John Harrison had as one of his most vivid memories of that January the sight of GIs pressed against the hot stones of the walls of burning houses, as flames came out of the roof and windows. They were not hiding from Germans; they were trying to get warm for a minute or two.

The GIs, and the Germans opposite them, went through worse physical misery than the men of Valley Forge. Washington's troops had tents, some huts, fires to warm by and provide hot food. They were not involved in continuous battle. By contrast, the conditions in Northwest Europe in January 1945 were as brutal as any in history, including the French and the German retreats from Moscow in midwinter, 1812 and 1941.

Another characteristic of the January fighting was the horror created by a high incidence of bodies crushed by tanks. Men slipped, tanks skidded. The wounded couldn't get out of the way. Twenty-year-old Pvt. Dwayne Burns of the 82nd Airborne saw a fellow paratrooper who had been run over by a tank. "If it hadn't been for the two pair of legs and boots sticking out of all the gore, it would have been hard to tell what it was. I looked away and thought for sure that I was going to vomit. I just wanted to throw my weapon away and tell them I quit. No more, I just can't take no more."

There was an awfulness about the fighting on the Western Front in 1945 that cannot be exaggerated. For the Germans, old men and boys mostly, it made no sense to be fighting the Americans while the Red Army invaded their homeland from the east. For the Americans, it was obvious that they had won the war, except that the damned Krauts kept fighting. For the veterans of the Battle of the Bulge, it seemed unfair that after having stopped the Germans cold it fell to them to undertake offensive action to finish the job. When replacements arrived at his company CP, bringing it up to strength in preparation for an attack, Sgt. John Martin of the 101st confessed, "I could not believe it. I could not believe that they were going to give us replacements and put us on the attack. I figured, Jesus, they'll take us out of here and give us some clothes or something. But, no, they get you some replacements and 'Come on boys, let's go.' And then that's when we start attacking."

It was the policy of the U.S. Army to keep its rifle companies on the line for long periods, continuously in the case of the companies in infantry divisions, making up losses by individual replacement. This meant the veteran could look forward to a release from the dangers threatening him only through death or serious wound. This created a situation of endlessness and hopelessness.

Combat is a topsy-turvy world. Perfect strangers are going to great lengths to kill you; if they succeed, far from being punished for taking life, they will be rewarded, honored, celebrated. In combat, men stay underground in daylight and do their work in the dark. Good health is a curse; trench foot, pneumonia, severe uncontrollable diarrhea, a broken leg are priceless gifts.

There is a limit to how long a man can function effectively in this topsy-turvy world. For some, mental breakdown comes early; Army psychiatrists found that in Normandy between 10 and 20 percent of the men in rifle companies suffered some form of mental disorder during the first week, and either fled or had to be taken out of the line (many, of course, returned to their units later). For others, visible breakdown never occurs, but nevertheless effectiveness breaks down. The experiences of men in combat produce emotions stronger than civilians can know—emotions of terror, panic, anger, sorrow, bewilderment, helplessness, uselessness—and each of these feelings drained energy and mental stability.

"There is no such thing as 'getting used to combat,'" the army psychiatrists stated in an official report on combat exhaustion.

"Each moment of combat imposes a strain so great that men will break down in direct relation to the intensity and duration of their exposure . . . psychiatric casualties are as inevitable as gunshot and shrapnel wounds in warfare. . . . Most men were ineffective after 180 or even 140 days. The general consensus was that a man reached his peak of effectiveness in the first 90 days of combat, that after that his efficiency began to fall off, and that he became steadily less valuable thereafter until he was completely useless."

But what could Eisenhower do? If he pulled his veterans out of the line, his rookies would take heavier losses for less gain. This was because for sure Hitler wasn't pulling back or giving his veterans a well-deserved rest. What Eisenhower saw was a German army that still had a fighting quality to it, supported by a steady flow of new and excellent equipment from the German industrial heartland along the Rhine River. At the end of January, Eisenhower told Marshall that "there is a noticeable and fanatical zeal on the part of nearly all German fighting men as well as the whole nation of 85 million people, successfully united by terror from within and fear of consequences from without."

He had it right and put it perfectly. The Germans knew what they had done as the conquerors and occupiers of Europe, and thus what they could expect when it was their turn to be conquered and occupied. As to terror, deserters could expect to be hanged and their families sent to concentration camps. The Nazi Party was still feared and obeyed. So long as Hitler was alive, it would be. Until then, the Germans would fight.

Eisenhower preferred to fight them west of the Rhine, and to close to the river from the Swiss border to Arnhem. At that point he could pull twenty divisions out of the line to create a reserve force that would then be capable of exploiting any opportunity that came along. "If we jam our head up against a concentrated defense at a selected spot," he said, "we must be able to go forward elsewhere. Flexibility requires reserves." By this stage of the war, flexibility was Eisenhower's outstanding tactical quality. What he had learned in the preceding twenty-eight months of combat was to expect to be surprised and to be ready to seize opportunities.

☐

Conditions in the February fighting were different from January, yet just as miserable in their own way. A battalion surgeon in the 90th Division described them: "It was cold, but not quite cold enough to freeze, this February in 1945. Rain fell continually and things were in a muddy mess. Most of us were mud from head to foot, unshaven, tired and plagued by recurrent epidemic severe diarrhea. . . . It was miserable to have to jump from one's blankets three or four times a night, hastily put on boots, run outside into the cold and rain and wade through the mud in the dark to the straddle pit. As likely as not the enemy would be shelling the area, and that did not help." He noted that the diarrhea was accompanied by severe abdominal cramps, vomiting, and fever.

"As usual, it was the infantrymen who really suffered in the nasty fighting. Cold, wetness, mud and hunger day after day; vicious attack and counterattack; sleepless nights in muddy foxholes; and the unending rain made their life a special hell." They were hungry because, much of the time, supply trucks could not get to them. Between heavy army traffic and the rain, the roads were impassable. The engineers worked feverishly day and night throwing rocks and logs into the morasses, but it was a losing battle.

On February 2, General Patton, plagued by impossible roads, ordered dogsled teams flown in from Labrador. His idea was to use them to evacuate wounded in the snow. By the time the first team arrived, however, the snow had melted, so the dogs were never used.

What was unendurable, the GIs endured. What had been true on June 6, 1944, and every day thereafter was still true: the quickest route to the most desirable place in the world—Home!—led to the east. So they sucked it up and stayed with it and were rightly proud of themselves for so doing. Pvt. Jim Underkofler, a former ASTPer, was in the 104th Division. Its CO was the legendary Gen. Terry Allen; its nickname was the Timberwolf Division; its motto was "Nothing in Hell will stop the Timberwolves."

"That might sound corny," Underkofler said in a 1996 interview, "but it was sort of a symbolic expression of attitude. Morale was extremely important. I mean, man alive, the conditions were often so deplorable that we had nothing else to go on, but your own morale. You know you're sitting there in a foxhole rubbing your buddy's feet, and he's rubbing yours so you don't get trench foot. That's only an example of the kind of relationship and camaraderie we had."

.. The straight line between Aachen and Cologne ran through Duren, on the east bank of the Roer River. But rather than going directly, Bradley ordered the main effort made with the veterans from Elsenborn Ridge and the Battle of the Bulge, through a corridor some seventeen kilometers wide south of the dreaded Hurtgen Forest. By so doing, the Americans would arrive at the Roer upstream from the dams and thus, once across the river, be free to advance over the Cologne Plain to the Rhine without danger of controlled flooding. The first task was to get through the Siegfried Line, still a formidable obstacle although in many places devoid of troops to utilize it. And every veteran in an ETO combat unit was well aware that this was where the Germans had stopped them in September 1944.

The generals were enthusiastic for this one. Gen. Walter Lauer, commanding the 99th Division, paid a pre-attack call on Sgt. Oakley Honey's C Company, 395th Regiment. Honey recalled that Lauer stood on the hood of a jeep, had the men gather around him, and gave a speech, saying, "We had fought the Krauts in the woods and the mountains and had beaten them. Now we were going to get a chance to fight them in the open." Honey commented, "Whoopee! Everyone was overjoyed." He added sarcastically, "You could tell by the long faces." Lauer went on: "We are in for a lot of new experiences and we are happy—happy because we are, at long last, to go on the offensive." Sgt. Vernon Swanson's comment: "How can a man be happier than that?"

On February 4, C Company pushed off, into the Siegfried Line. Swanson remembered that "our visibility was severely limited because it began snowing and shortly the heavy winds caused the snow storm to reach blizzard proportions. The order then came to fix bayonets." Honey recalled "charging into a snow storm with fixed bayonets and the wind blowing right into our faces. After moving through the initial line of dragon's teeth we began encountering deserted pillboxes. At one command post out came ten Germans with hands in the air offering no resistance."

Pvt. Irv Mark of C Company said, "I remember taking one

pillbox, and this stands out in my memory. The Krauts were waiting to surrender and the one in charge seemingly berated us for taking so long to come and get them. He said, *'Nicht etwas zu essen'* (nothing to eat). Strange we didn't feel one bit sorry for them." Swanson noted that "none of our company can recall any direct fire during our advance through the West Wall, although artillery shells dropped on us. We suffered no combat casualties possibly because we were much smarter than we had been six weeks earlier, particularly about booby traps and land mines."

Few companies were that lucky. Sgt. Clinton Riddle of the 82nd Airborne was in B Company, 325th Glider Infantry. At 0200, February 2, he accompanied the company commander on a patrol. "We walked to within sight of the dragon teeth of the Siegfried Line. We walked parallel with the line quite some distance. We could barely make out the pillbox on either side of the road that led through the dragon teeth. The teeth were laid out in five double rows, staggered. The Krauts had emplacements dotting the hillsides, so arranged as to cover each other with cross fire, and all zeroed in on the road where it passed through the teeth."

Returning from the patrol, the captain ordered an attack. "It was cold and the snow was deep," Riddle recalled. A company went first. It was met by small arms and mortar fire and was quickly driven to the ground. "There was more fire from the emplacements than I ever dreamed there could be," Riddle remarked, an indication of how well concealed many German fortifications were. "Men were falling in the snow all around me. That was an attack made on the belly. We crawled through most of the morning." Using standard fire-and-movement tactics, the Americans managed to drive the Germans beyond the ridge and over the road.

"When we reached the road leading through the teeth," Riddle said, "the captain looked back over his shoulder and said, 'Come on, let's go!' Those were the last words he ever said, because the Germans had that road covered and when he was halfway across he got hit right between the eyes. There was only three of us in our company still on our feet that we could account for when it was over."

Another twenty-five men turned up and the new CO, a lieutenant, began employing fire-and-movement to attack the pillboxes on either side of the road. But the Germans had been through enough. After their CO ordered the initial resistance, and then fired the shot that killed the American captain, his men shot him and prepared to surrender. So, Riddle related, "When we reached the pillboxes, the Germans came out, calling out *'Kamerad.'* We should have shot them on the spot. They had their dress uniforms on, with their shining boots. We had been crawling in the snow, wet, cold, hungry, sleepy, tired, mad because they had killed so many of our boys." They were through the initial defenses of the Siegfried Line, and that was enough for the moment.

The 90th Division reached the Siegfried Line at exactly the spot where the 106th Division had been hit and decimated on December 16. Pvt. Jack Ammons spent the night of February 5–6, 1945, in a bombed-out building on the edge of the line. "The village was eerie," he remembered. "It looked like a million ghosts of previous campaigns had passed through it." At 0400, February 6, the 359th Regiment of the 90th picked its way undetected through the dragon's teeth, minefields, barbed wire, and pillboxes in the outer ring of the fortifications. Shortly after dawn, pillboxes that had gone unnoticed came to life, pouring fire into the tanks and reinforcements following the infantry, stopping the advance. A week-long fight ensued.

The Germans employed a new tactic to confound the Americans. Captain Colby explained it: "Whole platoons of infantrymen disappeared as a result of the German tactic of giving up a pillbox easily, then subjecting it to pre-sighted artillery and mortar fire, forcing the attackers inside the shelter. Then they covered the doorway with fire, surrounding the pillbox after dark, and blowing it in. The men soon learned it was safer outside the fortifications than inside."

On February 9 regimental chaplain Father Donald Murphy noted a variation of the tactic in his diary: "K Company was in a pillbox. The GI outpost fell asleep and Jerries captured all of them, including Lts. Franklin and Osborne. The pillboxes are really death traps. You are helpless when you get in them."

Patton inspected a command pillbox: "It consisted of a three-story submerged barracks with toilets, shower baths, a hospital, laundry, kitchen, storerooms, and every conceivable convenience plus an enormous telephone installation. Electricity and heat were produced by a pair of diesel engines with generators. Yet the whole offensive capacity of this installation consisted of two machine guns operating from steep cupolas which worked up and down by means of hydraulic lifts. As in all cases, this particular pillbox was taken by a dynamite charge against the back door. We found marks on the cupolas where 90 mm shells, fired at a range of two hundred yards, had simply bounced."

To Patton, this was yet another proof of "the utter futility of fixed defenses. . . . In war, the only sure defense is offense, and the efficiency of offense depends on the warlike souls of those conducting it."

Captain Colby gives a vivid snapshot of American artillery in action: "We were looking at a day's assignment of about a dozen pillboxes. We were on a slightly higher ground and could see them plainly. As we studied the prospect with sinking feelings, a self-propelled 155 mm gun chugged and clanked up to us. A lieutenant dismounted and walked over.

" 'I hear you could use some fire,' he said.

"We did everything but hug him. We told him to pick out a pillbox and let fly.

"The lieutenant pointed to a pillbox. The gunner lowered the muzzle of the howitzer, opened the gun's breech-block, and peered through the barrel at the target. Satisfied with his aim, he told the loaders to stuff in a round."

A 155 mm shell weighed 100 pounds. It took two men to put it on a carrier equipped with handles like a litter, two others to pick up the carrier and hold the shell to the chamber of the gun. A fifth man shoved it in and stuffed in the bags of gunpowder. When the breech was closed and all was ready, the gunner yanked the lanyard.

The tremendous roar was, Colby said, "thrilling to an infantryman." He noted that the .30 caliber bullets he was shooting were 0.3 inch in diameter, while the 155 shell was 6.1 inches.

"The shell struck the pillbox and covered it with a sheet of flame from the explosive charge it carried. A perfect smoke ring popped out of an air vent in the top."

"Scratch one pillbox," the lieutenant said.

"It is still standing," Colby retorted.

"Yep. But there ain't anyone left alive inside. If there is, his brains are scrambled."

Colby felt that having revealed their position, they should take cover before the Germans started their counterfire. "Aw, hell," the lieutenant said, "let's blast some more before the fun starts. You wanta fire one?"

How could Colby resist? After another line-of-sight aim through the open bore, the gun was loaded and Colby gave a jerk on the lanyard. Scratch another pillbox. The lieutenant told Colby to get behind the gun where it next fired, saying he could watch the shell all the way to the target.

"He zeroed in on another pillbox. Sure enough, when the gun fired I could see a black dot arc swiftly toward the target. Again, there was a flash that covered the whole target. They fired a round or two at each pillbox out in front of us, then folded their equipment and clanked away to another scene. When we moved up, we found only dead or dazed men inside the pillboxes."

Colby's final comment was, "No matter how many pillboxes or bunkers there might be, the fact was that man had built them and man was tearing them down. The elaborate system of 'Dragon's Teeth' proved to be worthless and brought from us exclamations of amazement at the labor the Germans had expended."

That point was equally true when applied to the Atlantic Wall. At the Siegfried Line in February, as at the Atlantic Wall in June 1944, the Germans got precious little return on their big investment in poured concrete.

By the beginning of March, K Company, 333rd Regiment, had reached the Rhine. The men settled down in the village of Krefeld to await Montgomery's Operation Plunder, the crossing of the river; Monty was planning the operation with as much care as he had put into Operation Overlord, so the pause was a long one. By some miracle, the men found an undamaged high-rise apartment building in which everything worked—electricity, hot water, flush toilets, and telephones with dial tones. They had their first hot baths in four months. They found cigars and bottles of cognac. Pvt.

Ray Bocarski, fluent in German, lit up, sat down in an easy chair, got a befuddled German operator on the phone, and talked his way through to a military headquarters in Berlin. He told the German officer he could expect K Company within the week.

That was not to be. Having reached the river, K Company along with the rest of Ninth Army would stay in place until Montgomery had everything ready for Operation Plunder. The troops badly needed the rest. The night after taking Hardt, Pvt. Strawberry Craft was so totally exhausted that after getting into his foxhole he told the sergeant he was going to sleep that night. The sergeant warned him, "You might wake up dead." Craft replied, "I'll just have to wake up dead." Decades later he still remembered the exchange, and explained, "I needed the sleep, and I got it, too."

That kind of exhaustion was becoming endemic. Sgt. Joe Skocz of the 103rd Division was out on a night patrol. His lead scout was a veteran of sixty-five days of combat and had always done his duty. Suddenly the patrol stopped. Skocz went forward to see what was up. The scout, crouching behind a tree, pointed ahead and said, "There's people out there. They're waiting to nail us."

"They're not moving," Skocz pointed out.

"Neither are we."

Skocz ordered the scout to go forward and see what he could see. And as Skocz remembered it, "He leans up real close to my head and he says, 'Fuck you, Sergeant. You wanta find out, go up yourself.' " Skocz did and discovered there was nothing out there. "When we got back, I told him I never wanted to see him on the front lines again."

Sgt. William Faust of the 1st Division had been in combat in two continents and six countries. By March 1945, he said, "Those of us still remaining of the 'Big Red One' of 1942 had lost the desire to pursue; the enthusiasm we had for this sort of thing in Africa, Sicily, France, Luxembourg and Belgium was no longer with us."

On March 15, Pvt. Martin Duus of the 103rd Division, who had been in combat since the previous December, got hit in the neck. The bullet exited through his right shoulder. "My whole right arm was dead. I couldn't move it. I thought I'd lost it. I couldn't look." He never used it again; it was paralyzed. But his reaction belied the seriousness of the wound, while it spoke eloquently of the state of the old hands: "I was damn glad I was hit and could get out of there. Absolutely. My fear was I'd get well enough to go back."

On March 7 Patton's forces were still fighting west of the Rhine, trying to close to the river from Koblenz south to Mainz and in the process trap further German forces facing the U.S. Seventh Army. Patton was having divisions stolen from him, to dispatch south to help Seventh Army get through the Siegfried Line east of Saarbrucken. That made him furious, but he calmed down when Bradley agreed to move the boundary between Third and Seventh Armies some twenty kilometers south of Mainz. That put the best stretch of river for crossing south of Cologne in his sector. He was thinking of crossing on the run, and hoping he could do it before Montgomery's elephantine Operation Plunder even got started, and before Hodges, too, if possible.

But his men were exhausted. "Signs of the prolonged strain had begun to appear," one regimental history explained. "Slower reactions in the individual; a marked increase in cases of battle fatigue, and a lower standard of battle efficiency—all showed quite clearly that the limit was fast approaching." G Company, 328th Infantry Regiment, was typical. It consisted of veterans whose bone-weariness was so deep they were indifferent, or on the edge of battle fatigue, plus raw recruits. Still it had the necessary handful of leaders, and superb communications with the artillery, as demonstrated by Lieutenant Otts in the second week in March, during Third Army's drive toward the Rhine. Pvt. George Idelson described it in a 1988 letter to Otts: "My last memory of you—and it is a vivid one—is of you standing in a fierce mortar and artillery barrage, totally without protection, calling in enemy coordinates. I know what guts it took to do that. I can still hear those damn things exploding in the trees. I lost one foxhole buddy to shrapnel in that barrage, and then his replacement. I don't know who was looking after me."

□

On the morning of March 7, Lt. Harold Larsen of the 9th Division was flying in a Piper Cub, looking for targets of opportunity. To his astonishment, he saw the great Ludendorff Bridge at Remagen still standing. He radioed the news back to Gen. William Hoge, who immediately sent orders to the units nearest Remagen to take the bridge before the Germans could blow it.

The closest unit was A Company, 27th Armored Infantry Battalion. Its CO had been put out of action the previous day; Lt. Karl Timmermann, twenty-two years old, had replaced him. Timmermann fought his way to the approaches to the bridge. His battalion commander ordered him to get across.

"What if the bridge blows up in my face?" Timmermann asked.

The battalion commander turned and walked away without a word. Timmermann called to his squad leaders, "All right, we're going across."

There was a huge explosion. It shook Remagen and sent a volcano of stones and earth erupting from the west end of the bridge. The Germans had detonated a cratering charge that gouged a deep hole in the earthen causeway joining the main road and the bridge platform. The crater made it impossible for vehicles to get onto the bridge—but not infantry.

Timmermann called out, "Now, we're going to cross this bridge before—" At that instant, there was another deafening rumble and roar. The Germans had set off an emergency demolition two-thirds of the way across the bridge. Awestruck, the men of A Company watched as the huge structure lifted up, and steel, timbers, dust, and thick black smoke mixed in the air. Many of the men threw themselves on the ground.

Ken Hechler, in *The Bridge at Remagen,* one of the best of all accounts of the U.S. Army in action in World War II, and a model for all oral history, describes what happened next: "Everybody waited for Timmermann's reaction. 'Thank God, now we won't have to cross that damned thing,' Sgt. Mike Chinchar said fervently, trying to reassure himself.

"Pvt. Johnny Ayres fingered the two grenades hooked onto the rings of his pack suspenders, and nodded his head: 'We wouldn't have had a chance.'

"But Timmermann, who had been trying to make out what was left of the bridge through the thick haze, yelled:

" 'Look—she's still standing.'

"Most of the smoke and dust had cleared away, and the men followed their commander's gaze. The sight of the bridge still spanning the Rhine brought no cheers from the men. It was like an unwelcome specter. The suicide mission was on again."

Timmermann could see German engineers at the east end of the bridge working frantically to try again to blow the bridge. He waved his arm overhead in the "Follow me" gesture. Machine-gun fire from one of the bridge towers made him duck. One of A Company's tanks pulled up to the edge of the crater and blasted the tower. The German fire let up.

"Get going," Timmermann yelled. Maj. Murray Deevers called out, "I'll see you on the other side and we'll all have a chicken dinner."

"Chicken dinner, my foot, I'm all chicken right now," one of the men in the first platoon protested. Deevers flushed. "Move on across," he ordered.

"I tell you, I'm not going out there and get blown up," the GI answered. "No sir, Major, you can court-martial and shoot me, but I ain't going out there on that bridge."

Timmerman was shouting, "Get going, you guys, get going." He set the example, moving onto the bridge himself. That did it. The lead platoon followed, crouching, running, dodging, watching for holes in the bridge planking that covered the railroad tracks (put down by the Germans so that their vehicles could retreat over the bridge) but always moving in the direction of the Germans on the far shore.

Sgt. Joe DeLisio led the first squad. Sgts. Joe Petrencsik and Alex Drabik led the second. In the face of more machine-gun and 20mm anti-aircraft fire they dashed forward. "Get going," Timmermann yelled. The men took up the cry. "Get going," they shouted at one another. "Get going." Engineers were right behind them, searching for demolitions and tearing out electrical wires. The names were Chinchar, Samele, Massie, Wegener, Jensen. They were Italian, Czech, Norwegian, German, Russian. They were children of European immigrants, come back to the old country to liberate and redeem it.

On the far side, at the entrance to the tunnel, they could see a German engineer pushing on a plunger. There was nothing for it but to keep going. And nothing happened—apparently a stray bullet or shell had cut the wire leading to the demolition charges. Halfway across the bridge, three men found four packages of TNT weighing thirty pounds each, tied to I-beams under the decking. Using wire cutters, they worked on the demolitions until they splashed into the river. DeLisio got to the towers, ran up the circular staircase of the one to his right, where the firing was coming from, and on the fourth level found three German machine gunners, firing at the bridge.

"Hande hoch!" DeLisio commanded. They gave up; he picked up the gun they had been using and hurled it out the aperture. Men on the bridge saw it and were greatly encouraged. Drabik came running on at top speed. He passed the towers and got to the east bank. He was the first GI to cross the Rhine. Others were on his heels. They quickly made the German engineers in the tunnel prisoners. Timmermann sent Lt. Emmet "Jim" Burrows and his platoon up the Erpeler Ley, saying, "You know, Jim, the old Fort Benning stuff; take the high ground and hold it." Burrows later said, "Taking Remagen and crossing the bridge were a breeze compared with climbing that hill." He took casualties, but he got to the top, where he saw far too many German men and vehicles spread out before him to even contemplate attacking them. He hung on at the edge of the summit. But he had the high ground, and the Americans were over the Rhine.

Sixteen-year-old Pvt. Heinz Schwarz, who came from a village only a short distance upstream on the east bank of the Rhine from Remagen, was in the tunnel. "We were all still kids," he recalled. "The older soldiers in our unit stayed in the tunnel, but the rest of us were curious and went up to the bridge tower to get a better look." He heard the order ring out: "Everybody down! We're blowing the bridge!" He heard the explosion and saw the bridge rise up. "We thought it had been destroyed, and we were saved." But as the smoke cleared, he saw Timmermann and his men coming on. He ran down the circular stairs and got to the entrance to the tunnel just as DeLisio got to the tower. "I knew I had to somehow get myself out through the rear entrance of the tunnel and run home to my mother as fast as I could." He did. Fifteen years later he was a member of the Bundestag. At a ceremony on March 7, 1960, he met DeLisio. They swapped stories.

As the word of Timmermann's toehold spread up the chain of command, to regiment, division, corps, and army, each general responded by ordering men on the scene to get over the bridge, for engineers to repair it, for units in the area to change direction and head for Remagen. Bradley was the most enthusiastic of all. He had been fearful of a secondary role in the final campaign, but with Hodges over the river he decided immediately to get First Army so fully involved that Eisenhower would have to support the bridgehead.

First, however, Bradley had to get by Gen. Harold "Pinky" Bull, operations officer at SHAEF. The SHAEF G-3 was with Bradley when the word arrived. When Bradley outlined his plan, he related, Bull "looked at me as though I were a heretic. He scoffed: 'You're not going anywhere down there at Remagen. You've got a bridge, but it's in the wrong place. It just doesn't fit the plan.'

"I demanded, 'What in the hell do you want us to do, pull back and blow it up?' "

Bradley got on the phone to Eisenhower. When he heard the news, Eisenhower was ecstatic. He said, "Brad, that's wonderful." Bradley said he wanted to push everything across he could. "Sure," Eisenhower responded, "get right on across with everything you've got. It's the best break we've had." Bradley felt it necessary to point out that Bull disagreed. "To hell with the planners," Eisenhower said. "Sure, go on, Brad, and I'll give you everything we got to hold that bridgehead. We'll make good use of it even if the terrain isn't too good."

The next morning Eisenhower informed the CCS that he was rushing troops to Remagen "with the idea that this will constitute greatest possible threat" to the Germans. Because he had insisted on closing to the Rhine, SHAEF had sufficient divisions in reserve for Eisenhower to exercise flexibility and exploit the opportunity. Over the following two weeks he sent troops to Hodges, who used them to extend the bridgehead. The Germans made determined efforts to wreck the bridge, using air attacks, constant artillery fire, V-2 missiles, floating mines, and frogmen, but Hodges's defenses thwarted their efforts. By the time the big railroad bridge finally collapsed, the bridgehead was twenty miles long and eight miles deep, with six pontoon bridges across the river. It constituted a threat to the entire German defense of the Rhine. To the north, meanwhile, Montgomery was preparing his crossing, as was Patton to the south. Ike told Mamie, "Our attacks have been going well ... The enemy becomes more and more stretched ..." Unfortunately, "he shows no signs of quitting. He is fighting hard. ... I never count my Germans until they're in our cages, or are buried!"

Eisenhower spent the evening of March 16 with Patton and his staff. Patton was in a fine mood and set out to kid and flatter Eisenhower. He said that some of the Third Army units were disappointed because they had not had an opportunity to see the Supreme Commander. "Hell, George," Eisenhower replied, "I didn't think the American GI would give a damn even if the Lord Himself came to inspect them."

Patton smiled. "Well," he said, "I hesitate to say which of you would rank, sir!" The banter went on through the evening. Patton noted in his diary, "General E stated that not only was I a good general but also a lucky general, and Napoleon preferred luck to greatness. I told him this was the first time he had ever complimented me in 2½ years we had served together."

Historian Michael Doubler rightly judges that everything came together at Remagen. All that General Marshall had worked for and hoped for and built for in creating this citizen army, happened. It was one of the great victories in the army's history. The credit goes to the men—Timmermann, DeLisio, Drabik, through Hoge, Bradley, and Ike—and to the system the U.S. Army had developed in Europe, which bound these men together into a team that featured intiative at the bottom and a cold-blooded determination and competency at the top.

Up north, Montgomery's preparations for Operation Plunder continued. Down south, Patton's Third Army cleared the Saarland and the Palatinate in a spectacular campaign. As his divisions approached the Rhine, Patton had 500 assault boats, plus LCVPs and DUKWs, brought forward, along with 7,500 engineers, but with no fanfare, no fuss, no publicity, in deliberate contrast to Montgomery and so as to not alert the Germans. On the night of March 22–23 the 5th Division began to cross the river at Oppenheim, south of Mainz. The Germans were unprepared; by midnight the entire 11th Regiment had crossed by boat with only twenty casualties. Well before dawn the whole of the 5th and a part of the 90th Divisions were across. The Germans launched a counterattack against the 5th Division, using students from an officer candidate school at nearby Wiesbaden. They were good soldiers, and managed to infiltrate the American positions, but after a busy night and part of the next morning they were dead or prisoners.

At dawn German artillery began to fire, and the Luftwaffe sent twelve planes to bomb and strafe. The Americans pushed east anyway. By the afternooon the whole of the 90th Division was on the far side, along with the 4th Armored. Patton called Bradley: "Brad, don't tell anyone but I'm across."

"Well, I'll be damned—you mean across the Rhine?"

"Sure am, I sneaked a division over last night."

A little later, at the Twelfth Army Group morning briefing, the Third Army reported: "Without benefit of aerial bombing, ground smoke, artillery preparation, and airborne assistance, the Third Army at 2200 hours, March 22, crossed the Rhine River."

The following day Patton walked across a pontoon bridge built by his engineers. He stopped in the middle. While every GI in the immediate area who had a camera took his picture, he urinated into the Rhine—a long, high, steady stream. As he buttoned up, Patton said, "I've waited a long time to do that. I didn't even piss this morning when I got up so I would have a really full load. Yes, sir, the pause that refreshes."

By the first week of spring 1945, Eisenhower's armies had done what he had been planning for since the beginning of the year. Montgomery's elaborate crossing of the Rhine in Operation Plunder, featuring the largest airdrop in the history of war, had been successful. To the south, First and Third Armies were across. The time for exploitation had arrived. Some of the Allied infantry and armored divisions faced stiff resistance, others only sporadic resistance, others none at all. Whatever was in front of them—rough terrain, enemy strong points, more rivers to cross—their generals were as one in taking up the phrase Lieutenant Timmermann had used at the Remagen bridge—"Get going!"

The 90th Division, on Patton's left flank, headed east toward Hanau on the Main River. It crossed in assault boats on the night of March 28. Maj. John Cochran's battalion ran into a battalion of Hitler Youth officer candidates, teenage Germans who were eager to fight. They set up a roadblock in a village. As Cochran's men advanced toward it, the German boys let go with their machine gun, killing one American. Cochran put some artillery fire on the roadblock and destroyed it, killing three. "One youth, perhaps aged 16, held up his hands," Cochran recalled. "I was very emotional over the loss of a good soldier and I grabbed the kid and took off my cartridge belt.

"I asked him if there were more like him in the town. He gave me a stare and said, 'I'd rather die than tell you anything.' I told him to pray, because he was going to die. I hit him across the face with my thick, heavy belt. I was about to strike him again when I was grabbed from behind by Chaplain Kerns. He said, 'Don't!' Then he took that crying child away. The Chaplain had intervened not only to save a life but to prevent me from committing a murder. Had it not been for the Chaplain, I would have."

From the crossing of the Rhine to the end of the war, every man who died, died needlessly. It was that feeling that almost turned Major Cochran into a murderer. On the last day of March, Sgt. D. Zane Schlemmer of the 82nd had a particularly gruesome experience that almost broke him. His squad was advancing, supported by a tank. Six troopers were riding on the tank, while he and five others were following in its tracks, which freed them from worry about mines. A hidden 88 fired. The shell hit the gun turret, blowing off the troopers, killing two and wounding the other four. "The force of the blast blew them to the rear of the tank near me," Schlemmer recalled. "They lay as they fell. A second round then came screaming in, this time to ricochet off the front of the tank. The tank reversed gears and backed up over three of our wounded, crushing them to death. I could only sit down and bawl, whether out of frustration of being unable to help them, whether from the futility of the whole damn war, or whether from hatred of the Germans for causing it all, I've never been able to understand."

That same day Cpl. James Pemberton, a 1942 high school graduate who went into ASTP and then to the 103rd Division as a replacement, was also following a tank. "My guys started wandering and drifting a bit, and I yelled at them to get in the tank tracks to avoid the mines. They did and we followed. The tank was rolling over Schu [anti-personnel] mines like crazy. I could see them popping left and right like popcorn." Pemberton had an eighteen-year-old replacement in the squad; he told him to hop up and ride on the tank, thinking he would be out of the way up there. An 88 fired. The replacement fell off. The tank went into reverse and backed over him, crushing him from the waist down. "There was one scream, and some mortars hit the Kraut 88 and our tank went forward again. To me, it was one of the worst things I went through. This poor bastard had graduated from high school in June, was drafted, took basic training, shipped overseas, had thirty seconds of combat, and was killed."

Pemberton's unit kept advancing. "The Krauts always shot up all their ammo and then surrendered," he remembered. Hoping to avoid such nonsense, in one village the CO sent a Jewish private who spoke German forward with a white flag, calling out to the German boys to surrender. "They shot him up so bad that after it was over the medics had to slide a blanket under his body to take him away." Then the Germans started waving their own white flag. Single file, eight of them emerged from a building, hands up. "They were very cocky. They were about 20 feet from me when I saw the leader suddenly realize he still had a pistol in his shoulder holster. He reached into his jacket with two fingers to pull it out and throw it away.

"One of our guys yelled, 'Watch it! He's got a gun!' and came running up shooting and there were eight Krauts on the ground shot up but not dead. They wanted water but no one gave them any. I never felt bad about it although I'm sure civilians would be horrified. But these guys asked for it. If we had not been so tired and frustrated and keyed up and mad about our boys they shot up, it never would have happened. But a lot of things happen in war and both sides know the penalties."

Hitler and the Nazis had poisoned the minds of the boys Germany was throwing into the battle. Capt. F. W. Norris of the 90th Division ran into a roadblock. His company took some casualties, then blasted away, wounding many. "The most seriously wounded was a young SS sergeant who looked just like one of Hitler's supermen. He had led the attack. He was bleeding copiously and badly needed some plasma." One of Norris's medics started giving him a transfusion. The wounded German, who spoke excellent English, demanded to know if there was any Jewish blood in the plasma. The medic said damned if he knew, in the United States people didn't make such a distinction. The German said if he couldn't have a guarantee that there was no Jewish blood he would refuse treatment.

"I had been listening and had heard enough," Norris remembered. "I turned to this SS guy and in very positive terms I told him I really didn't care whether he lived or not, but if he did not take the plasma he would certainly die. He looked at me calmly and said, 'I would rather die than have any Jewish blood in me.'

"So he died."

18

Overrunning Germany

THE STANDARD STORY of how the American GI reacted to the foreign people he met during the course of World War II runs like this: He felt the Arabs were despicable, lying, stealing, dirty, awful, without a redeeming feature. The Italians were lying, stealing, dirty, wonderful, with many redeeming features, but never to be trusted. The rural French were sullen, slow, and ungrateful while the Parisians were rapacious, cunning, indifferent to whether they were cheating Germans or Americans. The British people were brave, resourceful, quaint, reserved, dull. The Dutch were regarded as simply wonderful in every way (but the average GI never was in Holland, only the airborne).

The story ends up thus: Wonder of wonders, the average GI found that the people he liked best, identified most closely with, enjoyed being with, were the Germans. Clean, hard-working, disciplined, educated, middle-class in their tastes and life-styles (many GIs noted that so far as they could tell the only people in the world who regarded a flush toilet and soft white toilet paper as a necessity were the Germans and the Americans), the Germans seemed to many American soldiers as "just like us."

Pvt. Ken Webster of the 101st hated the Nazis and wished more of the German villages would be destroyed, so that the Germans would suffer as the French and Belgians and Italians had suffered, and thus learn not to start wars. But despite himself, Webster was drawn to the people. "The Germans I have seen so far have impressed me as clean, efficient, law-abiding people," he wrote his parents on April 14. They were regular churchgoers. "In Germany everybody goes out and works. They are cleaner, more progressive, and more ambitious than either the English or the French."

With a growing area of western and central Germany under American occupation, the high command ordered a policy of non-fraternization. GIs were told they could not talk to *any* German, even small children, except on official business. This absurd order, which flew in the face of human nature in so obvious a way, was impossible to enforce. Still some tried. Webster recalled a replacement lieutenant who "became such a fiend on the non-fraternization policy that he ordered all butts field-stripped [torn apart and scattered] so that the Germans might derive no pleasure from American tobacco."

In some cases the GIs mistreated the civilian population, and they engaged in widespread looting, especially of wine, jewelry, Nazi memorabilia, and other portable items. Combat veterans insist that the worst of this sort of thing was carried out by replacements who had arrived too late to see any action. These American teenagers could be especially brutal in their treatment of German POWs. There were some rapes, not many because the army's policy was to identify, try, and, if found guilty, execute rapists (forty-nine GIs were shot for rape or murder). Overall, it is simple fact to state that the American and British occupying armies, in comparison to the other conquering armies in World War II, acted correctly and honorably. As a single example, a German woman in Konigsberg when it was occupied by the Red Army recalled how, after she and her friends had been repeatedly raped, "we often asked the soldiers to shoot us, but they always answered: 'Russian soldiers do not shoot women, only German soldiers do that.'"

Webster told a story that speaks to the point. "Reese, who was more intent on finding women than in trading for eggs, and I made another expedition a mile west to a larger village where there were no G.I.s. Like McCreary, Reese tended to show an impatience with hens and a strong interest in skirts; regardless of age or appearance, he'd tell me, 'There's a nice one. Boy that's a honey. Speak to her Web, goddamn!' Since I was shy, however, and those females invariably looked about as sociable as a fresh iceberg, I ignored his panting plaints. Besides, the Fraus weren't apt to be friendly in public, where the neighbors could see them. Maybe indoors or at night. Finally we came to a farm where a buxom peasant lass greeted us. Reese smiled. After I had gotten some eggs, Reese, who kept winking at her, gave her a cigarette and a chocolate bar, and, as love bloomed in the garden of D ration [a newly issued food package] and Chelseas, I backed out the door and waited in the sun. No dice, Reese later reported. I returned home with a helmetful of eggs, Reese with a broken heart. But it was, as he said, 'good fratranizin' territory.' He tried again that night before the six o'clock curfew went into effect. No luck."

Had Reese been a Soviet, German, or Japanese soldier, this little nonincident probably would have turned out differently.

So the Germans in areas occupied by the Americans were lucky, and they knew it. They did their best, most of them, to please the Americans, with considerable success. There was something approaching mutual admiration. That caused the GIs to wonder about what they had heard about the Germans. Glenn Gray spoke to the point: "The enemy could not have changed so quickly from a beast to a likable human being. Thus, the conclusion is nearly forced upon the GIs that they have been previously blinded by fear and hatred and the propaganda of their own government." The theme of German-American relations in the first week of April 1945 was harmony.

It helped immeasurably that the Germans were no longer putting up much of a fight. The 101st Airborne, for example, was headed southeast through Bavaria on its way to Austria. Contact with the enemy picked up as the convoy moved southeast, but not in the sense of combat. The men began to see German soldiers in small groups, trying to surrender. Then larger groups. Finally, more field gray uniforms than anyone could have imagined existed.

Easy Company was in the midst of a German army in disintegration. The supply system lay in ruins. All the German soldiers wanted was a safe entry into a POW cage. "I couldn't get over the sensation of having the Germans, who only a short time ago had been so difficult to capture, come in from the hills like sheep and surrender," Webster wrote. When the convoy reached the autobahn leading east to Munich, the road was reserved for Allied military traffic, the median for Germans marching west to captivity. Gordon Carson recalled that "as far as you could see in the median were German prisoners, fully armed. No one would stop to take their surrender. We just waved."

Webster called the sight of the Germans in the median, "a tingling spectacle." They came on "in huge blocks. We saw the unbelieveable spectacle of two G.I.s keeping watch on some 2,500 enemy." At that moment the men of the company realized that the German collapse was complete, that there would be no recovery this spring as there had been last fall.

There was still some scattered, sporadic resistance. Every single bridge was destroyed by German engineers as the Allies approached. Occasionally a fanatic SS unit would fire from its side of the stream. It was more an irritant than a threat or danger. The Americans would bring forward some light artillery, drive the SS troops away, and wait for the engineers to repair the old or make a new bridge.

Major Winters was struck by the German fanaticism, the discipline that led German engineers to blow their own bridges when the uselessness of the destruction was clear to any idiot, and "the total futility of the war. Here was a German army trying to surrender and walking north along the autobahn, while at the same time another group was blowing out the bridges to slow down the surrender."

On April 29 the company stopped for the night at Buchloe, in the foothills of the Alps, near Landsberg. Here they saw their first concentration camp. It was a work camp, not an extermination camp, one of the half-dozen or more that were a part of the Dachau complex. But although it was relatively small and designed to produce war goods, it was so horrible that it was impossible to fathom the enormity of the evil. Prisoners in their striped pajamas, three-quarters starved, by the thousands; corpses, little more than skeletons, by the hundreds.

Winters found stacks of huge wheels of cheese in the cellar of a building he was using for the battalion CP and ordered it distributed to the inmates. He radioed to regiment to describe the situation and ask for help.

The company stayed in Buchloe for two nights. Thus it was present in the morning when the people of Landsberg turned out, carrying rakes, brooms, shovels, and marched off to the camp. Gen. Maxwell Taylor, it turned out, had been so incensed by the sight that he had declared martial law and ordered everyone from fourteen to eighty years of age to be rounded up and sent to the camp, to bury the bodies and clean up the place. That evening the crew came back down the road from the camp. Some were still vomiting.

"The memory of starved, dazed men," Winters wrote, "who dropped their eyes and heads when we looked at them through the chain-link fence, in the same manner that a beaten, mistreated dog would cringe, leaves feelings that cannot be described and will never be forgotten. The impact of seeing those people behind that fence left me saying, only to myself, 'Now I know why I am here!' "

Eisenhower was free to send his armies wherever he chose. Montgomery wanted him to give First Army to Twenty-first Army Group and let it join Ninth Army for a drive on to Berlin—under his command. Hodges wanted Berlin, as did Simpson, Patton, Brooke, and Churchill. But Bradley didn't and neither did Eisenhower. Partly their reason was political. At the Yalta conference the Big Three had agreed to divide Germany into zones of occupation, and Berlin into sectors. In central Germany, the Elbe River was the boundary. If Simpson's Ninth or Hodges's First Army fought its way across the Elbe and on to Berlin, they would be taking territory that would have to be turned over to the Soviet occupation forces; if they fought their way into Berlin they would have to give up more than half the city to the Red Army. Eisenhower asked Bradley for an estimate on the cost of taking Berlin. About 100,000 casualties, Bradley replied, and added that was "a pretty stiff price to pay for a prestige objective, especially when we've got to fall back and let the other fellow take over."

Further, Eisenhower believed that if the Americans tried to race the Russians to Berlin, they would lose. Ninth and First Armies were four hundred kilometers from Berlin; the Red Army was on the banks of the Oder River, less than a hundred kilometers from the city. And the Red Army was there in great strength—more than 1.25 million troops.

Another consideration: Eisenhower's goal was to win the war and thus end the carnage as quickly as possible. Every day that the war went on meant more death for the concentration camp inmates, for the millions of slave laborers in Germany, for the Allied POWs. If he concentrated on Berlin, the Germans in Bavaria and Austria, where many of the POW and slave labor camps were located, would be able to hold out for who knew how long.

There is a parallel here with the end of the American Civil War. Just before Appomattox, some of Robert E. Lee's staff suggested to him that he disband the Army of Northern Virginia and instruct the troops to scatter into the West Virginia mountains, where as small groups they could carry on guerrilla warfare. Lee was appalled by the suggestion. He said there could be nothing worse for the South than having armed bands roaming the countryside without discipline or direction.

But Hitler was no Lee. And the SS and Hitler Youth were not only fanatics but were armed with the most modern weapons, which gave small groups of them a firepower greater than that of the Army of Northern Virginia at its peak. Even after the surrender of the Ruhr, the Germans never ran out of guns or ammunition. These boys could get all the panzerfausts, potato mashers, machine guns, burp guns, rifles, and Schu mines they could carry. If they were lucky enough to have fuel, they could have Tiger tanks, 88s, and more heavy stuff. This combination of fanatic boys and plenty of weapons and ammunition created a nightmare situation.

After the mid-April surrender of 325,000 troops (plus thirty generals) in the Ruhr pocket, the Wehrmacht packed it in. Lt. Gunter Materne was a German artilleryman caught in the pocket ("where everything was a complete mess"). Out of ammunition and fuel, he destroyed his self-propelled cannon. "At the command post, the CO of our artillery regiment, holding back his tears, told us that we had lost the war, all the victims died in vain. The code word 'werewolf' had been sent out by Hitler's command post. This meant that we were all supposed to divide up into small groups and head east." Not many did, Materne observed. The veterans sat down and awaited their American captors. There was no attempt by the regular army to maintain a front line.

The Volkssturm, the Waffen SS, and the Hitler Youth were another matter. They fought fiercely and inflicted great damage. The GIs never knew, when the lead jeep rounded a corner, what was ahead. If inexperienced boys were there, they would fire—most often a panzerfaust shell at the jeep. The Americans would proceed to smash the village. "I'm not going to be the last man killed in this war" was the feeling, so when some teenage boy fired on them, they brought down a tremendous amount of shells. It was chaos and catastrophe, brought on for no reason—except that Hitler had raised these boys for just this moment. The fanatics were forcing the Americans to do to the German civilians and cities what Hitler wanted to do to them, because they had shown themselves to be unworthy of him.

The Allied fear was that Hitler would be able to encourage these armed bands over the radio to continue the struggle. His voice was his weapon. If he could get to the Austrian Alps he might be able to surround himself with SS troops and use the radio to put that voice into action.

Exactly that was happening, according to American agents in Switzerland. SHAEF G-2 agreed. As early as March 11, G-2 had declared, "The main trend of German defence policy does seem directed primarily to the safeguarding of the Alpine Zone. This area is practically impenetrable. . . . Evidence indicates that considerable numbers of SS and specially chosen units are being systematically withdrawn to Austria. . . . Here, defended by nature the powers that have hitherto guided Germany will survive to reorganize her resurrection. . . . Here a specially selected corps of young men will be trained in guerrilla warfare, so that a whole underground army can be fitted and directed to liberate Germany."

In September 1944, SHAEF intelligence had declared the German army dead. In mid-December 1944, SHAEF intelligence had missed altogether the gathering of the largest army the Germans ever put together on the Western Front. Having paid so heavily for its complacency in December, SHAEF intelligence went the other direction in March 1945 when it gave Eisenhower a report that was grossly exaggerated ("armaments will be manufactured in bomb-proof factories, food and equipment will be stored in vast underground caverns, with the most efficient secret weapons yet invented") and alarmist. Yet there was a core of truth to it. If the factories and underground storage facilities were imaginative, the threat of Hitler and a radio was not. He could ask his fanatics to hold on and hold out, until the Western Allies and the Soviet Union went to war.

There was a receptive audience to that line. Capt. John Cobb of the 82nd Airborne remembered an incident on the day of the surrender of the Ruhr pocket. He was in charge of a temporary prisoner compound. "The German who was the ranking officer made a request to see me. I received him, expecting some complaint about living conditions or treatment. Instead, he requested that he be allowed to join us with German volunteers when we began our attack against the Russians. He was incredulous when I informed him that we had no intentions of fighting the Russians."

Cpl. Friedrich Bertenrath recalled how the war ended for him: "There were still about 150 of us, and forty vehicles. The Americans came up. They searched us but we did not hold up our hands. After a bit, a bottle of schnapps was passed around. Each took a sip. An American said, 'You are all prisoners.' Someone from our side said, 'Forget about taking us prisoners, let us join you to go fight the Russians.'

" 'Forget that,' one of the Americans replied. They were decent men. We were allowed to get into our vehicles—they gave us some gas—and we drove with them through the area as if it were peacetime. There was an American jeep in front and one behind us, and in between twenty German tanks and APCs [armored personnel carriers]. It was a beautiful spring day. There were no more planes, no more Jabos above us."

Sgt. Bruce Egger remembered a lieutenant who surrendered to him. The lieutenant spoke perfect English "and was as blond, sharp, and arrogant as a Hollywood version of a Nazi officer. He gave us a lecture about why the Americans should not have waged war on Germany; we should have joined them fighting the true enemy, which was Russia, and that it was not too late. We laughed at him, but as the Cold War developed, I often thought of his words."

□

Eisenhower's mission was to get a sharp, clean, quick end to the war. The Russians were going to take Berlin anyway. There were more German divisions in southern Germany than to the north. The best way to carry out the mission was to overrun Bavaria and Austria before the Germans could set up their Alpine Redoubt. Eisenhower ordered Ninth Army to halt at the Elbe, First Army to push on to Dresden on the Elbe and then halt, and Third Army and Seventh Army, plus the French army, to overrun Bavaria and Austria.

Put another way, he refused to race the Russians to Berlin. He was much criticized for this. It remains his most controversial decision of the war. It has been much written about, including by me. I have nothing to add to the debate, except this: In thirty years of interviewing GIs, reading their books and unpublished memoirs, corresponding with them, I have not yet heard one of them say that he wanted to charge into Berlin. For the GIs, what stood out about Eisenhower's decision was that he put them first. If the Russians wanted to get into the ultimate street fight, that was their business.*

Day after day over the last couple of weeks, more concentration camps were discovered. On April 15 the British got into Belsen. That day Edward R. Murrow went to Buchenwald, just north of Weimar. Like Eisenhower and every GI who saw one of the camps, Murrow feared that no one could believe what he saw. He gave a description on his CBS radio program. In his conclusion he said, "I pray you to believe what I have said about Buchenwald. I have reported what I saw, but only part of it. For most of it I have no words. . . . If I've offended you by this rather mild account of Buchenwald, I'm not in the least sorry. I was there."

Martha Gellhorn of the *New York Times* visited the main camp at Dachau. Then she flew out on a C-47 carrying liberated

---

* Gregori Arbatov was a rifle company commander in the Red Army in the Battle of Berlin. He took terrible casualties. Some of them were men he had led in the Battle of Moscow, and so many others. Fifty years later he still shook with fury at the thought of Stalin's insistence on taking the city. Arbatov said any sane man would have surrounded Berlin, pounded it with artillery, and waited for the inevitable capitulation. "But not that son of a bitch Stalin. He sent us into the city, with all those crazy Nazi kids, and we bled." The estimated casualty cost was 100,000.

POWs to France. She talked to them about Dachau, which they had just seen.

"No one will believe us," one soldier said. They all agreed. "We got to talk about it, see? We got to talk about it if anyone believes us or not."

Marguerite Higgins of the rival *New York Herald Tribune* was also there. She reported, "The liberation was a frenzied scene. Inmates of the camp hugged and embraced the American troops, kissed the ground before them and carried them shoulder high around the place."

On April 27 the 12th Armored Division approached Landsberg-am-Lech, west of Munich. There were a Wehrmacht unit and a Waffen SS unit in the town. The Wehrmacht commander decided to withdraw across the Lech River. The SS commander wanted to fight. The regular officer told him to do as he wished, but the Wehrmacht troops were getting out of there. When the civilians saw the soldiers leaving, they hung out white sheets. The sight infuriated the SS. "In their rage," Lt. Julius Bernstein related, "they went from house to house and dragged outside whomever they found and hanged them from the nearest tree or lamp post. As we rode into Landsberg, we found German civilians hanging from trees like ripe fruit."

Later that day an awful black, acrid smoke appeared. It came from one of the outlying camps of the Dachau system. When the Americans approached, the SS officer in charge had ordered the remaining four thousand slave laborers destroyed. The guards had nailed shut the doors and windows of the wooden barracks, hosed down the buildings with gasoline, and set them on fire. The prisoners had been cremated alive. Later, Bernstein helped load civilians from Landsberg into trucks to take them to see the atrocity. "Would you believe that no one admitted any knowledge of the camp?" he later wrote. "They told us they thought it was a secret war factory, so they didn't ask questions. They all defended Hitler, saying, 'The Fuhrer knew nothing of this!' They blamed Goering, Goebbels and Himmler, but not their dear Fuhrer."

Their dear Fuhrer, meanwhile, declared that "the German people have not shown themselves worthy of their Fuhrer," and on April 30 killed himself. He named Adm. Karl Doenitz as his successor. Doenitz's task was to surrender—hopefully to the Western Allies only. He therefore sent Gen. Alfred Jodl, the German Chief of Staff, to Eisenhower's headquarters in Reims to accomplish that goal. Jodl arrived on Sunday evening, May 6. He conferred with his aides Gens. Smith and Strong, emphasizing that the Germans were willing, indeed anxious, to surrender to the West, but not to the Red Army. Doenitz, he said, would order all German troops remaining on the Western Front to cease firing no matter what SHAEF did about the offer to surrender. Smith replied that the surrender had to be a general one to all the Allies. Jodl then asked for forty-eight hours "in order to get the necessary instructions to all their outlying units." Smith said that was impossible. After the talks dragged on for over an hour, Smith put the problem to Eisenhower.

Eisenhower felt that Jodl was trying to gain time so that more German soldiers and civilians could get across the Elbe and escape the Russians. He told Smith to inform Jodl that "he would break off all negotiations and seal the western front preventing by force any further westward movement of German soldiers and civilians" unless Jodl signed the surrender document. But he also decided to grant the forty-eight-hour delay before announcing the surrender, as Jodl requested.

Smith took Eisenhower's reply to Jodl, who thereupon sent a cable to Doenitz, explaining the situation and asking permission to sign. Doenitz was enraged; he characterized Eisenhower's demands as "sheer extortion." He nevertheless felt impelled to accept them, and was consoled somewhat by the thought that the Germans could still save many troops from the Russians during the forty-eight-hour delay. Just past midnight, therefore, he cabled Jodl: "Full power to sign in accordance with conditions as given has been granted by Grand Admiral Doenitz."

At 2 A.M. on May 7, Generals Smith, Frederick Morgan, Bull, Spaatz, Tedder, a French representative, and Gen. Ivan Susloparoff, the Russian liaison officer at SHAEF, gathered in the second-floor recreation room of the Ecole Professionelle et Technique de Garçons, Reims. Strong was there to serve as translator. The war room was L-shaped, with only one small window; otherwise, the walls were covered with maps. Pins, arrows, and other symbols showed how completely Germany had been overrun. It was a relatively small room; the Allied officers had to squeeze past one another to get to their assigned chairs, gathered around a heavy oak table. When they had all sat down, Jodl, accompanied by an aide, was led into the room. Tall, perfectly erect, immaculately dressed, his monocle in place, Jodl looked the personification of Prussian militarism. He bowed stiffly. Strong found himself, to his own surprise, feeling a bit sorry for him.

While the somewhat elaborate procedures for the signing went on, Eisenhower waited in his adjacent office, pacing and smoking. The signing took a half hour. In the war room Jodl was delivering the German nation into the hands of the Allies and officially acknowledging that Nazi Germany was dead; outside, spring was bursting forth, promising new life.

Eisenhower knew that he should feel elated, triumphant, joyful, but all he really felt was dead beat. He had hardly slept in three days; it was the middle of the night; he just wanted to get it over with. At 2:41 A.M., Strong led Jodl into Eisenhower's office. Eisenhower sat down behind his desk. Jodl bowed, then stood at attention. Eisenhower asked Jodl if he understood the terms and was ready to execute them. Jodl said yes. Eisenhower then warned him that he would be held personally accountable if the terms were violated. Jodl bowed again and left.

Eisenhower went out into the war room, gathered the SHAEF officers around him (aides Kay Summersby and Capt. Harry Butcher managed to sneak in too), and photographers were called in to record the event for posterity. Eisenhower then made a short newsreel and radio recording. When the newsmen left, Smith said it was time to send a message to the CCS. Everyone had a try at drafting an appropriate document. "I tried one myself," Smith later recalled, "and like all my associates, groped for resounding phrases as fitting accolades to the Great Crusade and indicative of our dedication to the great task just completed."

Eisenhower quietly watched and listened. Each draft was more grandiloquent than the last. The Supreme Commander finally thanked everyone for his efforts, rejected all the proposals, and dictated the message himself. "The mission of this Allied force was fulfilled at 0241 local time, May 7, 1945."

He had managed to grin while the newsreel cameras were on, to hold up the pens in a V-for-Victory sign, to walk without a limp. After signing the last message he slumped visibly. "I suppose this calls for a bottle of champagne," he sighed. Someone brought one in; it was opened to feeble cheers; it was flat. Utter weariness now descended; everyone went to bed.

It was not at all like the image Eisenhower had held before him for three years. From the time he left Mamie in June 1942, he had sustained himself with the thought of this moment. "When the war ends"—the image of that magic moment had kept him going. When the Germans surrendered, then all would be right again. The world would be secure, he could go home, his responsibilities would be over, his duty done. He could sit beside a lazy stream with nothing but a cane pole and a bobber, and Mamie there with him, so that he could tell her about all the funny things that had happened that he had not had time to write about.

By early 1945, he had been forced to modify the fantasy somewhat, as he realized that he would have to remain in Germany for some months at least, as head of the American occupying forces. Still, he clung to the thought that Mamie could be with him immediately after the shooting stopped. Now he had the sinking feeling that even that was not going to be possible.

As to escaping responsibility, decision-making, and the burden of command, he had already had to face the fact that such a release was impossible. Worst of all, he already feared that world security was threatened. There had been too many of his own officers who listened with approval to the German whisperings about an anti-communist alliance; on the other side, the Russian suspicions about Western motives struck Eisenhower as bordering on paranoia (even before he went to bed, Eisenhower received a message that said the Russians would not accept the surrender signed in Reims and insisted on another signing, in Berlin). It made him wonder if it would be possible after all to cooperate with them in rebuilding Europe. Going to bed on that morning of May 7, Eisenhower felt as flat as the champagne.

But Eisenhower's flatness should not preclude a glance at what he had accomplished and what he had to celebrate, had he had the energy to do so. The problem is that, like Smith, one searches in vain for the fitting accolades to acknowledge the accomplishments of Dwight D. Eisenhower in the Second World War—of what he had endured, of what he had contributed to the final victory, of his place in military history.

Fortunately, George C. Marshall, next to Eisenhower himself the man most responsible for Eisenhower's success, spoke for the nation and its allies, as well as the U.S. Army, when he replied to Eisenhower's last wartime message, "You have completed your mission with the greatest victory in the history of warfare," Marshall began. "You have commanded with outstanding success the most powerful military force that has ever been assembled. You have met and successfully disposed of every conceivable difficulty incident to varied national interests and international political problems of unprecedented complications." Eisenhower, Marshall said, had triumphed over inconceivable logistical problems and military obstacles. "Through all of this, since the day of your arrival in England three years ago, you have been selfless in your actions, always sound and tolerant in your judgments and altogether admirable in the courage and wisdom of your military decisions.

"You have made history, great history for the good of mankind and you have stood for all we hope and admire in an officer of the United States Army. These are my tributes and my personal thanks."

It was the highest possible praise from the best possible source. It had been earned.

Many units had a ceremony of some sort to mark the unconditional surrender. In the 357th Combat Team, 90th Division, the CO had all the officers assemble on the grassy slopes of a hill, under a flagpole flying the Stars and Stripes. The regimental CO spoke, as did the division commander. "I can't remember their words," Lt. Col. Ken Reimers said, but he remembered counting the costs. "We had taken some terrible losses—our infantry suffered over 250 per cent casualties. There was not a single company commander present who left England with us, and there were only a half dozen officers in the whole regiment who landed on Utah Beach."

The 90th Division had been in combat for 308 days—the

record in ETO—but other divisions had taken almost as many casualties. The junior officers and NCOs suffered most. Some of America's best young men went down leading their troops in battle. Dutch Schultz paid his officers and NCOs a fine tribute: "Men like Captains Anthony Stefanich, Jack Tallerday; Lieutenants Gus Sanders, Gerald Johnson; and Sergeants Herman R. Zeitner, Sylvester Meigs, and Elmo Bell, to name only a few, were largely responsible for my transformation to a combat infantryman able to do his job. They taught me to overcome my fears and self-doubts.

"Not only were these men superb leaders both in and out of combat, but, more importantly, they took seriously the responsibility of first placing the welfare of their men above their own needs."

There is no typical GI among the millions who served in Northwest Europe, but Bruce Egger surely was representative. He was a mountain man from central Idaho. At the end of 1943 he was in ASTP at Kansas State. When the ASTP program was cut, he got assigned to Fort Leonard Wood for training. In October 1944 he arrived in France and went into a Repple Depple. On November 6 he went on the line with G Company, 328th Regiment, 26th Division. He served out the war in almost continuous front-line action. He never missed a day of duty. He had his close calls, most notably a piece of shrapnel stopped by the New Testament in the breast pocket of his field jacket, but was never wounded. In this he was unusually lucky. G Company had arrived on Utah Beach on September 8, 1944, with a full complement of 187 enlisted men and six officers. By May 8, 1945, a total of 625 men had served in its ranks. Fifty-one men of G Company were killed in action, 183 were wounded, 116 got trench foot and 51 frostbite.

Egger rose from private to staff sergeant. After the war he got a degree in forestry in 1951 and served in the U.S. Forest Service for twenty-nine years.

In his memoir of the war, Egger speaks for all GIs: "More than four decades have passed since those terrible months when we endured the mud of Lorraine, the bitter cold of the Ardennes, the dank cellars of Saarlautern. . . . We were miserable and cold and exhausted most of the time, we were all scared to death. . . . But we were young and strong then, possessed of the marvelous resilience

of youth, and for all the misery and fear and the hating every
moment of it the war was a great, if always terrifying, adventure.
Not a man among us would want to go through it again, but we are
all proud of having been so severely tested and found adequate.
The only regret is for those of our friends who never returned."

19

The GIs

I FIRST BECAME AWARE of the phenomenon when I was interviewing the men of Easy Company, 2nd Battalion, 506th PIR, 101st Airborne. I ran into it again and again in doing the interviews for my books on D-Day and the campaign in Northwest Europe. Pvt. Ed Tipper summed it up with a question: "Is it accidental that so many ex-paratroopers from E Company became *teachers?* Perhaps for some men a period of violence and destruction at one time attracts them to look for something creative as a balance in another part of life. We seem also to have a disproportionate number of builders of houses and other things in the group we see at reunions."

Indeed. One became a roofing contractor in Sacramento, another a structural ironworker on buildings and bridges, another a supervisor for the Washington State Highway Department, another superintendent for a heavy construction contractor in Louisiana, another spent forty-five years working with granite in the polishing trade, another a supervisor for installing new lines for the Pacific Telephone and Telegraph Company, another a carpenter, another a worker on high-dam construction. Nine men from the company became high school or college teachers. In this, the men of Easy Company were typical of the GIs.

They were the men who built modern America. They had learned to work together in the armed services in World War II.

They had seen enough destruction; they wanted to construct. They built the Interstate Highway System, the St. Lawrence Seaway, the suburbs (so scorned by the sociologists, so successful with the people), and more. They had seen enough killing; they wanted to save lives. They licked polio and made other revolutionary advances in medicine. They had learned in the army the virtues of a solid organization and teamwork, and the value of individual initiative, inventiveness, and responsibility. They developed the modern corporation while inaugurating revolutionary advances in science and technology, education and public policy.

The ex-GIs had seen enough war; they wanted peace. But they had also seen the evil of dictatorship; they wanted freedom. They had learned in their youth that the way to prevent war was to deter through military strength, and to reject isolationism for full involvement in the world. So they supported NATO and the United Nations and the Department of Defense. They had stopped Hitler and Tojo; in the 1950s they stopped Stalin and Khrushchev.

In his inaugural address, President John F. Kennedy described the men and women of his generation: "The torch has been passed to a new generation of Americans—born in this century, tempered by war, disciplined by a hard and bitter peace, proud of our ancient heritage—and unwilling to witness or permit the slow undoing of those human rights to which this nation has always been committed."

The "we" generation of World War II (as in "We are all in this together") was a special breed of men and women who did great things for America and the world. When the GIs sailed for Europe, they were coming to the continent not as conquerors but liberators. In his Order of the Day on June 6, 1944, Eisenhower had told them their mission was: "The destruction of the German war machine, the elimination of Nazi tyranny over the oppressed peoples of Europe, and security for ourselves in a free world." They accomplished that mission.

In the process they liberated the Germans (or at least the Germans living west of the Elbe River). In Normandy, in July 1944, Wehrmacht Pvt. Walter Zittats was guarding some American prisoners. One of them spoke German. Zittats asked him, " 'Why are you making war against us?' I'll always remember his exact words: 'We are fighting to free you from the fantastic idea that you are a master race.' " In June 1945 Eisenhower told his staff, "The success of this occupation can only be judged fifty years from now. If the Germans at that time have a stable, prosperous democracy, then we shall have succeeded." That mission, too, was accomplished.

In the fall semester of 1996, I was a visiting professor at the University of Wisconsin-Madison. I taught a course on World War II to some 350 students. They were dumbstruck by descriptions of what it was like to be on the front lines. They were even more amazed by the responsibilities carried by junior officers and NCOs who were as young as they. Like all of us who have never been in combat, they wondered if they could have done it—and even more, they wondered how anyone could have done it.

There is a vast literature on the latter question. In general, in assessing the motivation of the GIs, there is agreement that patriotism or any other form of idealism had little if anything to do with it. The GIs fought because they had to. What held them together was not counry and flag, but unit cohesion. It has been my experience, through four decades of interviewing ex-GIs, that such generalizations are true enough.

And yet there is something more. Although the GIs were and are embarrassed to talk or write about the cause they fought for, in marked contrast to their great-grandfathers who fought in the Civil War, they were the children of democracy and they did more to help spread democracy around the world than any other generation in history.

At the core, the American citizen soldiers knew the difference between right and wrong, and they didn't want to live in a world in which wrong prevailed. So they fought, and won, and we all of us, living and yet to be born, must be forever profoundly grateful.

At the conclusion of interviews, I often asked the ex-GIs to sum up what it all meant to them. Most men dismissed the question as impossible to answer. Some talked about friendship, comrades, buddies. Not one ever talked about patriotism and pride. Yet it was there. The best expression of it I ever heard came at the end of a group interview. I've long since forgotten the name of the speaker, but I'll never forget what he said. "Imagine this. In the spring of 1945, around the world, the sight of a twelve-man squad of teenage boys, armed and in uniform, brought terror to people's hearts. Whether it was a Red Army squad in Berlin, Leipzig, or Warsaw, or a German squad in Holland, or a Japanese squad in Manila, Seoul, or Beijing, that squad meant rape, pillage, looting, wanton destruction, senseless killing. But there was an exception: a squad of GIs, a sight that brought the biggest smiles you ever saw to people's lips, and joy to their hearts.

"Around the world this was true, even in Germany, even— after September 1945—in Japan. This was because GIs meant candy, cigarettes, C-rations, and freedom. America had sent the best of her young men around the world, not to conquer but to liberate, not to terrorize but to help. This was a great moment in our history."

Another bright image came from a veteran who said that he felt he had done his part in helping to change the twentieth century from one of darkness into one of light. I think that was the great achievement of the generation who fought World War II on the Allied side. As of 1945—the year in which more people were killed violently, more buildings destroyed, more homes burned than any other year in history—it was impossible to believe in human progress. World Wars I and II had made a mockery of the nineteenth-century idea of progress, the notion that things were getting better and would continue to do so. In 1945 one had to believe that the final outcome of the scientific and technological revolution that had inspired the idea of progress would be a world destroyed.

But slowly, surely, the spirit of those GIs handing out candy and helping bring democracy to their former enemies spread, and today it is the democracies—not the totalitarians—who are on the march. Today, one can again believe in progress, as things really are getting better. This is thanks to the GIs—along with the millions of others who helped liberate Germany and Japan from their evil rulers, then stood up to Stalin and his successors. That generation has done more to spread freedom—and prosperity—around the globe than any previous generation.

John Lydon, a thirty-four-year-old attorney in Chicago, wrote me in 1998 that his father had served in SHAEF. "Most of my young life," Lydon confessed, "I never really understood my father. I blamed him and his generation for everything from McCarthyism to the Vietnam War to Watergate. I never gave them credit for the Interstate Highway System, IBM, NASA, the Civil Rights Act of 1965, the fall of Communism, or any of it. Then I read your book [*Citizen Soldiers*]. You have helped me understand my father. When my son is old enough, I will give him your book so he can get to know his grandfather."

Sgt. Henry Halsted, who won a Bronze Star, participated after the war in some experimental programs that brought together college-age German and American veterans in England, and a similar one in France. The idea was to teach through contact and example. In 1997, Halsted got a Christmas card from a German participant living in Munich: "I think often of our meetings and mutual ideals. Indeed, the 1948 program and everything connected with it was the most important, decisive event for me. Influenced my life deeply!"

And a French participant wrote, "In 1950 France was in ruins. I saw only a world marked by war, by destruction, by the shadow of war, and by fear. I believed that it was not finished, that there would be a next war. I did not think it would be possible to build a life, to have a family. Then came the group of young Americans, attractive, idealistic, optimistic, protected, believing and acting as though anything was possible. It was a transforming experience for me."

That spirit—we can do it, we can rebuild Europe and hold back the Red Army and avoid World War III—was the great gift of the New World to the Old World in the twentieth century. America paid for that gift with the lives of some of its best young men. When I read the letters from the veterans I'm almost always impressed by their brief accounts of what they did with their lives after the war. They had successful careers, they were good citizens and family men, and many of them made great contributions to their society, their country, and the world. Then I think about those who didn't make it, especially all those junior officers and NCOs who got killed in such appalling numbers.

These men were natural leaders. They died one by one. Of each of them, I wonder, What life was cut off here? A genius? It is impossible to imagine what he might have invented; we do know that his loss was our loss. A budding politician? Where might he have led us? A builder? A teacher? A scholar? A novelist? A musician? I sometimes think the biggest price we pay for war is what might have been.

Lt. Waverly Wray comes to mind. So do Capt. Anthony Stefanich and Lt. Col. Robert Cole and so many others, gone long before their time, their deaths depriving us of the gift of their lives. When they tolled the bell for Wray, Stefanich, Cole, and the hundreds of their buddies who went down, that bell tolled for all of us.

What I think of the GIs more than a half century after their victory was best said by Sgt. Mike Ranney of the 101st: "In thinking back on the days of Easy Company, I'm treasuring my remark to a grandson who asked, 'Grandpa, were you a hero in the war?'

" 'No,' I answered, 'but I served in a company of heroes.' "

So far as I am concerned, so did they all.

Sources

In this volume I've woven a narrative of the war based on the books I've done with my editor, Alice Mayhew, and Simon & Schuster over the past fifteen years. They are *Eisenhower: Soldier, General of the Army, President-Elect, 1890–1952* (1983); *Pegasus Bridge: June 6, 1944* (1985); *Band of Brothers: E Company, 506th Regiment, 101st Airborne from Normandy to Hitler's Eagle's Nest* (1992); *D-Day: June 6, 1944: The Climactic Battle of World War II* (1994); and *Citizen Soldiers: The U.S. Army from the Normandy Beaches to the Bulge to the Surrender of Germany, June 7, 1944–May 7, 1945* (1997). Where necessary and appropriate I've provided bridges between sections taken from the different books. To help the flow of the narrative, and to avoid repetition, I've eliminated notes from the text. Interested readers can go to the original works for specific citations. In this list of sources, I've included the names of the men and women I've interviewed over the past two decades, and those of men who have given written memoirs to the Eisenhower Center at the University of New Orleans. The bibliography of books and articles is not intended to be a comprehensive list of the major works on World War II; rather it is a list of the publications I've consulted and cited for the books listed above.

Oral Histories, Memoirs, and Interviews

Marion H. Adams
Robert Adams
Ray Aebischer

John L. Ahearn
Nicholas Aiavolasiti
Roger L. Airgood

Harold Akridge
Lloyd Alberts
Parker A. Alford
Bob Allen
Daniel Allen
Weldon J. Allen
Harry C. Allison
Alfred Allred
John S. Allsup
Will Alpern
Al Alvarez
R. Ambrose
Alan Anderson
Clifford Anderson
Franklin Anderson
Louise S. Armstrong
James E. Arnold
Benjamin Arthur, Sr.
Earl Asker
Edward A. Askew
William A. Atkins
Carl Atwell
Theo G. Aufort
C. R. Ault
John C. Ausland
Cyrus C. Aydlett

Peter P. Bachmeier
W. Garwood Bacon, Jr.
Steve Baehren
Jack Bailey
Roderick Bain
Arthur Baker
Fred J. Baker
Leland A. Baker
Ray Ballard
Charles A. Barbier
Harry C. Bare
Jack R. Barensfeld
Edward Barnes
John J. Barnes
Joseph Barrett
Robert B. Barrix

W. Arthur Barrow
Armond Barth
Farr H. Barto
Eugene H. Barton
James A. Batte
Harold Baumgarten
Sherman L. Baxter
Jacques Bayer
Goebel Baynes
James H. Bearden
Sam Walter Bears
Briand N. Beaudin
Gale B. Beccue
John A. Beck
Raymond F. Bednar
Howard Beebe
Charles Beecham
Frank Beetle
Daniel R. Beirne
Bryan Bel
Joe Belardo
Leo T. Bement
Donald Bennett
Ronald Bennett
Wilfred Bennett
Arden Benthien
Max Berger
William E. Bergmann
Edward Bergstrom
I. R. Berkowitz
Eugene Bernstein
Edward J. Best
Richard Betts
Bryan Beu
Briand Beudin
A. R. Beyer
John Biddle
Grandison K. Bienvenu
Ted Billnitzer
Dick Bills
Sidney V. Bingham
Doug Birch
Gordon D. Bishop

Wallace Bishop
John E. Bistrica
John R. Blackburn
Pat Blamey
Joseph S. Blaylock, Sr.
Earl Blocker
Rans Blondo
Edward C. Boccafogli
Jeff Bodenweiser
Robert L. Bogart
Oliver Boland
Vernal Boline
Calhoun Bond
Letterio R. Bongiorno
Milton Boock
John D. Boone
Everett L. Booth
Stan Booth
Stanley Borkowski
Charles Bortzfield
Donald E. Bosworth
Donald G. Botens
Paul Bouchereau
William Boulet
Bill Bowdidge
Robert Bowen
Ellis C. Boyce
Robert J. Boyda
James C. Boyett
Calvin Boykin
William Boykin
Leo D. Boyle
Bruce D. Bradley
Holdbrook Bradley
Omar Bradley
Felix P. Branham
James W. Brannen
John Braud
Cecil Breeden
Earle Breeding
Warren R. Breniman
John V. Brennan
William O. Brenner

Robert (Bob) Brewer
Michael A. Brienze
Eugene D. Brierre
Calvin Bright
Dorothy Brinkley
Harold E. Brodd
Geoff W. Bromfield
Anthony M. Brooks
John Brooks
Bob Brothers
Sam Broussard
Floyd L. Brown
John G. Brown
Owen L. Brown
Sid Brown
James J. Bruen
Roger L. Brugger
J. Frank Brumbaugh
August Bruno
Phil H. Bucklew
Morris Buckmaster
David Buffalo
Nile Buffington
J. R. Buller
Tom Burgess
Ferris Burke
Ralph R. Burnett
Dwayne T. Burns
Joe Burns
Thomas V. Burns
Chester Butcher
Robert Butler
Nicholas F. Butrico
C. D. Butte
Pat Butters

Tom Cadwallader
Paul Calvert
Joseph L. Camera
Bob Cameron
Donald Campbell
Herbert Campbell
Arthur R. Candelaria

Harold O. Canyon
Robert Capa
John C. Capell
Aaron Caplan
George Capon
Carl D. Carden
Homer F. Carey
Elmer Carmichael
Jim Carmichael
Harry Carroll
Gordon F. Carson
Donald Carter
Jack Carter
William A. Carter
Carl Cartledge
Kenneth H. Cassens
Richard Cassiday
Joseph Castellano
Coy Chandler
Sidney S. Chapin, Jr.
Eugene Chase
Angelos T. Chatas
N. J. Chelenza
Frank Chesney
Jules Chicoine
Aubrey Childs
Carl Christ
Burton P. Christenson
Burton Christianson
Donald C. Chumley
Arthur Ciechoski
Fred Claesson
Richard Clancy
Elmer W. Clarey
Asa V. Clark, Jr.
Richard C. Clawson II
William Clayton
Michel M. Clemencon
Nigel Clogstorm
B. A. Coats
John Cobb
Murray Codman
John Colby

Isaac Coleman
Lorell Coleman
John Collins
Richard H. Conley
Henry L. Conner
Ralph E. Cook
Charles M. Cooke, Jr.
Williard F. Coonen
Belton Cooper
W. R. Copeland
Ed Corbett
Jack Corbett
Tom Corcoran
Kenneth Cordry
Christopher Cornazzani
A. H. Corry
S. Coupe
Milton A. Courtright
Jerry Cowle
Clarence Cox
Joseph Cox
James J. Coyle
William Craft
Roy E. Creek
Ralph Crenshaw
Theodore Crocker
Michael Crofoot
Art Cross
Russell Crossman
Robert Crousore
Jack Crowley
Tom Cruse, Jr.
Jack T. Curtis
Robert Curtis
Rupert Curtis
Isador E. Cutler

Lord Dacre of Glanton
Mike Dagner
Joseph A. Gahlia
Carlton Dailey
Robert L. Dains
Edward Daly

Gerald Darr
Charles W. Dauer
Sam P. Daugherty
Dave Davidson
Phillip B. Davidson
Gary S. Davis
Robert L. Davis
Francis W. Dawson
John R. Dawson
Joseph Dawson
Robert Dawson
Victor J. Day
William Dean
William J. Decarlton
Arthur Defilippo
Louise Deflon
Arthur Defranco
Irish Degnan
Sir Francis de Guingand
Kenneth T. Delaney
Robert L. Delashaw
Vincent J. Del Guidice
Igor De Lissovoy
Ralph Della-Volpe
Michael Deloney
James M. Delong
John P. Delury
Richard H. Denison
William Denton
Roger Derderian
Morton Descherer
Howard R. Devault
John J. Devink
Ralph E. Deweese
Antonia R. Didonna
Dominic Diliberto
Gerard M. Dillon
William T. Dillon
David Doehrman
Joseph A. Dolan
Leo Dolan
Joseph Dominguez
Richard Donaghy

David Donald
Joseph Donlan
"Ike" Dorsey
Joseph Dougherty
Cliff Douglas
Dow L. Dowler
Ralph Dragoo
Joseph A. Dragotto
Ronald J. Drez
James H. Drumwright, Jr.
Stanley Dudka
Edward T. Duffy
Anthony Duke
Lewis Duke
John Dunnigan
Kenneth Dykes

Jerry W. Eades
James Eads
Ted Eaglen
B. Ralph Eastridge
Eugene E. Eckstam
James Edward
Arlo Edwards
Donald K. Edwards
Malcolm G. Edwards
J. Frank Ehrman
Thomas Eichler
James Eikner
Harry Eisen
Dwight D. Eisenhower
John S. D. Eisenhower
Milton S. Eisenhower
Gene E. Elder
George Eldridge
John B. Ellery
John S. Elleshope
George Elsey
John Englehart
Donald Ennett
John L. Erexson
Clay Ernest
Frank Ernest, Jr.

Rudi Escher
Joseph H. Esclavon
Don Eutzy
Carl Evans
Robert L. Evans
James M. Everett
Bill Everhard

Bobby Fachiri
Richard P. Fahey
John T. Fanning
Victor H. Fast
William E. Faust
Frank R. Feduik
Jacob A. Feigion
Bernard S. Feinberg
Max Feldman
Andrew A. Fellner
Leo Fenster
Col Ferguson
Mary Ferrell
Richard Ferris
H. Fielder
Lewis Finkelstein
Martin Finkelstein
James F. Finn
Richard Fiscus
P. L. Fitts
John E. Fitzgerald
Steve Fitzgerald
Barry Fixler
Maro Flagg
Tony Flamio
Richard S. Fleming
K. Fletcher
Arthur Flinner
Robert A. Flory
Hilton M. Floyd
Roger Foehringer
Edward J. Foley
Michael R. D. Foot
George Forteville
George P. Fory

Thomas J. Fournier
Dennis Fox
Benjamin T. Frana
Geoffrey B. Frank
Benjamin Frans
Richard A. Freed, Sr.
George Freedman
Roger Freeman
Herbert A. Freemark
Alfred J. Freiburger
Max Friedlander
J. C. Friedman
Murray Friedman
James T. Fudge
Dan Furlong

Steve Gabre
Francis Gabreski
Frank Gaccione
Clair R. Galdonik
Edwin M. Gale
Edward P. Gallogly
Paul Gardiner
Howard C. Gates
Parker Gathings
Ralph Gault
Paul E. Gauthier
Sims S. Gauthier
William Gentry
Henry Gerald
Edward Gerard
Edward "Buddy" Gianelloni
Sam M. Gibbons
Gerald Gibbs
William D. Gibbs, Jr.
Joseph P. Gibney
Edward S. Giers
Melvin R. Gift
Robert Giguere
Jack Gilfry
Edward B. Giller
Ed Gilleran
James L. Gilligan

Solon B. Gilmore
Thomas J. Gintjee
John Girolamo
Thomas J. Glennon
Emanuel E. Gluck
Edward J. Gnatowski
Franz Gockel
Russell C. Goddard
John Goetz
Harry Goldberg
Glen Golden
Henry L. Goldsmith
Lawrence Goldstein
Theresa Gondree
Bryan L. Good
Andrew Goodpaster
Geroge W. Goodspeed
Ralph E. Goranson
Walter Gordon
Victor Gore
Harry D. Graham
Dick Granet
Billy Gray
Dennis G. Gray
Jack Gray
Leslie B. Gray
Elmer R. Green
Joseph L. Green
David Greenberg
John Montgomery Greene
Gordon Emerson Greenlaw
Gabriel N. Greenwood
John Greenwood
Richard Gresso
Bill Grey
Leslie Grice
Len Griffing
O. T. Grimes
Maxwell Grimm
R. K. Grondin
Lyle Groundwater
Samuel N. Grundfast
Charlie Guarino

William Guarnere
Stanley Guess
Carroll Guidry
Grant G. Gullickson
Martin Gutekunst
Forrest Guth
Mariano Guy

Hyman Haas
George R. Hackett
Tim Hackney
Harry T. Hagaman
William J. Hahn
Earl Hale
Fred W. Hall, Jr.
Raymond Hall
Robert A. Hall
Patricia Hamas
J. H. Hamilton
Warner H. Hamlett
Dorr Hampton
Clayton E. Hanks
Curtis Hansen
Michel Hardelay
Randy Hardy
Herman Hareland
John Hargesheimer
David Harmon
William E. Harness
Charles E. Harris
Fred Harris
Leslie Harris
John Harrison
Clarence Hart
William Hart
Rainer Hartmetz
George E. Hartshorn
C. G. Hasselfeldt
J. K. Havener
Douglas Hawkins
Wallace B. Hawkins
Robert L. Hayes, III
Robert L. Healey

Gerald W. Heaney
Bennie L. Heathman
Charles W. Heins
Andre Heintz
Beatrice Heller
Joseph Heller
B. P. Henderson
Ted Henderson
Cyril Hendry
Gerald M. Henry
Leonard F. Herb
Paul Hernandez
Leo Heroux
Andrew Hertz
R. Hesketh
Clarence Hester
James W. Hewitt
Frederick von der Heydte
Victor Hicken
Henry Hickman
Howard W. Hicks
Lindley R. Higgins
Henry J. Hill
Howard Hill
James Hill
O. B. Hill
Ralph Hill
Ernest Hillberg
John D. Hinton
Herman Frank Hinze
Newal Hobbs
Robert A. Hobbs
G. K. Hodenfield
Jack L. Hodgkinson
Marion C. Hoffman
Ted Hoffmeister
Barnett Hoffner
James F. Hogan
David Holbrook
James G. Holland
Penny Gooch Holloway
Donald Holman
Bill Holmes
Frank Holmes

Bob Holsher
John Honan
Josh Honan
Ed H. Honnen
George Honour
C. Hooper
John Hooper
Thomas A. Horne
Merwin H. Horner, Jr.
A. W. Horton
Nathaniel R. Hoskot
Warren Hotard
Colin Howard
E. D. Howard
Frank O. Howard
John Howard
Joy Howard
Raymond Howell
Charles M. Huber
Tony Hubert
Jerry Hudson
Charles Huff
Dan Hugger
R. R. Hughart
A. H. Hultman
Harry Hunt
Albert W. Huntley
Ernie Husted
George Hutnick
Bernard F. Hydo

Jack Ihle
Jack Ilfrey
Bill Irving
Don Irwin
Jack R. Isaacs
Orville Iverson

Ed Jabol
Sam Jacks
C. L. Jackson
Sir Ian Jacob
Quiles R. Jacobs
Jack Jacobsen

Arthur Jahnke
Alma Jakobson
Herbert M. James
Charles Jarreau
Ralph Jenkins
Steve Jenkins
Henry D. Jennings
James Jennings
Leroy Jennings
Richard Jepsen
Edward J. Jeziorski
Harry Johnson
Lagrande K. Johnson
Russell Johnson
Steve Johnson
George H. Johnston
Roland Johnston
David M. Jones
Edward G. Jones, Jr.
George A. Jones
J. Elmo Jones
J. W. Jones
James A. Jones
Oscar W. Jones
William E. Jones
William H. Jones
Captain Jordan
Erik M. Juleen

John Kaheny
Stanley Kalberer
Albert Kamento
Chris Kanaras
Robert Karwoski
Thomas S. Kattar
M. B. Kauffman
Robert E. Kaufman
Jack Keating
Elbert Keel
Ned F. Kegler
Steve Kellman
Edward J. Kelly
Robert Kelly
John Kemp

Edward Kempton
Frank J. Kennedy
Harry Kennedy
George Kerchner
Ester Kesler
Leslie W. Kick
Maurice Kidder
William C. Kiessel
R. H. Kilburn
William Kilgore
Jack D. Kill
Jerry R. Kimball
John T. King, III
Russell King
William L. King
Lorin D. Kinsel
Trenton L. Knack
George Kobe
Harvey W. Koenig
Vincent A. Kordack
Werner Kortenhaus
Walter T. Kozack
David Koziczkowski
Chester Kozik
Weldon L. Kratzer
Herb Krauss
E. Krieger
Raymond Kristoff
James A. Krucas
M. G. Kruglinski
L. M. Kuenzi
Frank J. Kuhn, Jr.
Clemens Kujawa
Peter Kukurba
William Kupp
A. W. Kuppers
Bob Kurtz
James Q. Kurz
R. Ben Kuykendall

Ivan Ladany
Richard G. Laine, Jr.
George Lane
Gilbert H. Lane

Devon G. Larson
Lance Larson
John L. Latham
Wood Lathrop Lawrence
George Lawson
Howard A. Lawson
Bill Layton
Ken Lease
Leonard Lebenson
Thomas Lee
Wesley T. Leeper
William Leesemann
William H. Lefevre
Elbert E. Legg
George Leidenheimer
Paul Lello
G. W. Levers
Ronald Lewin
John R. Lewis, Jr.
Robert L. Lewis
William Lewis
Leo K. Lick
Elinor Lilley
R. J. Lindo
Ruth S. Linley
C. Carwood Lipton
Lou Lisko
Al Littke
John Livingston
Warren R. Lloyd
Bill Lodge
Ralph Logan
Donald E. Loker
Joe Lola
Noah F. Lomax
Leonard Lomell
James A. Long
William R. Long, Sr.
Paul Longrigg
Kenneth P. Lord
Roger V. Lovelace
David Lownds
Hans von Luck

Walter Lukasavage, Jr.
Ewell B. Lunsford
George Luz
Lou Lyle
Edward Lynch, Jr.
Thomas Lynch

Frederick Macdonald
Edward P. Mackenzie
John Mackenzie
John H. MacPhee
George W. Madison
Donald J. Magilligan
Salva P. Maimone
Lou Mais
Frederick C. Maisel, Jr.
Don Malarkey
Edith Manford
Ray A. Mann
Moses Defriese Manning
Bob Maras
Jim Marine
Maynard C. Marquis
John Marshall
Paul M. Marshall
Billy Martin
Herbert F. Martin
Homer Martin
John Martin
Peter Martin
Russell Martin
Thomas Martin
Walter Martini
Alexander Marzenoski
Stan Mason
Peter Masters
John Mather
Russ Mathers
S. H. Matheson
Robert Mathias
Robert Mattingly
William W. Maves
John G. Mayer

Craig Mays
Buddy Mazzara
Herbert E. McAdoo
Sidney McCallum
Joseph E. McCann, Jr.
Donald McCarthy
Dick McCauley
William H. McChesney
Earl E. McClung
Billy McCoy
Robert McCrory
Francis H. McFarland
Leroy D. McFarland
John S. McGee
Daniel A. McGovern
George McGovern
Rieman McIntosh
Frank E. McKee
Clarence McKelvey
Anthony W. McKenzie
Benjamin F. McKinney
Ernest J. McKnight
Colin H. McLaurin
John McLean
John W. McLean
Stephen J. McLeod
G. F. McMahon
Allen M. McMath
Howard McMillen
Raleigh L. McMullen
Robert McMurray
Neil McQuarrie
G. V. McQueen
Jack A. McQuiston
Joe Meckoll
Mac Meconis
Stan Medland
J. Medusky
Jay H. Mehaffey
Kenneth G. Meierhoefer
Walter Melford
Anthony J. Mennella
Guillaume Mercader

Don Mercier
Douglas Meredith
Dillon H. Merical
James G. Merola
Robert Merriman
Kenneth J. Merritt
Frank Mertzel
John E. Meyer
Bruce F. Meyers
Larry J. Micka
Charles Middleton
John R. Midkiff
Jim Mildenberger
George E. Miles
Charles H. Miller
Robert H. Miller
Robert M. Miller
Robert V. Miller
Victor J. Miller
Stanley E. Mills
Woodrow W. Millsaps
William J. Milne
James L. Milton
Leslie D. Minchew
Wallace E. Minnick
Peronneau Mitchell
Michael Mitroff
Woodrow R. Mock, Jr.
Jack Modesett
Joseph S. Moelich, Sr.
John Moench
Charles D. Mohrle
Albert Mominee
David E. Mondt
John Montgomery
William C. Montgomery
John Montrose
Peter R. Moody
Raymond E. Moon
Ferdinand Morello
Rocco J. Moretto
Aubrey Morgan
Sir Frederick Morgan

William J. Moriarity
Jesse Morrow
John R. G. Morschel
Dan J. Morse
Richard Mote
Andrew Mouton
Armin Mruck
Bert Mullins
Placido Munnia
Gilbert E. Murdock
James Murphy
Claude Murray
Frank Murray
F. L. Mutter

Romuald Nalecz-Tyminski
E. Ray Nance
Roger D. Nedry
William S. Nehez
Charles Neighbor
Don Nelson
Donald T. Nelson
Albert Nendza
Cliff Neumann
Kenneth C. Newberg
George K. Newhall
Arthur L. Nichols, Jr.
Roy W. Nickrent
R. J. Nieblas
Julius R. Noble
Harry Nomburg
Francis M. Norr
Frank J. Nowacki
Alfred Nuesser
Ralph J. Nunley
Donald W. Nuttall

William Oatman
Edward Obert
E. O'Donnell
Ralph G. Oehmcke
Lou Offenberg
Harold J. O'Leary

Ingvald G. Olesrud
Ross Olsen
James C. O'Neal, Jr.
William T. O'Neill
John B. O'Rourke
Lawrence Orr
William Otlowski
James Ousley
William T. Owens
Sherman J. Oyler
Jim Oyster

Joseph J. Palladino
Clifford Palliser
N. L. Palmer, Jr.
Francis A. Palys
Ellison W. Parfitt
Arnold Parish
Bill Parish
Darel C. Parker
Richard Parker
W. E. Parker
William Parker
John Parkins
Harry Parley
Irene Parr
Wally Parr
Tony B. Parrino
Harold L. Parris
Philip J. Parrott
Clifton Parshall
Tom Parsons
Fred C. Patheiger
Mario Patruno
J. Robert Patterson
Ralph Patton
Michael C. Paul
Vernon L. Paul
Anthony J. Paulino
Joe Pavlick
John M. Peck
James O. Peek
Al Pekasiewicz

John Pellegren
James Pemberton
Aaron D. Pendleton
Ken Penn
Julius Perlinski
Marvin Perrett
John A. Perry
Gene Person
Debs H. Peters
Earl W. Peters
H. B. Peterson
Jerry Peterson
Joseph L. Petry
Elvin W. Phelps
Woodrow W. Phelps
Jack Phillips
James Phillips
Jerry L. Phillips
Robert M. Phillips
Paul Phinney
Robert Piauge
Harold Pickersgill
Gregory Pidhorecki
Dewey Pierce
Exum L. Pike, Sr.
Malvin R. Pike
Joe Pilck
Kenneth Pipes
Pierre Piprel
Sidney S. Platt
Leonard Ploeckelman
Edward Plona
Tom Plumb
Felix C. Podalok
George T. Poe
Nigel Poett
Forrest Pogue
Lee Polek
John Polyniak
Tom Porcella
Mario Porcellini
Angelo Porta
Pat Porteous

Donald Porter
Dennis Pott
Vincent Powell
Cecil Powers
Darrell Powers
Ralph Powers
Lee Pozek
Orvis C. Preston
Walter Preston
L. A. Prewritt
John Price
Virgil T. Price
Walter Pridmore
Jack B. Prince

Richard H. Quigley
Tom Quigley
Louis F. Quirk, Jr.

John C. Raaen, Jr.
Duwaine Raatz
Robert J. Rader
Paul Q. Radzom
Emerald M. Ralston
John Ramano
Oswaldo V. Ramirez
Bill Ramsey
Denver Randleman
Louis Rann
Glen Rappold
Charles Ratliff
Bill Ray
Larry Raygor
Samuel Reali
Paul Ream
Quinton F. Reams
William C. Reckord
Robert E. Reed
Russell P. Reeder, Jr.
Richard Reese
Sandy Reid
Joe D. Reilly
Harry L. Reisenleiter

Bill Rellstab
John J. Reville
K. B. Reynolds
Oscar Rich
John R. Richards
John W. Richards
Elliot Richardson
Robert Richardson
Samuel Richardson
Wilbur Richardson
Samuel Ricker, Sr.
Clinton E. Riddle
James R. Rider
Ross Riggs
John W. Ripley
Jason Rivet
George V. Roach
Arthur E. Roberts
Douglas Roberts
Elvy B. Roberts
James M. Roberts
Javis Roberts
John W. Robertson
Robert T. Robertson
William S. Robilliard
John H. Robinson
Dean Rockwell
Charles W. Rodekuhr
Edward K. Roger
Paul Rogers
Robert E. Rogge
Charles Roland
Edgar M. Rolland
Nick Romanetz
Kenneth L. Romanski
Edward L. Ronczy
Andy Rooney
Bob Rooney
James M. Roos
Theodore Roosevelt
Robert Rose
Zolman Rosenfield
George Rosie

William Rosz
Wayne Roten
William J. Roulette
Frank Rowe
G. Royster
Mike Rudanovich, Jr.
David W. Ruditz
Thomas R. Rudolf
Eugene W. Rule
Warren Rulien
Mel I. Rush
Charles P. Rushforth, III
Carlton P. Russell
Ken Russell
James A. Russo, Jr.
Peter N. Russo
H. A. Rutherford
Ron Rutland
George Ryal
Bob Ryan
Charles J. Ryan
George Ryan
William F. Ryan

Werner Saenger
Edwin Safford
Harvey Safford
Robert L. Sales
Robert Salley
Sidney A. Salomon
Lawrence F. Salva
Charles E. Sammon
James Sammons
Otis Sampson
Raymond Sanders
Archie Sanderson
Hector J. Santa Anna
Alfred J. Sapa
Joseph E. Sardo, III
Jack R. Sargeant
William E. Satterwhite
Cliff Saul
Robert Saveland

Jeff Savelkoul

William M. Sawyer

Michael Sayers

Dennis Scanlan

Franklin J. Schaffner

Irl C. Schahrer

Leonard Schallehn

Eldon Schinning

D. Zane Schlemmer

Vincent H. Schlotterbeck

Roy F. Schmoyer

Rudy Schneider

Robert Schober

Donald P. Schoo

Edgar A. Schroeder

Herbert W. Schroeder

Oliver A. Schuh

William G. Schuler

Everett P. Schultheis

Arthur B. Schultz

Edward R. Schwartz

William F. Schwerin

John Scilliere

Don Scott

W. Murphy Scott

Donald L. Scribner

Richard Scudder

Ronald Seaborne

Larry J. Seavy-Cioffi

Elmer Seech

Irvin W. Seelye

John Seitz

Henry E. Seitzler

Cletus Sellner

William Sentry

Jack R. Sergeant

Roy G. Settle

Ohmer D. Shade

Edward Shames

Don Shanley

Fred Shaver

Horace G. Shaw

Walter P. Shaw

J. T. Shea

Brian Shelley

Joseph Shelly

Charles G. Shettle

K. F. Shiffer

Alex Shisko

Tom Shockley

C. Richard Shoemaker

Ron Shuff

Walter Sidlowski

Stan Silva

Frank L. Simeone

Thomas A. Simms

Walter Simon

W. A. Simpkins

Louis Simpson

Ralph H. Sims

Clifford H. Sinnet

Wayne Sisk

Charles E. Skidmore, Jr.

C. B. Jack Skipper

Paul L. Skogsberg

John R. Slaughter

John K. Slingluff

Albert H. Smith, Jr.

Allen T. Smith

Anthony M. Smith

David M. Smith

Douglas Smith

George A. Smith

Helen Smith

Jim Smith

Joe G. Smith

John F. Smith

Lewis C. Smith

R. Smith

Ronald E. Smith

Thor Smith

W. B. Smith

William C. Smith

Bob Smittle

Irving Smolens

Harry Smyle

Ernie Snow
Ronald Snyder
William N. Solkin
Clifford R. Sorenson
John Souch
Joe J. Sousa
Frank E. South
John Spaulding
Doug Spitler
Albert Spoheimer, Jr.
Floyd Stanard
Edward H. Stanton
Phillip Stark
William D. Steel
Ralph V. Steele
David Steinberg
Tom Steinhardt
Ralph Steinway
Allen Stephens
Roy O. Stevens
Charles W. Stockell
Clayton E. Storeby
John J. Storm
Raymond Stott
Joshwil Straub
Bob Strayer
Francis H. Strickler
Robert F. Stringer
Raymond L. Strischek
Wallace C. Strobel
Rod Strohe
Sir Kenneth Strong
Clyde Strosnider, Sr.
Ray Stubbe
John C. Studt
Lewis Sturdovon
Phillip Sturgeon
Jon Sturm
Stanley Stypulkowski
Charles R. Sullivan
Sigurd Sundby
S. S. Suntag
Frank Swann

H. Sweeney
J. Leslie Sweetnam
Oscar F. Swenson
Fred Swets
William L. Swisher
Edward Szaniawski

Ralph Tancordo
Fred R. Tannery
Arthur Tappan
E. Tappenden
Vernon W. Tart
Wayne Tate
Manuel Tavis
Amos Taylor
Frank Taylor
James R. Taylor
John R. Taylor
Nigel Taylor
Ron Taylor
W. B. Taylor
Sir Arthur Tedder
Alan Tequseay
Joseph Terebessy, Sr.
Terry Terrebonne
Charles H. Thomas
David E. Thomas
Paul Thompson
James M. Thomson
Charles C. Thornton, Jr.
Jacqueline Thornton
John Thornton
M. Thornton
Wagger Thornton
J. Tillett
Jack L. Tipton
Richard Todd
Lynn C. Tomlinson
Joseph Toughill
Benno V. Tourdelille
Arthur W. Tower
Joe Toye
Charles R. Trail Travett

Dewey O. Tredway
Frank A. Tremblay
Raymond A. Trittler
K. A. J. Trott
John F. Troy
William True
William H. Tucker
Arthur W. Tupper
Thomas B. Turner
William A. Turner
Robert S. Tweed

Alexander Uhlig
Sidney M. Ulan
James Underkofler
Matthew Urban
Willis L. Ure

Thomas Valance
Norman Vance
Howard Vander Beek
Benjamin Vandervoort
James Van Fleet
John Vaughan
Elmer Vermeer
Ernest Vermont
Sarifino R. Visco
Raymond Voight
Walter Vollrath, Jr.
Kurt Vonnegut
Walter Voss
Willis L. Vowell

Martin Waarvick
Orville Wade
Orval Wakefield
Frank Walk
Robert E. Walker
Sir Patrick Wall
James Wallwork
Martin Walsh
George R. Walter
Marion G. Wamsley

William Wangaman
Simon V. Ward, Jr.
Lawrence Waring
Adolph Warnecke
Lloyd Warren
Wilfred Washington
Homer E. Wassam
John Watkins
Orville Watkins
James H. Watts
James L. Watts
Carl Weast
E. R. Webb
Glover Webb
David K. Webster
Fritz Weinschenk
Dean Weisert
Robert Weiss
James Weller
Harry Welsh
Wendell E. Wendt
Floyd West
Henry F. West
William Westmoreland
Albert Nash Whatley
Elmer M. Wheeler
Brian T. Whinney
Harry T. Whitby
F. S. White
George White
James A. White
Don Whitehead
J. J. Whitmeyer, Jr.
Frank Whitney
Don T. Whitsitt
Eldon Wiehe
Arthur B. Wieck
Herbert H. Wiggins
Felix P. Wilkerson
Robert A. Wilkins
James Wilkinson
George Williams
Joe B. Williams

Thomas E. Williams
George E. Williamson
Harvey Williamson
Kenneth R. Williamson
Robert J. Williamson
Richard Willstatter
Leonard Wilmont
William Wilps
Alan R. Wilson
J. E. Wilson
Seth Wilson
William Wingett
Edgar R. Winters
Richard D. Winters
William R. Winters
Tom Winterton
Walter F. Wintsch
Gene Wirwahn
J. J. Witmeyer
C. L. Witt
Willie B. Wolfe
David Wood
George R. Woodbridge
Julian R. Woods

Frank Woosley
Carroll Wright
Joseph N. Wright
Kenneth Wright
Richard Wright
Ted Wright
Brony Wronoski

Edward L. Yarberry
Willie Yates
Dick Young
Edwin P. Young
Samuel Young

Robert Zafft
Walter F. Zagol
Charles Zalewski
Charles Zeccola
Lester Zick
John Zink
Walter Zittats
Sam Zittrer
John Zmudzinski

Bibliography

Air Ministry. *By Air to Battle: The Official Account of the British First and Sixth Airborne Divisions.* London: H. M. Stationery Office, 1945.
Allen, Max. *Medicine Under Canvas: A War Journal of the 77th Evacuation Hospital.* Kansas City, Mo.: The Sosland Press, 1949.
Ambrose, Stephen E. *Band of Brothers: E Company, 506th Regiment, 101st Airborne: From Normandy to Hitler's Eagle's Nest.* New York: Simon & Schuster, 1992.
———. *Citizen Soldiers: The U.S. Army from the Normandy Beaches to the Bulge to the Surrender of Germany, June 7, 1944–May 7, 1945.* New York: Simon & Schuster, 1997.
———. *D-Day: June 6, 1944: The Climactic Battle of World War II.* New York: Simon & Schuster, 1994.
———. *Eisenhower: Soldier, General of the Army, President-Elect, 1890–1952.* New York: Simon & Schuster, 1983.
———. *Eisenhower: Soldier and President.* New York: Simon & Schuster, 1990.

SOURCES 373

———. *Eisenhower and Berlin, 1945: The Decision to Halt at the Elbe.* New York: W. W. Norton, 1967.

———. *Ike's Spies: Eisenhower and the Espionage Establishment.* Garden City, N.Y.: Doubleday, 1981.

———. *Pegasus Bridge: June 6, 1944.* New York: Simon & Schuster, 1985.

———. *Rise to Globalism: American Foreign Policy Since 1938.* New York: Penguin, 1972.

———. *The Supreme Commander: The War Years of General Dwight D. Eisenhower.* Garden City, N.Y.: Doubleday, 1971.

Ambrose, Stephen E., and James A. Barber, editors. *The Military and American Society: Essays and Readings.* New York: The Free Press, 1972.

Astor, Gerald. *The Mighty Eighth: The Air War in Europe as Told by the Men Who Fought It.* New York: Donald Fine Books, 1997.

Baldridge, Robert C. *Victory Road.* Bennington, Vt.: Merriam Press, 1995.

Balkoski, Joseph. *Beyond the Beachhead: The 29th Infantry Division in Normandy.* Harrisburg, Pa.: Stackpole, 1989.

"B" Battery. *The "B" Battery Story: The 116th AAA Gun Battalion with the First U.S. Army.* Passaic, N.J.: The B Battery Association, 1990.

Bischof, Gunter, and Stephen Ambrose, eds. *Eisenhower and the German POWs: Facts Against Falsehood.* Baton Rouge: Louisiana State University Press, 1992.

Blair, Clay. *Ridgway's Paratroopers: The American Airborne in World War II.* Garden City, N.Y.: Doubleday, 1985.

Blumenson, Martin. *Breakout and Pursuit.* Washington, D.C.: U.S. Department of the Army, 1961.

Booth, Michael T., and Spencer Duncan. *Paratrooper: The Life of Gen. James M. Gavin.* New York: Simon & Schuster, 1994.

Boritt, Gabor, ed. *War Comes Again: Comparative Vistas on the Civil War and World War II.* New York: Oxford University Press, 1995.

Bradley, Omar. *A General's Life.* New York: Simon & Schuster, 1983.

———. *A Soldier's Story.* New York: Henry Holt, 1951.

Bradley, Robert. *Aid Man!* New York: Praeger, 1970.

Brown, Anthony Cave. *Bodyguard of Lies.* New York: Harper & Row, 1975.

Bryant, Sir Arthur. *Triumph in the West.* London: Collins, 1959.

———. *The Turn of the Tide.* New York: Doubleday & Co., 1957.

Campbell, D'Ann. "Servicewomen of World War II." *Armed Forces and Society,* Vol. 16, No. 2 (winter 1990).

Capa, Robert. *Robert Capa.* New York: Grossman, 1974.

Carell, Paul. *Invasion—They're Coming: The German Account of the Allied Landings and the 80 Days' Battle for France.* New York: Dutton, 1963.

Center for Military History. *The Army Nurse Corps.* Washington, D.C.: GPO, CMH Publication 72-14, 1993.

Chandler, David, ed. *The D-Day Encyclopedia.* New York: Simon & Schuster, 1994.

Chernitsky, Dorothy. *Voices from the Foxholes, by the Men of the 110th Infantry.* Published by Dorothy Chernitsky, 18 Country Club Blvd., Uniontown, PA 15401, 1991.

Churchill, Winston S. *The Second World War* (especially *The Hinge of Fate, Closing the Ring,* and *Triumph and Tragedy*). Boston: Houghton Mifflin Co., 1948–1953.

Clark, Mark Wayne. *Calculated Risk.* New York: Harper & Bros., 1950.

Colby, John. *War from the Ground Up: The 90th Division in WWII.* Austin, Tex.: Nortex Press, 1991.

Cole, Hugh M. *The Ardennes: The Battle of the Bulge.* Washington, D.C.: Office of the Chief of Military History, 1965.

———. *The Lorraine Campaign.* A volume in the *United States Army in World War II: The European Theater of Operations* series. Washington, D.C.: Department of the Army, 1950.

Colley, David. "Operation Northwind: Greatest Defensive Battle." *VFW Magazine,* January 1995.

Cosby, Harry. *A Wing and a Prayer.* New York: HarperCollins, 1993.

Cosmas, Graham, and Albert Cowdrey. *The Medical Department: Medical Services in the European Theater of Operations.* Washington, D.C.: Center of Military History, U.S. Army, 1992.

Cowdrey, Albert. *Fighting for Life: American Military Medicine in World War II.* New York: The Free Press, 1994.

Craven, Wesley Frank, and James Lea Cate, eds. *Europe: Argument to V-E Day, January 1944 to V-E Day.* (Vol. 3 of *The Army Air Forces in World War II.*) Chicago: University of Chicago Press, 1951.

Crookenden, Sir Napier. *Drop Zone Normandy: The Story of the American and British Airborne Assault on D-Day 1944.* New York: Macmillan, 1976.

Dank, Milton. *The Glider Gang: An Eyewitness History of World War II Glider Combat.* Philadelphia: Lippincott, 1977.

Davis, Kenneth S. *Soldier of Democracy. A Biography of Dwight Eisenhower.* Garden City, N.Y.: Doubleday, Doran & Co., 1945.

de Gaulle, Charles. *The War Memoirs of Charles de Gaulle,* Vol. II, *Unity.* New York: Simon & Schuster, 1959.

de Guingand, Sir Francis. *Operation Victory.* New York: Charles Scribner's Sons, 1947.

D'Este, Carol. *Decision in Normandy.* London: Collins, 1983.

Doubler, Michael D. *Closing with the Enemy: How GIs Fought the War in Europe, 1944–1945.* Lawrence: University of Kansas Press, 1994.

Durand, Arthur. *Stalag Luft III: The Secret Story.* Baton Rouge: Louisiana State University Press, 1988.

Durnford-Slater, John. *Commando: Memoirs of a Fighting Commando in World War Two.* Annapolis, Md.: Naval Institute Press, 1991.

Egger, Bruce E., and Lee M. Otts. *G Company's War: Two Personal Accounts of the Campaigns in Europe, 1944–1945.* Tuscaloosa: University of Alabama Press, 1992.

Eisenhower, Dwight D. *At Ease: Stories I Tell to Friends.* Garden City, N.Y.: Doubleday & Co., 1967.

———. *Crusade in Europe.* Garden City, N.Y.: Doubleday & Co., 1948.

———. *Letters to Mamie.* Edited by John S. D. Eisenhower. Garden City, N.Y.: Doubleday & Co., 1978.

———. *Mandate for Change.* Garden City, N.Y.: Doubleday & Co., 1963.

———. *The Papers of Dwight David Eisenhower* (Vols. I through V edited by Alfred D. Chandler, Jr., et al.; Vols. VI through IX edited by Louis Galambos, et al.). Baltimore: Johns Hopkins University Press, 1970, 1978.

———. *Waging Peace.* Garden City, N.Y.: Doubleday & Co., 1974.

Eisenhower, John. *The Bitter Woods: The Battle of the Bulge.* New York: G. P. Putnam's Sons, 1969.

Ellis, John. *On the Front Lines: The Experience of War Through the Eyes of the Allied Soldiers in World War II.* New York: John Wiley & Sons, 1980.

Ellis, L. F. *Victory in the West,* Vol. 1, *The Battle of Normandy.* London: H. M. Stationery Office, 1962.

English, John A. *A Perspective on Infantry.* New York: Praeger Special Studies, 1988.

Fane, Francis. *Naked Warriors.* New York: Prentice-Hall, 1956.

Farago, Ladislas. *Patton: Ordeal and Triumph.* New York: Astor-Honor Inc., 1964.

Foot, M. R. D. *SOE: The Special Operations Executive 1940–1946.* London: BBC, 1984.

Fraser, David. *Knight's Cross: A Life of Field Marshal Erwin Rommel.* New York: HarperCollins, 1993.

Frisbee, John. "Operation Varsity." *Air Force Magazine,* March 1996.

Fussell, Paul. *Doing Battle: The Making of a Skeptic.* Boston: Little, Brown, 1996.

———. *Wartime: Understanding Behavior in the Second World War.* New York: Oxford University Press, 1989.

Gabel, Kurt. *The Making of a Paratrooper: Airborne Training and Combat in World War II.* Lawrence: University of Kansas Press, 1990.

Gale, General Richard. *Call to Arms: An Autobiography.* London: Hutchinson, 1968.

———. *With the 6th Airborne Division in Normandy.* London: Sampson Low, Marston, 1948.

Garland, Albert N., and Howard McGaw Smyth. *Sicily and the Surrender of Italy.* Washington, D.C.: U.S. Department of the Army, 1965.

Gilbert, Martin. *The Day the War Ended: May 8, 1945—Victory in Europe.* New York: Henry Holt, 1995.

Glassman, Henry. *"Lead the Way, Rangers:" A History of the Fifth Ranger Battalion.* Printed in Germany, 1945.

Goebbels, Joseph. *The Goebbels Diaries: The Last Days.* Edited and translated by Louis Lochner. New York: Doubleday, 1948.

Gray, Glenn. *The Warriors: Reflections on Men in Battle.* New York: Harper & Row, 1959.

Gregory, Barry. *British Airborne Troops, 1940–45.* New York: Doubleday, 1975.

Haffner, Sebastian. *The Meaning of Hitler.* Translated by E. Osers. Cambridge, Mass.: Harvard University Press, 1979.

Harrison, Gordon A. *Cross-Channel Attack.* Washington, D.C.: U.S. Department of the Army, 1951.

Hastings, Max. *Overlord: D-Day and the Battle for Normandy.* New York: Simon & Schuster, 1984.

Hatch, Gardner, ed. *4th Infantry "Ivy" Division: Steadfast and Loyal.* Paducah, Ky.: Turner Publishing, 1987.

Havener, J. K. *The Martin B-26 Marauder.* Blue Ridge Summit, Pa.: Tab Books, 1988.

Hawkins, Ian L., ed. *B-17s Over Berlin: Personal Stories from the 95th Bomb Group.* Washington, D.C.: Brassey's, 1990.

Hechler, Ken. *The Bridge at Remagen.* Missoula, Mont.: Pictorial Histories Publishing Company, 1993.

Heinz, W. C. "I Took My Son to Omaha Beach." *Collier's,* June 11, 1954.

Hemingway, Ernest. "How We Came to Paris." *Collier's,* October 7, 1944.

———. "Voyage to Victory." *Collier's,* July 22, 1944.

Hickey, Michael. *Out of the Sky: A History of Airborne Warfare.* New York: Scribner, 1979.

Hinsley, F. H. *British Intelligence in the Second World War: Its Influence on Strategy and Operations.* New York: Cambridge University Press, 1981.

Historical Section European Theater of Operations Staff, eds. *Utah Beach to Cherbourg*. Nashville, Tenn.: Battery Press, 1984.

History of the Joint Chiefs of Staff, 4 vols. Washington, D.C.: GPO, 1982.

Hoegh, Leo, and Howard Doyle. *Timberwolf Tracks: The History of the 104th Infantry Division*. Washington, D.C.: Infantry Journal Press, 1946.

Howarth, David. *Dawn of D-Day*. London: Collins, 1959.

Huie, William Bradford. *The Execution of Private Slovik*. New York: Duell, Sloan and Pearce, 1954.

Hynes, Samuel, et al., eds. *Reporting World War II: American Journalism 1938–1946,* 2 vols. New York: Library of America, 1995.

Ingersoll, Ralph. *Top Secret*. New York: Harcourt Brace, 1946.

Irving, David. *Hitler's War*. New York: Viking, 1977.

———. *The Trail of the Fox: The Search for the True Field Marshal Rommel*. New York: Dutton, 1977.

———. *The War Between the Generals*. New York: Congdon & Lattes, 1981.

Ismay, Hastings L. *The Memoirs of General Lord Ismay*. New York: Viking Press, 1960.

James, D. Clayton. *The Years of MacArthur,* Vol. I, 1880–1941. Boston: Houghton Mifflin, 1970.

Johnson, Gerden. *History of the Twelfth Infantry Regiment in World War II*. Boston: 4th Division Association, 1947.

Keegan, John. *Six Armies in Normandy: From D-Day to the Liberation of Paris*. New York: Penguin Books, 1983.

Keeler, Owen. "From the Seaward Side." *U.S. Naval Institute Proceedings*, August 1989.

Knight, James. "The DD That Saved the Day." *U.S. Naval Institute Proceedings,* August 1989.

Kornitzer, Bela. *The Great American Heritage: The Story of the Five Eisenhower Brothers*. New York: Farrar, Straus and Cudahy, 1955.

Lale, Max. "My War." *East Texas Historical Journal,* Vol. 32 (1994).

Lane, Ronald. *Rudder's Rangers*. Manassas, Va.: Ranger Associates, 1979.

Lang, Daniel. "Letter from Rome." *New Yorker,* June 17, 1944.

Langdon, Allen. *"Ready": A World War II History of the 505th Parachute Infantry Regiment*. Indianapolis, Ind.: 82nd Airborne Division Association, 1986.

Lee, Ulysses. *The Employment of Negro Troops*. Washington, D.C.: Office of the Chief of Military History, 1966.

Leinbaugh, Harold P., and John D. Campbell. *The Men of Company K: The Autobiography of a World War II Rifle Company*. New York: William Morrow, 1985.

Lewin, Ronald. *Ultra Goes to War*. London: Hutchinson, 1978.

Liebling, A. J. "Reporter at Large." *New Yorker,* July 8 and 15, 1944.

Litoff, Judy Barrett, and David C. Smith, eds. *Since You Went Away: World War II Letters from American Women on the Home Front*. New York: Oxford University Press, 1991.

———. " 'This Is War and I Guess I Can Take It:' The World War II Letters of American Red Cross Women Overseas." Paper given at annual meeting of the American Red Cross Overseas Association, July 2, 1994.

———. " 'Today We Have Lived History:' The D-Day Letters of U.S. Women." Paper given at the Eisenhower Center, May 16, 1994.

———. *We're in This War, Too: World War II Letters from American Women in Uniform*. New York: Oxford University Press, 1994.

Luck, Hans von. *Panzer Commander: The Memoirs of Colonel Hans von Luck.* New York: Praeger, 1989.

MacDonald, Charles. *The Mighty Endeavor: American Armed Forces in the European Theater in World War II.* New York: Oxford University Press, 1969.

Macmillan, Harold. *The Blast of War: 1939–1945.* New York: Harper & Row, 1968.

Marshall, S. L. A. "First Wave at Omaha Beach." *Atlantic Monthly,* November 1960.

———. *Night Drop: The American Airborne Invasion of Normandy.* Boston: Little, Brown, 1962.

Martin, Pete. "We Shot D-Day on Omaha Beach." *American Legion Magazine,* June 1964.

Masterman, J. C. *The Double-Cross System in the War of 1939–1945.* New Haven, Conn.: Yale University Press, 1972.

Mauldin, Bill. *The Brass Ring.* New York: W. W. Norton, 1971.

McCann, Kevin. *Man from Abilene.* Garden City, N.Y.: Doubleday & Co., 1952.

McKeogh, Michael, and Richard Lockridge. *Sergeant Mickey and General Ike.* New York: G. P. Putnam's Sons, 1946.

Memorable Bulge Incidents: Living Legends. Published by Veterans of the Battle of the Bulge, P.O. Box 11129, Arlington, VA 22210.

Miller, Edward G. *A Dark and Bloody Ground: The Hurtgen Forest and the Roer River Dams, 1944–1945.* College Station: Texas A&M University Press, 1995.

Miller, Robert. *Division Commander: A Biography of Major General Norman D. Cota.* Spartanburg, S.C.: The Reprint Co., 1989.

Mitcham, Samuel. *Rommel's Last Battle: The Desert Fox and the Normandy Campaign.* New York: Stein & Day, 1983.

Moench, John O. *Marauder Men: An Account of the Martin B-26 Marauder.* Longwood, Fla.: Maalia Enterprises, 1989.

Montgomery, Bernard Law. *Memoirs.* Cleveland: World Publishing Co., 1958.

Morgan, Kay Summersby. *Past Forgetting: My Love Affair with Dwight D. Eisenhower.* New York: Simon & Schuster, 1976.

Morison, Samuel Eliot. *The Invasion of France and Germany, 1944–1945.* (Vol. 11 of *History of United States Naval Operations in World War II.*) Boston: Little, Brown, 1959.

Move Out: The Combat Story of the 743rd Tank Battalion. n.p., n.d. Copy in Eisenhower Center, University of New Orleans.

Mrazek, James. *Fighting Gliders of World War II.* London: Hale; New York: St. Martin's Press, 1977.

Murphy, Edward F. *Heroes of WWII.* New York: Ballantine, 1991.

New York Sun, October 24–27, 1944.

Panter-Downes, Mollie. "Letter from London." *New Yorker,* June 10, 1944.

Parrish, Thomas, ed. *The Simon & Schuster Encyclopedia of World War II.* New York: Simon & Schuster, 1978.

Patton, George S., Jr. *War As I Knew It.* Boston: Houghton Mifflin Co., 1947.

Perret, Geoffrey. *There's a War to Be Won: The United States Army in World War II.* New York: Random House, 1991.

Pogue, Forrest C. *George C. Marshall: Ordeal and Hope, 1939–1942.* New York: Viking Press, 1966.

———. *The Supreme Command.* A volume in the *United States Army in World War II: The European Theater of Operations* series. Washington, D.C.: Office of the Chief of Military History, 1954.

Province, Charles M. *Patton's Third Army: A Daily Combat Diary.* New York: Hippocrene Books, 1992.

Pyle, Ernie. *Ernie's War: The Best of Ernie Pyle's World War II Dispatches.* Edited by David Nichols. New York: Simon & Schuster, 1986.

Rapport, Leonard, and Arthur Northwood. *Rendezvous with Destiny: A History of the 101st Airborne Division.* Greenville, Tex.: 101st Airborne Division Association, 1965.

Reeder, Russell. *Born at Reveille.* New York: Duell, Sloan & Pearce, 1966.

Reid, Pat. *The Latter Days at Colditz.* London: Hodder and Stoughton, 1952.

Rommel, Erwin. *The Rommel Papers.* Edited by B. H. Liddell Hart. New York: Harcourt, Brace, 1953.

Rooney, Andy. *My War.* Holbrook, Mass.: Adams Media Corp., 1995.

Roush, John H., ed. *World War II Reminiscences.* Reserve Officers Association of California, P.O. Box 4950, San Rafael, CA 94913, 1995.

Roy, Reginald. *1944: The Canadians in Normandy.* Ottawa: Canadian War Museum, 1984.

Ruppenthal, Roland. *Logistical Support of the Armies,* 2 vols. A volume in the *United States Army in World War II: The European Theater of Operations* series. Washington, D.C.: Office of the Chief of Military History, 1953.

Ryan, Cornelius. *A Bridge Too Far.* New York: Simon & Schuster, 1974.

———. *The Last Battle.* New York: Simon & Schuster, 1966.

———. *The Longest Day: June 6, 1944.* New York: Simon & Schuster, 1959.

Salomon, Sidney. *2nd U.S. Ranger Infantry Battalion.* Doylestown, Pa.: Birchwood Books, 1991.

Saunders, Hilary St. George. *The Red Beret: The Story of the Parachute Regiment at War 1940–1945* with a foreword by Viscount Montgomery of Alamein. Nashville, Tenn.: Battery Press, 1985.

Schott, Matthew. "Prisoners Like Us: German POWs Encounter Louisiana's African-Americans." *Louisiana History,* Vol. 36, No. 3 (Summer 1995).

Smith, Walter B. *Eisenhower's Six Great Decisions.* New York: Longmans, Green and Co., 1956.

Sommers, Martin. "The Longest Hour in History." *Saturday Evening Post,* July 8, 1944.

Sorvisto, Edwin. *Roughing It with Charlie: 2nd Ranger Bn.* Pilzen, Czechoslovakia, 1945.

Sperber, A. M. *Murrow: His Life and Times.* New York: Freundlich, 1986.

Stannard, Richard M. *Infantry: An Oral History of a World War II American Infantry Battalion.* New York: Twayne, 1993.

Steckel, Francis C. "Morale Problems in Combat: American Soldiers in Europe in World War II." *Army History,* Summer 1994.

Steinhoff, Johannes, Peter Pechel, and Dennis Showalter, eds. *Voices from the Third Reich: An Oral History.* New York: Da Capo Press, 1994.

Summersby, Kay. *Eisenhower Was My Boss.* New York: Prentice-Hall, 1948.

Swanson, Vernon, ed. *Upfront with Charlie Company: A Combat History of Company C, 395th Infantry Regiment, 99th Infantry Division.* North Royalton, Ohio: 1995.

Tedder, Sir Arthur. *With Prejudice.* London: Cassell, 1966.

Tute, Warren, John Costello, and Terry Hughes. *D-Day.* London: Pan Books, 1975.

U.S. Army, Historical Section Staff. *Omaha Beachhead: June 6–June 13, 1944.* Nashville, Tenn.: Battery Press, 1984.

U.S. War Department. *Handbook on German Military Forces.* Baton Rouge: Louisiana State University Press, 1990.

Vallavieille, Michel de. *D-Day at Utah Beach.* Coutances, Normandy, 1982.

Viorst, Milton. *Hostile Allies: FDR and Charles de Gaulle.* New York: Macmillan Co., 1965.

Vonnegut, Kurt, Jr. "Memoirs." *Traces of Indiana and Midwestern History,* Vol. 3, No. 4 (special Issue, Fall 1991).

———. *Slaughterhouse-Five, or The Children's Crusade.* New York: Delacorte Press, 1994 edition.

Wandrey, June. *Bedpan Commando: The Story of a Combat Nurse During WWII.* Elmore, Ohio: Elmore Publishing, 1989.

Warlimont, Walter. *Inside Hitler's Headquarters, 1939–1945.* New York: Praeger, 1964.

Webster, David Kenyon. *Parachute Infantry: An American Paratrooper's Memoir of D-Day and the Fall of the Third Reich.* Baton Rouge: Louisiana State University Press, 1994.

Weigley, Russell. *Eisenhower's Lieutenants: The Campaign of France and Germany.* Bloomington, Ind.: Indiana University Press, 1981.

Werth, Alexander. *Russia at War, 1941–1945.* New York: Dutton, 1964.

Wheldon, Huw. *Red Berets into Normandy.* Norwich: Jarrold, 1982.

Whiting, Charles. *Death of a Division.* New York: Stein and Day, 1980.

Wills, Deryk. *Put on Your Boots and Parachutes! Personal Stories of the Veterans of the U.S. 82nd Airborne Division.* Published 1992 by Deryk Wills, 70 Hidcote Road, Oadby, Leicester LE2 5PF, England.

Wilmot, Chester. *Struggle for Europe.* New York: Harper, 1952.

Wilson, George. *If You Survive.* New York: Ballantine, 1987.

Ziemke, Earle. "Operations Kreml: Deception, Strategy, and the Fortunes of War." *Parameters: Journal of the U.S. Army War College,* 9 (March 1979): 72–81.

INDEX